Emotions, Advertising and Consumer Choice

Flemming Hansen & Sverre Riis Christensen

Emotions, Advertising and Consumer Choice

With research assistance
by Steen Lundsteen, MSc

Copenhagen Business School Press • Liber • Universitetsforlaget
2007

Emotions, Advertising and Consumer Choice

© Copenhagen Business School Press, 2007
Printed in Denmark by Narayana Press, Gylling
Cover design by O.K. Petersen & Søn
Cover pre-press by BUSTO | Graphic Design
First edition 2007

ISBN 978-82-15-01184-4 (Norway)
ISBN 978-91-47-08765-5 (Sweden)
ISBN 978-87-630-0198-4 (Rest of the world)

Distribution:

Norway
Universitetsforlaget AS
Postboks 508 Sentrum
NO-0105 Oslo, Norway
Tel +47 24 14 75 00, fax +47 24 14 75 01
post@universitetsforlaget.no
www.universitetsforlaget.no

Sweden
Liber AB, Baltzarsgatan 4
SE-205 10 Malmö, Sweden
Tel + 46 40 25 86 00, fax +46 40 97 05 50
www.liber.se
Kundtjänst tel +46 8 690 93 30, fax +46 8 690 9301

Rest of Scandinavia
DJOEF/DBK, Mimersvej 4
DK-4600 Køge, Denmark
Tel +45 3269 7788
Fax +45 3269 7789

North America
International Specialized Book Services
920 NE 58th Ave., Suite 300
Portland, OR 97213, USA
Tel +1 800 944 6190
Fax +1 503 280 8832
Email: orders@isbs.com

Rest of the World
Marston Book Services, P.O. Box 269
Abingdon, Oxfordshire, OX14 4YN, UK
Tel +44 (0) 1235 465500, fax +44 (0) 1235 4656555
E-mail Direct Customers: direct.order@marston.co.uk
E-mail Booksellers: trade.order@marston.co.uk

Table of Contents

Foreword

Two developments in the late 20th century have together formed the background for the writing of the book "Emotions, Advertising and Consumer Choice".

On the one hand, the growing realisation of the problems inherent in exploring consumer choice and advertising effects departing in traditional cognitive models of choice and communication effects. Multi-attribute models modified with levels of involvement, attitude attribution, degrees of self-regulation etc. have left large parts of consumer choice behaviour unexplained. Effect hierarchies as a basis for studying communication effects have proven unsatisfactory.

On the other hand, recent insight gained among brain neurologists and psychologists, often with the use of brain scanning devises such as PET and FMRI Scanning, have drawn attention to the row of very basic emotional processes in the brain and their governing influence on human behaviour, not only in disabled individuals under medical treatment but also in the behaviour of ordinary individuals in everyday life.

It is time that emerging fields of "neuroeconomics" is introduced into the traditional consumer choice theories. In the present book consumer choice is dealt with in a more narrow sense than consumer behaviour in general. Such topics as social influence, learning, segmentation, retailing consumer policy and many others are not included. Rather focus is on the role of the more affective aspects of contemporary approaches to the study of emotions and their relations with feelings. In this sense the book will present a new view on affective factors.

Center for Marketing Communication (CMC) was started at the Copenhagen Business School in 1999 with the purpose of studying the effects of advertising and other mass communication. Over the years a number of projects have been completed in cooperation with the many company sponsors of the center, many of which were guided by a search for explanation beyond those proposed by traditional cognitive thinking.

The authors are particularly grateful to all our colleagues at the CMC who in different ways all have influenced the work leading to the present book.

As of the fall 2006 CMC comprises the following researchers:
Flemming Hansen (ekon. dr., professor), Birgitte Tufte (doctoral degree in Pedagogy, professor), Lars Grønholdt (PhD, professor), Larry Percy (PhD, visiting professor), Christian Alsted (PhD, adjunct professor), Steffen Gulmann (MSc, adjunct professor), Joergen Kai Olsen (senior associate professor), Anne Martensen (PhD, associate professor), Richard Jones (PhD, associate professor), Tore Kristensen (PhD, associate professor), Jeanette Rasmussen (MSc, PhD-

student), Lars Bech Christensen (MSc, PhD-student), Kristina Birch (MSc, PhD-student), Sverre Riis Christensen (MSc, senior researcher), Jens Carsten Nielsen (MSc, Centre Director), research Assistant Steen Lundsteen (MSc) and Maiken Lerche Møller (MSc).

In the years 2000 to 2004 important contributions also have been made by the PhD candidates from the center, Lars Pynt Andersen and Pernille Schnoor.

Particularly two major research activities have been of importance for the publication which is introduced here. First very extensive work sponsored by Taylor Nelson Sofrès/Gallup Denmark on emotions quantified through responses to brands and products with the use of batteries of feeling words. This has been crucial to several of the chapters of the book. The authors are particularly grateful to the Managing Director Henrik Hansen and Research Director Rolf Randrup at TNS Gallup in Copenhagen. In early phases of this work the cooperation with visiting professor, Larry Percy has been extremely valuable.

Other very important contributions have come from research done on the TNS/Carlton Television single source database from UK 1985-89. CMC was given access to these data in the late 1990'ies thanks to the efforts of Colin McDonald in London. Much advice on the analysis of these data has also been received from Professor John Philip Jones.

From its start in 1999 work, which also feeds into the present book, has been going on on this database. Particularly research has been carried out and reported by the senior author of this book with the assistance of research assistants Lotte Yssing Hansen and Lars Bech Christensen. A special thank is due to research assistant Steen Lundsteen, who in the last phases of the project has been responsible for the huge task of editing and data analysis. In this work the advice of Colin McDonald, Robert Heath and John Phillip Jones has been very important. The authors are grateful for these contributions.

Other projects have been carried out in the first part of the 20th century and here the contributions by research assistants Jens Halling, Morten Hallum Hansen and Pernille Christiansen have been instrumental. Also projects have been carried out in close cooperation with the various sponsors of CMC. Particularly the cooperation with the Danish Cancer Association has been valuable and the contributions by this organization's marketing director Poul Møller and his co-workers are highly appreciated. Research assistants Katrine Kristensen and Ina Andresen Mance have also been very instrumental in finalizing the project.

CMC has been able to support the work published in the present book not the least by the sponsoring members of the center and through budgets made available by the management of the Copenhagen Business School. In this process the support of the president, Finn Junge Jensen, has been instrumental but also valuable support has been granted from the Dean of the Business Faculty, Ole Stenwinkel Nilsson and the Head of the Department of Marketing, Ricky Wilke. The sponsor members of CMC to whom the authors wish to express their gratitude are:

- DAF
- DMU
- DMF
- DRRB
- FMD
- Initiative Universal Media A/S
- Kræftens Bekæmpelse
- TV2/Reklame A/S
- Danish Award for Research in Marketing
- Bates A/S
- BRF Kredit A/S
- Carat Danmark A/S
- Danske Spil A/S
- Danske Bank A/S
- DDB
- DSB
- Ekstra Bladet
- Epinion A/S
- Forbruger-Kontakt a-s
- GordioS A/S
- House of Prince A/S
- IAA - International

- Advertising Association
- idé-nyt a-s
- Ingeniøren A/S
- JP Politikens Hus
- Lowe
- Lån&Spar Bank A/S
- Mediacom A/S
- Mediaedge:cia A/S
- Novo Nordisk A/S
- OMD
- Post Danmark
- Radio 100 FM
- SAS Scandinavian Airlines Denmark A/S
- Sepia Proximity A/S / BBDO
- Stryhn's A/S
- TDC A/S
- TNS-Gallup A/S
- TrygVesta

Findings from projects, many of which are integrated into the present book have been presented over the years at numerous conferences organized by the European Advertising Academy (EAA), the European Marketing Academy (EMAC), the Association for Consumer Research (ACR), the European Association for Research in Economic Psychology (EAREP), the American Academy of Advertising (AAA), the Advertising Symposium International (ASI) and others. Particularly the cooperation with other researchers established through the EAA Annual Advertising Research Conference has been valuable. But also ASI, at whose Annual Advertising Symposium the senior author and colleagues have presented findings and received valuable feedback each year since the late 20th century, is to be thanked. This thank is particularly directed to its never tiring organiser, Mike Sainsbury.

The book draws more upon applied research than many other theoretical works. It does so because the concern with emotions – as different from feelings – in many ways have appeared earlier amongst researchers working with applied research rather than among consumer and communication academics. Thus the present book is not written as a text book in the strict sense of the word although the authors are using it as such. To do this they work with selections of papers complementing the text and by giving the students access to the databases based on which several of the chapters of the book are written. The book as a whole is written aimed at graduate students in their final year, PhD students, and practitioners with an MBA or similar background.

The book focuses on how traditional measures of feelings in consumer behaviour and psychology can be interpreted in the light of contemporary neuro-physiological insight in emotional processes. Also it makes suggestions as to how psychologically based measures can be used meaningfully when working with an emotional concept rooted in brain research.

The background of both authors with many years of practice in marketing management together with the close contact with sponsors of CMC has made the book different from most traditional books in the area in the sense that it is more practically oriented and closely related to managerial decisions as they occur in the marketing context.

We hope that this will help the book finding many readers not only within the academic marketing community but also in business and practitioner circles.

Part I

Emotions in Consumer Choice

In the first part of the book we look at the development of the traditional cognitive theories of consumer choice. From here the attention is directed to more recent treatments of affect among consumer researchers. Next a distinction between feelings and emotions is introduced, with emotions seen as the more physiological unconscious mechanisms governing simple choices and influencing more complex ones. Following this some important observations made by neurologists are introduced, and a measurement procedure enabling the researcher to estimate emotions based on questions about feelings that may be activated by the emotions is suggested. The use of this procedure is illustrated in the last two chapters of Part One, where also emotionally based mental brand equity is estimated for 126 brands, some of which in two upon each other following years. This enables the researcher to demonstrate the stability of mental brand equity, and show major changes in market conditions from one year to the next may influence these.

Chapter I

The Origin of Consumer Choice Theory

1. Marketing Theory

Interest in consumer choices grew up among marketers in the process of formulating a more general marketing theory. Some of the factors accounting for marketing becoming an important element in society were mass production, mass distribution, and product branding. With the economic advantages of mass production, producers became fewer and fewer, and their distance to their final consumers became larger. In the traditional small city society, there was an affluent number of shoemakers in each town, each with their own small shop and each with their own personal contact with a smaller or larger number of customers. When the shoe manufacturing moved into factories the direct contact between the consumer and the manufacturer disappeared. The shoe maker had to make shoes to fit average feet at averagely acceptable prices and to make them available in larger markets, and eventually, in specialized stores offering shoes made by many different manufacturers. In the process, the need grew for the manufacturer to understand what kinds of shoes, what kind of people demanded, what they were willing to pay for them, and how they preferred to have them made available in special stores, department stores, supermarkets etc.

As a function of this process, a parallel development in retail stores emerged. Where in the traditional city society the baker sold bread, the butcher sold meat, the tailor sold dresses, the shoe maker sold shoes etc, stores began to emerge where the same store sold shoes from many manufacturers, the same confectionary stores sold dresses from many manufacturers etc. Already in the traditional society, the "general store" grew up. This combined store was selling most fast moving consumers goods, and maybe also other more durable items. However, in the 19th century, and with accelerated speed in the 20th century, stores combining different product lines grew up. The department store, the super market, the mail order store were early such inventions. Later, additions were such as the building shops, brown goods shops (radio, television, VCR etc.), white goods shops. Still later in the development, as manufacturers found themselves becoming more and more dependent upon large retailers, they began again to take interest in having own retail facilities. This was of course only possible in areas where a sufficient demand could be accumulated around a rather limited assortment. The automobile dealers, banks, insurance companies were early such phenomena. In later years, highly specialized stores carrying only one brand of fashion clothing, television, radio equipment etc. emerged. In this entire process, the need grew for understanding what consumers prefer, what they are willing to pay, and how much time they are willing to spend on the purchasing process. The bulk of decisions made by consumers are made in the many different types of stores. To understand how these choices are made is mandatory to the student of consumer behaviour, and this realization initiated early studies of consumer behaviour.

A particular development in this process was the invention of the branded goods. Essentially, brands appeared as the single manufacturer's attempt to maintain a link to his final consumer by providing a standardized product, at a standardized quality and sold at a standardized price in a standardized packaging with a standardized name. For instance the butter market moved from cask butter to branded butter, soap moved from loose weight to hard soap etc. Some of the earliest brands invented still exist in the market today such as Lurpak, Colgate, Coca Cola, Levi's, Nestlé etc. These brand manufacturers needed still more information about consumers. How they used their products, what they preferred, what they disliked etc. As a curiosity, one may in later years observe a development in the branded product areas where all the different brands in a particular area become more and more alike. All the manufacturers are able to provide the same quality at the same price and sell it through the same stores. Left for the manufacturer to differentiate his offer to the market was the branding and the building of confidence in the brand. The brand name has become an extremely important issue in contemporary market thinking. "Pleasures of the Mind" more and more dominate pleasures of the body provided by the product and brands (Kubovy, 1999).

Summing up this brief description of the development of marketing as a field, we can observe that was happened has been that the proportion of cost associated with selling the product and that of manufacturing it, has changed dramatically over the last centuries. In many product areas today, manufacturing costs are but a fraction of the total sales price, and estimates at the aggregate level are that in the economically most developed countries, more costs go into marketing products than into manufacturing them. With the shoemaker example again in the little village in the 17th century, he spent most of his time on making shoes and only a few hours on talking to customers. The shoe manufacturer of today spends a majority of his total budget on packaging, communication, distribution etc.

2. Early Consumer Behaviour Research

Consumer choice is that part of consumer behaviour theory that focuses on how the individual consumer goes about making choices.

As concern with marketing theory grew, topics such as merchandising, personal selling, and retailing became early issues at international universities, and eventually, formed the background for the business schools of today. The concern with advertising came a little later and not the least derived from this an interest in understanding consumer motivation and consumer use of information emerged. In the early days, consumer behaviour took up a few pages in the chapter on advertising in marketing textbooks. The real development of consumer behaviour as a discipline began, following the Second World War. The very first academic approaches to the understanding of consumer behaviour may be ascribed to four outstanding personalities, three of which were Jews moving out of Vienna in the 1930s.

George Gallup's contribution was first and foremost the development of the marketing research instrument as a tool for getting information about consumers. But also on the theoretical level, he made important contributions. His concept of proven recall as a measure of advertising effectiveness was a very early contribution (Lipstein, 1985). Ernest Dichter, a psychologist, also made important methodological contributions. He is more or less father of qualitative consumer research as we know it today, and the group-depth interview was one of his tools. A major work from his hands "Handbook of Consumer Motivation" (1964) is still an inspiring source for hypotheses regarding motives behind many different kinds of consumption. The third outstanding Viennese Jew in early consumer behaviour research is Lazarsfeld (Katz and Lazarsfeld 1955). His and his co-workers' work with personal influence, originally in connection with American elections, but later at a more general level finds its expression in the two-step hypothesis of personal influence suggesting that some people, relatively few, pick up the new products, political opinions etc. from external sources media, books etc. and then transmit this information on to other members of the social groups to which they belong.

A final contribution to the very early foundation for contemporary consumer behaviour research comes from social psychologists such as the Hovland group at Yale University (Hovland et al., 1953). These researchers examined factors influencing attitudes covering a wide range of topics such as order of presentation, use of positive versus negative argumentation, assimilation and contrast effects in reaction to communication attitude change and personality etc. Hovland also was one of the earlier proponents of cognitive multi-attribute theory based on comparison with computer programming (Hovland and Janis, 1959). Neither of these authors were particularly concerned with consumer choice behaviour, but rather their approach to the study of human behaviour in a more general way became the fundament for consumer behaviour theory.

Other researchers made early contributions to how consumers behaved in real life. Ferber (1954) was concerned with the decision process preceding particularly major purchases of durable goods (Ferber, 1954). But he also became interested in how information about consumers' expectation about their purchasing, income and saving could predict actual economic behaviour (Ferber, 1967). In this area, other important contributors were Katona (1955) and Juster (1964) who, based at Michigan State University, made the foundations for the continuous measures of consumer expectations, still an important instrument in American economic policy. To other researchers household behaviour became an issue (Foote, 1961) and so did household purchase decisions Mueller (1958). In continuation of the work on consumer expectations, Katona (1955) also contributed with his more speculative "The Powerful Consumer". Here he anticipates much of what today is considered consumer policy research, i.e. research on how consumers may influence the products and brands they are being offered.

Out of this early work on consumers also grew the family-life cycle hypothesis (Clark, 1955). Here the researcher studied how consumption changes as the family develops from the single individual to young, married couples, couples with younger children, couples with older children, elderly families without children and single, elderly people. This typical pattern of life development was a good description of how things were in the 1940s and 1950s. Today, divorces, second marriages, single mothers etc. have made the concept less useful.

3. Consumer Behaviour as a Discipline

Today, the number of business schools all over the world offering courses in consumer behaviour is astronomical. The number of different basic textbooks available in the market exceeds 100, and a number of copies sold makes it one of the most profitable textbook markets for publishers. In the same manner, the number of scholars concerned with consumer behaviour has grown. The Association for Consumer Research (ACR) was founded at a small meeting at Ohio State University in 1968.

Today, ACR has two annual main conferences, one in the US, and one outside the US mostly in Europe and the Far East. The total number of members of the Association for Consumer Research now exceeds 4000. To this comes that the concern for consumer behaviour has spread out all over the world, first with a large number of universities offering consumer behaviour courses in different locations in Europe, and the number of researchers concerned with consumer behaviour growing in a manner like it has been seen in the US. In the later 10-15 years, the same development has been observed in the Far East, not the least in Australia, Hong Kong, Korea, New Zealand, China, India and Singapore.

The Journal of Consumer Research was started in 1972 and is now the highest rated publication among academicians in the area. In addition to this, today 20-30 other English language journals on consumer behaviour exist, such as Journal of Consumer Behaviour, Journal of Consumer Policy Research, Journal of Economic Psychology etc.

As mentioned before, the first contributions concerning consumer behaviour appeared as parts in marketing textbooks and were part of the curriculum in classes teaching marketing at a basic and at a graduate level. Today, however, the discipline exists in its own right with, in addition to the many textbooks, an extremely large literature on more specialized topics in the consumer research area.

Typically textbooks exist, targeted for the undergraduate market, and more extensively covering books aimed at the graduate market. Examples of such textbooks are Engel et al., now in its 11th edition; Peter and Olson (1987), Solomon et al. (1999), Walters (1978), and Schiffman and Kanuk (1978). At the PhD level, but also at the graduate level in major marketing schools, the discipline is offered in terms of a number of different specialized sub- areas. Examples are such as Innovations, consumer values centering on such extensive systems as VALS, Risk, Kompas (Hansen et al., 1998) etc, but also companies as customers is being studied.

Basic work on business to business marketing was done by Webster and Wind (1972), on consumer policy research (Ölander, 1986) sponsoring (Waliser, 2003) satisfaction research (Mooradian and Oliver, 1997), direct marketing (Roberts and Berger, 1989) and information processing Bettman (1979) etc. The typical textbook defining the discipline as it is being taught in most places includes such topics as motivation, personality, life style, attitudes, buying behaviour, social influence, opinion leadership, income, effects, innovation, culture, perception, learning and involvement, etc.

The core of all these areas is the understanding of the individual choice the consumer makes between brand, product types, price levels, stores, saving versus spending, public services etc. This core itself, however, in most textbooks take up only a little percentage of the total material presented. The chapters on choice-models and attitudes typically cover 15 to 20 per cent of the material presented in most textbooks.

In the present book also affective processes are given much more attention than in traditional consumer behaviour books. This is so because contemporary findings in areas such as neuroeconomics demonstrate the extreme importance of particularly emotions for consumer choices.

4. The Content of the Present Book

The purpose of the present book is to focus on the core of consumer choice theory: How choices are made and how information influences this. In this context the book relies heavily on attitude measurement, attitudes and choice. Thus consumer choice is here studied in its broadest sense, looking at all the factors influencing the individual consumer. It is intended to do so aimed at an audience of graduate students in the advertising and marketing field. In the existing literature, attempts to understand choices all depart in cognitive theories.

That is computer-like models of brains making choices based upon choice criteria along which alternatives are evaluated. As we shall see in following chapters, these attempts have far from always been successful. A number of observations have been made over the years suggesting that other fundamentally different processes may be of importance for consumer choice behaviour. Extended research into affective aspects of choice and, particularly, into the role of emotions governing individual behaviour has given consumer behaviour research a new direction, which is the main theme for the present book. Apart from seeing consumer choice in the light of the traditional cognitive multi attribute models (Chapter II), we shall look at the role of affective elements in influencing choices. We shall do this in Chapter III by reviewing available evidence, and we shall more directly approach the topic in Chapter IV where we shall introduce contemporary thinking about emotions in a manner made appropriate for studies of consumer choice. In Chapter V, we present findings from an initial study of emotional responses to brands and product areas, covering 66 brands in 16 product areas. Here we confirm the importance of emotional responses and demonstrate operational ways of quantifying emotional response potential associated with brands, products etc.

In the process of working with our first project (Chapter V), we learned a lot of things, not the least concerning limitations and possibilities of different methodologies used for quantifying emotional response. Also the importance of large samples has become obvious from the results from the first study. Therefore, TNS/Gallup also sponsored the second study covering 4,000 respondents using a modified measuring methodology and in many ways improving the approach based upon experiences from the first round of data collection. Still, comparability between the results from the first and the second study is maintained. This whole major 2nd study is reported in Chapter VI.

Next in the second main part of the book, we narrow our focus on effects of advertising and other marketing communication. This is done in an attempt to understand the feasibility of using emotional response measures in tracking advertising and other campaigns and in using emotional response tendencies in pre-testing of communication.

Prior to this, however, we introduce the reader to the basic theories about advertising and advertising effects in chapters VII, VIII, IX and X, where we more specifically review traditional and contemporary approaches to measuring advertising effects in pre-testing and tracking. In Chapter XI, we look into a number of specific cases where we can see the role of emotions in understanding market structures. In Chapter XI, we also raise the question to what an extent, emotional response potentials remain stable over time, and we ask the question about what kind of factors seem to be causing the changes. Then, in Chapter XII we suggest ways in which net emotional response strength (NERS) can be used as an instrument in measuring the effects of the marketing communications of the company and in testing alternative ways of organizing such communication. In the final chapter (XIII) we summarize the major views put forward in the preceding chapters, and we discuss the need for future research in the area and point at the directions researchers may go to make useful contributions to the whole area.

5. The Aim of the Book
The book in its totality is a useful textbook at the graduate level focusing on consumer choice and communication effects.

In one of the early formulations of marketing theory, the so-called Copenhagen School (Kjær Hansen, 1960 and Mickwitz, 1959), demand for a particular product is seen as a function of three kinds of determinants.

1) The price, the quality, the availability (distribution) and the
2) Price, promotion for the product, quality, availability and promotion for competing products.
3) Other variables such as income, basic needs of the consumers etc.

In this model the concept of elasticity, as it is also known in economic theory, is important. The elasticity of advertising reflects how much a certain amount of increased advertising spending (dA) in relation to the total amount of advertising (A) influences the sales (dq) relative to the total sales, (q). This elasticity concept is borrowed from economic theory where it is important when studying the effect of income changes and price changes. Applied to advertising it looks

$$\frac{dq \, / \, q}{dA \, / \, A}$$

Closely related to the concept of elasticities is the way in which we look at markets. Markets somehow have to be defined. When should we talk about the market for cola drinks and when should we talk about the market for soft drinks? Generally, in marketing theory when defining markets, the cross elasticities between the items on the different markets are important. In the ideal situation, a market is one where changes in price, advertising, distribution or quality of the products have no effect on demand of products in any other market, and similarly no other market exists where changes in product quality, price, availability and promotion have any effect on the market in focus. Put formally, when the marketer will talk about a pure market then he says that the cross elasticities must be zero. The cross price elasticity between prices on apple juice and prices on Coca Cola for instance is defined as

$$dp = dq_{apple} / q_{apple} \Big/ dp_{cola}/p_{cola}$$

The larger this price cross elasticity (or any other elasticity) between two products, the larger the competition, and vice versa, the smaller the more independent the particular market is. In essence of course, cross price elasticities of a certain magnitude exist between all markets since income is limited, and price increases in one product area make less money available for spending in other areas. Generally, however the marketer disregards this kind of price cross elasticity. Also, in practice the marketer requires the cross elasticities to be of a certain magnitude before he includes a particular type of product into the market.

However, some of the major disasters in applied marketing have had to do with this cross product competitive phenomenon. In the 1940s, the large Hollywood moviemakers considered themselves as moviemakers. With the appearance of television and other means of distributing entertaining material, they too late realized that they were not in the market for movies, but rather in the market for entertainment, and found their major competitors being not the other moviemakers, but the large national television companies; ABC, NBC and CBS.

In our book we are particularly concerned with those aspects of consumers' behaviour that determines – in different markets - what products and what brands they purchase, where they purchase them, in what quality they purchase them and to what prices, and particularly in its 2nd part, how communication influences this.

Overview
It may be useful to the reader to have an overall view of how the many topics taken up in this book relate to each other.

In its simplest form consumer behaviour can be seen as consisting of three groupings of elements (Peter and Olson, 1987):

- Consumer cognition and affect
- Consumer behaviour
- Consumer Environment

The three elements are interrelated so that elements in the environment (an ad, a product on a shelf in a supermarket) may interact with consumer cognition and affect (increasing awareness of a brand, increasing positive responses toward a brand) and so influence behaviour (purchase of the brand) at some later time.

Most textbooks on consumer behaviour will elaborate on these three basic elements, however not many contemporary textbooks are offering a "total model" of consumer behaviour as it was the case earlier. The reason for this, naturally, is the realization that consumer behaviour as a total phenomenon is so complicated and with so many possible factors interacting – and on top of that, they interact in a reciprocal fashion, so that any modeling attempt would most likely create more confusion than simplicity for the student of consumer behaviour.

The present book takes a stand in relation to the general system of three elements - three elements which are eminently relevant across a plethora of consumer choices, both frequently recurring choices of low importance and choices rarely made and of extreme importance. It takes as its point of departure the world of Fast Moving Consumer Goods (FMCGs), not omitting all other areas of consumer choices, but focusing on FMCGs, since that is where a lot of strong brands exist, that is where a lot of marketing planning effort is going in and that is where a lot of money is spent on advertising and promotion.

From this viewpoint, a number of reservations concerning existing and traditional theory on consumer choices become apparent:

- Most consumer decisions are made by adults who have several years of exposure to brands and advertising and deal with phenomena which the consumer is reasonably used to dealing with – so learning about new products and features is the exception rather than the rule
- Brands are managers' prime tool to differentiate their offering from that of competition, thus brands serve the consumer as a quick-reference to choices, circumventing reflection and deliberation
- Advertising is so proliferated and ubiquitous for FMCG brands that it is unreasonable to expect that consumers will pay much – or any, for that matter – attention to it, except in rare cases

In spite of the first reservation, most modeling of consumers assume that a cognitive and conscious mental activity in connection with choices is important, not really acknowledging the fact that the process must be routinized to an extreme degree.

In spite of the quick-reference role of brands, branding theory assumes extensive mental activity over time in order to develop the deep and lasting relationship between consumer and brand.

And in spite of the third reservation, cognitive modeling of advertising's effects is still prevalent – not the least amongst practitioners.

On the other hand, consumers make numerous decisions as witnessed by ever-increasing private consumption, branding does work as witnessed by various attempts at estimating the financial value of brands. And advertising seems to work even though it is not paid attention to, judging from empirical evidence on correlations between market share and ad spending.

So the stand that we have taken in writing this book is, that affect in the form of emotions, feelings, and moods plays a much larger role in consumer choice and processing of advertising than is generally accepted, particularly when we look at FMCGs. We do not discount cognition in consumer choice, rather we are of the opinion that both affect and cognition are at play, but that cognition is much less important than affect in choices concerning brands within FMCGs.

From this standpoint we have structured our thinking and the present book. Part I of the book deals with the elements that are embedded in the consumer, namely functions of the brain in the form of cognition and affect and actual behaviour. Part I is intended to outline the current knowledge of these elements and to that knowledge add our thinking and work on the role of emotions, the affective part of the individual.

Figure I.1:   Structure of the book (Chapter numbers in Roman Figures)

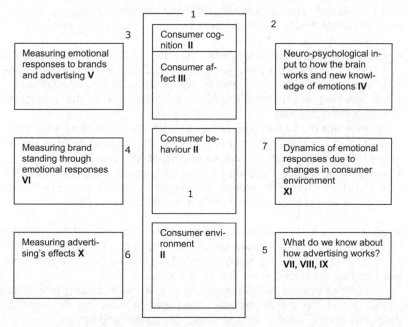

Part I of the book covers topics 1 through 4. We start by reviewing the fields of Consumer Behaviour, consciousness, cognition and affect as a precursor to a discussion of the limitations of this kind of theory – topics numbered 1 in Figure I.1.

Neuro-psychological science has progressed in recent years in its understanding of how the brain works under various conditions. We broaden the perspective on particularly consumer affect through this input and through input on emotions, what they are, what their functions are assumed to be – all in order to be able to see emotions as an important basis in controlling how consumers respond to environmental stimuli or internal stimuli – topics numbered 2 in Figure I.1.

We then progress to develop a method that can measure the direction and intensity of emotions so that we will be able to determine the extent to which an emotional theory of consumer choice has merit – topics numbered 3 in Figure I.1.

With the measurement instrument in place, we can indicate the behavioural consequences of emotional responses through actual measurement of brand standing across a number of categories. And this concludes Part I of this book – topics numbered 4 in Figure I.1.

Part II deals with the aspect of the environmental influence on the consumer, and again, we have limited ourselves as stated above to the marketing mix variable of advertising – for reasons cited earlier. We review the current knowledge on the practice of advertising in connection with marketing of FMCGs – topics numbered 5 in Figure I.1 - and we review the practice of advertising testing, particularly in the light of the emotional nature of consumers' information processing, since that must call for different measures of advertising than the predominantly cognitively oriented testing practices employed so far – topics numbered 6 in Figure I.1.

The final chapters in part II deal with what we already know from studies about how behaviour may change over time driven by changes in marketing actions or by changes in competitive situations or simply by changes in the market. We see these case illustrations as examples of how environmental changes – or external forces – drive changes in emotional responses and through those change market performance – topics numbered 7 in Figure I.1.

Chapter II

Consumer Behaviour and Cognitions

CHAPTER OUTLINE
This chapter reviews the foundations of contemporary consumer behaviour theory to lay the background for the book's subsequent discussions on consumer behaviour. Also it serves as a frame of reference for the discussion on cognitive vs. affective modeling of consumer choice. The chapter further reviews the existing forms of cognitive consumer choice models and concludes with a discussion of the limitations that are found in these models when they are applied to a contemporary marketing environment. This discussion is exemplified by looking at alternative views on consumers' information processing when they are exposed to advertising.

CHAPTER OBJECTIVE
In this chapter it is our objective to provide the reader with an overview of the state of consumer modeling from a cognitive point of departure. This takes up the larger part of the chapter. At the end of the chapter we attempt to establish the link between modeling of information processing and the much broader field of modeling consumer behaviour. Our purpose with this is to argue that such a link is particularly important in low involvement situations so commonplace in most FMCG choice situations, situations that are the prime focus of this book.

A. Consumer Behaviour

In contemporary society the role as consumer takes up a major part of the time and energy used by most individuals. Consumer behaviour comprises at least all activities related to purchasing, consuming and exchanging information about brands, products and services. These activities occur with high frequency during most or all of our time. Even our sleep is not consumption free: the bed, sleeping clothes, sleeping pills etc. It therefore makes sense to look at consumer behaviour as a particular class of human behaviour.

The mere fact that the disposition of practically all individual income – after income tax - directly or indirectly relates to our behaviour as consumers also emphasizes the importance of consumer behaviour in the total lives of contemporary individuals. In addition to this, our use of public services and our relationship and dealings with the public sector may in many instances be looked upon as consumer behaviour.

The act of purchasing comprises the purchase itself and the related activities prior and posterior to this. Here, a number of minor and major conflicts arise and choices have to be made. In these situations, the individual is faced with alternatives of various kinds. The choice between coffee brands on the shelf in the supermarket may be governed solely by the – possibly weak – approach/avoidance tendencies activated in the situation. Here it makes sense to emphasize that studies show that very many purchasing decisions are made very fast (Ruso and LeClerc, 1994), (Pieters and Warlop, 1999) and in less than 5 seconds at the point of purchase. Popai (1999) show that in US 70%, France 76%, UK 70%, Belgium 70% and Germany 55% of all Fast Moving Consumer Good purchases are made in front of the shelf. A different situation occurs when the consumer is faced with a new car model in the process of buying a car, considerable motivation may be aroused and this in turn may give rise to extensive cognitive evaluations.

The same applies to the actual consumption of products. A number of specific decisions are made and a number of related events occur prior to, during and after the consumption situations. Taking a sip from a glass of wine may be done more or less automatically. Enjoying the aftertaste of the wine may give rise to emotionally based feelings. The choice of a particular bottle to serve on the occasion may involve cognitive activities like remembering experiences from past drinking situations.

The role as a consumer also includes a number of instances where we communicate about products, consumption experiences etc. In a specific social setting with friends, colleagues or acquaintances we may talk about what we have consumed in previous similar situations. In some cases, the individual provides information, in other cases the individual receives information from mass media or through personal communication. The appearance of the brand name in the deodorant ad may arouse reactions, which in turn influence the reception and processing of the adjoining factual information about the brand.

All in all, we are faced with a large number of situations where choices are made and where products, individuals and media play an important role as stimuli to the individual.

Even with children as they mature and are socialized to become contemporary consumers (John, 1999) their environment is crowded with stimuli and situations where the child learns appropriate consumption responses. This process is dominated by learning. The social meaning of the thing appearing to the child as it grows up is learned and the appropriate responses are stored in memory.

The relative importance of the consumer role is suggested by such observations as the role of brand names in the vocabulary of young children. Hansen et al. (2002) find that 5 to 7-year-old children on average know 500 or more brand names – a number which constitute a significant proportion of their total vocabulary – all of which relates to their role as consumers.

B. Consciousness and Cognition

In consumer behaviour there is a traditional distinction between simple, semi-complex and extended decision-making. Simple choices may be controlled solely by simple and unconscious processes. The semi-complex choices give rise to more cognitions - possibly conscious - whereas extended decision-making is a highly complex phenomenon, usually associated with conscious and cognitive processes, often extended over time and with rather complex information search and problem solving involved.

We as humans are first and foremost concerned with phenomena that we are conscious about. It is automatically so because "we do not know about" the unconscious activities. In very early psychology much concern was with studying various kinds of conscious states of the mind (James, 1890). Later with the advent of behaviourism this "introspection" was rejected. One should study the relationships between observable behaviours and observable stimulations acting upon the individual only (Hull, 1943). Still later in the development of psychology, cognitive modeling became more flexible but still very biased towards cognitive and conscious information processing, even though it became more and more evident that unconscious cognitive processes played an important role to the individual.

Consciousness as we think about it, when we describe how we feel, what we experience and when we process information, is something that has been developed quite recently in the evolutionary history. Jaynes (1976) in his fascinating "The origin of consciousness in the breakdown of the bicameral mind" speculates that consciousness does not date longer back as possibly 8-10.000 years. Unconscious brain processes, thus, are by far much older and also more widespread than their cognitive counterparts. Early in the development of animals they probably were the only kind of information processing. In a sense, it is strange that today we see unconscious processes merely as the opposite of consciousness – in spite of the fact that they came first in the development of humans as opposed to the conscious processes, which appeared much later.

Unconscious processes rely to a large extent upon their own memory system, the implicit memory. This applies to processes regulating the blood flow, stomach processing and many other fundamental processes ongoing in the body. Also many aspects of seeing, tasting, feeling, thinking, evaluating and judging rely on unconscious processes drawing upon implicit memory. When judging or evaluating takes place, we may sometimes be able to become aware of these processes or the results stemming from them.

Even the use of language relies heavily upon unconscious processes and information stored in implicit memory. We decode what is being said using phonology, we give meaning to it with the use of semantics, we make sense of the relationship between the words with the use of syntax and we see it in the light of the world as we perceive it, pragmatics. The phonology, the semantics, the syntax and pragmatic processing all occur unconsciously and have been labelled "the psychology of the cognitive unconsciousness" (Ledoux, 2002).

1. Cognitive Consumer Choice Models

The study of consumer choice behaviour departs in cognitive approaches. Early attempts are made by Nicosia (1966) and Andreasen (1965). The first more structured models are found in works by Howard and Sheth (1969), by Engel et al. (1971) and by Hansen (1972).

These early students of consumer behaviour largely study human choice behaviour as information processing much in line with general problem solving, known from organizational psychology, and not uninspired by computer developments contemporary to their time. This said, however, they all, to different degrees, allow for unconscious cognitive processes to occur.

Important contributions along these lines are also made by Fishbein (1965) on measuring attitudes, McGuire (1976) and Bettman (1979) on cognitive processes and association theory and leading publications of the 1970's and 80's were dominated by contributions based on this thinking. Important journals all covered multi-attribute cognitive models of choice, information processing and similar topics. Even today hypotheses derived from these models in different forms are the most frequently found topic for PhD-research and contributions in leading journals.

It is not the purpose here to review this entire line of research. Rather we shall try to outline some of the major characteristics of the models used and the thinking brought forward. This is done to form a background for the subsequent treatment of emotions in consumer choice.

The building blocks of cognitive theories are cognitive elements. In its entire life span the individual receives an astronomical number of informational impressions. Even in a single moment the number of aspects that could be perceived is enormous. Estimates have been made, that put the number of commercial stimuli received by an average citizen of an industrialized country is more than 3000 in one average day.

To be able to handle such almost unlimited numbers of colour, form, sound, taste and other impressions, as well as all possible combinations of these, the individual systemises the impressions he receives. The cognitive theorist holds that he does so by establishing categories into which each of the different elements are classified. Such categories may be seen as cognitive elements in their own right. One should imagine as many and more cognitive elements available to the individual as the number of words in the spoken language. To categorise is to place things, events and people around us in classes. A cognitive element represents a number of units, acts, phenomena, which have something in common. Responses are based rather on common traits of the category than on the single unit's individual character.

Cognitive elements are learned. They are general in the sense that people are able to classify a new phenomenon into a category even though one exactly like the one in question has never previously been encountered. The complete set of cognitions that an individual has may be compared to a language, even though the two systems are not identical. There are cognitive elements corresponding to combinations of words, and there are cognitive elements to which no words correspond: that is elements that can be used to handle impressions from the environment without those having to be verbalised. Examples of such elements can be those related to taste, music and the arts.

Contemporary neuropsychology does not think of cognitive elements as specific information units stored in particular places in the brain. They rather see them as something which in particular situations can be activated based upon connections between many different sub-elements entering into the picture of the overall category. Nerve cells in the brain are interlinked. Exactly how a cognitive element becomes activated depends on what cells and what links are activated. For our discussion here it is useful to think of all the latent cognitive elements of the individual as a huge store of information units that may be activated consciously or unconsciously in different situations and with different links between them. Such information storages are also discussed as associate networks.

The cognitive elements as associate networks serve a number of purposes.

- Firstly they represent the coding system of the individual. And they are used in perceiving and classifying things in the environment.
- Secondly, they represent the informational units with which thought processes work. When humans solve problems, think or engage in other cognitive activities, it involves work with such activated cognitive elements. They connect them, compare them, and out of this come activity and conclusions.
- Thirdly, the concepts are important in communication between individuals. As suggested, the language can be seen as part of the total system of concepts.
- Fourthly, the conceptual system, the informational parts of cognitive elements are the key to understanding information storing occurring in memory.

One can imagine a cognitive element as a unit of information like a record in an IT-system. It may represent a complex phenomenon, like a person's image, or it can be as simple as the number "1". The total number of records in the system represents the latent cognitive elements. Those aroused for actual treatment represent the activated cognitive structure.

As in all other information coding systems each element has an identification tag. Each element is described in a number of dimensions and everything corresponding to this description is placed as belonging in the category.

Cognitive elements are interrelated. For instance, a sports car may to some people be related to traffic accidents. Such relations also represent information stored in connection with the various cognitive elements.

Cognitive elements may also be more or less positively evaluated. We may like steaks and not stews or vice versa. That is, information about the evaluation of the element must be stored. This is generally referred to as the attitude towards the cognitive element.

In any particular situation a set of cognitively related elements may be activated. Such cognitive structure can be of different kinds. The elements can be linked positively (for instance: likes, helps, serves), negatively (for instance: dislikes, counteracts) or neutrally (for instance: has no influence on, or is irrelevant to).

Insko (1967) in a now classical paper classifies cognitive relations as shown in Table II.1.

Table II.1: Cognitive relations (Insko, 1967)

Sign	Affective	Instrumental	Logical	Spatial or proximal
Positive	Like	Make easier	Follow from	Holds on to
	Love	Evoke /Provoke	Corresponding /Equivalent	Second to
	Admire	Help	Same	Close to
	Interested in	Cause	Equal to	
Neutral	Not care	Without effect	Not the same	
Negative	Hate	Obstruct	Concordant	Far from
	Have antipathy	Act against	Conflict with	
	Talk condescendingly about	Harm	Different from	

An activated cognitive structure may be illustrated as done in Figure II.1. Here are three cognitive elements: "I", "chocolate" and "fattening" related as illustrated. "I" "like" "chocolate", "chocolate" is "fattening" and "I" "dislike" being fat.

Figure II.1: Example of evoked cognitive structure

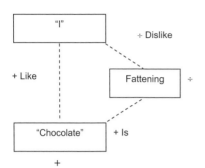

This structure has two positive and one negative connection. All structures with this character are in one way or the other conflicting to the individual. An unconflicting similar situation would occur if either "I disliked chocolate" or "chocolate was non-fattening". In both instances the conflict is eliminated from the cognitive structure. When coping with problems, individuals form such cognitive structures and in problem solving they try to eliminate the conflict. They may do so by preferring choice alternatives represented by balanced structures or they may do so by changing conflicting relationships between elements. The individual aims at avoiding conflict in such associate networks and this process is sometimes referred to as balancing the cognitive structure (Hovland et al., 1953). Social psychologists have pointed at many strategies that can be applied in this connection. Heider's congruence theory (1958) describes one such strategy and the dissonance theory (Festinger, 1957) describes another. Here the individual after a choice – and in order to resolve the seeming conflict - tends to avoid positive information about the rejected alternatives and negative information about the one chosen.

In consumer choice behaviour attitudes are seen as related to the special cognitive elements and they are of particular importance. Attitudes can be seen as the total evaluation associated with a cognitive element. The attitude has a cognitive, an evaluative and a conative (behavioural intention) element (Osgood et al., 1957).

The attitude may be towards a brand, towards some aspects of that brand, about how it may fulfil choice criteria or any other element appearing in the total cognitive information system. The relationship between the latent total information storage and the activated part is important. The capacity to cope with information is limited and only relatively few cognitive elements will be available at the same time in short term memory ready for treatment. How many and what elements depend upon stimulation from the environment, the total activity of the brain system, physiological conditions such as hunger or thirst, and the links existing between the different elements. If some elements are activated those closely linked with them are likely to become activated also.

To explain choices made in such cases, the student of consumer behaviour has traditionally looked at cognitive elements and the relations among these. An illustration of such an activated cognitive structure is shown in Figure II.2 of an individual's hypothetical cognitive structure of a brand (Dove shampoo) and related choice criteria influencing attitude and choice intentions of the brand. Figures associated with choice criteria $(a^1 - a^4)$ reflect the importance to the criteria. Figures with arrows $(b^1 - b^4)$ reflect the degree of association between the cognitive elements: The image of the brand. The process is seen as a Schemata (Rumelhart, 1984) with declarative (a's in Figure II.2) and procedural elements (b's in Figure II.2).

Figure II.2: Activated cognitive structure for Dove Deodorant Brand

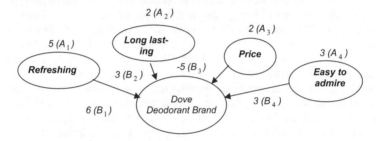

In some researchers' work with cognitive attitude models, choice criteria that reflect a certain aspect of "feeling" elements occur (see for instance, Mazis et al. 1975). Here are found criteria such as the extent to which the (cigarette) brand makes you feel "socially accepted" or a visit to an amusement park "makes you feel happy". Thus some choice criteria in cognitive choice models may reflect such feeling elements. Many authors, however, find that multi-attribute choice models work the best when the elements activated are of an informational/cognitive nature.

As suggested earlier in activated cognitive choice structures (like Figure II.2), the way in which a cognitive element (a choice alternative, a brand etc.) is evaluated is seen as the attitude towards the choice alternative, brand, etc. In turn, this attitude is seen as a function of its positive and negative association with other cognitive elements. In Figure II.2 the attitude towards the brand Dove is positively influenced by the way it relates to "Refreshing" and negatively by its relationship with "Price".

The role that these relationships have in forming behavioural intention towards the item to be evaluated is treated in multiattribute theories (Hansen, 1972, and Bettman, 1979) of which the Fishbein model is a special version (Fishbein, 1965). Here the evaluation (EA_i)

of a brand is the sum of the strength (A_j) of all the j attitudes associated with the brand multiplied with the strength of these associations (b_{ij}):

Formula II.1:

$$A_j = \sum_i B_{ij} * A_i$$

Thus the cognitive evaluation of the alternative may be seen as a computer like treatment of the importance of the different needs, the alternative is expected to fulfil, weighted with the extent to which they are seen to do so.

In this connection the concept of involvement is important as a central determinant of the nature of the decision making process. The degree of involvement of a consumer in a particularly task increases with, the risk and the importance of the consequences of the choice, with the nature of the specific choice situation (time pressure, social consequences etc.) as well as with a predisposition for involvement in the consumer brands in the choice situation (Zaichowsky, 1985).

With high involvement from the consumer such complex computations may actually take place. With lower involvement the consumer is likely to rely on less complex cognitive evaluations. He/she may choose the one alternative (brand, item on the menu etc.) that is best on the most important criteria and thereby skip the weighting.

The nature of the needs being satisfied by the alternative (brand, product, etc.) is important. In some instances the consumer is primarily faced with what can be labelled problem avoidance, that is to remove a headache, to avoid a risk of fire to one's house, to remove stains from the teeth, etc. These situations are referred to as informational problem solving situations (Rossiter and Percy, 1997, and Rossiter and Bellman, 2005). In contrast to these situations are the transformational situations where positive need fulfilment is at stake and the consumption is rewarding in its own right, such as in choice of a perfume to obtain a pleasant smell, choice of a select brand of whisky to gain a positive taste experience, to buy a new dress to give oneself a felling that one looks better etc.

In contemporary marketing concern with experience marketing and the whole complex of the experience economy (Pine and Gilmore 1998) and (Kubovy, 1999) leads to contemplation about "pleasures of the mind", where the focus is upon the transformational aspects of consumer behaviour as it occurs in varying degrees in almost all marketing alternatives. In contrast to this these authors see "pleasures of the body" where the satisfaction of basic needs is in focus.

2. Decision Processes

In contrast with many simple routinized choices, other consumer decisions may be seen as sequences of choices made, leading to the final purchase, consumption or communication decision. Trial of a new coffee brand may involve a preceding situation where new information makes the individual aware of the existence of the new brand. Also preceding may be another situation in the store where the individual is faced with the new brand together with competing existing coffee brands. When even more involving problems are at stake, such as the purchase of a new refrigerator, the number of steps in the sequence may be quite considerable. Still, however, in cognitive theory what is studied is what happens in each single of these choice situations constituting the complete decision process.

3. The Activated Cognitive Structure

The potential number of cognitive elements that an individual can bring into a given choice situation is extremely large. In principle, it can be anything stored in memory. It is, however, only a minor part of this which is activated in any single situation. The short term memory's limited capacity accounts for this. The distinction between the latent system of choice criteria, images, preferences, attitudes, schemata, etc. and those activated from here in the specific choice situation is very important. In cognitive models of choice it is the interaction between the activated cognitive elements which is in focus.

As suggested previously, the activated cognitive structure in a consumer choice situation may comprise:

- a number of alternatives to be chosen from (brands, products, stores, etc.)
- a number of choice criteria (with related attitudes towards these) of importance for the alternatives.
- information about how the alternatives are evaluated relative to the choice criteria (that is, their image or the beliefs about them)
- and possibly earlier, formed evaluations and preferences for the alternatives activated

Already in the 50's Miller (1956) reviewed a large number of studies that dealt with the number of elements entering into different kinds of choices. His overall conclusion is contained in the title of his paper: "The magic number 7 plus minus 2". His conclusion was that the maximum number of cognitive elements entering into choice situations almost always would be between 5 and 9, depending upon the type of problem, individual conditions, situational conditions, etc.

This observation has been confirmed later and it has played a major role in consumer behaviour studies. Jacoby (1977) introduces the concept of "information load" and "information overload". Information load is a measure of the complexity of the activated cognitive structure in a particular situation. Information overload occurs when the consumer is brought into a situation where there is more information than he can handle. Many studies show that the limits to the informa-tion handling capacity are real. For instance, Bither and Wright (1977) in a study of alternative birth control methods show that, even in such involving situations, the number of attitudes entering into the consid-erations are limited. In spite of this, consumers may be able to handle even very complex problems (Alba and Hutchinson, 1987). They do so by organizing single aspects into more complex groups. The ex-perienced photographer does not look at all alternative exposure in-tervals that a particular camera offers. Rather he "chunks" or groups information on different closer systems. The more experienced the consumer is in a particular area, the larger "chunks" he may make use of. The connoisseur of vintage cars may have such complex chunks of information as "12 cylinder, 2 doors, open, German sports cars from 1920-1938".

Other consumer researchers have been concerned with the econ-omy of information treatment. Departing from economic theories about optimal information use, Shugan (1980) illustrates the relation-ship between the advantages associated with using a slightly more complex choice strategy on the one hand and the disadvantages as-sociated with errors that may result when wrong decisions are made on the other hand.

The same arguments about economy in information processing have led to the concepts of acceptable alternatives or evoked set. Howard and Sheth (1969) emphasize that for the individual consumer in most product areas this is much less than the number of brands and other alternatives available. Urban and Hauser (1980) operation-alize this concept by asking the following questions about brands:

- Which brands do you like?
- Which brand did you buy last time?
- Which brand did you buy the second last time?
- Which brand do you have in the household presently?
- Which brands have you used lately?
- Which brands have you ever used?
- Which brand would you not consider to buy?

The acceptable alternatives are here defined as the brands men-tioned in reply to one ore more of the six first questions minus those mentioned as answers to the last question.

Figure II.3: Sherif's subjective grouping (Sherif et al., 1965)

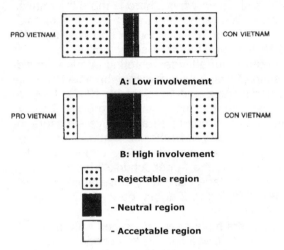

Sherif et al. (1965) in their "Social judgement involvement approach" (1965) make a distinction between acceptable, neutral and rejectable alternatives. The idea is illustrated in Figure II.3 with the three regions illustrated for more or less involved individuals in pro et con Vietnam attitudes (Sheriff's own example). Here the individual has a number of possible statements that can be accepted, some towards which the individual is indifferent and others which he clearly rejects. For the more involved individual the acceptable region is narrower and the extent of the region of rejection is much larger.

This has implications when formulating messages aimed at influencing individual attitudes. If your claim is more or less identical with the individuals initial position it will have little or no affect on the stand the individual takes. If on the other hand the communication position is to deviate from what the individual already thinks, then it will be reflected also and have little or no effect. Only with messages providing some newness to the receiver, but not too much conflicting information, effective information processing will occur.

Similarly Brisoux and Laroche (1980), Church et al. (1985) and Laroche et al. (1985) emphasize the importance of considering alternatives that are neither rejected nor accepted. An indifference ascribable either to the lack of insight or following from the combination of attributes which the alternatives have. In line with this Hüber and Puto (1983) illustrate how it may have considerable influence on the choice conflict if one alternative is extremely good on one dimension but worse on others.

4. Multi-Attribute Models
Under the heading of multi-attribute models, a number of different rules are discussed that the individual may apply in coping with vari-

ous cognitive structures representing choice alternatives. Another representation of such a structure is presented in Figure II.4.

Figure II.4: *Cognitive structure with choice criteria and image, 4 central boxes. In decision (lines connecting choice criteria) about the alternatives; gas (G) or oil (O) heating (Hansen, 1987)*

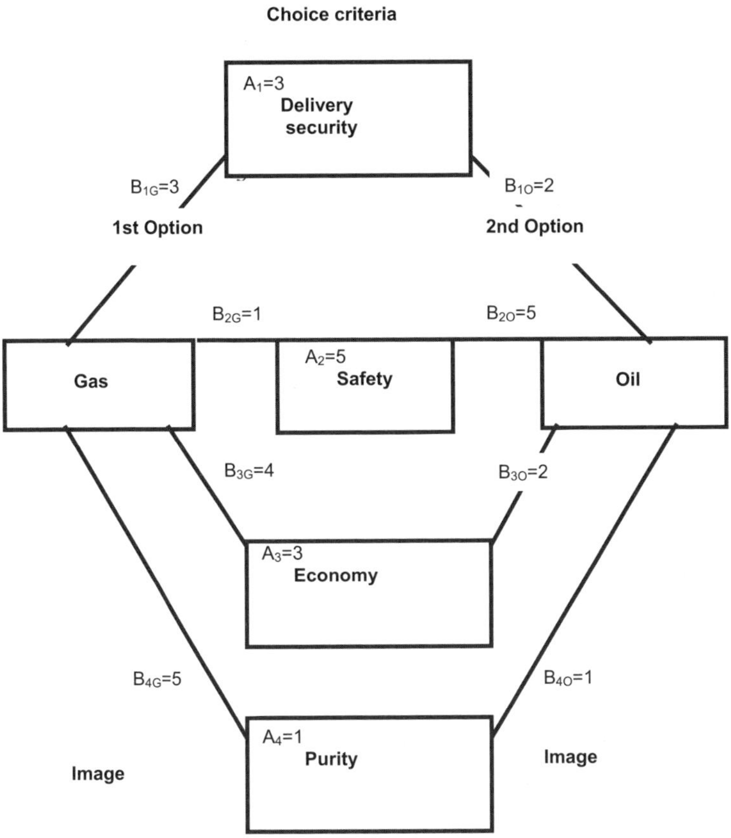

Choice criteria

Here attitudes towards security of delivery, security, economy, and cleanliness are determining choice criteria in a choice between having gas or oil installed as energy source for a private household. The figures in the boxes indicate the importance assigned to each of the attitudes (the A_j, in Figure II.4) and the extent to which the two alternatives are believed to provide services favouring the choice criteria (B_{ij}, in I) are suggested by the numbers connected with each of the lines in the diagram.

Essentially, the figure illustrates a choice situation between oil and gas for home heating. This can be analysed in several different ways.

In terms of the Fishbein model it can be illustrated as done in Table II.2 where the 2nd and 3rd columns (2A and 2B) give beliefs about image of the two alternatives. If these are added up it appears that Gas has the most positive image (most positive beliefs associated with it) and if image alone is governing the choice, the prediction would be that gas would be chosen. As illustrated in the figure, however, the choice criteria are not equally important. Importance is given in the first column of Table II.2. If one weights the image of the alternative with the importance consumers associate with the different attitudes related to the choice, then the image for gas in Table II.2 (column 2A) can be multiplied with importance of the choice criteria (column 1), resulting in the overall evaluation of gas in column 3A.

Table II.2: Computation of total image value and attractiveness-score (Hansen, 1987)

	1. Importance of choice Criteria	2A Evaluation of Alternatives (images) Gas	2B Oil	3A Attractiveness Gas	3B Oil
Delivery certainty	3	3	2	9	6
Safety	5	1	5	5	25
Economy	3	4	2	12	6
Purity	1	5	1	5	1
		(13)	(10)	31	38

When these figures are added combined attraction measures of 31 and 38 respectively emerges for the two alternatives. These imply that the predicted choice is now oil.

Cognitive multi-attribute models of choice study how attitudes and beliefs may be thought of as governing the choice. The two models described here are both compensatory in the sense, that strength on one particular attitude dimension may compensate weakness on another in the evaluation of the alternative.

The first model where the choice criteria's importance is neglected may be labelled a pure image model whereas the second model is the already introduced Fishbein model. Different authors have used different terminology in coping with the elements in such choice situations as shown in Table II.3.

Table II.3: Different multi-attribute terminology (Hansen, 1987)

	Perceptual	Evaluating	Intention
Fishbein (1965):	Belief	Attitude	Intention
Rosenberg (1959):	Instrumentality	Value	Attitude
Osgood et al. (1957):	Cognition	Affect	Conation
Hansen (1972)	Image	Choice criteria	Attractiveness or intention

In the choice between the image model and the more complex compensatory Fishbein model Fishbein and Ajzen (1975) argue for the importance of the rating, whereas Woodside and Clokey (1974) only find moderate improvements in the predictions by using weighting compared with the straight image model. Also Curry and Menasco (1983) suggest that in some situations it may be difficult operationally to distinguish between image and importance of criteria. Even in quite complex decisions the simple image model has proven to function well (Asthon, 1980). Generally it has been found that weighting of alternatives is important where more consequential choices are at stake such as choice among political parties, line of education, etc.

Interesting in this connection is Woodside and Clokey's (1974) test of three different varieties of the model applied to the choice between headache remedies. Here three models – 1, 2, 3 (Figure II.5) – were applied to nine headache brands and nine choice criteria that possibly could be important for each of these.

Figure II.5: 3 alternative multi-attribute models

$$1^{st} \text{ model: } A_J = \sum_{I=1}^{9} B_{IJ}$$

$$2^{nd} \text{ model: } A_J = \sum_{I=1}^{9} B_{IJ} A_I$$

$$3^{rd} \text{ model: } A_J = \sum_{I=1}^{3} B_{IJ} A_I$$

Preferences for brands are computed in three different ways:
1. The already mentioned image model
2. The traditional Fishbein model
3. A modified Fishbein model, where only the three most important choice criteria are applied.

Even though all three models made good predictions of the actual choices made by the respondents, the first and the third model were slightly better than the more complex Fishbein model.

5. The Theory of Reasoned Action

The Fishbein model has also been criticized for not taking sufficient care of how social influences may have impact on the choices made. In a modified version of the model, the theory of "Reasoned action", Ajzen and Fishbein (1977) propose an extended model where social beliefs in terms of individuals' perceptions of different reference groups multiplied with the belief about the acceptability of the alternative to the group is introduced. Here it explicitly is the Behaviour Intentions (I) which is predicted. The model suggests:

Formula II.2:

$$I_j = \alpha \sum_1^N B_{ij} A_i + (1-\alpha) \sum_1^m NB_{kj} MC_k$$

Where,

I_j = The intention towards alternative j

NB_k = The person's perception of reference (group) "k"'s estimation of how acceptable the alternative "j" is

MC_k = The importance of the views of person "k" to the respondent

α = A weight reflecting the relative importance the two components of evaluations. With $\alpha = 1$ the formula reduces to the traditional Fishbein Model.

… and can be illustrated as shown in Figure II.6.

Figure II.6: *Structure in Fishbein's extended attitude model (Hansen, 1987)*

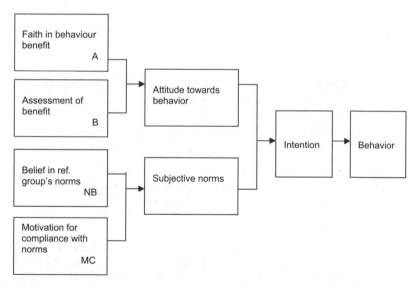

The first part of the model is the traditional Fishbein model. The second part introduces what the authors label normative beliefs (NB). These represent the individuals' view of how important it is to consider different reference groups or persons when the actual choice is made. The relative importance of the social influence is labelled motive to comply (MC). It is weighted by a parameter, Alpha, where the larger the Alpha the less important the social influence and with Alpha taking on the value of one, the model reduces to the traditional Fishbein multi-attribute model.

Ryan and Bonfield (1980) have illustrated the usefulness of the model in some consumer behaviour connections and so have Lutz (1977), Bearden and Woodside (1977) and Ryan and Bonfield (1980). Others, however, have had difficulties in applying the model. Miniard and Cohen (1981 and 1983) argue that the model in many situations does not give better predictions than more simple models and they suggest that it may be difficult to estimate the value of the variables in it. And Shimp and Kavas (1984) propose a modified Theory of Reasoned Action model incorporating interaction between attitudes towards the alternative and subjective norms. With data on coupon they demonstrate their model to be superior to the basic model.

And, also, Ryan (1982) finds that there may be close relationships between the attitude elements and the normative social influence elements making it difficult to distinguish between them. The latter suggesting that some aspects of social influence may already be contained in straightforward choice criteria. Nevertheless Bagozzi et al. (1992) finds support for the Theory of Reasoned Action and so does Janiszewski (1993).

6. The Theory of Planned Behaviour
The Theory of Reasoned Action has been shown to work best when consumers have reasonable actual influence on the choices they are making (Shimp and Kavos, 1984). When they are only little concerned the Theory of Reasoned Action often falls short. Sheppard et al. (1988) after reviewing earlier research on the Theory of Reasoned Action find that in cases where individuals themselves judge that they have strong influence on the actual outcome of the choice the model works the best; "Action that are at least in part determined by factors beyond individuals volitional control fall outside the boundary conditions established for the model". The Theory of Planned Behaviour is proposed by Ajzen (1991) to cope with this phenomenon. The essence of this model is illustrated in Figure II.7.

Figure II.7: The Theory of Planned Behaviour (Aizen 2002)

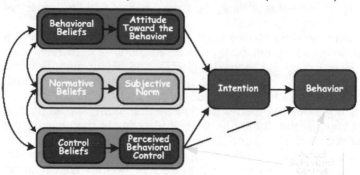

In essence the model says that the more the controlled the individual perceive to have over the act in question the better the Reasoned Action model will predict behaviour (the upper parts of Figure II.7).

The superiority of the Planned Behaviour Model is illustrated by findings by Chang (1998), Shim et al. (2001) and Hansen et al. (2004), but also earlier finding such as Bagozzi (1986) points in that direction. That people actually do perceive differences in the extent to which they can influence what happens to them, researchers working with attribution theory have demonstrated. In a thorough review of studies concerned with people's perception of causes for what has happened to them, their attribution of causes influence their choices (Weiner, 2000, and Campbell and Kirmani, 2000).

7. Identifying Choice Criteria

Different techniques exist for estimating choice criteria in a particular product area and at the same time these techniques can illustrate how the alternatives are perceived along these. Multidimensional scaling (Carmone and Green 1981) of various kinds are used in this connection. Here departing in how alternatives are perceived relatively to each other (perceived similarity) a representation is looked for where the distances between the points in the plot correspond as much as possible to the differences as they are seen by the respondents participating in the study. As many as needed dimensions are included in the analysis. The more dimensions, the better fit obtained.

Figure II.8: Aggregated perceptual picture of 8 toothpaste brands with ideal point embedded (Neidell, 1969)

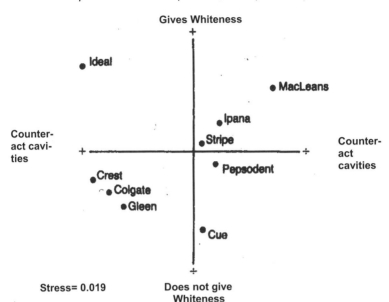

To illustrate the underlying idea, consider Figure II.8, where different toothpaste brands are positioned relative to two dimensions judged to reflect two important choice criteria regarding toothpaste: "gives white teeth" and "protects against cavities".

The distance from any brand to the two axes may be seen as the beliefs about the brand's ability to fulfil the criteria on the two dimensions. Thus McLean's is believed to give white teeth but not to be good for protection against cavities whereas Crest is believed to be active against cavities but not to give white teeth.

In such a diagram an ideal can be identified as illustrated with a dot in the upper left corner of the diagram. The preference for the brand can then be interpreted as a distance from the brand to the ideal and choices are predicted based upon these preference estimates. In such a model the preference can be computed as follows:

Formula II.3:

$$A_i \text{ (preference)} = \sum_{J=1}^{N} \frac{1}{(B_{ij} - ID_j)A_j}$$

where B and A are image and attitudes as in Figure II.8 and ID_j is the value of the ideal product on the dimension *j* and *i* are the different brands.

In some instances the ideal can be seen as a vector pointing in the direction of the ideal.

Here, the better the alternatives are perceived in way of need fulfilment measured along the axes, the better. The one alternative, the projection of which is further out along the vector, is the best. The angle of the dimensions reflects the relative importance of (here two) choice criteria.

8. Non-Compensatory Cognitive Models

The models described so far are all compensatory in the sense that they assume that the individual makes some computations weighting the possible contributions (image values) for each choice alternative. It is possible, however, for the individual to apply less complex non-compensatory models also. This may particularly be so when perceived control is low. These non-compensatory models are simple and often very easy for the consumer to apply. There are many different ways in which individuals can compare alternatives without weighting or making other compensatory considerations.

The consumer may simply be looking for the alternative which scores the best on the most important (image) dimension. Or he or she may inspect whether the alternative is satisfactory ("good enough") on some more important (image) dimensions.

It has been argued that the individual consumer, in addition to having a number of standard methods available, is able to develop new choice methods if the already known ones are less suitable. Bettman and Park (1980) have coded and studied protocol data about decisions for consumers in a manner so that it has been possible to identify such individually constructed processes.

The two main categories of non-compensatory models are disjunctive and conjunctive. In a conjunctive type of model the consumer requires that an alternative is satisfactory in regard to two or more attitudes (choice criteria). The disjunctive decision rule implies that a consumer requires that one particular condition must be fulfilled. In Table II.4 choice among different apartments with different rents are illustrated. If the decision rule is conjunctive, the criteria could be that the apartment should cost less than or equal to Euro 1,500 pr. month and that the distance should be 1.5 kilometres or less. This means that the alternatives 1, 2 and 3 are acceptable. With a disjunctive choice process where, for instance, either the rent should be below Euro 1,000 or the distance equal to or below 1.5 kilometres the only feasible alternatives become 1.

Table II.4:   9 alternative housing options with varying prices and location

Apartment	Monthly rent (EURO)	Distance from work (km)
1	1000	1.5
2	1800	1.5
3	2000	1.5
4	1000	2
5	1800	2
6	2000	2
7	1000	3
8	1500	3
9	2000	3

A special version of the conjunctive model is a lexicographic model suggested by Tversky (1969). He assumes that the decision maker has formulated minimum requirements regarding each attitude along which the alternatives are evaluated. The choice then is made by first examining what alternatives satisfy the most important dimension. If more than one is available the process continues by asking which of the alternatives are acceptable on the second most important dimension. This process continues until only one alternative is left. The process here is also labelled "processing by attribute" – or lexicographic – and it requires that the decision maker can formulate minimum demands on the different dimensions.

Such minimum criteria rely upon experiences with previous use, knowledge about the alternatives, communication etc. If too many satisfactory alternatives are available the minimum demands tend to increase. The reverse occurs if no alternatives fulfil the requirements. This may lead to reconsideration of the minimum level for acceptability. It would be expected that the procedure is used where many alternatives are available.

In some situations, however, alternatives are not easily available but have to be sought out. Here a processing by alternative or processing by brand is possible. Such a model is described in Hansen (1972) based upon Cyert and March's (1963) organisational search model. Wright (1980) discusses such behaviour as making satisfactory choices. In research on consumer satisfaction (Oliver, 1980 and Õlander, 1986) such models are fundamental.

As with the lexicographic decision process it is assumed that minimum levels for the attitudes associated with the alternatives exist. The procedure, however, is different. The most nearby alternative is inspected first. This is examined on all relevant criteria. If it satisfies the minimum conditions on all areas it is chosen and the process terminates. If the alternative is not satisfactory the next alternative is inspected. If this is satisfactory it is selected. If it is not satisfactory, the process continues until a satisfactory alternative is found. If repeatedly the process does not lead to satisfactory alternatives, downward modifications of expectations may be expected. And reverse, if the conditions are all too easily fulfilled the minimum demands may be heightened.

The non-compensatory choices are simple and require uncomplicated judgements. They are most likely to be applied where the individual is only involved in a limited way, that is where there is only little energy available for the decision process. Johnson and Meyer (1984) illustrate how the use of non-compensatory models vary, depending upon the complexity of the problem. When many alternatives are to be compared it is more likely that non-compensatory processes are used. Thus non-compensatory processes will more frequently appear early in more extensive decision processes where many alternatives are involved. Later compensatory alternative evaluations can be applied. In this fashion the least attractive alternatives are sorted out early.

C. Limitations of Cognitive Choice Models

1. Attitude and Choice

Fundamental for the usefulness of the attitude-based cognitive consumer choice models is the underlying basic assumption that attitudes somehow precede behaviour.

However, several authors have presented evidence throwing doubt upon the validity of this proposition. Most comprehensively this is discussed by Ray (1976) who, departing in the classical attitude theory's conceptualisation that cognition precedes attitudes which precedes behaviour (cognition affect behaviour), discusses how in many instances things may happen in a different order.

A somewhat reversed order of things "behaviour, cognition, attitude" may prevail when choices are made with limited time available, low familiarity with the choice alternatives and with limited involvement.

Similarly "attitude, cognition, behaviour" relationships may occur where strongly held attitudes conflict with externally determined behaviours calling for a solution of the conflict using cognitive processing prior to execution of the behaviour.

Much research has been reported, suggesting discrepancies between attitudes and subsequent behaviours. In later years an often-recorded topic, where this discrepancy is evident, is the attitudes towards environmental issues and their limited influence on environmental behaviour (Beckmann and Kilbourne, 1998). More fundamental research has suggested that processes very different from those assumed in cognitive models may be at work when consumers make choices. Another way of bringing additional power to the classical cognitive approach is to bring feelings or emotions in as a separate component in line with the cognitive elements. For instance Allen et al. (1992) show that adding feelings/emotions to predictions of consumer choice improves the prediction made by attitudes alone.

2. Alternative Views on the Role of Cognitive Processes

In parallel with the above-described mainstream line of thinking, a number of observations have been made by different researchers, observations that are difficult to interpret in terms of the cognitive effect hierarchy way of thinking (Hansen, 1984). Picture perception has been studied by psychologists and Nickerson (1968), for instance, presents highly relevant findings for our purpose. We will not be reviewing the entire line of this particular research here, but it is worth illustrating the underlying idea: imagine an experiment where you show 200 pictures for two seconds each to an audience of 200. On the following day, you do the same; only you this time include 200 new pictures to make a total of 400 pictures. Following the exposure of each picture, you ask a question to test if people can recognise the pictures from the day before. The overall observation in such an experiment is that 95-100 % of the stimuli presented on the first day are recognised. The research has gone on to look into how such recognition persists over time, the role of the length of the exposure time, the nature of the pictures presented, the motivation of the subjects in the audience etc. We shall not go into details with this, but it is a basic observation that provided two seconds are allowed for exposure (or one second for exposure and one second for undisturbed information processing before the next exposure), the recognition process is extremely efficient and documents an enormous capacity for storing of visual information in the brain. This information storage is not limited to short or medium-term memory and may persist for years.

Another line of research has been reported by Zajonc (1968). Here, the purpose was to study how the positive evaluation of items, to which subjects are exposed, increase with the number of exposures. In classic studies, Chinese characters and nonsense words have been used. The experimental design is simple. On the first day, respondents are exposed to a sequence of for instance Chinese characters, but the stimuli are controlled so that some of the characters are shown 1, 2, 5, 10, or even 25 times. The following day, the same respondents are asked what they think the meaning is of the different Chinese characters in terms of being more or less positive. Findings from such a study are illustrated in Figure II.9. The obvious effect of an increased number of exposures is seen. This line of research has led to the formulation of the so-called 'mere exposure' hypothesis. Similar results have been reported by many authors as for instance lately by Beaver et al. (2005) who shows that fear reactions being unconsciously associated with stimuli such as spiders, flowers and mushrooms also reappear subsequently with exposure to the conditional stimuli. Findings that also confirm the existence of such subliminal effects are also reported by Naccache et al. (2005).

Figure II.9: Average positive assessment of the meaning of Chinese character at low and high number of exposures on a 5 point scale (Zajonc, 1968)

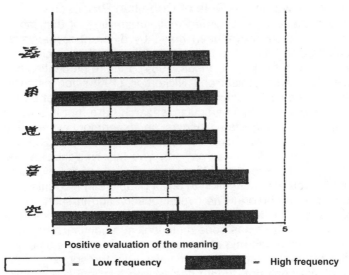

In many situations, it seems that mere exposure improves evaluation; but, of course, there are limits. If the words are not nonsense words, but rather meaningful ones such as names of known persons or of cities or brands, the prior knowledge and evaluation of the persons or cities may inhibit the mere exposure effect.

This is illustrated with findings from another classical piece of psychological research. In the 1940s, Torqerson and Lorge (reported in Zajonc, 1968) had students counting the frequency with which different words occurred in a sample of literature from Chicago University Library. With a different sample of students, they ranked the average positive, negative evaluation of the different words. Findings reflecting evaluation of cities are shown in Table II.5.

The mere exposure relationship is evident, but, remarkably, exceptions can be observed too. The frequency with which Chicago occurs in literature sampled from a university library does not compensate for the way in which people seem to view Chicago relative to for instance Boston. Conversely, the relatively rare frequency with which San Diego appears does not overrule the generally positive impression people have of the city.

Table II.5: Preference ranks and frequency counts of 10 cities (Za-jonc, 1968) (High preference score means low preference)

City	Frequency	Average preference rank
Boston	255	2.75
Chicago	621	3.08
Milwaukee	124	3.83
San Diego	9	4.25
Dayton	14	5.75
Baltimore	68	6.08
Omaha	28	7.08
Tampa	5	7.08
El Paso	1	7.50
Saginaw	2	7.58

Similar results are found in studies of corporate image. This has been of major concern for companies for many years. Some of the major findings from the Mori group in London are reported in Worchester and McIntyre (1979). The basic observation here is that if you measure how frequently a person has heard about a particular company (self-rated awareness) and how positively/negatively the same person evaluates that company (self-rated attitude); a classical image-positioning picture emerges (see Figure II.10). Here, it appears that the better known a company is, the more positively it is evaluated.

Again, there are exceptions. A local company may be very well known, but its bad behaviour may also be known to an extent that results in a relatively more negative evaluation compared with the average. On the whole, however, the results from such studies are dramatic. In a particular Danish case where 50 companies were evaluated and response data was separated into 'those who claim to know the company the best' and 'the rest', it was found that only one company was more negatively evaluated among those claiming to know it the best (a chemical company with extreme waste problems) (Hansen, 1984).

At this point a word is to be said about an issue occasionally occurring in the public debate. In a published book in the 50's by Vance Packard (1956), the idea was proposed that words placed in a movie with exposure so short that it could not be perceived consciously still had effect on consumers. It was claimed that after such exposure consumption of coke and popcorn in the cinema increased dramatically. In later replications similar, but much smaller, effects than those originally claimed were found. It has by the way never been possible to identify the original study and the general opinion today is that if such effects exist, they are of a magnitude making them economically uninteresting. A related issue of increasing contemporary interest is the placement of brands in movies and other entertainment (Tiwsakul et. al. 2005). Here such placement is found to be more effective the more the product presented is integrated into the content of the movie, the better known it is, and the more perceivably it is presented (Andersen, 2006). All factors suggesting more cognitive information processing.

Figure II.10: Familiarity and favourability of companies (Worcester and McIntyre, 1979)

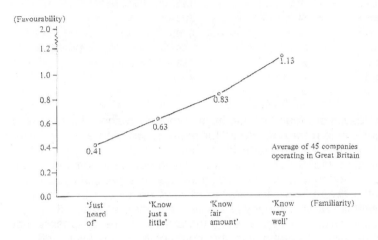

In an extension of the mere exposure research, Zajonc and co-workers studied what they labelled emotions without cognitions. Here they show that the mere exposure effect occur even stronger when the exposure time for the alternative has been so low that the respondents cannot possibly have been aware of it. This becomes important for our subsequent discussion of emotions. Findings are reported in Zajonc and Marcus (1985). In this line of research, the basic idea is very simple and can be illustrated with one of their classical studies. You ask two groups of respondents to evaluate Walkmans (personal tape recorders) by listening to music and speech from these, which they have mounted on their head. The respondents (students) are told that it is an experiment designed to evaluate the quality of a new type of Walkman.

The two groups listen to the same content under the same conditions and with the same instructions. The only difference between the two groups is the following: In the test it is explained that when you use a Walkman in real life, you will often do so when moving around. You may be walking, running or in other ways be occupied with parallel activities. To simulate the effect of these other activities in the listening situation, the respondents in one group are asked to nod their heads while listening, whereas the respondents in the other group are asked to shake their heads. Surprisingly enough, the group nodding their heads evaluate their Walkmans significantly better than those shaking their heads.

Research concerned with left and right-brain information process-ing should be mentioned also. The whole issue is complicated and it is doubtful whether its applicability to the study of consumer informa-tion processing has been properly demonstrated. However, it is worth pointing at some of the characteristics normally associated with left-brain versus right-brain information processing. This is done in Table II.6. Here, the left-brain is shown to be concerned with conscious, verbal, analytical, sequential, arithmetic information processing. This coincides with what we here talk about as cognitive information proc-essing. The right-brain, in contrast, is much more involved with un-conscious, non-verbal, musical, synthetic, holistic, geometrical or spatial information processing. The basic research is reviewed in Sperry (1982) and some results relating to its applicability to the study of consumer behaviour are reported by Hansen (1981), who finds that the measurement problems arising when working with nor-mal (not brain disabled) individuals are so, that the direct applicability of the distinction in applied consumer research is limited.

Table II.6: Characteristic left-right brain aspects of information proc-essing (Hansen, 1981)

"Left"	"Right"
Consciousness	Unconsciousness
Verbal	Non-verbal
Analytical	Synthetic
Sequential	Holistic
Arithmetic	Geometrical (Spatial)

In more recent years however brain scanning experiments have shown the importance also when more trivial tasks are performed by normal individuals. For instance Rueckert (2005) demonstrates that happy faces are perceived differently by right and left brains, and Sim and Martinez (2005) demonstrate that emotional words are remem-bered the better when transmitted to the left ear, - and thus first re-ceived in the right hemisphere. A similar result is reported by Naka-mura et al. (1999) demonstrating that the right (inferior frontal) cortex plays an important role both in processing and interpreting facial ex-pressions. The complexity of the interaction between the brain halves is however documented by Wildgruber et al. (2005) whose respon-dents were to recognize earlier exposed feeling words (happy, sad etc.). Here activities in both brain halves were identified, but also some right hemisphere specialization when emotional variations in the presentation of the stimuli were at stake.

All in all, the findings reviewed here suggest that when we receive information in situations like those in which we are exposed to adver-tising and other forms of marketing communication processes and phenomena occur that are very different from the processes that the cognitive psychologists assume.

3. Peripheral and Low Involvement Information Processing
Different authors have tried to adjust the cognitive modeling of consumer choice with the phenomena just discussed in mind. In this context the concept of involvement has been important. Emphasised by Krugman (1977) and Mitchell and Olson (1981), involvement has been made operational by Zaichkowsky (1985). In many studies of consumer information processing, it has been demonstrated that with low involvement, consumers are less accessible, have fewer defences and are little motivated to cope with complicated information.

Probably one of the more integrated approaches to dealing with low involvement information processing is found in the Rossiter and Percy informational grid (Rossiter and Percy, 1997 and Rossiter and Bellman, 2005). Here, two important distinctions are made. One of them has to do with the kind of motivation that drives consumers in connection with different purchases. This distinction relates to positive transformational consumption (such as obtaining good taste in food, feeling happiness by demonstrating good taste in clothes) and negative/avoidance motivation informational consumption (such as avoiding a headache by using headache remedies, avoiding too much trouble in winter by having a good snow shovel etc.). The second distinction relates to high and low involvement in the already mentioned terminology of Zaichkowsky (1985).

Figure II.11: The Rossiter-Percy Grid (Rossiter and Percy, 1997) or Rossiter/Percy-Bellman Grid (Rossiter and Bellman, 2005)

Type of Motivation

	Informational (negatively originated motivations)	Transformational (positive-ending motivations)
Low involvement (trial experience sufficient)	Typical product categories (brands may differ): • aspirin • light beer • detergent • routine industrial products	Typical product categories (brands may differ): • candy • regular beer • fiction novels
	• Brand loyals • Routinized favorable brand switchers	
High involvement (search and conviction required prior to purchase)	Typical product categories (brands may differ): • microwave oven • insurance • home renovations • new industrial products	Typical product categories (brands may differ): • vacations • fashion clothing • cars • corporate image
	• New category users • Experimental or routinized other-brand switchers • Other-brand loyals	

Type of Decision

Recall occurs when the individual is able to name the item analysed (brand, advertisement, company etc.), when asked what items he knows in a particular area. Recognition on the other hand requires that the individual is shown the item (brand, advertisement, etc.) and asked if he has seen it.

From this platform, the authors propose four different kinds of communication situations shown in Figure II.11. Whereas the high involvement and particularly high involvement/informational processing comes close to what we traditionally find in the effect hierarchy cognitive type of modeling, the low involvement/transformational kind of processing is of a much more emotional nature, it occurs at a low level of consciousness and is stored in the implicit memory.

In this conceptual framework, a distinction between recognition versus recall is important also. In many purchase situations where involvement is low and little factual information is available, recognition of the alternative to be chosen is of major concern. Here, a parallel to the subsequently discussed peripheral processing appears. This is the case when the consumer makes his choice in front of the shelf (Popai, 1999)

In contrast, in other purchasing tasks of a more elaborate nature with planning and comparison of alternatives, the ability to recall relevant alternatives and information about them is extremely important. It is suggested that communication resulting in recall is stored structurally differently from information solely providing recognition. As we shall see subsequently, this is very relevant for some of the aspects of contemporary thinking about emotional information processing.

Figure II.12: How Advertising Works: Planning Model (Vaughn, 1979)

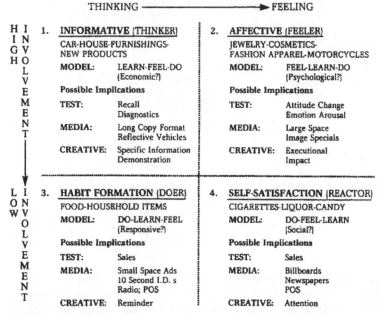

THINKING ⟶ FEELING

H I	1.	**INFORMATIVE** (THINKER)	2.	**AFFECTIVE** (FEELER)
I N G V H O L V E M E N T		CAR-HOUSE-FURNISHINGS- NEW PRODUCTS		JEWELRY-COSMETICS- FASHION APPAREL-MOTORCYCLES
		MODEL: LEARN-FEEL-DO (Economic?)		**MODEL:** FEEL-LEARN-DO (Psychological?)
		Possible Implications		Possible Implications
		TEST: Recall Diagnostics		**TEST:** Attitude Change Emotion Arousal
		MEDIA: Long Copy Format Reflective Vehicles		**MEDIA:** Large Space Image Specials
		CREATIVE: Specific Information Demonstration		**CREATIVE:** Executional Impact
L I O N W V O L V E M E N T	3.	**HABIT FORMATION** (DOER)	4.	**SELF-SATISFACTION** (REACTOR)
		FOOD-HOUSEHOLD ITEMS		CIGARETTES-LIQUOR-CANDY
		MODEL: DO-LEARN-FEEL (Responsive?)		**MODEL:** DO-FEEL-LEARN (Social?)
		Possible Implications		Possible Implications
		TEST: Sales		**TEST:** Sales
		MEDIA: Small Space Ads 10 Second I.D. s Radio; POS		**MEDIA:** Billboards Newspapers POS
		CREATIVE: Reminder		**CREATIVE:** Attention

The same kind of thinking is also found in the way in which major advertising agencies structure their planning. Thus Vaughn (1979) describes what he calls the FCB-Planning model with a quadrant consisting of four different assumptions about the consumer's information processing. This is illustrated in Figure II.12.

Here the dimensions are thinking/feeling and high/low involvement. In this model the high involvement/thinking purchases are seen to represent the classical cognition, evaluation, conation (think – learn – do) sequence. The other quadrants are characterized by "feel – learn – do", "do – learn – feel" and "do – feel – learn" (see Figure II.12). Here it is assumed that advertising should be the more emotional or feeling based when self satisfaction and affect are at stake. On the other hand involvement allows for more informational content in the message. A similar model used by BBDO (Franzen and Borgmann, 2001) makes a distinction between active/passive and positive/negative feelings (see Figure II.13). Again the dimensions are of great similarity with the transformational/informational dimensions of the Rossiter/Percy Grid and the active/passive dimensions with the high/low instrument dimensions.

Figure II.13: Types of emotional responses (BBDO Worldwide, un-published, in: Franzen and Borgmann, 2001)

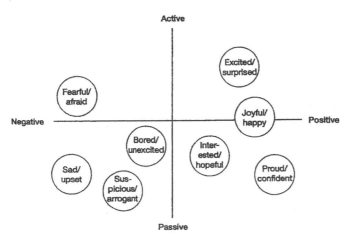

The similarity between the three ways of looking upon advertising (Figures II.11, II.12 and II.13) is striking. Undoubtedly they reflect basic viewpoints adhered to by creatives and others. In subsequent chapters we shall keep the distinctions high/low involvement and transformational/informational in mind.

4. The Elaboration Likelihood Model
Another theoretical approach to the study of consumer information processing is presented by Petty and Cacioppo (1986a) in their Elaboration Likelihood Model. Here, the distinction between peripheral versus central information processing is fundamental. Central information processing is pretty much what we think of in terms of the cognitive hierarchical treatment of information (think – feel – do), whereas peripheral information processing relies on less elaborate, less conscious activity and probably also with more feelings involved.

The authors themselves write: "We have outlined two basic routes to persuasion. One route is based on the thoughtful (though sometimes biased) consideration of arguments central to the issue, whereas the other is based on affective associations or simple inferences tied to the peripheral cues in the persuasion context."

When variables in the persuasion situation render the elaboration likelihood high, the first kind of persuasion occurs (central route). When variables in the persuasion situation render the elaboration likelihood low, the second kind of persuasion occurs (peripheral route). Importantly, there are different consequences of the two routes to persuasion. Attitude changes via the central route appear to be more

persistent, resistant, and predictive of behaviour than changes induced via the peripheral route" (Petty et al., 1983). And Singh (2003)
describes emotional processing as it relates differently to peripheral
and central information processing.

The Petty and Cacioppo (1986a) Elaboration Likelihood Model
(ELM) is modified by Hansen (1997) in terms of an Elaboration Likelihood Advertising Model (ELAM). This model is illustrated in Figure
II.14. Here, central information processing focuses first and foremost
on product and brand relevant information, which generates brand
awareness, brand perception, image preferences and eventually buying intentions. Variables used to reflect the central processing are
brand-related in terms of brand recall, brand recognition, brand processing, attitude towards the brand, preferences for the brand, purchase intentions and possibly changing purchase behaviour.

Figure II.14: The Elaboration Likelihood Advertising Model (ELAM)
(Hansen, 1997)

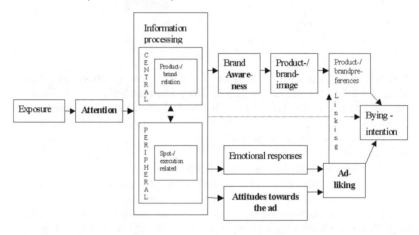

Peripheral information processing following exposure and attention
concerns itself more with how the message looks, what the story is,
what perceptual representations such as e.g. music, pictures, etc.
appear in the advertisement or commercial. These, in turn, generate
attitudes towards the ad (rather than towards the brand) and ad-
liking. These in turn may influence the extent and nature of the parallel central information processing when that occurs. It may also lead
to implicitly stored memories that may eventually be generated as
recognitions that possibly have an influence in purchase situations.
Measurements related to peripheral information processing are more
concerned with ad recall, ad recognition, ad processing, attitudes towards the ad-feelings and ad-liking. Particularly in connection with
advertising processing, different studies have been conducted to
identify the characteristics of peripheral versus central processing at

the Center for Communication Research at the Copenhagen Business School. One of these shall be reported here (Hansen and Hansen 2001b).

5. The Role of Peripheral versus Central Information Processing

Center for Marketing Communication has had access to 18 standardized advertising pre-tests conducted by Gallup/TNS in Denmark 1998-1999. Each of these included 120-150 respondents. They follow the lines described in the ELAM model (Figure II.14) and include the measures specified here. In each test, questions are partly formulated at the brand level (brand recall, attitudes toward the brand etc.) and partly at the advertising level (advertising recall and A-Ad). A more detailed account of this study is found in Hansen (1997) and Hansen and Hansen (2001b).

The products included are fast moving consumer goods. In this reporting, we are particularly concerned with the extent of peripheral versus central information processing and the nature of the responses depending upon which data processing approach is dominating. For this purpose, responses from three open questions asked in the course of the test, partly evaluating positive and negative aspects of the ads and partly asking for what the respondent thinks the advertising is supposed to communicate, were analysed.

A standardised procedure for probing respondents was used and responses were coded by two independent coders along the following lines: All responses were reduced to their basic elements; for instance a "good-looking girl in beautiful car" was divided into "good-looking girl" and "beautiful car". Subsequently, all such informational items were categorised depending on whether they were positive or negative, and depending on whether they primarily related to the product, its use, its advantages etc. (central) or whether they primarily reflected the story in the ad, its pictures, its underlying music, its execution etc. (peripheral). The relatively few items that were unclassifiable along these dimensions were excluded.

Between two and three informational elements were registered for each respondent. Based on these, respondents' use of central or peripheral information processing can be classified. This is shown in Table II.7. Several observations can be made from these figures. First, more than three times as many peripheral statements can be identified relative to the number of central informational ones.

Secondly, when central information processing dominated, responses tended to be slightly more positive. With peripheral information processing however, negative statements are more frequent than positive ones.

*Table II.7: Number of predominantly central and predominantly pe-
ripheral responses in a study of 18 ads (Hansen and Hansen, 2001a) Some respondents may report both positive
and negative statements.*

Central positive	353
Central negative	231
Central no. of respondents	540
Peripheral negative	1209
Peripheral positive	1008
Peripheral no. of respondents	1627

*respondents with no classifiable responses are excluded

Summary results regarding the nature of central versus peripheral communication effects are shown in Table II.8.

*Table II.8: Advertising responses among respondents with predomi-
nantly central vs. peripheral processing (Hansen and Hansen, 2001a).*

	Central	Peripheral
No. of statements	3.2	1.9
Ad recall	2.4	1.1
Ad liking	3.9	2.2
Brand preference	2.4	1.1

Here, it appears that when central information processing dominates, the ad is recalled better, liking is higher, brand preference is higher and buying intention (here measured as positive self-rated changes in buying intention following the exposure) is higher. Also, attitudes towards the ad show the same picture. The items here are borrowed from the Gallup-Robinson standardised advertising pre-testing procedure (Metha, 1994). Two statements from each of the four factors underlying this instrument (informative, entertaining, evaluative, and negative attitudes) are used (Table II.9). Five out of six positive attitudes score are (significantly) higher when central information processing is involved, and the negative ones do the opposite.

Table II.9: Attitudes towards the ad. Number of times the A-ad word is chosen (Hansen et al., 2002)

	Central (N=1190)	Peripheral (N=3668)
Exciting	22%	19%
Credible	42%	33%
Sensitive	31%	27%
Warm	22%	21%
Entertaining	36%	32%
Informative	32%	29%
Stupid	19%	24%
Irritating	17%	24%

It is obvious that all measures suggest that better communication re-sults are achieved when central information processing is generated.

There is, however, one exception to this (Table II.10). The test in-cluded 12 feeling words. Here it is found that peripheral information processing results in more positive feeling responses and fewer negative ones. Of the 12 items used, 9 show significant differences in the direction indicated here.

Table II.10: Self-rated feelings/emotions associated with central and peripheral information processing (Hansen and Hansen, 2001a)

	Central (N = 1038)	Peripheral (N = 3418)
Pleasure	26%	40%
Hope	29%	33%
Acceptance	22%	34%
Happiness	27%	41%
Dominate	9%	13%
Enjoyment	46%	58%
Inspiring	29%	28%
Surprising	19%	23%
Mistrust	8%	9%
Sorrow	7%	5%
Anger	12%	7%
Fear	3%	5%

All in all, we may summarize these findings as follows:

When predominantly concerned with fast moving consumer goods advertising, 75 % of the information processing is peripheral. When central information processing occurs, it is always more efficient as indicated by practically all commonly used measurements of the communication effect. When peripheral information dominates, only the feeling responses tend to be more expressed.

An overall conclusion may be that the advertiser may like to stimulate central information processing as much as he can, however, when he cannot achieve this, he must be concerned particularly with the feeling responses following the peripheral information processing. In designing campaigns, it is likely to be a basic issue whether one should emphasise central information processing by providing lots of relevant product and use information or whether one should focus on creating more attention and thereby possibly also ending up with more peripheral information processing.

The more creative advertising executions may have a tendency to do the latter. That is, high attention is achieved at a price in terms of lesser informational content. Of course, the good, creative solution generates both central and peripheral information, but the good creative solution is difficult to get at.

6. Revitalising the Think-Feel-Do Advertising Attitude Model

In later years much research has been concerned with defending the cognitive choice models either by isolating factors which may influence the extent to which attitudinally based choices occur, or by focusing on an extended view of the affective part of the attitude element.

We shall look a little into the first here, the latter will be the topic for the subsequent chapter. The emphasize on reasoned action is such an attempt. Here focus is on situations where attitudes are better able to explain consumer choice, much in line with central processing in the ELM model.

A basic view held in explaining discrepancies between attitudes and subsequent behaviour is that situational factors may influence the actual behaviour. Already Fishbein and Aizen argue that basically attitudes do not predict behaviour, they predict intentions towards behaviour. The extent to which these intentions lead to actual behaviour is a study object in its own right.

Such behaviour-intention discrepancies are well documented. In a study of consumer garbage Cote et al. (1985) illustrate the effect of unexpected situations on relationships between behaviour and behavioural intentions. In the garbage they find many items not XXXX from the attitudes of the consumers. In line with this, Allen et al. (1992) demonstrate that in situations where situational factors influence the formation of meaningful attitudes, other affective measures related to the situation improve predictions. Also Fazio et al. (1989) stress the importance of what they label "attitude accessibility" for the strength of the attitude-to-behaviour relationship. They argue that some attitudes are more easily accessible to the decision maker than others. When such attitudes are dominant, greater attitude-to-behaviour correspondence is expected. But also in line with other research they find that when these accessible attitudes are dominating, situational factors such as the actual placement of the choice alternatives in front of the respondent play a more important role. Findings confirmed by Hansen et al. (2004).

Also Bettman et al. (1998) has been concerned with these issues in what they have labelled constructive choice making. Their argument is that due to limited processing capacity consumers often do not have well defined decision preferences but construct them using a variety of strategies depending upon the actual choice situation.

Finally, Howard and Genglet (2001) review findings suggesting that affective elements may play a greater role in choices where the situation leaves little time for cognitive processing. With low involved or motivated consumers, predictions based on straight forward cognitive processing work less well. Particularly here situational factors may interact with the cognitive processes and overrule pre-existing attitudes and cognitions.

In line with these findings the focus in the 90's is put on the role of the appraisal that individuals give to the feelings generated by events or cognitions. In the work of Frijda (1993) feelings appear when something appeals to the individual and is being judged by the individual to be of interest to him. Cognitive appraisal is a judgement about what interest is at stake. In that sense it can be seen as an attempt to expand cognition theory to also cope with feelings (emotions) (Johnson and Stewart, 2004). Also the work by Lazarus (1991 and 1999) is based on individuals' cognition appraisal of whether an emotional stimulus is to be evaluated positively or negatively, and to whether the individual can cope with the situation to which the appraisal is associated. In appraisal theory (and the related attribution theory) cognitive processes play a dominant role in explaining feelings (emotions).

Other attempts to circumvent the problems of making attitude scores predict behaviour in a straight forward manner are presented by researchers applying different phenomenological approaches to the study of consumers. A frontrunner is Belk being concerned with what he has been labelled "naturalistic enquiry and the symbols of consumption" (Belk et al. 1988, Belk and Pollay 1982). A fascinating account of a large scale observational study carried out with researcher travelling from west to east in the USA and observing consumers and their behaviour is described in Belk et al. (1989), but also Hirschman has been concerned with the symbolic value of consumption (Hirschman 1990 and Hirschman 1992).

More structured approaches to this study of the meaning of consumption depart in semiotic methodology. An early attempt to structure such interpretations of advertising are presented by Mick and Buhl (1992). An instructive report of text interpretation in advertising using semiotic methodology is found in McQuarrie and Mick (1996).

But also Meyers-Levy and Tybout (1997) combine linguistic analyses with information processing models of choice.

In line with this concern has also been the use of ethnographic methodology. Oswald (1999) studying a Haitian family in the Midwestern US is concerned with how ethnic consumers use consumption as a way of moving from one cultural identity to another.

The concept of advertising literacy has come into fashion. Goodstein (1993), Kitchen and Spickett-Jones (2003), Grayson and Shulman (2000) discuss how consumers may interpret advertising differently depending upon their advertising literacy. The media literate post-modern young consumer can shift around between different modes of advertising interpretation. They have a sophisticated appreciation of the conventions, styles and trends of advertising and they can give plausible accounts of what the advertising objective and marketing thinking behind a campaign were and would be (Kitchen and Spickett-Jones). In line with this Broadbent (1999) writes:

> *"In information processing terms, this suggests a high level of reflective ability certainly among some parts of the population (media literate youth) towards understanding what advertising is trying to achieve. This suggests a level of consumer reflection about the purpose of a message and the intent of those who created it, both agency and advertiser".*

Lately, in a reaction to this post-modern research a neo-post-modern approach departing in rhetorical methodology is appearing. Andersen (2004) is concerned with the rhetorical aspect of advertising messages and points at an emerging concern with ESP (Emotional Sales Proposition) versus the trend in classic and contemporary advertising to highlight one or a few number of differentiating points – typified by the USP (Unique Selling Proposition) concept of advertising.

This whole line of research has interesting implications and may in time become integrated with emotional approaches to the study of communication effects as they will be discussed in subsequent chapters.

Much research, occupied with these phenomena, point at affective variables of various kinds as important elements to introduce into the choice model. The treatment of affective variables in cognitive consumer choice models is the topic of the next chapter.

D. Summary
Departing in a general discussion of consumer behaviour as representing an extraordinary large proportion of the wake time of the individual, the paradox between the assumed cognitive mental process and the time spent on most choices is highlighted. Although consumers do make complicated decisions in complex and risk filled situa

tions – such as buying a house, buying a car, choosing to change the whole family environment by relocating, refinancing a home mortgage, expanding the home and other such rare, but involving decisions – by far the largest number of consumer decisions are taken in split seconds, almost automatically. Alternative models of consumer choice and information processing are examined, also models that in one way or the other point at possibilities of persuading the individual through ways that are much less attention filled for the individual or that function at much lower level of consciousness. The earliest of these models are the so called "mere-exposure-effect" model, that documents the simple phenomenon that liking or developing a positive reaction can be achieved simply by exposing the individual repeatedly to the same stimulus. Similar results have been documented in corporate image surveys where it is an established fact that the more well-known a company is, the more it is evaluated positively. Finally a number of models are examined that point to the very different ways of information processing that are associated with situations where the consumer is low involved – the majority of consumption situations – and where therefore persuasion is created more by the advertising stimuli as such than by factual messages. This body of knowledge is reviewed so that the reader is aware of the overwhelming amount of evidence that most consumer choices are not made according to primarily cognitively oriented and sequential models assuming rationality.

Chapter III

Affective Information Processing

CHAPTER OUTLINE
This chapter reviews the body of knowledge that concerns the roles of affect in information processing in relation to consumer behaviour. The review opens with a discussion of the two concepts: emotions and feelings, since both are used more or less synonymously by authors that are concerned with affect. We present our definition of the two concepts and their interrelationship with emphasis on the concept of feelings, since this concept is the one that most research on affect is dealing with – either under the heading of feelings or emotions. The chapter discusses affect in consumer choice and information processing under the following broad headings: Personality, attitudes, mood and emotion. The number of feelings that are relevant are discussed, as are the possible relations between feelings and underlying, innate or learned emotional responses. From this point of departure the role of feelings in consumer behaviour research is reviewed. The chapter concentrates on that part of research in affect that covers concepts similar to the definition of feelings in this book. We present various ways of measuring feelings that have been used by researchers, including our own research.

CHAPTER OBJECTIVE
In this chapter we aim to provide a deeper understanding of the non-cognitive mechanisms at play when consumers make choices or process information in relation to choices. We do this by reviewing existing knowledge as far as the role of affect in consumer choice is concerned. We attempt - through our discussion of affect – to provide the reader with an increased awareness of the many interpretations of this concept that have been presented over time and across studies. From the presented knowledge, we infer some conclusions regarding the role of feelings, as we use the term, in consumer choice, particularly in low involvement situations or when alternatives are not very differentiated. Our objective is to provide the reader with the initial arguments for looking deeper at emotional responses as the controlling mechanisms in much consumer behaviour.

A. The Role of Affect in Consumer Choice
The concept of affect has undergone changes in the last half century. Today, most authors would agree with contributors such as Erevelles (1998), Bagozzi et al. (1999) in making a distinction between affective and cognitive processing. Basically, the cognitive processing term is reserved for the kind of multi-attribute evaluation of information in

connection with choices among alternatives as described in the preceding chapter.

Erevelles (1998) and Bagozzi et al. (1999) rather than multi-attribute modeling talk about two parallel types of modeling: cognitive and affective. Petty et al.'s (1983) distinction between central and peripheral processing is in line with this, although central as well as peripheral information processing may have emotional as well as cognitive aspects. Finally Janiszewski (1988 and 1990), when documenting how affective processing can occur independently of cognitive processes, also propose that the two kinds of processes should be studied separately.

Affect is not a new term in consumer psychology. In the classical, three-dimensional attitude definition of Osgood et al. (1957): the cognitive, affective and conative dimensionality of meaning is introduced. Here, the affective element takes up a central role, accounting for the evaluative side of the meaning of words. In most contemporary literature, affect is seen as something like "a valenced feelings state" (Cohen and Areni, 1991).

In this sense, Bagozzi et al. (1999) see affect as an overall terminology for such different, mental processes as feelings or emotions, moods, some elements of attitudes, and even personality. Our main focus in the following chapters is the affective processes as they are represented by emotional responses and emotional response potentials. We shall, however comment on the different meanings affect takes on according to Bagozzi et al. (1999).

1. Affect and Personality

Within psychological theory, a large number of personality inventories have been developed over the years, many departing in Murray's (1938) classical work on personality. One such inventory, commonly used in consumer psychology, is Edwards' personal preference schedule (EPPS) (Edwards, 1955), with classical applications in a marketing context, reported by Evans (1959) and Koponen (1960). Other classical instruments that have been used by marketers are Thurstone's temperament schedule (Thurstone, 1953), and Gilford-Zimmermann's temperament survey (Freeman, 1962).

All of these and others try to describe individuals along a limited number of dimensions, such as altruistic, social, aggressive, sexual, cognitive, empathic, etc. Almost always, among these are dimensions that reflect individual differences in the tendencies to demonstrate more or less affective behaviour. It is not our aim here to discuss individual differences in emotional and cognitive processing, but when looking at emotionally guided behaviour in subsequent chapters it should be kept in mind that individual differences may play a role also.

Directly focused on this aspect of personality is Plutchik and Kellerman's emotion profile index (1974), where the authors with the use of 62 forced choice questions arrive at descriptions of emotional traits of individuals, such as sociable, affectionate, adventurous, resentful, impulsive, quarrelsome, shy, cautious, self-conscious, obedient, etc. Interesting as they may be, such expectedly more stable individual differences in behavioural patterns are less likely to be of importance in most consumer choices, and their usefulness in studies of consumer behaviour is limited (Kassarjian and Kassarjian, 1979). Their contribution has been of modest significance for the study of individual consumer choice. We shall leave it to the reader to pursue the rich psychological literature on such personality systems (Freemann, 1962) and go on to the next affective meaning.

2. Attitudes and Affect
Attitudes were a central theme in the preceding chapter. Most definitions of attitude contain elements of an affective nature. This is very obvious in Osgood et al.'s (1957) three-dimensional attitudinal model, but in all balance models, consistency models and similar attitude models, affect appears in the sense that some cognitive elements are more liked, preferred, or positively or negatively evaluated.

The multi-attribute models all try to estimate some kind of attitude preference, action potential, behavioural intentions or the like. Kroeber-Riel (1979) in his thought provoking approach to the study of consumer choice explicitly treats attitudes as such.

It is not the purpose here to pursue the entire attitude literature which, to some extent, has been dealt with already in the preceding chapter. However, it should be pointed out that in classical attitude theory, affect is a more or less integrated element in the central attitude variable. Lately however, authors have been increasingly critical of this view. In more recent years some researchers have worked with a two-dimensional attitude construct (cognitive and affective) (Holbrook and Hirschman, 1982), and Allen et al. (1992) have shown that the impact of affect is better accounted for by being represented separately rather than seen as an aspect of attitudes.

In line with this Batra and Ahtola (1990) have developed separate scales for the measurement of cognitive and affective elements of evaluation. Thus, it is becoming more and more common to make a distinction between affective and cognitive models of choice. Erevelles (1998) writes "attitude is distinguished from affect in, that attitude is an evaluative judgement, while affect is a valenced feeling state." The work by Zajonc (1980), favouring a separate affective model has been introduced already, and in line with this the work by Janiszewski (1988) concludes, that affective processes can occur independently of cognitive processes, and both propose that one should study them separately.

In the early 1980's, Van Raaij (1983) points at affect without cognition in consumer choice, and also Pham et al. (2001) illustrate how evaluations, based on feelings, give faster, more stable and consistent predictions of the choice of an individual.

In line with these and other authors, we will in the following, when talking about cognitive information processing, limit ourselves to the computer-like computations as assumed in multi-attribute models with focus on the more cognitive informational elements in this process. In this connection it is important to emphasize that the distinction between cognitive and affective has nothing to do with the distinction between conscious and unconscious processing as it will be discussed later in more detail. Cognitive processing can be conscious as well as unconscious, and affective processing may at least give rise to parallel conscious cognitive activities.

3. Affect and Mood

With affective personality variables and affective elements in attitude put aside, we are left with feelings (or in the terminology of some authors: emotions) and mood. Mood is generally perceived as a longer lasting state, often of a lower intensity than feelings (emotions). Like personality, moods are rarely directly associated with any particular stimulus object in the environment. Feelings, on the other hand, are higher in intensity, and associated with one or more particular elements in the environment.

It is generally believed, for feelings to be of relevance, that an individual has a personal stake in what the feeling is about, and at the same time perceives the event as advancing or counteracting that stake. This kind of appraisal can occur consciously or unconsciously (Lazarus, 1982; Frijda, 1993).We shall leave the further treatment of feelings until the subsequent section, and here only have a little more to say about moods. As early as 1985 Gardner (1985) reviewed 40 early studies of the effects upon mood in consumer behaviour. She summarizes her findings in a model shown in Figure III.1.

Figure III.1: *Determinants of consumer moods (Gardner, 1985, p. 288)*

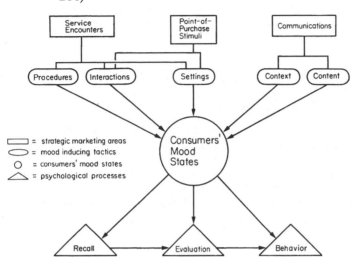

Here mood effects are measured as recall, evaluation and behaviour and are seen to occur created by service encounters, point of purchase stimuli and communication. These findings are replicated in many later studies. Milotic (2003); Morrin and Ratneshwar (2000) and Erevellles (1998), in reviewing marketing-relevant literature on moods, characterise moods as "mild pervasive generalised affective states, not usually associated with a stimulus object" (p. 202). He finds that positive moods influence information processing positively as well as information retrieval. An observation also confirmed by Kumar and Krishman (2004). In a German study Siemer (2001) shows how induced moods may influence different feelings.

One reason for the limited concern with moods in consumer behaviour research may be the belief that mood plays only a small role in consumer choice evaluations. Still, it may be important in less involving situations, and for instance Swinyard (1993) demonstrates that moods generated in retail environments play a role for a consumer's shopping experience, and Hansen (2002) demonstrates that moods, as they appear in usage situations, may influence the perception of food quality.

When moods generated by advertising stimuli have effect on brand and communication evaluations, Batra and Stayman (1990) find that positive moods may limit the amount of cognitive elaboration of advertising messages. In the same way, the media can generate moods, and they have been shown to have an overflow effect on the evaluation of advertising material (Goldberg and Gorn, 1987). Similarly Keller et al. (2003) find that loss versus gain framed messages influence consumers differently depending upon whether they are brought into a positive or a negative mood prior to the exposure. Although moods may not always be easily distinguishable from feelings, as we shall focus on them subsequently, we shall a following section (III.C.8) have a little more to say about research on moods.

4. Affect and Emotion

The concept of emotion appears early in psychological theory. It is a major topic in James' (1890) psychology and it is an implicit part in Freudian psychology (1925). Way back to Aristoteles emotions are central in man's thinking of life and its psychology.

"The emotions are all those feelings that do so change men as to affect their judgements and that are also attended by pain or pleasure" (Aristoteles: Rhetoric, 1378 A 21-2, in Agres et al., 1990). In his treatment of emotions he sees them as "not only natural but for a purpose" (Robinson, p. 21, in Agres et al. 1990).

Several things are made clear here that we shall find important in our subsequent treatment of emotions and emotional response potential:

- Firstly in much traditional literature, the words "feelings" and "emotions" are synonymous but not identical. An issue we shall return to shortly.
- Secondly, emotions influence how people judge things in their environment.
- Thirdly, they have positive and negative sides – they give rise to positive and negative responses.
- Fourthly, they are basically inherited mechanisms and largely bodily controlled.

B. Emotions are Different from Feelings

At this point we shall introduce a distinction, which is becoming more and more common in contemporary thinking about emotions, particularly in neuro-psychological approaches, and which we shall adhere to in all of the following pages on this issue.

Feelings are different from emotions. Emotions are unconscious, basically inherited, responses to stimuli in the environment and to changes in inner states of bodily needs and cognitive activity. The latter means that we may arouse emotions as a result of cognitive activities. Thinking about something, may arouse emotions. Emotions of which the individual may be unaware and which may or may not influence conscious and unconscious cognitive processes, particularly feelings. Feelings, thus, are the cognitively conscious or unconscious counterparts of the basic underlying physiological emotions. We make this distinction here since it will be useful for our entire treatment of affect as a governing force in consumer choice. As we shall see in much existing literature in psychology, social psychology and consumer behaviour, the terms are used more or less interchangeably. To use both terms, however, only makes sense if it is clearly understood how feelings may be aroused from underlying emotions (Hansen, 2005). In a consumer behaviour context, particularly Franzen and Bouwman (2001) and Heath (2006) have been concerned with this issue, which will be in focus in the next chapter. Also other authors have pointed at the need for such a distinction (for instance Izard, 1992, and Bagozzi et al., 1999) and in practical use it is reported in Faseur and Geuens (2004).

Thus, here and in the following, we shall talk about two different but related phenomena "emotions" and "feelings". The feelings are those cognitively, whether consciously or unconsciously, perceived elements about which the individual may tell his environment and which he himself may experience more or less strongly.

In this terminology the topic for the rest of the present chapter are feelings as they have been dealt with by psychologists and consumer psychologists.

We do not intend a criticism towards the authors to be quoted in the following that again and again they use the words "emotions and feelings" as if they are either interchangeable or of the same nature. It is with the purpose to clarify things that we have chosen to concentrate on the term "feelings" when we are talking about the cognitively activated counterparts of the basic underlying emotions. In doing so we are in line with contemporary neurological findings such as reported by Damasio (1994) and LeDoux (1998), and the distinction by Rossiter (2004) between Type 1 and Type 2 emotions is very similar.

For instance, in "Emotion in advertising – theoretical and practical explorations" edited by Agres et al. (1990), most of the contributions in reality talk about feelings as we see them here. So do Bagozzi et al. in "The role of emotions in marketing" (1999), Huang in "The theory of emotion in marketing" (2001), Journal of Advertising Research in its special issue on Emotions in 2004, and many earlier authors. We shall however strongly recommend the reader to keep this distinction between feelings and emotions in mind, since, as we shall see in the subsequent chapters, it will enable us to enrich our understanding of how consumer choice is governed.

We realize the potential confusion that lies in using this distinction and do does Bechara and Damasio (2005) who suggest the term "somatic marker" for what they and other neurologists see as emotions "because the term emotion tends to mean different things to layman, the psychologist and others, we have here used the term "somatic marker" to refer to the collection of body-related responses that hallmark an emotion" (p. 337). Here, however we have chosen not to go that far, but rather emphasize the difference between emotions and feelings.

1. The Neglect of Feelings in Early 19th Century's Psychology

With the shift from the classical and introspectively based psychology to behaviourism, where the possibility of studying the individual's own perception of its internal processes is almost rejected, feelings largely disappear from early 19th century's psychology. With the reintroduction of the individual as an intervening variable that explains behaviour - from an SR-psychology to an SOR-psychology, where the O represents the individual as an object between stimuli and responses - this changes. Feelings, however, do not to any great extent become reintroduced in psychology. Rather the cognitive world as described in the preceding chapter emerges and the period from around the 2nd World War until very recently may be labelled the period of cognitive psychology.

Only as the weaknesses of the cognitive approach in explaining human choice and behaviour become more and more evident, the interest slowly begin to include also affect in its own right and particularly feelings. Concern arises with their structure and with their influence on human choice.

2. Feelings in Psychology

In the 60's a few psychologists began to study how people may express themselves about their feelings and various theories about basic, secondary and social feelings (emotions) emerged. Thus, under the heading of emotions, feelings or affective behaviour, social psychologists and students of consumer behaviour have made studies that deal with other than directly cognitive information processing.

Most concern has been with feeling and feeling words. As already suggested in this literature, the distinction between feelings and emotions to be used here is not always evident. Classifications of different basic feelings are proposed by several authors. By now classical contributions are made by Plutchik (1980) trying to classify individual differences in people's use of self descriptive feeling words. Previously Tomkins (1962) works with 8 basic dimensions (surprise, interest, joy, rage, fear, disgust, shame and anguish). Similar lists are proposed by Izard (1977) and Ekman (1980) who has a shorter list of 6 feelings covering: happiness, disgust, anger, fear, surprise, and sadness. These feelings are supposed to be innate and largely defined through studies of body and facial expressions or they are derived from answers to a longer list of feeling words.

Also secondary, often social, feelings are proposed by these authors. Many of these secondary feelings are seen as mixes of the more fundamental ones and a theory of how they combine is presented by Plutchik (1980). He sees how different feelings relate to each other is the circumplex model as illustrated in Figure III.2. Here basic (horizontal and vertical) dimensions are positive – negative evaluation and degree of arousal and activation (Russell et al., 1989). It should be noted that here positive and negative feelings are seen as opposing each other on the same dimension. An issue to which we shall return.

Figure III.2: The Circumplex Model (Larsen and Deiner, 1987)

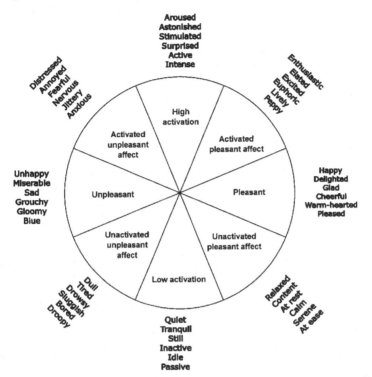

In the same category as circumplex models are dimensional models working with few dimensions such ad PAD (Russell and Mehrabian (1977). Here the dimensions are pleasure – displeasure (P), arousal (A) and dominance – submission (D). Again we note that also this model assumes positive and negative feelings to appear on a uni-dimensional bipolar scale. It is also worth noticing the three dimensions have a close relationship with the three dimensions in the Osgood et al. (1957) attitude concept.

Table III.1: A summary of scaled measurements of feelings (Ortony and Turner, 1990)

Psychologist	Basic feelings	Reasons to name the basic feelings
James (1884)	fear, sadness, love, fury	involvement in the body
McDougall (1926)	anger, disgust, delight, fear, subjugation, tenderness, admiration	related to instincts
Watson (1930)	fear, love, fury	'hardwired'
Mowrer (1960)	pain, pleasure	not acquired
Izard (1971)	anger, contempt, disgust, suffering, fear, guilt, interest, joy, shame, surprise	'hardwired'
Arnold (1980)	anger, aversion, courage, separation, yearning,, desperation, fear, hate, hope, love, sorrow	imply a behavioural tendency
Plutchik (1980)	acceptance, anger, anticipation, disgust, joy, fear, sorrow, surprise	related to adaptive body processes (based on the evolution theory)
Ekman *et al.* (1982)	anger, disgust, fear, joy, sorrow, surprise	have a universal facial expression
Gray (1982)	fury and terror, worry, joy	'hardwired'
Panksepp (1982)	expectation, fear, fury, panic	'hardwired'
Tomkins (1984)	anger, interest, contempt, disgust, fear, joy, shame, surprise	tightness of the firing of neurons
Weiner and Graham (1984)	happiness, sorrow	independent of attributes
Frijda (1986)	yearning, happiness, interest, surprise, admiration, grief	cause various forms of action willingness
Oatley and Johnson-Laird (1987)	anger, disgust, worry, happiness, sorrow	require a proportional content

Most studies of such feelings have relied upon interviewing respondents using words describing the different feelings and asking to what extent they are relevant in different contexts. Underlying dimensions are then identified using factor analysis or other ways of clustering the feeling words. A now classical review of a large number of such early studies is provided by Ortony and Turner (1990) and shown in Table III.1. Other interesting studies of feeling words are reported by Kamp and Macinnis (1995). The authors use a large number of different feeling words resulting in feelings that can be labelled differently, some being positive and other negative. Some authors have worked with as many as 5-600 different feeling words. They all end up, however, with relatively few groups like in Table III.1.

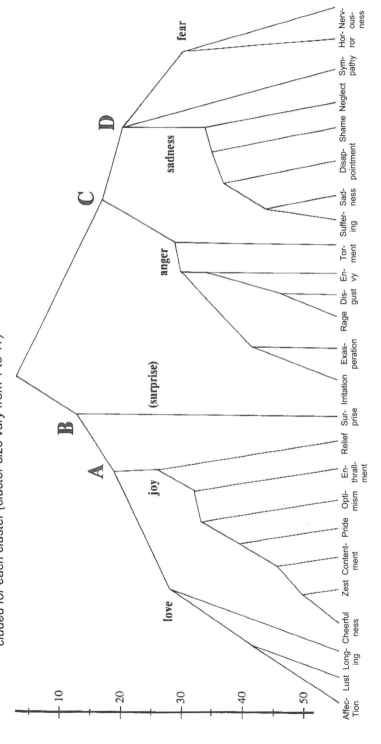

Figure III.3: Cluster analysis of 118 feeling words (Shaver et al., 1987). In the bottom line only one feeling word is included for each cluster (cluster size vary from 1 to 17)

The almost invariable result coming from grouping feeling words, that classify these into two groups: positive and negative, is demonstrated by Shaver et al. (1987) (Figure III.3). Using an hierarchical clustering procedure on the 135 feeling words two major clusters arise. One with positive and one with negative feelings words. As we shall see later this may reflect two fundamental underlying emotional response tendencies: approach/avoidance. Each of the two categories in turn, are then divided into different aspects of Joy/Love, with lower level groupings such as happiness, hope, pride etc, and anger/sadness/fear with lower level groupings such as hate, aggression, guilt etc. All these lower level groupings correspond to feelings about which individual may be able to speak.

In a consumer behaviour context, a very good list of such feeling words (labelled emotions) is the list of 28 'consumer basic feelings (emotions) by Richins (1997). Those are tied to the perception of consumption situations (Table III.2).

Again these feelings represent cognitive counterparts of emotions about which the individual may be able to inform.

Table III.2: The consumption emotion set (Richins, 1997). Values in parentheses represent the Pearson correlation for two-item scales and Cronbach's alpha for scales with more than two items.

Anger (α = .91, .87):
    Frustrated
    Angry
    Irritated
Discontent (r = .73, .67):
    Unfulfilled
    Discontented
Worry (α = .77, .77):
    Nervous
    Worried
    Tense
Sadness (α = .83, .72):
    Depressed
    Sad
    Miserable
Fear (α = .82, .74):
    Scared
    Afraid
    Panicky
Shame (α = .82, .85):
    Embarrassed
    Ashamed
    Humiliated
Envy (r = .39, .46):
    Lonely
    Homesick
Romantic love (α = .82, .82):
    Sexy
    Romantic
    Passionate
Love (α = .86, .86):
    Loving

Sentimental
Warm hearted
Peacefulness (r = .55, .68):
    Calm
    Peaceful
Contentment (r = .60, .58):
    Contended
    Fulfilled
Optimism (α = .82, .86):
    Optimistic
    Encouraged
    Hopeful
Joy (α = .91, .88)
    Happy
    Pleased
    Joyful
Excitement (α = .88, .89):
    Excited
    Thrilled
    Enthusiastic
Surprise (N.A., α = .81):
    Surprised
    Amazed
    Astonished
Other items:
    Guilty
    Proud
    Eager
    Relieved

In the research on feelings, among the basic feelings the negative ones are far more common than the positive ones. When looking upon the basic commonly accepted feelings, proposed by Ekman, the negative ones (disgust, anger, fear and sadness) dominate against the positive (happiness) and the ambivalent (surprise).

In spite of the large number of feelings often introduced by the different authors, what happens in most cases of variable reduction down to a small number of factors – either through factor analysis or through cluster analysis of variables - a 2-4 dimensional feeling solution results. This always includes an approach (positive) and an avoidance (negative) dimension, and sometimes arousal or involvement or similar dimensions.

Particularly the issue about positive and negative feelings (emotions) being bipolar or representing two basically different dimensions is important. This view adhered to here is supported by findings reported by Lang (1995), Edell and Burke (1987), Edell (1989) and many findings to be reviewed subsequently.

Of course, the amount of variance explained with these two higher order level factors is lower than when a larger number of factors are included, but the uniformity of the dimensions and their face validity is such, that the solutions can still be judged to be operationally useful. Most commonly also, the amount of explained variance picked up by the 3rd factor or each of the following factors is much smaller.

The fundamental observation made here is that in the terminology of an SOR model, and with the use of self-administered questionnaires, we may identify 10-20 different factors corresponding to the many feeling dimensions in the classical feeling literature (Table III.1). However, it seems that in forcing solutions with fewer dimensions upon the data, more basic dimensions emerge. These underlying fewer dimensions we may rightfully think reflect emotions. Thus, a major observation at this point is that we may still gain insight into emotional responses based on a distinction between feelings and emotions, and that the measurement of feelings and concentrated analysis of the data end up in emotional like dimensions. This topic shall be explored further in the following chapter.

C. Feelings in Consumer Behaviour Research and Advertising

As discussed already, the limited ability of information processing modeling to explain all aspects of consumer choice behaviour became more and more evident in the 1970's and 80's.

Wright (1980) points out, that consumers quite frequently may make very simple satisfactory feeling based choices. Krugman (1977) talks about exposure without recognition and memory without recall. Kroeber-Riel (1979) bases his thinking on consumer behaviour and advertising effects on arousal theory (Berlyne, 1960) and what he labels activation research. Here, unconscious, feeling based information processing is a central element. As suggested earlier, Zajonc (1968) already in the 1960's talked about effects of mere exposure on evaluative attitudes and in Zajonc and Marcus (1982) emphasize the basic differences between affective and cognitive factors in forming preferences for alternatives. Holbrook and Hirschman (1982) suggest that the hedonic element may be fundamentally important in many kinds of consumption. In line with these more theoretical considerations operational research began to be reported also. Schlinger (1979) presents findings, based on a standardized emotional profile measuring responses to nonverbal elements of advertising. Similarly, Edell and Burke (1987) suggest a three-dimensional model of how consumers respond with feelings to advertising. Aaker et al. (1986) departing in a large choice of consumer relevant feeling words identify 16 positive and 15 negative feeling clusters describing different kinds of feelings aroused by advertising.

A very good review of this early research on feelings in advertising is available in Agres et al. (1990). And that feelings (emotions) actually influence consumer behaviour where feelings (emotions) are used as explanatory variables is shown by Allen et al. (1992), who measured feelings using the Izard Battery (Izard, 1977) and improve predictions made of donating blood.

In a later review of the role of feelings in consumer behaviour research, Huang (2001) summarized four major attempts with feeling and related affect models in consumer behaviour. These will be summarized here. When dealing with the quantification of feelings she talks about "Differential emotion (feeling) theory", which is based upon Isaacs's early work and applied particularly in research on consumers' post-purchase satisfaction (Westbrook and Oliver 1991). In the view of these authors a rather simple two-dimensional representation of positive and negative amount of feelings is satisfactory for understanding post-purchase satisfaction. An observation which has been repeated by several authors, for instance by Martensen and Grønholdt (2002).

In another category she treats measurements departing in "The Circular model of emotion (feeling)". Departing in Plutchik's work using a limited number of primary feelings (emotions), Huang holds that all other feelings emerge as combinations of these. The circular model proposed was shown in Figure III.2. Here feelings (emotions) are seen as partly inherited and they play a basic role for the survival of human beings. The basic feelings (emotions) interact with each other. The work by Holbrook and Batra (1987) is based on such affective feeling responses to products and consumption.

Thirdly Huang talks about: "Panas: The Positive and Negative Affect Schedule". This approach relies particularly upon the work by Watson et al. (1988). An important aspect of this theory is that positive and negative affective dimensions are seen as mutually independent, and that they are the two primary feeling dimensions. These ideas have been applied particularly in connection with the study of mood effects, but also Dubé and Morgan (1998) find them useful in work with service satisfaction, and Huang (2001) does so in advertising. Mooradian and Oliver (1997) interpret post purchase behaviour as guided by negative and positive feelings. Another proposal for independent positive and negative feeling dimensions is Herr and Page (2004) who writes "We find that liking and disliking judgements appear asymmetrically linked in memory". Also Russell and Carroll (1999a and 1999b) and Watson and Telkgen (1999) debate whether positive and negative feelings can exist at the same time. It is a reappearing finding that the structure of self-reported feelings includes both a positive and a negative grouping (Laros and Steenkamp, 2005, and Hansen, 2005).

As a fourth category of measurement Huang points at "The PAD-model of affect". PAD stands for Pleasure/Displeasure, Arousal/Non-arousal and Dominance/Submissiveness as the three fundamental feeling dimensions also found in Osgood et al.'s (1957) attitude theory. They are the key components in Russell and Mehrabian's (1977) three-factor theory of emotions (feelings). In 1997 Mehrabian points at similarities and differences between the PAD and the PANAS approaches, suggesting that the 3rd dimension in the PAD model to some extent accounts for that variance which particularly the negative dimension in the PANAS model picks up.

The work by Holbrook and Batra (1987) discussed earlier confirms this theory, but Havlena and Holbrook (1986) report more questionable findings. This theory has been most successful when applied to behaviour in retail environments (Donovan and Rossiter 1982) and Dhar and Sherman (1996).

Common for all of the four categories discussed here is that a relatively few positive and negative feeling dimensions are essential (from 8-10 to 2-3). All of the models emphasize the existence of positive and negative dimensions, but sometimes a few other general arousal or activation-like dimensions appear also.

In a sense summarizing these and other contributions, Richins (1997) proposes his consumption emotion (feeling) set, CES, already introduced in Table III.2. The feeling words here are equally distributed on positive and negative ones and thereby providing finer discriminations among positive feelings than are found in the basic psychological models such as Plutchik, Ekman, Tomkins, and others. A modification justified by the related relatedness of the items to consumption situations, all of which most include some positive elements, otherwise they would be sorted out by the consumer.

In the following we shall summarize more recently reported findings on feelings (emotions).

1. Hedonic Consumption and Feelings/Emotions

In the early treatment of emotional phenomena in consumer behaviour the discussion takes place at a rather general level. Holbrook and Hirschman (1982) are talking about experiential aspects of consumptions: consumer fantasies, feelings and fun. Lazarus et al. (1980) discuss emotions as cognitive phenomena, and Lutz (1985) discuss attitudes towards the ad and points at the existence of affective elements also in this construct.

In this work a uni-dimensional affect is normally assumed. A good representation of this is found in Aaker et al. (1986) in their concern with "warmth in advertising". As they see it, their concept of warmth may be interpreted as an overall positive emotional response tendency in ads and their warmth monitor attempts to measure this "warmth" as it develops while commercials are being watched. In a later replication of the work, Abeele and MacClachlan (1994) confirm Aakers original findings but also point at the difficulties in interpreting what "warmth" in advertising really means.

2. Mere Exposure

Another line of research which also deals with affect in a uni-dimensional manner is represented by Janiszewski (1990 and 1993) and Janiszewski and Meyvis (2001). Here the concern is with mere exposure. Building on the original work by Zajonc (1968 and 1980) they see mere exposure as occurring as a subconscious affect formation which may take place in the pre-processing stage of information processing. They interpret the mere exposure effect as a result from an improved ability to recognise different stimuli and they talk about the result of the process as "processing fluency". This approach may be seen as an attempt to keep the affective responses associated with mere exposure within the realm of (unconscious) cognitive processing.

3. Consumer Satisfaction
In an entirely different line of research, Oliver (Westbrook and Oliver, 1991, and Mano and Oliver, 1993) relates emotional (feeling) processes to post consumption experiences. In addition to satisfaction being a result of cognitive information processing about the consumption experiences they see an emotional evaluation emerging in parallel with this and as a factor in its own right. In the customer satisfaction model with which Grønholdt and Martensen (2004) work, it is evident that satisfaction and loyalty is determined also by emotional tendencies reflected in feeling words associated with the evaluation of the product experience.

4. Attitudes and Emotions as Separate Constructs
Already Batra and Ray (1986a) argue for distinguishing between affective responses and cognitively based evaluative responses to advertising. In reviewing different empirical evidence they conclude that affective responses influence attitudes towards the ad and may have significant influence on brand attitudes also. In the early 1990's different authors begin to work with cognition and attitudes as constructs separated from affect in terms of feelings, mood and emotions. And as mentioned Allen et al. (1992) in a study of 361 blood donors demonstrates that peoples' own account of feelings may provide information that meaningfully supplement cognitive attitude judgements in predicting behaviour.

In a different context, MacInnis and Park (1991) demonstrate how music may interfere with consumer choices. They find different effects in low and high involvement situations operationalized as central versus peripheral information processing. In this context, they report that if the music fits with previous positive experiences on behalf of the respondent, music has the greatest impact on choices in connection with central information processing whereas unfitting music to a larger extent influences choices when peripheral information processing was dominating.

5. Social Feelings
In a special study, Howard and Gengler (2001) show how social influence may take the form of emotional transfer or, as labelled by the authors, contagion effects. Respondents observing friendly, smiling sources of personal communication tend to replicate and internalize the feelings expressed in the faces of the senders by mimicking – a phenomenon that has been utilized in sales training courses under the label: Creating rapport. Where the idea is that the salesman by mimicking the body language of the prospective client can make him

feel more comfortable and at ease. In turn, the extent to which the respondents adopt the emotions expressed by the sender. This influenced their evaluation of different products. In a subsequent experiment it was further demonstrated that involvement strengthened the influence of the emotions expressed by the sender.

6. Influence on the Nature of Choices

Adaval (2003) explores the extent to which affect, when it influences brand evaluations, does so primarily by influencing the image properties of the brand or the choice criteria governing the choice. With an experimental manipulation of affect in terms of showing different movies prior to the choices, Adaval found affect primarily influencing how the alternatives were perceived, - i.e. their images - rather than the choice criteria used for evaluating them. Thus, Adaval demonstrates how an emotional state in terms of a mood generated prior to the choice may influence the choice behaviour. The experiment is much in line with the research on moods.

7. Moods

As emphasized earlier, mood can be seen as a weaker, longer lasting emotional tone, different on the one hand from personality differences, that are more stable and long lasting, and on the other hand from emotions specifically aroused by the choice alternatives in the choice situation. Swinyard (1993) manipulated mood by giving respondents more or less positive (false) feedback to an assignment task in class. Subsequently, they made choices regarding shopping activities and a positive influence of the mood was found on shopping intentions.

In a different context Kahn and Isen (1983) manipulate mood by giving a gift of candy, chewing gum etc. prior to making a choice and find more variety seeking behaviour among respondents receiving the positive affect manipulation prior to the choice. Thus, again mood has an impact on how the choice process functions.

In a study on evaluation of different brand extensions, Barone et al. (2000) demonstrate an important effect of the mood respondents were in. Again here, mood was manipulated by giving false feedback placing subjects in more or less positive mood states. In their study, Barone et al. found that the largest effect of mood upon the evaluation of brand extensions came when the brand extension evaluated was not too similar or neither too different from the original brand to which it was an extension.

Pham et al. (2001) demonstrate how feelings, that are consciously perceived, influence judgemental properties of choice, so that the choices are made faster with more stable outcome and consistency. In the study, an ingenious design was used to manipulate feelings. Subjects were asked to list feelings they had in response to different pictures each shown for ten second. After all pictures had been seen, subjects reviewed their own feelings and the extent to which they judged them to be positive or negative. Subsequently, choice of pictures was related to reported feelings and cognitive evaluation of the same pictures. In reality, this manipulation comes close to what in research is termed mood manipulation.

Lee and Sternthal (1999) show how moods, experimentally manipulated by exposing respondents to more or less entertaining advertisement, facilitate learning of brand names and the related elaboration of brand information. In line with these findings, also Murry et al. (1992) demonstrate how feelings aroused by television programmes influence the evaluation of advertising inserted in blocks in the programmes. The influence is measured in terms of the attitudes towards the advertisement and eventually the attitudes towards the brands advertised. And Meloy (2000) demonstrates how mood induced by candy gifts influence preferences for brands with preferred brands becoming even more preferred. And finally, Keller et al. (2002) demonstrate how mood may influence the evaluation of factual health information about health cancer risk.

All in all, mood manipulations are demonstrated to influence choices and choice processes and the emotional factor acting in a specific choice may be a function both of the emotional response potential of the choice items and of the mood in which the person enters into the choice situation.

8. Affective Responses to Advertising
Particularly in the 1990's many researchers have been concerned with feelings and advertising. Erevelles (1998) reviews these issues. He talks about studies of selection of advertising appeal and goes back to Vaughn's (1979) proposal that cognitive information advertising is more effective for what he calls "thinking products" such as cars etc (Figure II.13). Affective advertising should be more useful for "feeling products" such as perfume etc. This distinction is also underlying the Rossiter/Percy grid introduced earlier (Figure II.12).

Affect and attitude towards ads is a whole issue in its own right, which is already touched upon in the previous section on attitudes. Effect and context effects on advertising are concerned with the extent to which the medium as such or the immediate surroundings of the commercial in the medium influence the way in which the commercial or the ad is processed. And, for instance, Celuch and Slama (1993) suggest that generally affectively oriented programmes and ads result in better advertising effectiveness than cognitively oriented programmes and ads.

In a now classical study, Edell and Burke (1987) demonstrate how viewing different television commercials generate different feelings. And in turn these feelings influence the perception of the ad, thus documenting that emotions generated in exposure situations influence the advertising processing. Kumar and Krishman (2004), find what they label "contextual interference" as influence on feelings associated with brands featured in an ad. In these studies the contextual interference reflects what happens, when the consumer has been exposed to other ads, particularly competing ones at almost the same time as the exposure of the tested ad.

Feelings depicted in an ad, and the extent to which feeling appeals are integrated in different ways in the ad execution, relate to how the consumer responds. Particularly, humour has been studied in some detail and, for instance Scott et al. (1990) find that humour works best for what they call humour relevant socially oriented issues whereas for more business-like events it is less effective.

Batra and Stayman (1990) manipulate mood by having respondents reading different stories and controlling the effect of mood by having respondents responding to feeling statements after the manipulation. They find their mood manipulation efficient in terms of influencing how print ads are perceived.

Also in a classical study, Goldberg and Gorn (1987) demonstrate how manipulating moods by the selection of different television programmes shown prior to exposure to commercials, influence the mood reported by respondents as well the effects of commercials broadcasted following the programmes. These effects are seen to vary with the extent to which the advertisements are informational rather than transformational in nature with the greatest influence coming in connection with transformational advertising messages.

In a later study, Murry and Dacin (1996) demonstrate that the influence of positive emotions towards programmes influence the extent to which they are liked. Particularly they show that whereas positive emotions influence cognitive processing directly, negative emotions may give rise to more detailed cognitive analysis of the emotional stimuli. This is in line with earlier findings (Murry et al., 1992), a large scale study where they classify responses to 150 ads. They find that emotional responses (together with ad content and attitudes towards the ad) influence viewing time of the ads.

9. Coping with Positive and Negative Emotions

In recent years, a particular concern has been with the way in which consumers handle situations in which there are both positive and negative emotional elements involvement. This may be the case in practically all consumer choices but of course more expressed in some than in others. This particularly relate to the debate of feelings measured with the three dimensions preference, arousal and dominance (PAD) versus measurement relying upon primarily two positive and negative affect dimensions (PANAS).

Luce (1998) in a now classical study demonstrates how negative emotional response potential in conflicting choice situations may make the respondent choosing strategies whereby conflict is avoided by preferring choices where the status quo is maintained.

Status quo may be maintained by making brand loyal choices or by making no choice at all. She illustrated this in an experiment where she manipulated trade off value in connection with car purchases (car safety level versus price, and styling versus pollution system).

In a similar experiment, Shiv and Fedorikhin (1999) study what they label 'coping responses in dealing with choices involving positive and negative emotional elements'. In choosing between chocolate cake (affective attraction) versus fruit desserts (cognitive attraction), they demonstrate that when processing resources (mental energy available for the choice) are experimentally manipulated, then more affective choices are made when processing resources are limited. Translated to our terminology we would say that in less involving situations emotionally based choices are more likely to be made.

Another conclusion regarding the way in which emotionally conflicting choices are made is reported by Raghunathan and Irwin (2001). They manipulate what they label 'domain match' - that is the similarity with which brands to be judged are presented together with other alternatives in the choice situation. High domain match would be comparing coffee with other coffee brands whereas low domain match would be comparing coffee with coke, whiskey, beer etc.). With this manipulation they find that with closer domain match much more emotional, hedonic choices are made.

Also Williams and Aaker (2002) have concerned themselves with coping. They demonstrate how individual differences may influence coping with mixed emotions. They expose Anglo-Americans (supposed to have lower propensity to accept duality) and Asian-Americans (who accept higher duality) to communication appeals highlighting conflicting emotions (happiness and sadness). Here, they find more positive attitudes towards alternatives among respondents with higher propensity to accept duality (Asian-Americans).

Baumeister (2002) and also Aaker and Lee (2001) demonstrate individual differences in coping with conflicting goals. They introduce a concept they call "distinct self-view" as a moderator of choice behaviour. "Distinct self-view" is measured by having respondents rate their concern in a specific choice situation – here a choice between competing grape juices – as the extent to which they "thought about themselves" in contrast to the extent to which their "thoughts were focused on you and your family". In the study they find more hedonic emotional choices made when people are more self-centred.

In another coping experiment, Pham and Avnet (2004) concern themselves with what they call: ideals and "oughts" in consumer choice. In the study respondents were primed to focus upon ideals or "oughts" by having them think about their past hope aspirations and dreams and to list them. Similarly "oughts'" condition was manipulated by having respondents think about their current duties, obligations and responsibilities. As a result they find that with ideals in focus, consumers rely more on subjective affective responses to adver-tisements whereas when "oughts" are brought to mind they tend to cope more with the substance of the message.

Garg et al. (2005) in reviewing 25 years of research on the influ-ence of incidental affect on choice behaviour report such effects upon recall and recognition, risk assessment and attitude. Incidental affect in their terminology is not unlike mood as discussed earlier and they demonstrate that such moods may activate cognitive pre-dispositions with influence on the appraisal of future events. They also demon-strate that task related affect increases the more difficult it becomes to determine the trade off between alternatives.

In line with this, Garg et al. (2005) replicate Luke's findings that people are more likely to rely upon status quo options when making emotionally difficult trade offs. But they also demonstrate that inciden-tal affect (mood) moderates this effect such that angry individuals are more influenced by task related affects. Additionally, Duhachek (2005) claims that coping behaviour is even more complicated than suggested by the already reviewed work in the sense, that he identi-fies different coping strategies depending upon different feeling states. He reports findings on conflicting choices in an experiment where respondents are choosing between a hedonically superior (and functionally inferior) cell phone versus a functionally superior but hedonically inferior one. Here his concern is not so much with the choice itself, rather with the feelings experienced following the choice, where he finds that consumers feel more guilt after a hedonic choice, but they report more sadness with the functionally superior choice.

Finally Kumar and Krishman (2004), find what they label "contex-tual interference" as influence on feelings associated with brands fea-tured in an ad. In these studies the contextual interference comes from consumers having been exposed to other ads, particularly com-peting ones at almost the same time as the exposure of the tested ad.

The entire coping literature argues for the coexistence of positive as well as negative feelings at the same time.

10. Feeling Dynamics

Kamp and MacInnis (1995), Young (2004) and Hollis (2005) empha-size the dynamic aspect in studying feelings portrayed in commer-cials. They are looking at what they call "emotional flow", represent-ing not what is portrayed in the ad, but rather what the viewers feel in response to the ad's different stages or elements. In theirs and other research of this nature a handheld dial, administered by the respon-dents during their watching the ad, is used. Particularly TV commer-cials have been studied in this manner by comparing the magnitude of the response with the different elements appearing in the course of the commercial that give rise to feelings. With different ads they find that the emotional flow has an influence upon as well positive, as negative feelings, involvement, empathy, and attitudes towards the ad.

An important issue in this line of research is whether the content of commercial communication concerned with either of the four categories in the Rossiter/Percy grid (Figure II.11) should be concurrent or discurrent with the nature of the purchase motivation. Dubé et al. (1996) raise this issue inspired by George Mandler's (1982) hypothesis about an inverted u-shaped relationship between incongruity and evaluation in a context of new product evaluation.

It has generally been found that if congruity between brand and its advertising is perceived to be moderate, the ad will change the purchase motivation. It will also be evaluated more favourably than the ad matching the purchase motivation or the ad extremely discongruent with the brand. The same observation is made by Loef et al. (2001). This may be seen in the light of the work by Sherif et al. (1965) and the work on subjective grouping discussed earlier (Chapter II).

Finally, Hall (2002) proposes an interesting model of advertising effect in which a distinction between pre-experience exposure and post-experience exposure is important. Particular feelings and related affective processing is dominant in the pre-experience phase, whereas more cognitive processing may occur in the post-experience phase. In the pre-experience phase an expectation for the advertised issue is created. This forms anticipations about the kind of satisfaction to gain by the product, which is involved.

Hall (2002) illustrates with an example:

"In beer advertising the moment when the cap is opened to release the carbonation is an essential pre-exposure element. The pre-experience processing may include the construction of a rationale for the anticipation generated."

In discussing the application of his model he emphasizes the necessity for advertising pre-testing being concerned with the brand or the issue advertised rather than with advertising itself. A point also made by Heath (2001), who also – in line with Du Plessis (2005a) stresses the importance of emotional responses for the generation of attention.

D. Investigating Feelings

We shall briefly review methodologies used for measuring feelings in a consumer context. We shall later (in Chapter X) return to findings obtained with some of these methods.

1. Interview Based Measures

As it has been seen in the preceding pages feelings are most frequently measured with the use of lists of feeling words. Richins (1997) is a good example of this. The use of such measures is also illustrated last in this chapter.

2. Manipulating Feelings

Experimental manipulation has also been used to generate different feelings, the effects of which then have been quantified by other means. Many of the studies reported above have relied on such manipulation.

3. Psycho-Physiological Measures

Also in marketing studies various measurements have been used in attempt to reveal feeling responses using other than questioning. Kroeber-Riel (1979) in his work on activation has reported several studies using what he labels psycho-physiological measures. Here he has respondents respond by pressing a lever, fixing the length of a line with the use of a ruler, and the like. For instance the work by Aaker et al. (1986) on warmth also illustrates this.

4. Physiological Measures

Over the years a long list of measurement devices originally developed for other purposes have been used in attempt to quantify emotions. EEG measures have been used to track the electrical activity in the brain, and by studying the size of pupil underlying emotional responses have been quantified. Galvanic skin response measuring arousal by measuring the amount of electricity transmitted over the surface of the hand owing to sweating has also been applied and so has measures of heart beat. This will be dealt with in more detail later.

5. Facial Expressions

The use of facial expressions as indicators of feelings (emotions) has a long tradition in research. Probably Darwin (1872) is the first to observe the similarity in facial expressions across cultures, and even across different kinds of primates, as indicators of emotions. Work by Ekman (1980) relies on facial expressions as indicators of basic emotions existing across existing cultures. A special coding system is developed by Mammucari et al. (1988) and discussed by Parkinson (2005). To use these coding schemes some kind of registration of facial expression has to be made. The use of cameras is one possibility, but recently methodologies have been developed where electrodes are taped to central locations of the face, and the registration of the muscles in these locations thereby registered. More recently advanced technology has been developed using radiology to map faces and Verma et al. (2005) show how facial expressions reflect the same emotional pictures as does functional Magnetic Resonance Imaging (fMRI).

The fact that facial expressions may reveal emotions more or less independent of cognitive control made the idea obvious that by having people choosing among faces expressing different feelings (emotions) one might learn about the underlying emotions. The fact that facial expressions reveal feelings and underlying emotions is used for measuring emotional responses (feeling responses) in a different manner also. The smiling face scale may be seen as a particularly simple version of such measurements.

The first serious attempt using pictorial material for testing were made by the psychologist Lang (1985) and applied in an advertising context by Morris (1995). The test Self-Assessment Manikin (SAM) is developed with reference to the Mehrabian and Russell three dimensional PAD model. It measures different degrees of preference, activation and control are shown. Morris, in testing a large number of running campaigns for well known companies, finds the advertisements can be placed in a space with "pleasure" and "arousal" as axis, whereas dominance seems to play a minor role.

The most extensive later work by Desmet (2002) departs in the psychological feeling theories by Fridja and work with seven positive and seven negative feelings. The use on this PR-EMO measurement device will be taken up in Chapter XI together with related commercial applications.

E. CMC Evidence

At the Center for Marketing Communication at the Copenhagen Business School work has been done over the last five years on the effects of marketing communication in the form of advertising, sponsoring, design, logo colours, etc. In much of this work a feeling battery has been included. The feeling words selected are derived from the Richins' (1997) battery with some additions from the work by Holbrook and Batra (1987) selected with the purpose of measuring communication effect in mind.

In most instances around 20 feeling words have been used, but in some of the tests the list of words used has been reduced further. The findings are derived from a large scale test of advertising effectiveness (Hansen, 1997), studies of design (Kristensen et al., 2000b), logo colours (Hansen et al. 2001) and sponsoring (Hansen et al., 2002a). In most tests the same 12 feeling items appear. An integrated reporting is found in Hansen (2005).

The ad tests are described in the previous chapter in the discussion of the extent of central and peripheral information processing. All tests are based on the variables used in the ELAM test (Figure II.15). There is good reason to look at the joint findings across the different applications in the different contexts involving the short list of the feeling words. It makes sense to briefly review the findings of these studies here. In all cases, it appears that a 2 dimensional factor solution is meaningful; all include an approach (joy/positive) and an avoidance (sadness/negative) emotional dimension, a finding also Laros and Steenskamp (2005) confirm with the use of similar data.

In one of the Danish data cases where the negative dimension is only vaguely confirmed (Designs) the addition of a third dimension introduces a new dimension. At the same time the definition of the negative dimension becomes more clear and the third dimension reflects involvement with the issue, strength of the arousal or similar.

The amount of variance explained with the relatively limited number of factors is of course lower than ideally wished, since low dimensional solutions exclude explained variance by subsequent minor factors. However, the consistency of the dimensions across the different data sets confirms the general validity of the underlying dimensions identified. A summary of the findings from the forced two dimensional solutions is shown in Table III.3.

Table III.3: Loadings on two factors (positive/negative emotional responses) in analyses of data on sponsoring, ad-test, design and colours of logo

	Sponsoring		Ad test		Design		Colours of logo	
	Positive	Negative	Positive	Negative	Positive	Negative	Positive	Negative
Happiness	.39	.03	.70	.01	.72	-.16	.63	.07
Joy	.61	-.11	.67	-.04	.78	-.06	.71	.23
Pleasure	.48	.01	.58	-.21	.75	.03	.54	-.05
Accept	-.45	-.56	.56	.08	.06	-.55	-.02	-.68
Inspiring	.38	-.16	.54	-.05	.62	.43	.50	.13
Hope	.33	-.02	.51	.12	.43	-.30	.38	-.13
Surprise	-.02	.16	.40	.19	.16	.81	.22	.51
Anger	-.07	.61	-.01	.67	-.84	-.11	-.53	.47
Fear	-.03	.45	.17	.65	-.73	-.13	-.49	.48
Mistrust	x)	x)	-.06	.60	-.71	.07	-.55	.53
Trust	.32	-.36	x)	x)	x)	x)	x)	x)
Sorrow	-.07	.40	-.07	.50	-76	-.31	x)	x)
Dominant	-.10	.08	.23	.44	-47	.30	-.25	.10
Trustworthiness	x)	x)	x)	x)	x)	x)	.08	-.72
None of these	x)	x)	-.50	-.13	x)	x)	x)	x)

X) data not available

These data demonstrate the consistency with which the positive-negative dimensions occur. Only the negative dimensions in the case of the design test comes out a little bit weaker than in other cases. Difficulties with associating some of the negative feeling words with the kind of designs represented may account for this. Here the negative feeling words load negatively on the seemingly overall evaluative first dimension. Also the unexplained variance associated with particularly "surprise" and "dominance" suggests the presence of an "arousal" dimension in the data.

1. Arousal or Not?
Consistently across own and most others' research two independent feeling dimensions, a positive feeling – joy -and a negative – sadness, have been identified. When models reduced to very few dimensions are at stake two of them always represent these positive and negative (approach/avoidance) tendencies. Also the two dimensions tend to appear relatively independent of each other.

In some of our own preliminary studies and in findings reported from several other authors, however, one or additionally two dimensions occur, which often deal with arousal or involvement. There is no doubt that the extent to which the individual is involved, and thereby more or less arousal is produced, is an important determinant of responses to feeling statements.

To cite but a few of the instances where the same observations appear in the marketing literature: Batra and Ray (1986a) work with three dimensions, among which the third, is labelled activation and reflects arousal. Edell and Burke (1987) talk about upbeat (arousal), negative and warm dimensions, the latter two reflecting approach/avoidance tendencies, whereas the first may be interpreted as some aspects of involvement or arousal, and the PAD model include and arousal dimension for instance found important in Morris and McMullen's (1999) work with the Self Assessment Pictorial test (SAM).

Finally, Batra and Holbrook (1987) also talk about pleasure, arousal and dominance. Again arousal appears as one facet of the feelings, people associate with marketing stimuli. The importance associated with "The Activation Concept" by Kroeber-Riel (1979) should be kept in mind here also.

All this leaves the question, whether two dimensions, a positive and a negative (approach/avoidance), alone best represent the underlying common traits in feeling responses or whether a dimension of an arousal kind should be included also, and if so, how should it be quantified.

The issue is not to be settled here but will be taken up again after a more thorough treatment of contemporary research of emotions (Chapter IV). Here it is sufficient to emphasize that somehow the degree to which people are involved with what is at stake, when feelings are expressed, may result in different levels of arousal or may activate more or less extensive processing of feelings.

F. Summary
Affect is discussed in the forms that consumer behaviour research and literature have covered over the years: Personality, moods, attitudes and feelings. These are all seen by researchers as variables

that intervene and modify choice results that would have come out of the purely cognitive and conscious multi-attribute models. Personality as the most stable form has the least influence on choices, the influence of mood as a longer-lasting state is documented, but the largest influence is typically found, when affective aspects of attitudes and particularly feelings are introduced in the modeling of consumer choice. Of particular interest here are feelings that we see as the counterparts – or derivatives – of underlying emotions. Where emotions are unconscious and non-cognitive in nature as we will discuss in the next chapter, feelings may well be conscious phenomena that individuals can not only experience – joy, sorrow – but can also express: I am happy, I am sad. Researchers over the years have worked with varying numbers of specific feelings, however it is shown in the chapter that these feelings more often than not lend themselves to grouping in two basically different groups: Positive and negative, expressing two basic behavioural tendencies: approach and avoidance. And the review of the literature concerning feelings – in the terminology of this book – in relation to information processing, in spite of the somewhat tentative nature of the findings reported here, give rise to a number of possible conclusions that we would like to direct the attention of the reader to.

1. It is evident that there are more and different things under the sun when studying marketing communication responses than what is suggested in AIDA and similar cognitive effect hierarchy formulations.

2. A distinction between central/peripheral, high/low involvement or more or less cognitive information processing seems useful.

3. The central information processing is informational in its nature and when it occurs, it is, by far, more efficient in terms of achieving positive effect scores such as those traditionally used in marketing communication studies.

4. In contrast, peripheral information processing of a transformational nature seems to lead to higher emotional responses.

5. In the real world, the marketer may wish to generate strong concentrated central information processing. However competition from other communication, other advertising, low involvement on behalf of the receivers etc. set limits to the extent to which this is feasible.

6. In reality, at least when talking about fast moving consumer goods, peripheral information processing seems to be dominant in most instances and here feeling responses are important.

7. Feeling responses to marketing communication are basically of a positive and a negative nature. The positive and negative feeling responses are largely independent.

8. Feeling responses contain a more or less expressed element of arousal/involvement.

9. With a distinction introduced between feelings and emotions, it is suggested here that an operational measure of more basic emotions can be derived from scores based on responses to statements of feelings of a more cognitive-conscious nature. In any event, emotions (feelings) contribute significantly to the overall effectiveness of communication. This is particularly the case when peripheral processing of communication is taking place.

10. It is not obvious from the data analysed here whether the effect of feelings primarily makes other information processing more efficient, or whether they, in terms of emotions, have a more direct effect with information being stored at an implicit level which can be reactivated in purchasing and other situations.

Chapter IV

Neuroeconomics: Emotions in Contemporary Neuropsychologial Theory and in Consumer Choice

CHAPTER OUTLINE
This chapter deals with the development of our understanding of the brain and its functions, particularly as they address the concepts of emotions and emotional responses. The chapter takes neurological and neuropsychological research as its point of departure, since the developments within these areas of science provide much more detailed understanding of what is actually going on in the human brain as the individual deals with making choices. Obviously much of the cited research has a character of basic research rather than of applied research, which is what most of the consumer behaviour research is. However, as the chapter progresses, the parallel between "serious" life-preserving behaviour and more mundane consumer behaviour should become obvious. The chapter provides a formulation of contemporary consumer choices in terms of emotional and cognitive processes under the heading: Emotions in Consumer Choice Behaviour, in order to demonstrate the potential in developing these types of models from neurological findings. The chapter concludes with a discussion of neuroeconomics as the heading of a new type of research field, where – as the concept name states – neurology and economics are combined in order to understand human decision making under uncertainty.

CHAPTER OBJECTIVE
It is our objective to provide the reader with an understanding of what is currently actually known about how humans make decisions through reviewing and discussing contemporary neurological knowledge and research on the functioning of the human brain. This serves as a precondition to our discussion of the implications for building models of consumer choice.

We aim to develop two links to consumer behaviour theory from this understanding:

1. Integrating an emotional view of choice behaviour with the existing models of consumer choices to provide a deeper explanation of those existing models, and
2. Building on neuroeconomic findings to sketch the future potential for neurologically based emotional theories as the foundation of consumer choice behaviour modeling.

A. Background

> *"The picture is the essence of our knowledge in itself. It is in the picture our intellectual activity begins, not only as a passing situation, but as a lasting foundation for all intellectual activity." (Thomas Aquinas: "De Malo")*

Emotions – inner guiding unconscious processing – are aroused to a varying degree by all external stimuli such as pictures, sounds, and all kinds of perceptions as well as by many internal bodily and cognitive processes.

In the following, we shall review contemporary approaches to the study of emotions. Any perception gives rise to some emotional response. Recent neurological and physiological research has pointed at the importance of emotions in understanding human behaviour. Emotions as they capture the essence of the pictures we meet in our daily world or recall from our memory. Particularly brands, products and adverts are all such pictures. Emotions may also be aroused by all kinds of cognitive activity and other internal stimuli – also cognitive activity such as thinking about brands, products, or communication about brands and products may give rise to emotions. In this way all kinds of consumers' decision making generate accompanying emotions.

Many researchers have emphasized that emotional processes are unconscious brain processes resulting in observable bodily changes such as freezing behaviour, rising blood pressure, increasing production of stress hormones and startling reflexes. Here it is postulated that a relatively simple positive-negative emotional response potential is associated with any internally or externally generated picture the individual encounters. All items of consumer choice: brands, categories, public services, are represented by such pictures.

In this context, the important viewpoint is put forward that feelings depend upon emotions and both emotions and feelings influence consumer choices, although they do so in different ways. Here it is held that feelings are conscious or unconscious counterparts of the underlying more elementary emotional processes governing behaviour. It is also proposed that systematically studying feelings may allow us to infer about the underlying emotional processes. Thus the important distinction between feelings and emotions already introduced in the preceding chapter is maintained.

1. Emotions in Contemporary Neurological and Neuropsychological Research

Neuropsychologists have looked at human decision-making and found that emotions always play a role with simple as well as well as with complex choices. This is a relatively new view on human decision-making. As early as in 1994, Damasio argues that cognitive thinking has preoccupied the behavioural sciences in general and psychology and brain research in particular – and at the expense of the role of emotions and feelings.

Early psychologists, like James (1890) and Freud (1925), have had little influence in the late 20th century on mainstream thinking about human decision-making and choice. Darwin's (1865) observations about the development of emotional expressions in different species have largely been forgotten and the biological functions of emotions were never a research topic in experimental psychology and neurology. However, it is argued by Damasio (1994), Goldman (1993), McGaugh (2003), Gazzaniga (1998) and Ledoux (1998) that emotions should be seen in the light of the development of the brain, and that they can be traced to the most ancient parts of the brain, the pre-reptilian brain. For the interested reader Manstead et al. (2004) gives an excellent overview of contemporary contributions.

Basically the view is, that emotional responses such as freezing in front of threatening stimuli, aggressive or defensive reactions when in danger, approaching when pleasant stimuli are encountered, etc., are all behavioural patterns learned very early in the development of the species and are inherited in a conform way across many different races and are found among all human individuals. In Darwin's 1872 publication he, among other things, demonstrates how facial expressions of fear, anger and love have great similarities among very different species.

It would take us too far to go into details with the neurological evidence on the role of emotions. We would among other things be looking at studies based upon mentally disabled individuals, animal experiments, functional Magnetic Resonance Imaging studies on normal individuals, etc. Rather we will review knowledge of some of the more basic functioning of the brain and particularly the role of emotions - or somatic markers, as they are some times labelled.

2. The Nature of Emotions

But then what are emotions in humans?

The present senior author is a (not too good) golfer. Occasionally it happens – in spite of all good efforts – that he does not hit the ball at all. When in the early days of his golf career this happened his immediate reaction was to throw away the club or to bang it into the ground. This was a completely emotionally controlled reaction where important related feelings were anger, disgust, sadness, and the like. This being an unwise reaction, both for the sake of the golf club and for the social reactions of the other players, he soon learned to suppress the immediate emotional response. In this process unpleasant feelings first were observed and later the violent behaviour was suppressed – controlled by sensible cognitive processes.

But what does the neurologist have to say about such emotions?

First they are very well defined neurological processes occurring in the central and oldest part of the brain. They are associated with areas in the pre-reptilian brain such as hypothalamus, amygdala, the brainstem and the basal forebrain.

Figure IV.1: The structure of the human brain (Percy, 2004)

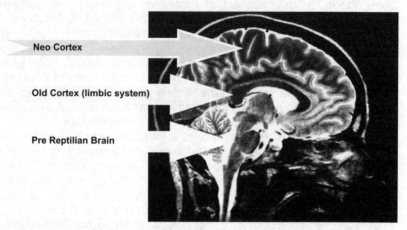

Basically, the brain can be seen as composed of three elements (Figure IV.1). One part is the so-called neo cortex, that is, the exterior part of the brain and in humans by far the largest. Cognitive processes primarily take place here and they do so with some specialization with areas reserved for seeing, hearing, talking, etc. Also specialization occurs in terms of the left and right side of the brain. This is shown in Figure IV.2.

The second part, the so-called old (cingulate) cortex, is found in mammals and in all animals at the reptilian or higher stage of development. This system functions as the brain controlling system (the only operating system of the brain in animals, below a certain level of development) and in humans it plays an important role in interaction with the cortex and it is where hypothalamus, amygdale, thalamus and insula are found.

Finally, the inner central or oldest part of the brain, the brain stem or - the pre-reptilian brain is where the most basic, elementary, controlling processes originate and to which hypothalamus, amygdale, thalamus and insula are linked. The structure of the brain, with the parts most important for emotions, is shown in Figure IV.3.

Figure IV.2: Specialized areas in the right and left neuro-cortex (Franzen and Bouwman, 2001, p. 6)

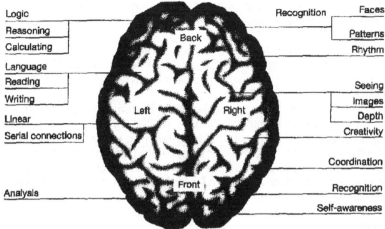

Figure IV.3: Areas in the Brain of Particular Importance to Emotional Processes (Damasio, 2003)

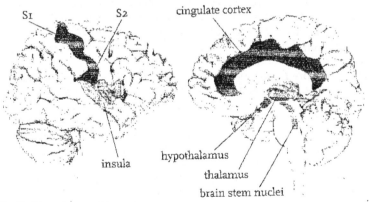

S_1, S_2: Somato-sensing regions

Figure IV.3 shows the main somato-sensing regions, from the level of the brain stem to the cerebral cortex. These regions are important, since they receive stimulation from bodily processes. Normal feelings of emotion require the integrity of all these regions, but the role that each region plays in the process is different. All regions are important but some regions (insula, cingulate cortex, and brain stem nuclei) are more important than others.

Emotional responses can be identified with the use of physiological measurements. EEG response, galvanic skin responses, eye movements, heart rate, voice and facial expressions are measures that researchers frequently use. Galvanic skin responses, for instance, are based on a measure of the capacity of the surface of the hands' (because of increased or decreased dampness) ability to transmit more or less electric current. When more aroused or agitated the hands sweat more and this is measured as an ability to transmit electricity.

The classical work with single respondents by Krugman (1977) should be recalled also. Here the measurement of brain (EEG) responses is taken to demonstrate different levels of involvement in particular TV spots.

In this area, Hazlett and Hazlett (1999) demonstrate that electronically registered electromyography (EMG), which is measuring changes in electrical activity in different facial muscles reflecting very small changes in the muscles' tension, relate to responses to advertising. These measures make it possible to distinguish between changes in facial musculature indicating positive or negative emotions. Also in their findings covering six different product categories they demonstrate EMG measures significantly related to (positive) feelings.

With these as with other measures such as heart rate, pupils' size, EEG responses, however, only the strength of the response is registered – not it's more specific nature (positive negative, defensive, aggressive, etc.). In later years, the PET (Positron Emissions Topography) scanning has been an important tool and so has functional Magnetic Resonance Image scanning (fMRI-scanning). These technologies are among the more important reasons for the new insight we have about emotional processes today.

With these brain scanning techniques it is being measured, exactly where in the brain activity occurs, when a certain process is ongoing (talking, feeling fear, solving problems etc.). These tools have become extremely important in the treatment of mental disorders. For instance, it can be detected what part of the brain is involved or out of order when such phenomena as severe depression, schizophrenia, reduced memory functions, etc., occur.

The technique, however, can also be used to identify exactly which brain parts are involved when different tasks are performed by normal individuals. In this way it can be identified what happens when, in the middle of a road, an individual observes a car approaching at fast speed. Then the perception is channelled from the sensory cortex through amygdala, basal forebrain, hypothalamus, and the brain stem, generating an increased heart rate (autonomous response), sweating in the hands (glandular response) and freezing or running away (behavioural response). All this may occur before any further activity takes place in cortex, where cognitive information processing takes place. Only later, when information has been transmitted here, the more precise nature of the danger is identified, and feelings and information processes occur that sometimes are registered consciously.

This has been summarized in the so-called low/high road hypotheses about how (particularly fear) stimulation controls the behaviour. Along the low road, stimulation from the environment is transmitted extremely fast and unconsciously to the amygdala of the oldest inner part of the brain which in turn elicits behavioural response. Along the high road, information goes through the cerebral cortex and gives rise to (possibly conscious) cognitive processes which in turn - somewhat later - may adjust the initial behaviour generated by the low road (Figure IV.4).

Figure IV.4: Low and High Roads to the Amygdala (Ledoux, 1998)

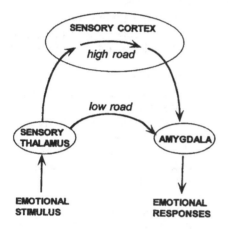

3. On Rats and Fear

Since emotional responses always contain a basic element which is inherited from the past and is ready at the birth of the individual, it is possible to study some basic elements of emotional responses by studying the behaviour of animals. Rats have been the preferred experimental tool in this endeavour. The work by LeDoux and his co-workers (LeDoux 1998 and 2002) has been fundamental for the insight we now have into the nature of emotional responses.

An important question in this and other lines of research on emotions has been whether emotional responses are completely innate or whether they are learned also - to a smaller or larger degree. In dealing with this phenomenon researchers have looked at the cells of the brain and their inter-relatedness. Basically a brain cell consists of a cell body with a number of very long "hairs" attached. This is illustrated in Figure IV.5.

Figure IV.5: Components of a neuron (LeDoux, 2002, p. 40)

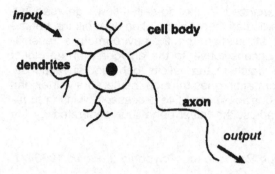

This functioning of the cells of the brain is not unique to emotional processes, but occurs in connection with all processes in the brain. Understanding this mechanism, however, helps clarify the nature of emotional processes.

The "hairs'" in Figure IV.5 denoted dendrites provide input to the cell from other cells and the "hairs'" denoted axons provide the connections reaching out to other cells. The dendrites and the axons connect the cell with a large number of other cells. The number of axons and dendrites is large and particularly the axons are very long. They give access to other parts of the brain and they may be as long as stretching from one part of the cortex to another. Through the dendrites the cells receive input from other cells and through the axons they provide output to other cells.

The connection between two cells that takes place is called synapse; it functions between the axons of one cell and the dendrites of another cell. The connection between these cells is in the form of electrical stimulation. Experiences, conscious or unconscious (in the rat always unconsciously), are represented by connected structures of brain cells, which may become activated and influence the behaviour of the individual. Also innate behaviour governing information is permitted through dendrites originating in the body or in the brain's very innermost parts.

The rat, when facing danger in its experimental condition or in real life, will have activated cells transmitting innate threat as well as learned aspects associated with threat. Freezing, it is believed, is a completely automatic innate response initiated when facing danger. In some instances it may not be that useful after all, for instance when a deer freezes in front of an oncoming car. But like most of the responses created by the evolution of animals it is good for most of them most of the time.

But learned modifications to the innate responses are important. A rat, which previously has been in danger encountering a cat, will store information about this experience in such a manner, that it can be used in adjusting behaviour in a subsequent danger situation. In the terminology of Damasio a somatic marker is being formed. Basically what has occurred is illustrated in Figure IV.6.

Figure IV.6: The fear system (LeDoux, 2002, p. 7)

Thus nature or nurture, or inherited or learned impulses, activate the fear system, which generates defensive responses. In this fear system a particular part of the most inner part of the brain, the amygdala, plays an important role.

These very fundamental processes studied in great detail and with many kinds of animals are found also to be at work in humans. Here PET and fMRI scanning have been valuable tools. Since coming into common use in the treatment of psychiatric patients in the early 90's it has given insight into exactly what parts of the brain are involved when various tasks are performed and when various diseases are encountered.

In humans, whose capacity in cerebral cortex is much larger than that of animals, the individual may parallel the process known from the study of rats when exposed to danger signals: send the signal directly onwards from the sensory cortex to the amygdala, similarly to the emotional processes when they reach the amygdala directly from the sensory cortex. But the individual may also pass the signal on to the cerebral cortex for processing when the signal is transmitted to the amygdala.

These two ways in which central stimulations from the environment or from internal processes may reach the amygdala, are those that have been characterized as the low versus the high road. Where the low road is the direct, quick and less specific generating very fast responses, the high road is the indirect road which takes a longer time since a larger number of brain cells and connections between these are involved, but which results in stimulation which is much more specific. This is illustrated in Figure IV.7.

Figure IV.7: Auditory stimuli elicit defence responses through the Amygdala (Le Doux, 2002, p. 121)

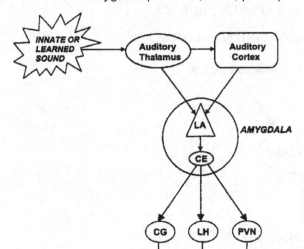

4. Emotions and Feelings

As suggested earlier, the distinction between feelings and emotions is important. In contemporary neuro-psychology feelings are seen as cognitive processes activated by the underlying emotions and possibly interacting with other elements in the short term cognitive memory. "The term feeling should be reserved for the private mental experience of an emotion, while the term emotion should be used to designate the collection of responses, many of which are publicly observable." (Damasio 2000, p. 42), and (Ledoux 1998, p. 282): "I'm saying that feelings come about when the activity of specialized emotion systems gets represented in the system that gives rise to consciousness."

In this connection, we shall again emphasize that the distinction between emotions and feelings is not synonymous with the distinction between conscious and unconscious processes (Shweder, 2004). Emotions are always unconscious, whereas feelings may be conscious as well as unconscious. It is also important to emphasize that cognitive processes may be of a high or low involvement character, but they will always be influenced by emotional activities, also.

One must realize that the automatic, very little demanding, fast and energy-saving emotional responses are unconscious and occur alone in many situations where cognitions, comparisons and information searches would have been unnecessarily time demanding and complicated.

The emotion formation process was illustrated in Figure IV.6. Whereas the individual is unable to inform about the underlying / emotional processes – although we talk about its behavioural expressions such as measured heart rate, freezing etc. – he can easily tell about his conscious feelings and forced to do so, he may even make unconscious feelings conscious and tell us about them. In Table IV.1 we summarize the differences between feelings and emotions.

Table IV.1: Summarized differences between emotions and feelings

Emotions	Feelings
- Activated by internal and external stimuli	- Activated by emotions or body state
- Unconscious	- Conscious or unconscious
- Not including cognitive activities	- Including cognitive activities
- Not controllable	- Partly controllable
- Often find expression in visible, bodily reactions	- Often finds expression in non visible, mental reactions

5. The Evolution of Emotions

Darwin's observations about similar emotional responses in species at very different developmental stages and their purposeful role in individuals were introduced earlier. To understand the nature of the brain system that regulates emotions, it is useful to take en evolutionary view on the brain.

The brain system underlying emotional behaviour "has been preserved throughout many levels of brain evolution" (Ledoux 1998, p. 425) and "to the extent that consciousness is recent, in evolutionary time, feelings came after responses in the emotional chicken-egg problem" (Ledoux 1998, p. 125). About this Ledoux (1998, p. 208) also writes: "the amygdala is like the hub of a wheel. It receives low-level inputs from sensory specific regions of the thalamus, higher-level information from sensory specific cortex and still higher-level sensory independent information about the general situation from the hippocampus formation. Through such connections, the amygdala is able to process the emotional significance of individual stimuli as well as complex situations. The amygdala is in essence involved in the appraisal of emotional meaning".

This pattern of neurological processing has been studied in animals at many levels of development and has been found mirrored in humans. Our previous review of rats and fear highlights this. Or to put it differently: "Emotions were probably set in evolution before the dawn of consciousness and surfaces in each of us as a result of inducers we often do not recognize consciously, on the other hand feelings perform the ultimate and longer lasting effects in the theatre of the conscious mind" (Damasio 2003, p. 111).

Emotions occur to us by the responses they elicit. Generally, they may be grouped as autonomous responses (increased heart rate, increased blood pressure etc.), glandular responses (sweating and different hormonal productions etc.) and behavioural responses (withdrawal, freezing, approaching) and in particular facial expressions. Such responses can be identified in even very primitive organisms. The biological causes underlying these emotional responses are outlined by Damasio (2000, p. 51):

"Emotions are complicated collections of chemical and neural responses, forming a pattern; all emotions have some kind of regulatory role to play, leading in one way or another to the creation of circumstances advantageous to the organism exhibiting the phenomenon; emotions are about the life of an organism, its body to be precise, and their role is to assist the organism in maintaining life."

"Notwithstanding the reality that learning and culture alter the expression of emotions and give emotions new meanings, emotions are biologically determined processes, depending on innately set brain devices, laid down by a long evolutionary history."

"The devices which produce emotions occupy a fairly restricted ensemble of sub-cortical regions, beginning at the level of the brain stem and moving up the higher brain; the devices are part of a set of structures that both regulate and present body states. All the devices can be engaged automatically, without conscious deliberation; the considerable amount of individual variation and the fact that culture plays a role in shaping some inducers does not deny the fundamental stereotypicity, automaticity, and regulatory purpose of the emotions."

"All emotions use the body as their theatre (internal milieu, visceral, vestibular and musculosceletal systems), but emotions also affect the mode of operation of numerous brain circuits: the variety of the emotional responses is responsible for profound changes in both the body landscape and the brain landscape. The collection of the changes constitutes the substrate for the neural patterns, which eventually become feelings of emotion."

In a consumer behaviour context emotions are aroused by the consumer encountering brands, products, other marketing stimuli, or by his thinking about them. These emotions may or may not give rise to cognitions; and the more involving the stimuli the consumer is faced with; the more likely it is that these will become conscious.

6. Consciousness, Feelings and Emotions

We as humans are first and foremost concerned with our consciousness. It is automatically so, because "we do not know about" the unconscious activities. In very early psychology much concern was with studying various kinds of conscious states of the mind (James 1890). Later with the widespread adoption of the behaviouralistic school of thought it was rejected entirely for what became labelled "introspection". The core tenet of this school was, that one should study the relationships between observed behaviours and observed stimulations acting upon the individual (Hull 1943). Still later in the development of psychology cognitive modeling became more flexible, but still very biased towards cognitive information processing even though it became more and more evident that also unconscious cognitive processes played a role to the individual.

Consciousness as we think about it, when we describe how we feel, what we experience and when we manipulate this information, is something which has been developed quite recently in the evolutionary history, (Jaynes, 1976). Unconscious brain processes, thus, are by far much older and also more widespread than their cognitive counterparts. Early in the development of animals they were the only kind of information processing. In a sense, it is strange that today we define unconscious processes which came first in the development of humans in relationship to and as the opposite of consciousness which actually appeared much later in the development of the brain.

Unconscious processes to a large extent rely upon their own memory system, the implicit memory. This applies to processes regulating the blood flow, stomach processing and many other fundamental processes ongoing in the body. Also many aspects of seeing, tasting, feeling, thinking, evaluating and judging rely on unconscious processes drawing upon implicit memory. When judging or evaluating takes place we may sometimes be able to become aware of these processes or the results stemming from them. Even the use of language relies heavily upon unconscious processes and information stored in implicit memory. We decode what is being said using phonology, we give meaning to it with the use of semantics and we make sense of the relationship between the words with the use of syntax and we see what is said in the light of the world as we perceive it, pragmatics. The phonology, the semantics, the syntax and pragmatic processing all occur unconsciously and have been labelled "the psychology of the cognitive unconsciousness" (Le Doux, 2002).

The role of consciousness in connection with emotions is worth special consideration. Damasio (2000, p. 155): "Emotions are seen as stereotype, unconscious, complex patterns of response whereas feelings are seen as patterns at the level of consciousness which may or may not become conscious. Reasoning and information processing is conscious. But it is through feelings, which are inwardly directed and private, that emotions, which are outwardly directed to the public, begin their impact on the minds. I separate three stages of processes along a continuum; a state of emotions, which can be triggered and executed unconsciously, a state of feeling, which can be represented unconsciously and a state of feeling made conscious that is known to the organism having both emotions and feelings (Damasio, 2000, p. 36). And spelling the three resulting phenomena out, Damasio (2000, p. 8) talks about three different things: "An emotion, a feeling of that emotion, and knowing that we have a feeling of that emotion".

What we mean when we say "I do not feel like it" is that an emotion has made us feel negatively, more or less consciously, about the phenomenon in question. Similarly, when we argue "I feel more for the red than the blue dress" or when we explain that this dinner course makes us feel better than another, underlying emotional responses generate the feelings we express.

7. Basic and Social Emotions: Few or Many Different Emotional Brain Processes?

Often a distinction inherited from older studies of feelings is maintained between social and basic emotions. They are seen to differ in the degree to which they are innate or socially acquired, but even social emotions include some innate elements. The basic emotions most frequently referred to by neurologists are those corresponding with Ekman's (1980) feelings of happiness, disgust, fear, anger, sadness and surprise. Here as in other theories on feelings it is remarkable that the number of negative feelings exceeds the number of positive ones. Among those fear, anger, and disgust are probably less frequent in connection with brands and products.

Thus Ekman has only one positive feeling, "happiness", and the same is the case with other studies of feelings (see Table III.1 in Chapter III). The social or second order feelings are seen as derived from the basic emotions. In the terminology of Plutchik (1980) they are combining aspects of the more basic emotions. They contain an important element acquired through learning, but social responses may contain innate elements also and social responses may in some instances be entirely controlled by emotional processes.

It is not clear exactly how many and what emotional systems one can separate. Ledoux argues (1998, p. 126): "I think starting with universal behavioural functions is a better way of producing a list of basic emotions than the more standard ways: facial expression, emotion words in different languages or conscious introspection." And moreover, (p. 127): "Different classes of emotional behaviour represent different kinds of functions that take care of different kinds of problems for the animals that have the problems." In particular, Ledoux concentrates much of his work on the fear system of the brain, but doing this with the clear intention that other emotional systems function in a much similar way. Damasio (2003) points at different sub areas of the brain being activated when such emotions as social versus basic emotions are involved, but on the whole, neurologists and neuro-psychologists see that different emotional response systems have very much in common, even though they may also activate different sub-parts of the brain.

As pointed out, among the emotions only one positive is normally referred to: like Ekman's "happiness" or Damasio's "joy". In the study reported subsequently we shall focus on this positive basic emotion and a more general negative one, possibly combining: distress, sadness, and the like. In consumer behaviour more explicit defensive and other negative responses like fear, anger, etc. are rarely at stake. Thus, it seems warranted in connection with consumer behaviour to focus on basic emotions "joy" (approach) and "sadness" (avoidance). These two basic positive and negative emotions when quantified as response potential may also reflect elements of secondary derived social emotions. For instance, "pleasant company" may involve some amount of happiness. By emphasizing the positive estimates relative to the negative ones we reflect the reality that products, brands and companies that survive, tend to be looked upon positively, otherwise they would disappear. Recent neurological findings also point in the direction of fewer and more simple basic emotions than generally believed (Russell and Peterson, 2005).

8. Emotions, Arousal and Involvement

It is generally observed that the more involvement, the more cognitive information processing is likely to occur, but also involvement may be of a different nature. It may be related to the product (utilitarian) or value expressive, affective kinds of problem involvement. The different kinds of involvement are suggested to influence the extent to which feelings are aroused. In line with this Kapferer/Laurent (1992) talk about emotional involvement, and Kroeber-Riel (1993) about situational involvement.

Levels of involvement are related to the arousal level of the cortex (Berlyne, 1960). Generally, arousal is quantified with the use of measures of electrical activity in the brain (EEG) (Krugman, 1971), and when arousal occurs, the brain becomes more alert and sensitive to impressions from the environment. Among those different systems that contribute to arousal, several are related to the processes in the brain stem area of thalamus, amygdala and hippocampus. In general, amygdala, in addition to influencing specific processing in the brain, induces generally triggered arousal. Among the feelings "surprise" may in its own right reflect arousal.

It is also worth remembering that in our review of studies of feelings (Chapter III) we found arousal-like dimensions to appear. The neurological interplay between arousal and positive/negative emotional responses is not yet fully understood. One may look upon arousal as a separate – in our terminology third – emotional dimension, or one may chose to consider arousal as a separate factor, that influences the magnitude of any separate positive/negative emotional response. In this sense arousal takes on a meaning much like involvement as it is occurring in theories of consumer behaviour. Here and in the following we shall chose the latter approach.

Thus emotions, when involvement is high, generate considerable arousal, activating feelings and cognitive activity. Less strong emotions may still give rise to some arousal, maybe not enough to secure conscious cognitive activity, but still enough to arouse unconscious feelings influencing behaviour. One may speculate that the more surprise, change, newness (Berlyne, 1960) the more arousal associated with an emotion-triggering phenomenon or situation; and the more arousal, the more likely it is that the emotion or its related feelings will influence the actual behaviour chosen in response to the emotion. Particularly in situations where there is low involvement from the consumer, some authors claim that emotions are especially important (Heath, 2001).

The whole issue relates to a classical debate in psychology between adherents to a bipolar versus a two dimensional positive/negative affect dimension (Watson et al., 1999 and Russell and Carroll, 1999). In summary in the following we shall adhere to the two dimensional views, but take involvement into separate account. In giving preference to a basic two-dimensional solution - as done in our own research (Chapter V and VI) - we do not neglect that situations where emotions prevail may differ in involvement, or the arousal level generated by the situation may differ. This however we think may lead to more strong positive and/or negative emotions. Thus the numeric sum of the positive and the negative emotions may suggest different arousal levels or degrees of involvement.

9. Background Emotions and Moods

Emotions are responses to stimuli and changes in the inner state of the individual or to happenings in the environment. The cause may be internal imbalances as registered (thirst, hunger) or external when relevant phenomena appear to the senses (i.e. a well known brand on the shelf in the supermarket). Additionally, the organism may maintain a certain emotional state over an extended period of time. This is often referred to as background emotions or mood as discussed previously.

Mood is distinguished on the one hand from specific emotions in the particular situations and on the other hand from more general personality-like traits. Moods or background emotions may, in a consumer behaviour context, be generated by the overall environment in which the consumer acts: the store, the mall, the kitchen, the restaurant, etc. Background emotions may also be influenced by one or more dominating phenomena in the environment such as the weather on the day of action, the movie on the screen, the looks and nature of the voice of the sales person in the store, or for the mother, the behaviour and the attitude of the child at breakfast. Such background emotions may in turn influence more specific emotions appropriate to what is going on: The choice of a brand in the store, the commercial watched in the break, the cereal brand to offer to the child.

B. Memory System

The memory system of the individual is important in many connections in the study of emotional and controlled responses by individuals (Schacter, 2001, McGaugh, 2003 and Percy, 2004). We have already used the distinction between short term and long term memory. The first represent information stored for very brief periods in the cerebral cortex of the brain. The second may be thought of as the place where whatever we are thinking about consciously at any given time is represented. The content of the short-term memory may come from sensory impressions or it may come from long-term stored information in the brain.

Again what is in the short-term memory may or may not be stored in the long term memory depending upon whether conditions for such storage are occurring. Much "irrelevant" information passing through the short term memory system never reach long term memory and fades out and does not influence the capacity of the brain's memory system. At this point it is important to emphasize that what is stored in long term memory is not stored as units of information like we think of in the terms of the computers' storing of specific records and particularly it is not stable and existing for ever.

Neither do we have all the different categories discussed earlier in connection with cognitive models of choice represented directly. Rather what is stored in the brain are numerous electrical connections between different elements stored in a pattern that makes it possible upon appropriate stimulation to retrieve in short term memory representations like our category elements - our concept - or whatever we intellectually are working with.

The storing itself, however, takes place for each informational item in a number of different places in the brain and our ability to recall specific events rests on the interconnectedness between all the different elements needed for reconstructing the impression of the event in question.

We may get a feel for what is happening with an example. If we think about the home we live in, this may be represented in more or less detail in short term memory. Actually the completeness of the home is never present but we may mentally move around in the house by changing the specific content of short term memory by having some brain connections activated and others deactivated in our memory.

Remembering that long-term memory as such is not in reality represented in the brain as the informational units we normally cope with, but rather in terms of combinations of connections established between elements in different locations in the brain, it is still useful to talk about the long-term memory as composed of two distinctively different kinds of elements.

The distinction is between declarative and non-declarative memory. The declarative memory refers to all of that stored information that can be made conscious or verbally declared, whereas the non-declarative brain system involves forms of memory that do not depend upon conscious processes. The first we may also call explicit and the second implicit memory.

Figure IV.8   A taxonomy of long-term memory. Long-term memory is often divided into two broad classes, explicit and implicit, each of which has further divisions. Based on Squire 1987 and Squire and Squire and Kandel, 1999

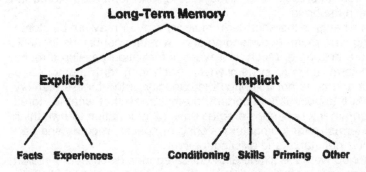

Squire and Kandel (1999) propose a classification of the explicit and implicit memory as shown in Figure IV.8. In early days the implicit memory was thought to primarily consist of programmes stored in order to enable the individual to perform the different procedures needed for it to survive (breathing, walking, writing etc.). Today it is realized that the implicit memory also contains a number of elements of importance for controlling, among others, emotional responses. Basically the distinction between explicit or implicit (declarative and non-declarative) memory rests upon the observation that in the explicit memory system the hippocampus located in what is sometimes labelled the cerebrellum (the second, in-between level of the brain) is important whereas implicit memory does not involve this particular part of the brain.

1. Memory and Emotions

In the role memory plays in the emotional as well as in the cognitive system, the distinction between explicit and implicit memory is important (Jacoby, 1991; Goode, 2001; Heath, 2001). Implicit memory includes a lot of information available for the performance of a number of different acts ranging from skilled learning over conditioning to a number of bodily functions. Explicit memory contains such information, which can be made conscious and enter into cognitive processing.

Regardless of whether explicit or implicit memory is involved, exactly how cognitive elements look to the individual may vary widely, and the same phenomenon may look different in the individuals' memory on different occasions. What is recalled is not a fixed well-defined informational research, but rather different memory traits stored in different locations. What will be activated depends on what the actual situation is and what associations are activated.

It is evident that emotions rely solely or mostly on implicit memory. In a sense, what is happening when an emotion is activated may be that what is available in implicit memory is coming into action, but emotions may also influence the choice process directly. With more emotions the feeling of remembering may be enhanced (Sharot et al., 2004 and Maxwell et al., 2005).

Important is also the distinction between short and long-term memory. The short-term memory is supposed to last for less than a minute and only if what is in the short-term memory is transferred to long-term memory, will it be possible to retrieve the information later. The distinction is treated by Damasio (2000) in what he calls core consciousness and extended consciousness. The core consciousness is that of which the individual is aware in any particular situation, whereas the extended consciousness may include information relating to the past or to expectations about the future. Emotions aroused as feelings occur first as a short term memory phenomenon, and they may influence behaviour by arousing feelings in conscious or unconscious processes determining what to be chosen: the brand from the shelf in the supermarket, the choice of blouse to wear for the day, etc.

To sum up, emotions may control behaviour alone, they may do so by activating conscious or unconscious feelings, and they may do so as parts in more or less extended problem solving.

With these viewpoints from contemporary brain research in mind, we shall return to our main topic, the study of consumer choice behaviour.

2. The Somatic Marker Hypothesis
Obviously many emotional responses are not solely innate they become modified by experience. In explaining this Damasio (1994) introduces "The Somatic Marker Hypothesis", in a similar manner Le Doux (2000) talks about "Emotion Circuitry in the brain".

In their purest form emotions are innate responses to basic stimuli such as fear, arousal, and threats. In the complex world of humans such elementary responses are rare. Rather, emotional responses occur to stimuli that have acquired the ability to arouse emotions.

Such stimuli may be internal (something we remember) or external (something we observe in the environment). To explain the functioning of such acquired emotional responses, Damasio introduces the concept of "somatic markers".

Somatic (bodily) responses are intrical parts of all emotions. When first it has been learnt that a stimulus is positively or negatively evaluated (associated with approach or avoidance tendencies) this learnt predisposition is labelled "a somatic marker". A brand name is a typical somatic marker. When internal or external stimuli activate such an acquired somatic marker, an emotional response is activated. This may or may not include the activation of unconscious or conscious emotional cognitions in the form of feelings, the important thing being that it is the somatic marker that is activated and that this functions as an emotion.

Recently Damasio and Bechara (Bechara and Damasio, 2005) suggest that one can substitute the word "emotion" with "somatic", and they talk about "somatic markers" rather than "emotional states". They do so, they claim, to avoid the confusion arising from the psychologists and others using terms, like emotions and feelings interchangeably. Here, however, we have chosen to use the term emotion as something different from feelings occurring at the non-cognitive level. In this connection it is worth recalling Damasio's (2002) definition of an emotion: "An emotion is defined as a collection of changes in body and brain states triggered by dedicated brain systems that respond to specific content of one's perception, actual or recalled, relative to a particular object or event".

Bechara and Damasio themselves provide evidence in favour of somatic markers' ability to guide human decision making in a useful manner. Similar evidence is recorded by Dunn et al. (2005) and also Maljkovic and Martini (2005) reports confirmatory findings. And Hare et al. (2005) report fMRI-scanning results from a study where respondents should make a go or a no go decision based upon emotional stimuli provided in the experiment. Finally Phelps (2006) presents findings from a study that suggests that the classical division between emotion and cognition may be unrealistic. An understanding of human cognition requires a consideration of emotions.

C. Emotions in Consumer Choice Behaviour

Emotional theory does not represent an alternative to traditional multi-attribute models of consumer choice. Rather, it improves their usefulness, and attitudes as studied in many multi-attribute models are still important.

Across all consumer behaviour situations involving product categories, brands, public and private services or communication about these items, emotions are aroused and in different ways they influence the responses made.

The responses in turn, generate information about and experiences with brands and products and this results in new or modified stored information, which influences future emotions. This follows from much of the research reviewed in the preceding pages and is convincingly demonstrated in an impressive study in an unexpected area. Greene et al. (2001) use functional Magnetic Resonance Imaging (fMRI) on 100 respondents to show how emotions influence what they call "Moral Judgments". Among the 60 moral judgments studied we find cases such as the choice between different coupons to use in a store and the choice among bus and train for travelling. In all cases different levels of emotional activity is observed with the use of brain scanning (fMRI).

In consumer behaviour we will work with a positive emotional response tendency like liking, joy, pleasure etc., and a negative tendency like harm, anger disgust etc. We see these as two dimensions, independent of each other, rather than two opposite poles on the same scale. This basic issue has been dealt with earlier here and in the literature in a number of studies that show, that they can occur at the same time, such as studies of "coping with positive and negative feelings" (for instance Luce, 1998, Aaker and Lee, 2001 and Duhachek, 2005). Where only positive or only negative emotions are present - as we shall see in some of the cases reported in our own research - the affect dimension may of course look uni-dimensional.

In a consumer behaviour context we also think of impressions such as taste, music, pictures, texture as integrated parts of many buying, consumption and communication situations. They all produce emotional responses. Particularly smell acts directly on those parts of the brain that are critical for emotional processing (Morrin and Ratneshwar, 2000, and Hansen, 2000), but also taste and music may have more direct access to emotional centres in the brain than more cognitively structured stimuli such as brands, information about brands etc.

Depending on the specific items (categories, brands or services) involved, different emotions may or may not become activated by the basic emotions. However, the similarity between all these instances is so that it makes sense to find in each of them a more or less strong positive (like joy) and a more or less strong negative (like disgust) emotional response tendency.

That is, something in the consumption situation or something about the alternatives considered may give rise to behaviour which has a clear positive – approaching - tendency (purchasing, upgrading preferences, recommending etc.) related to "joy". Or it may give rise to behaviour, which has a clear negative – avoiding - response related to "disgust" (rejecting, downgrading preferences, expressing negative opinions, etc.).

The intensity of the positive and negative emotional response tendencies may vary and so may the specific nature of the feelings (if any) aroused by the emotions. Compared with the emotions found in most clinical studies of individual behaviour such as depression, schizophrenia and other disorders, consumer emotions are weak, but as we shall see in different ways, they do influence the choices made by consumers.

The emotions generated by a severe traffic accident, major deceases, marriage decisions etc. are much more elaborate than those aroused by the observation of a brand or by the consideration of spending money on either of several product categories. In the previous section, it was suggested that we might distinguish between

1. emotions without consciousness whatsoever, commonly occurring with routinized choices
2. emotions giving rise to unconscious feelings, commonly occurring with semi complex choice, and
3. emotions giving rise to conscious feelings, most frequently with complex choices.

With the least complex consumer choices unconscious feelings are most likely whereas with semi complex choices more conscious feelings are frequent. Finally with more complex choices, cognitive evaluations with feelings playing a minor role are likely.

There is no one-to-one relationship between the three types of emotionally generated processes and the kinds of consumer choices. As the same choices gradually over time change from semi complex to routinized or from complex to semi complex choices, emotions without cognitions may become more and more dominant.

In the first case – the routinized choice- we would expect the emotions aroused by the alternatives, the brand or the brand category, to control the actual choice made with no cognitive information processing involved whatsoever. The consumer picking the usual detergent brand from the shelf in the supermarket and not really realizing that it has been done when having to pay for it at the cash register, is an obvious exemplification of this situation. These may account for as many as 60% of all purchases in super markets (Esch et al., 2005). The smoker's lighting of a cigarette, the TV-viewer's picking a candy from a box placed in front of the television set are other examples. The unconscious observation of a television spot forced upon the individual facing the screen may also be accompanied by emotions completely without cognitions. The basic structure of such choices is illustrated in Figure IV.9

It is perfectly possible, though, that the emotional responses give rise to some cognitive activity of which the individual never becomes aware. This will often be the case with semi-complex choices. The choice of the coffee brand may involve cognitively stored information about preferences for brands or acceptability of different brands. The perception of the television commercial may make some unconscious cognitive associations with previous exposures or the message may relate to other information already stored. The choice of the place for lunch in the large-scale shopping center may involve unconscious processing of feelings aroused by the emotions triggered by the consideration of the alternatives.

It might be argued also that some instances of impulse purchases take place with conscious feelings playing a decisive role for choice, and that these purchases take place with a certain level of conscious feelings. The shopper who – by impulse – selects the premium alternative from the shelf to be nice to himself probably does so as the result of a positive emotional stimulus which gives rise to the conscious feeling: Be nice to myself.

In many other instances of complex choices, cognitive evaluations may dominate in the control of consumer behaviour. Here, often processes occur like those assumed in multiattribute models of consumer choice. However, also in such situations the specific stimuli give rise to emotional responses that occur prior to any cognitive activity. These may in turn generate a "knowing feeling" of "I like", "I dislike" or of a more specific nature, say in the case of a perfume, "nice smell", "socially acceptable" and they may enable the consumer to speed up the choice process by more or less entirely relying upon emotional response tendencies.

Figure IV.9: Straight emotional choices

Figure IV.10: Extended emotional choice

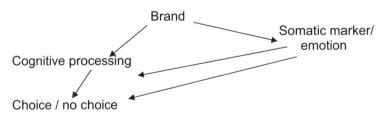

The important thing is that the emotions will always be there, but the extent to which cognitive processes occur may reduce, or may almost rule out, the direct impact of emotions upon the consumer choice. In many instances the immediate emotional response tendency – say to buy the good-looking, expensive perfume – may be completely over-ruled by cognitive considerations, such as: "I do not have that much money to spend right now".

Finally in the most extended cases of complex consumer choices the entire decision process can be broken down to a sequence of choices in each of which emotions may or may not play a role. The car purchaser's decision as to the price range for the new car may result following a very conscious consideration with few emotional elements involved. In a later state in the process the choice of the make of the car and the colour of the car may be greatly influenced by feelings aroused by observing or thinking about car brands and colours. Later, when a passing car reminds the car buyer of a re-cently observed commercial, the response may be completely emo-tional and only later when the driver reconsiders his purchase, con-scious cognitive processing may dominate.

All in all, the way in which emotions work will vary with the situa-tion in which the consumer finds himself, the brands and product al-ternatives he is faced with, or with the information – pictures or words – he is exposed to. These more or less elaborate and extended choices are illustrated in Figure IV.10.

1. Three Kinds of Choice Situations

To sum up, a parallel may be seen between the different levels of emotional responses discussed and the classes of consumer choice behaviour suggested by Howard and Sheth (1969), Engel et al. (1971 and later) and Hansen (1972), as well as in other cognitive choice theories. The low involving impulse-like repeat purchase of the loyal consumer comes close to the situation where only emotions without conscious feelings and cognitions are involved.

In some instances where a little more conflict is involved and maybe two or three alternatives are considered briefly, the choice may be explained in terms of unconscious feelings aroused by emo-tions in combination with more or less unconscious cognitive activity.

In contrast, the more involving kinds of consumer behaviour often described in the form of extended decision processes may involve emotions represented as consciously perceived feelings influencing outcome of the choice. Studying more extensive consumer behaviour such as the taking of a meal may involve a sequence of instances with unconscious emotions controlling behaviour alone.

Other instances may have emotions arousing unconscious feel-ings playing a role and still others will have conscious feelings aroused by the underlying emotions being of importance. The latter, for instance, may relate to the choice of the menu as such. The in-termediate choice category may occur in choices among different seasonings or dressings, and the completely, emotionally controlled choice could for instance be the 'mechanical' stopping of the meal because of being satisfied.

Similarly in connection with information processing, the careful reading of a brochure on a new washing machine may involve many instances of consciously perceived feelings, aroused by emotions. In the opposite extreme, the passing of a poster while driving by in a car may give rise to some emotional response triggered by the brand name or some illustrative or other element in the billboard.

In general, it is expected that when any kind of reading is involved, at least some unconscious activation of feelings derived from the emotions occur. The distinction introduced earlier between central and peripheral information processing (Petty et al., 1983) makes much sense here. In the peripheral information processing, emotions without cognitions are much more important than in the central information processing. Here, the emotions aroused constitute only a minor part of all the elements entering into the complete information handling process. And the primary effect of the emotions is in the form of more or less consciously derived feelings.

The extent to which information becomes stored, to be recalled or to be recognized only later, depends also upon the degree of involvement in the information processing situation. There can be no doubt that in instances where the situation gives rise to unconscious feelings of the emotions aroused. The possibility of storing of such impressions is there. It is argued, that the possibility for information storing is available in the form of somatic markers also even if emotional responses do not give rise to any kind of conscious or unconscious cognitive activity. This may to a large extent be the case with many exposures to marketing communication such as TV commercials, print ads, posters, IT-banners, etc. Studies employing recall and recognition measurements are clear indicators that unconscious storing of information does take place, since individuals with recall (cognitive activity has been present) exhibit much less favourable attitudes towards an advertised brand than do individuals who "only" recognize the specific ad (Heath, 2001).

In relation to consumer choice we may summarize this discussion in the diagram in Figure IV.11, where the upper half of the diagram is represented by processes such as those illustrated in Figure IV.11, whereas the processes corresponding to the lower half of the diagram are more like Figure IV.9.

Figure IV.11: Different consumer decision processes depending on level of consciousness and cognitive/emotional processing

Level of consciousness

		Unconscious	Conscious
	Cognitive	Limited problem-solving	Extended problem-solving
Type of process			
	Emotional	*Routinized problem-solving*	Impulse purchase/ Variety seeking

D. Neuroeconomics

The concern with emotional processes among neurologists has predominantly been concerned with mentally ill or retarded individuals. Lately however, it has become generally accepted that the findings have important implications for normal individuals, in particular for economic and consumption related issues. We shall not recapitulate the classic economic theory or consumer choice and the concept of multi dimensional utility, which has been central in these (Lancaster (1971). This is reviewed in Lee (2005), Glimcher et al. (2005) and Huang (2005).

A basic paper in contemporary neuroeconomics is Bechara and Damasio (2005). In a card game task they show how the Somatic Marker Hypothesis may explain normal individuals' better ability to make good decisions in social and risky situations as compared with individuals with brain damage to regions important for emotional processing.

Lately the professional arena is being overflowed with publications on neuroeconomics. The journals "Brain Research Bulletin" (vol. 67, issue 5, 2005) and "Games and Economic Behaviour" (vol. 52, no. 2, 2005) have special issues each with 5-6 contributions, and good contributions are also Camerer et al (2005), Glimcher et al. (2005), Phelps and Le Doux (2005), Coy (2005), and early contributions are found in Bechara (2003) and Glimcher (2003). A good review is available in Kenning and Plassmann (2005).

Most of this work is concerned with how people make decisions under uncertainty, and several of the contributions have interesting marketing implications. This is the case with the many gamble experiments where choices under uncertainty are explored. The actual observation that consumers do not make rational choices under such circumstances is made already by Tversky and Kahnemann (1974) and elaborated on in Kahneman's Nobel Price essay (2002). A more recent example is found in animal experiments by Lee (2005), and Chen et al. (2005) shows how uncertain choice activate the "posterior amygdale cortex" an area demonstrated by Bechara and Damasio (2005) to be involved in emotionally based decision making and similar findings are reported by Walter et al. (2005) from a fMRI study with humans. Another study of how varying willingness to trust others in money matters (Miller, 2005) is reflected in neural imaging.

In line with this also Lowenstein and Schkade (1999) concern with emotions' influence on welfare economic decision making is interesting. He points at three ways in which emotions influence economic behaviour:

1) Bargaining: Feelings of being treated badly by the opponents or pre-existing anger against them may cause irrational behaviour.
2) Intertemporal choices: For instance the decision to continue smoking may be seen as an irrational upgrading of the immediate pleasure of smoking against the risk of future possible diseases.
3) Decision making under risk and uncertainty: People's cognitive evaluation of risks often deviate from their emotional reactions to these risks. People may prefer 1,000 Euro right away from 2,000 Euro a year from now in spite of any calculation involving the amounts at stake

More related to everyday consumer behaviour are findings that the extent of credit card use is related to prefrontal cortial dysfunctioning (Spinella et al., 2005) and similar findings on investment decisions exist.

Also several studies of picture perceptions have relevance for advertising. Bermpohl et al. (2005) demonstrate how emotional pictures influence brain activities (again predominantly in the prefrontal cortex), and Pollatos et al. (2005) use EEG measures to demonstrate the same, and also show the effects to be more expressed with respondents who are better able to perceive their own heart rate, demonstrating the importance of the bodily (somatic) input to emotions. Similar emotional effects are discussed by Anderson and Shimamura (2005) and Mucha (2005) discuss the immediate importance of these and similar findings for advertising.

Of particular relevance are a few studies concerned with brand choice. In an attempt to reveal the role of brand names in terms of their impact on brain functioning, McClure et al (2004) conducted an experiment involving Coca Cola and Pepsi Cola. In the experiment 67 subjects were divided into 4 groups, one tasting a Coca Cola with the brand name attached to it. The second group tasting a Pepsi Cola with the brand name attached. The third and the fourth group tasted

Coke and Pepsi respectively without the brand names being known. Following the tasting the respondents were asked to express their preferences for the drink tasted. For the anonymous tasks, prefrontal brain activities were correlating with the degree of preference reported. In the branded version, knowing the Coca-Cola brand name had a dramatic effect on the experienced preferences, and brain activity occurred, reflecting strong thalamus/midbrain activity normally associated with emotional brain activities. The authors claim to have several so far unpublished cases of the same nature.

In a somewhat similar experiment, Deppe et al. (2005) and Plassmann et al. (2005) use FMRI to study choices between functionally similar brands. These authors report findings involving coffee and beer brands. When the targeted chosen brand was subjects' initial favourite brand strong activity in those brain areas normally associated with emotional activity was observed. As the authors put it: For products made distinguishable by brand name "a winner takes all" effect for participants' favourite brands appeared; on the one hand by reduced activation in brain areas associated with working memory and reasoning and on the other hand with increased activation in areas involved in processing of emotions and self-reflections during decision making. Finally another study of car brand preferences (Erk et al., 2002) has findings in line with the findings of Deppe et al. (2005).

In spite of the extremely high costs involved in conducting FMRI scanning and as a consequence of this the small samples, researchers are enforced to work with, the increasing availability of FMRI equipment at universities for research purposes will undoubtedly result in much more insight in the specific nature of emotional processes associated with brands, products and companies.

At a more general level some of these findings document the validity of verbal emotional responses relative to emotional brain functioning. The validity of positive and negative verbal responses as predictors of emotional brain activity is documented by Paulus and Frank (2003). With the use of FMRI they found that when people experienced more positive emotions towards stimuli they also show marked activity in those brain areas supposed to control emotional responses (again the ventromedial prefrontal cortex and related areas). These and other results are in different ways finding their way to the advertising and marketing research world. Havermans (2005) report on undocumented commercial applications of fMRI. Laybourne and Lewis discuss a methodology using EEC measures applying a portable device which it is possible to use in hall test designs. Similarly Page (2005) reports correlations between EEG measures and traditional interview based pretest data. Finally Addison (2005) reviews the commercial possibilities and dangers associated with the use of different neuroimaging techniques.

E. Summary
The chapter presents a view of emotions as psychological and physiological processes that originate in the older parts – in an evolutionary sense – of the brain, parts that humans have in common with many lower species, such as animals. The purpose of these processes in their origin seems to be to enable the individual to react swiftly and economically to situations where danger suddenly appears or the opportunity to hunt down food and the like. Present neurological research points to the continued existence of such emotional processes and illustrate the "new" paradigm, that emotion supports and guides rational decision making rather than interfering with it, as is the popularly interpretation of the role of emotions. The neurological findings on the role of emotions are that they are unconscious processes that enable the individual to act without much in the way of deliberation - by swiftly integrating prior, stored impressions with an interpretation of the present situation and issuing directions for actions from this basis. The Somatic Marker Hypotheses is a modeling and formulation of this role of emotions that fits very well with models of consumer behaviour.

The chapter discusses how emotional processes can be integrated in existing, cognitively based models of consumer choice – differentiating between routine, limited and extensive problem solving – and how recent findings, based on either brain scanning technology or galvanic skin responses point to a type of decision making where emotions guide the individual through complexity to swift and advantageous decisions, giving rise to a new field of cross-disciplinary academic study: Neuroeconomics.

Chapter V

Measuring Emotional Response Tendencies

CHAPTER OUTLINE

Contemporary neurology leaves little doubt about the importance of emotions in consumer choice. Left to answer is the question about how and if emotions in a neurological sense also can be quantified with the use of more traditional scaling techniques. This is the question that is raised in this chapter. The chapter opens with a discussion of how a questionnaire based measurement of unconscious emotional responses can be done through inferring the emotional responses through answers to feeling questions. The chapter then progresses through a detailed walk-through of how a large-sample survey was carried out and how the data were eventually analysed in order to arrive at the desired measures of positive and negative emotional response.

A number of basic propositions are established as a sort of yardstick by which the relevance of the methodology and its performance can be measured. The propositions and their "testing" is closely related to measurements of emotional responses to brands that are widely differently positioned in terms of buying motives and consumer involvement. The measurements give a lot of credence to not only the methodology but also to the theoretical assumptions underlying the role of emotions in consumer choice behaviour.

The chapter closes with integrating the theory of emotional responses into contemporary modeling of the subject of brand equity and a discussion of various ways of interpreting the emotional response data.

CHAPTER OBJECTIVE

We have two objectives with this chapter: To convince the reader of the possibility of measuring emotional responses to brands and categories of products in a valid and reliable fashion and secondly to confirm our theory about the role that emotional responses play in a consumer behaviour context. To strengthen the arguments about the role of emotions in consumer behaviour, the chapter also provides a strong integration of emotional responses into the broader theories of brand equity, particularly the element commonly referred to as Consumer Based Brand Equity or mental brand equity.

A. Background

In the preceding chapter we have made a number of observations on the nature of emotions. Some of them are still debated among psychologists, brain researchers and others. Others are more generally agreed upon. The more important observations are the following:

1. Emotions are different from feelings
2. Emotions come before feelings (if any) and are not conscious
3. Feelings are the cognitive counterpart to emotion and may become conscious
4. Emotions may differ depending upon the degree of involvement with, and the informational / transformational / nature of the underlying motivation.
5. Emotions vary both along a positive and along a separate negative emotional dimension.
6. Involvement as reflected in arousal accompanying an emotion may vary in terms of the strength of the positive and negative emotions.

These observations may be summarized in a number of testable hypotheses – or more precisely propositions.

1. From Emotions to Feelings - and Back

To study emotions associated with phenomena in the consumer behaviour context we must be able to quantify these. The brain scientist has a repertoire of tools available for the quantification of more or less strong positive and negative emotional responses. As suggested earlier, he may use blood pressure, heart beat rate, galvanic skin response, electroencelographic measures, etc., and in later years PET and fMRI-scanning have become important tools.

For the student of consumer behaviour, these tools are rarely available and rarely usable in the field, where most research on consumers takes place. However, the preceding discussion of the relationship between feelings and emotions may suggest a way in which we can get insight into the magnitude of the emotional responses generated in different consumer situations.

In cases where the consumer is consciously aware of the feelings associated with the underlying emotions, he should also be able to respond meaningfully to scaled questions about such feelings. The same is the case when we by asking questions force him to become aware of feelings linked with underlying emotions associated with stimuli (brands, products, communications about brands and products, etc.).

This is the methodology used in many previously quoted studies of feelings. When emotions give rise to only unconscious feelings or no feelings at all, it may still be possible to force a cognitive perception of feelings related to the underlying emotions by asking explicit questions regarding these.

Figure V.1:   From emotions to brand feelings to brand evaluation. Brand stimulus gives rise to (conscious or unconscious) feelings about brand

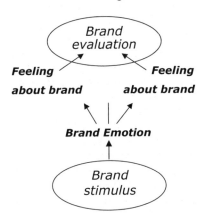

To put it differently, when an emotion occurs it may give rise to feelings. When a consumer meets a certain brand name (Figure V.1) the resulting emotion may give rise to the feelings labelled F1 to FN in the figure. This is well established among neuro-psychologists. Inversely, when the person is asked to judge the strength of the feelings F1 – FN in connection with the brand B, he gives answers making it possible to infer some things about the strength of the emotions that brand B may arouse (Figure V.2).

Figure V.2: From brand feelings to emotions. Answers to questions about feelings about brand reflections underlying brand emotion

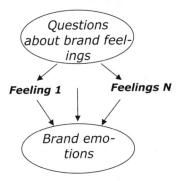

In psychology it is fundamental to talk about stimuli (S) that influence the organism and its processing (O), which in turn determines the response (R) of the individual. In this S-O-R model only "S" and "R" can be observed. The real psychological "O" processes are seen as intervening variables. The nature of these can be estimated from the measurement of other related phenomena. Thus to estimate emotions – O variables – from questions about feelings derived from the emotions is not the same as equalizing feelings and emotions.

Thus, we propose that the respondent's answering of specific questions about feelings associated with brands or product categories or communication, typically in the form of advertising about brands or product categories, may give information which can be used to estimate the underlying emotional response tendency. The feelings measured rely upon the specific feeling questionnaire used such as those already discussed (Izard 1977, Plutchik 1980, Holbrook and Batra 1987, Richins 1997 and others).

In addition to giving specific information of a more detailed nature of the feelings aroused, the answers also contain information about the more general underlying strengths of the positive/negative emotional response tendencies. Thus a number of propositions are suggested below, that will form the basis of a subsequent project encompassing measurement and analysis of emotional responses to brands and categories of products.

2. Propositions
The preceding discussion of the dimensionality of emotions, particularly in a consumer behaviour context, gives rise to the following proposition:

P1a: Consumers generate positive and negative emotional response tendencies faced with consumer choice alternatives such as brands, categories or information about the same. Such responses can be measured by a questionnaire containing scaled answers to feeling words and appropriate data analysis.

And since feelings are much more differentiated and varying with the nature of the stimuli, since the individual has learned to respond differently to different emotion-arousing stimuli:

P1b: The feeling statements most useful in identifying positive / negative emotional response tendencies for different brands or categories of brands differ among brands and categories.

Since arousal, as it relates to involvement, is an aspect of the emotions generated, we propose:

P2: The strength of the emotional response tendencies vary with the consumers' involvement in the specific product, brand, etc.

As brands and products may appeal more or less to informational or transformational needs (Rossiter and Percy, 1997) we propose:

P3a: The strength of the emotional response depends upon the kind of need satisfaction involved in connection with the particular brand category or brand category information considered. When the consumer is faced with a situation where he wants to minimize troubles, avoid problems etc. In the terminology of Rossiter and Percy, one which gives rise to "informational" based choice, relatively less emotional response strength is likely to occur.

P3b: When the situation is one where the consumer is expecting need gratification (that is positive pleasure of one kind or another deriving from the outcome of the choice) relatively more positive emotional response tendencies are likely to be observed.

P4: The more positive or the less negative emotional response tendencies an alternative gives rise to, everything else being equal, the more likely the choice of the alternatives or the more positively influenced the subsequent preference for it will be.

P5: When the stimuli giving rise to emotions are more arousing or involving, the magnitude of the emotion would be larger i.e. the sum of the numeric values of the emotions will be larger.

All these propositions must be seen in the light of the role emotions play in "straight" and "extended" consumer choices.

B. The Project

1. Data Collection
To test the propositions stated above, the following project has been carried out. In cooperation with TNS Gallup, Copenhagen, approximately 800 randomly selected consumers are interviewed with the use of self-administered questionnaires regarding their feelings for different categories and brands. Respondents are approached by random telephone dialling and asked if they are willing to participate in a scientific study of feelings for brands and product categories.

From the returned questionnaires a quota samples of age, sex and geographical regions was secured and the total number of willing respondents was divided into four matched groups. The response rate for the questionnaires returned was 67% and the number of usable questionnaires in each of the four categories was between 192 and 202.

Figure V.3: Categories and brands included in the study, grouped in the Rossiter-Percy grid (Rossiter and Percy, 1997) in co-operation with Larry Percy.

	Low Involvement		High Involvement
Informational	**Shampoo:** • Dove • Head & Shoulder • Sanex **Detergents:** • Ariel • BioTex • Neutral • Persil	**Pain killers:** • Panodil • Magnyl • Aspirin **Gasoline:** • Shell • Hydro Texaco • OK Benzin • Q8	Cell phone companies Computers Banks Newspapers
Transformational	Coffee Cereal Bread Cosmetics		Perfume Cars Airlines Amusement parks TV-Sets

2. The Choice of Brands and Stimuli
To carry out the study, a systematic variation of the stimuli along the dimensions proposed in hypotheses 3a and 3b was introduced. Thus, a number of categories and brands were selected to cover the four cells in the Rossiter/Percy matrix shown in Figure V.3. In each cell, a total of four categories were chosen (five in the case of high involvement transformational products, since additional data were available from a separate data collection).

Within each category four brands were included. In choosing categories and brands, it was secured that a sufficient number of respondents knowing the particular products and brands would emerge. The product categories and brands are all important in the Danish market, where data collection took place. In each product category, the leading brands were chosen together with one or two additional ones, ideally with differentiated images when such existed.

The total number of brands included was 69, representing 17 categories of fast moving consumer goods and services.

3. The Choice of Feeling Words
It was important to ensure that the feeling words included in the study were meaningful words for Danish consumers in connection with categories and brands in the study. Consequently, two pre-studies were conducted, each involving approximately 100 graduate students. Here students were exposed to different advertisements in different product categories. (Percy et al. 2004)

In the Danish language around 500 feeling words can be identified (possibly a little more in English). To arrive at an operational list of

feeling words representing these feeling words the following procedure was chosen.

First students were asked in writing to express their feelings for
the brands or categories. They were asked to write down feeling
words, they felt they could associate with the particular brand or
category. In this task, no aid was given as to the possible feeling
words to be used, but in the second of the tests, respondents additionally completed a translated version of the original 47 consumer
emotional items in Richins battery (Richins, 1997).

In the data set where the Richins consumer emotional statements
were included, the statements proposed from the open questions
were analysed relative to the answers given to the Richins' questionnaire. This suggested that some of the feeling words in the Richins'
battery made good sense for the particular respondents in the particular rating tasks.

Comparing also with the Izard (1977) and Plutchik (1980) batteries and that used by Holbrook and Batra (1987), a reduced list of
feeling words were decided upon in a manner to secure that no important feeling words from either of the theoretical frameworks were
excluded, and none were missing that could be of importance in a
consumer behaviour context.

In conducting the research the length of the questionnaire was a
major issue. The number of items to be rated and the number of feeling words combined to make the questionnaire potentially very long.
To make it possible nonetheless to include a wide variety of products
and brands, great efforts were put into minimizing the number of feeling words. The authors do not attempt to claim, that the final list of 24
words in itself represents the one and only possible list of feeling
words. As suggested by the findings reported in Chapter VI the positive / negative emotional dimensions may be identified with different
and more or less extensive lists. However as it will be shown as long
as the concern is with identifying feeling words that first and foremost
pick up the positive and negative emotional aspects of stimuli, the results are not very sensitive to precisely what words are used.

The fact is that for any single product category or brand, the use
of as few as 4 to 6 words may be sufficient to identify the underlying
positive / negative emotional dimensions. As proposed in H2, different words are likely to be the most suitable for different products and
brands. Since, however, it was not known exactly what words are
most meaningful for what products and brands, the complete list of
24 items was initially administered for all test items.

Apart from testing the hypotheses already stated, part of the purpose of the project was to identify a relatively shorter list of feeling
words, which would be sufficient to measure emotional response tendencies for different brands and brand categories. The research
questions raised by this purpose will be dealt with in the subsequent
discussion of the data analysis.

Still, with 24 feeling words (shown in Figure V.4) for each respondent to relate to for each brand and category, the potential number of ratings was astronomical. Therefore, the sample was divided into the four groups: one for each of the four cells in Figure V.3.

Thus, each questionnaire included 24 feeling questions for four (five) product categories and around 16 brands. The question used for a particular brand is shown in Figure V.4. Obviously not all brands were known to all consumers, and not all feeling statements made sense for all brands and categories. On the average, each respondent for each brand or category identified three to four feeling words that they could relate to.

Additionally, in the questionnaire for some brands, data were available on brand usage, preferences, loyalty and for durable product possession and purchase intentions. Data collection took place in Denmark in the fall of 2003.

4. Data Analysis and Raw Data

People's ability and willingness to respond to a complex questionnaire like the one in Figure V.4 is less than perfect.

Figure V.4: Questionnaire

On the following pages, different brand names are mentioned. We are now interested in how you feel when you think of each brand name. Under each brand name there is a list of feelings that one may have when thinking of a brand. For each brand that you know, please tick the box next to the word that matches the feelings you have, when you think of the brand. There are no right or wrong answers, and you may tick a box next to many or few words – all depending on what you think is most fitting when you think of the specific brand. After this, and next to each feeling box you have ticked, please show how strong the feeling is. This is done by use of the 7-point scale, where 1 means "Not very strong feeling" and 7 means "Very strong feeling".

This question is about the mobile phone brand/mobile phone company "Sonofon". If you do not know "Sonofon", please, go to the next brand question.

Please, tick off the words that describe your feeling when you think of the brand.	Please, tick off according to how strong the feeling is.							
	Not very strong						Very strong	
271.	1	2	3	4	5	6	7	
Desire	☐	☐	☐	☐	☐	☐	☐	☐	272.
Sexy	☐	☐	☐	☐	☐	☐	☐	☐	273.
Exciting	☐	☐	☐	☐	☐	☐	☐	☐	274.
Stimulating	☐	☐	☐	☐	☐	☐	☐	☐	275.
Happy	☐	☐	☐	☐	☐	☐	☐	☐	276.
Fine	☐	☐	☐	☐	☐	☐	☐	☐	277.
Calm	☐	☐	☐	☐	☐	☐	☐	☐	278.
Fresh, healthy	☐	☐	☐	☐	☐	☐	☐	☐	279.
Pretty	☐	☐	☐	☐	☐	☐	☐	☐	280.
Expectation	☐	☐	☐	☐	☐	☐	☐	☐	281.
Pride	☐	☐	☐	☐	☐	☐	☐	☐	282.
Success	☐	☐	☐	☐	☐	☐	☐	☐	283.
Aggressive	☐	☐	☐	☐	☐	☐	☐	☐	284.
Smart	☐	☐	☐	☐	☐	☐	☐	☐	285.
Relief	☐	☐	☐	☐	☐	☐	☐	☐	286.
Critical	☐	☐	☐	☐	☐	☐	☐	☐	287.
Doubt	☐	☐	☐	☐	☐	☐	☐	☐	288.
Boring	☐	☐	☐	☐	☐	☐	☐	☐	289.
Sad	☐	☐	☐	☐	☐	☐	☐	☐	290.
Pain	☐	☐	☐	☐	☐	☐	☐	☐	291.
Loneliness	☐	☐	☐	☐	☐	☐	☐	☐	292.
Worry	☐	☐	☐	☐	☐	☐	☐	☐	293.
Irritating	☐	☐	☐	☐	☐	☐	☐	☐	294.
Fear	☐	☐	☐	☐	☐	☐	☐	☐	295.
Nothing								

From the example of the questionnaire it can be seen that for any particular feeling, for each product or category respondents may be divided into 4 categories.

A. No response whatsoever.
B. Response in the first column ("271") indicating that the feeling word mentioned has meaning in relation to the brand or category presented, but no further scaling of the strengths of this feeling is given.
C. Same as B) followed by an indication of the strength of the feeling by marking 1-7 on the scale.
D. Only indication of strength.

In coding these observations, the final solution – arrived at after experimentation with various other solutions - is as follows:
All category A statements are given a value of zero.
All category B statements are given a value of 1.
All category C+D statements are given the value indicated by the response provided by the respondent on the rating scale.

As mentioned, there are several other possible solutions. Testing various solutions it turned out, that the factors derived are not highly sensitive to such modifications, as long as a data structure is maintained that includes all respondents with at least one answer in any single data line for each individual brand and category.

The 24 feeling words were administered to a total of 17 product categories and 69 brands. The number of respondents with only category A answers for a brand or a category vary between brands and categories. Such responses occur either because the brand is unknown to the respondents, or because they have been unable to associate any feeling words with it. Such respondents are deleted from the analysis of the particular brand. That means that for any brand or category all those respondents are included in the analysis that have given at least one category B, C, D answer to at least one feeling word for that category or brand.

For each brand, 50-250 of such responses are registered. On average three feeling words are checked.

The pattern for the shampoo category is shown in Table V.1. Being a low involvement informational product category, the number of feeling responses registered, 527, is among the lowest. For other categories, it runs as high as 1400.

Table V.1: Number of Non-Zero (B+C+D) Responses to 3 Shampoo Brands and to the Shampoo Category

Feeling	Total	Dove	H&S	Sanex	Category
Desire	27	7	1	6	13
Sexy	14	6	1	2	5
Exciting	5	3	0	0	2
Stimulate	32	4	3	12	13
Happy	44	10	5	11	18
Fine	50	17	5	12	16
Calm	28	10	0	11	7
Fresh/healthy	110	23	8	33	46
Pretty	39	7	4	4	24
Expectation	28	3	5	4	16
Pride	4	1	0	2	1
Success	15	2	4	3	6
Aggressive	5	1	1	1	2
Smart	15	2	5	1	7
Relief	14	3	3	4	4
Critical	14	3	5	1	5
Doubt	13	5	4	0	4
Boring	20	4	4	8	4
Sad	9	4	1	0	4
Pain	4	1	1	0	2
Loneliness	5	1	2	0	2
Worry	10	2	3	1	4
Irritating	16	4	6	2	4
Fear	6	2	0	1	3
Total	527	125	71	119	212

5. Standard Analytical Procedure

The procedure described below has been used for all 69 brands and 17 categories. It is described with a single brand as an example: the case of the brand 'Dove' belonging to the shampoo category.

First, an N-factor exploratory principal component factor analysis is carried out. This results in a 7-factor solution (explaining 79% of the variance). The results are shown in Table V.2. It appears that the first of these factors suggests a positive emotional dimension with feeling words such as sexy, excited, stimulated, happiness, pretty, success, smart loading high on the factor. The second factor suggests a general negative emotional response factor where aggressiveness, pain, loneliness and fear have high loadings.

Table V.2: Rotated Component Matrix for the Shampoo Brand Dove (Explained variance 79.8 %)

Feeling	N	1	2	3	4	5	6	7
Desire	7	0.10	0.05	0.29	-0.02	0.02	-0.81	-0.01
Sexy	6	0.61	0.00	0.37	-0.06	0.02	0.09	-0.02
Exciting	3	0.96	0.08	-0.06	0.05	-0.02	0.06	0.02
Stimulating	4	0.74	0.02	0.27	-0.04	0.02	0.09	-0.01
Happy	10	0.57	0.06	-0.64	-0.07	0.02	0.21	-0.01
Fine	17	0.02	0.03	-0.85	0.26	-0.04	0.23	0.00
Calm	10	-0.05	0.09	-0.71	0.36	-0.07	-0.25	0.03
Fresh. Healthy	23	0.27	0.01	-0.71	-0.09	0.00	0.25	-0.04
Pretty	7	0.67	0.06	-0.50	-0.11	0.05	0.09	-0.03
Expectation	3	0.01	0.11	0.03	0.04	-0.03	0.84	0.02
Pride	1	0.98	0.08	0.04	0.08	0.05	0.07	0.05
Success	2	0.97	0.09	-0.07	0.04	-0.02	-0.07	0.01
Aggressive	1	0.08	0.98	0.04	0.08	0.05	0.07	0.05
Smart	2	0.97	0.12	-0.06	0.05	-0.02	-0.06	0.02
Relief	3	-0.03	0.12	0.22	0.79	-0.10	-0.09	0.05
Critical	3	0.00	0.09	0.00	0.03	-0.89	-0.02	0.09
Doubt	5	0.00	0.04	-0.05	0.13	-0.87	0.01	0.05
Boring	4	0.01	0.05	0.02	-0.89	0.19	0.02	-0.04
Sad	4	0.01	0.06	0.02	-0.88	0.09	0.08	-0.03
Pain	1	0.08	0.98	0.04	0.08	0.05	0.07	0.05
Loneliness	1	0.08	0.98	0.04	0.08	0.05	0.07	0.05
Worry	2	0.01	0.09	-0.01	0.01	-0.08	0.02	-0.96
Irritating	4	-0.01	0.03	0.00	-0.04	0.48	-0.01	0.83
Fear	2	0.01	0.41	-0.01	-0.01	0.00	-0.02	-0.02

At this stage, the overall purpose is to derive a battery of a limited number of feeling statements that can be employed to identify the underlying positive-negative aspects (happiness / distrust or approach / avoidance) of the emotional states aroused by the brand. For this reason it was decided to concentrate the analysis on a two-factor solution with 44% of the total variance explained. This solution after rotation is shown in Table V.3.

*Table V.3:   Rotated Component Matrix - 2 factors only for Shampoo Brand
Dove. (Small loadings are deleted, explained variance 44%)*

Feeling		Component	
	N	1	2
Desire	7	0.361	
Sexy	6	0.714	
Exciting	3	0.840	
Stimulating	4	0.791	
Happy	10	0.820	
Fine	17	0.426	
Calm	10	0.219	0.203
Fresh. Healthy	23	0.588	
Pretty	7	0.824	
Expectation	3	0.183	0.175
Pride	1		0.932
Success	2	0.822	
Aggressive	1		0.932
Smart	2	0.824	
Relief	3		0.352
Critical	3		0.263
Doubt	5		0.244
Boring	4		0.353
Sad	4		0.349
Pain	1		0.932
Loneliness	1		0.932
Worry	2		0.212
Irritating	4		0.227
Fear	2		0.365
	125		

The two-factor varimax rotated component matrix clearly suggests a positive and a negative emotional interpretation. However, there are statements that for different reasons do not contribute very much to the explanatory power of either of the two factors. These can be deleted. For instance, 'expectations' loads very low on both of the two dimensions and so does the statement 'calm'. Other statements rest upon so few observations that they cannot be of much use in the subsequent analysis. They are deleted for this reason. Examples are 'exciting', 'pain', 'pride', 'aggressive' and others.

Following this step, a feeling battery of 16 items was arrived at (not shown here) and a new principal component analysis with varimax rotation was carried out on this battery. From this we have chosen to concentrate on the highest loading feeling statements. This leaves us with a battery of 10 statements including 6 positive and 4 negative feeling statements shown in Table V.4. A factor analysis on these 10 words explain 63% of the variance in two factors.

Table V.4: Rotated Component Matrix for the Shampoo Brand Dove
(Exp. Variance 56.0 %), N = number of responses

Statement	Component	
	1	2
Desire	0.585	0.004
Stimulating	0.737	0.019
Happy	0.900	0.004
Fine	0.680	-0.033
Fresh. Healthy	0.752	-0.044
Pretty	0.822	0.011
Critical	-0.005	0.753
Doubt	-0.021	0.719
Worry	0.007	0.539
Irritating	-0.014	0.898
Other statements	-	-
Statements in total	-	-

The imbalance between positive and negative statements reflects the imbalance in the number of responses given to positive and negative feeling statements. The battery derived in this manner is the supposedly best 'Dove' feeling battery. A note of caution, however, should be made here: it would be perfectly feasible to include or to delete 2 or 3 more statements based upon loadings and number of responses without changing the results very much.

We have, however, decided to stay with the 10 statements. This conclusion is supported by the results of the analysis of the remaining brands, for all of which it has been possible to identify 10 (6 positive and 4 negative) statements loading significantly on the two dimensions. These differ from category to category, but they are all drawn from the same original 24 feeling words.

The choice of exactly 10 statements for each category and brand warrants a few comments. As suggested earlier an emotional response strength estimate can be computed with the use of 4 to 6 statements for most items included in the study. However, to avoid having a different number of feeling words entering into the solution for the different items analyzed, it was decided – after inspecting the individual solutions for each brand and category – to settle on 10 feeling words in all cases analyzed. Thereby comparisons between brand and categories also become more meaningful. By doing this in the case of Dove – and in most other cases – as many as 2/3 of all ratings given are included in the analysis.

6. Analyzing the Shampoo Category

In Table V.5, the three last sets of two columns provide results in terms of 2-factor loadings for all three brands analyzed in the shampoo category: 'Sanex', 'Head and Shoulders' and 'Dove', together with the category solution (this is based on questions asked about the category as such, and not the individual brands). All loadings higher than 0.4, from the 24 items in the two factor solution (with a few exceptions of loadings of interest for the overall interpretation) have been included in the table. A clear similarity appears between the solutions in the 4 cases. This similarity suggests a solution where the responses to all three brands and the category as such are combined. Since the number of respondents for some brands is quite low this stabilizes the factor solutions.

Table V.5: Positive and Negative Emotional Loadings: Low Involvement- Informational 2-factor Solution. Category: Shampoo

Total	527		Category		Sanex		H&S		Dove	
	+emotion	-emotion	+emotion	-emotion	+emotion	-emotion	+emotion	-emotion	+emotion	-emotion
Exp. Variance:	33%		45%		45%		35%		45%	
# of respondents										
Desire 27	0.64		0.55	0.69	0.76		0.57		0.36	
Sexy 14	0.54					0.45			0.74	
Exciting 5									0.84	
Stimulating 32	0.68			0.70	0.68		0.68		0.79	
Happy 44	0.74			0.60	0.65		0.70		0.82	
Fine 50	0.64			0.59	0.70		0.68		0.43	
Calm 28				0.43	0.41					
Fresh 110	0.73			0.72	0.58	0.42	0.59		0.59	
Pretty 39	0.71			0.58	0.66		0.60		0.82	
Expectation 28	0.41			0.58	0.43		0.40			
Pride 4				0.41	0.58					
Success 15	0.54		0.80	0.50	0.59		0.80		0.82	
Aggressive 5			0.44		0.74	-0.63	(0.34)			0.93
Smart 15	0.44			0.48			0.48		0.82	
Relief 14	(0.36)		0.44		0.74	0.63				
Critical 14		0.56	(0.29)	(0.23)	(0.24)	-0.63		0.81	(0.29)	(0.24)
Doubt 13		0.55	0.80			-0.22		-0.27		(0.24)
Boring 20		0.48	0.69					-0.79		(0.35)
Sad 9				0.40						
Pain 4		0.64	0.79					0.88		0.93
Loneliness 5			0.80							0.93
Worry 10		0.71	0.69					0.87		0.22
Irritating 16		0.73	0.77					0.67		0.23
Fear 6		0.44	0.72							0.37

Still the meaningfulness of all the individual solutions is remarkable considering the relatively few respondents some brands are based upon. Combining data for all brands and those for the categories gives a data set of a total of 527 non-zero responses and it results in the two-factor solution shown in the "all brands + category" columns of Table V.5.

Applying the same criteria to this solution as we did with the Dove solution results in a 10-item battery (the solid words in Table V.5). On the whole, the 10 items have high loadings for the brands 'Dove', 'Head and Shoulders' and 'Sanex'. Thus, we may conclude that it is feasible to work with one standardized shampoo battery applied in the same fashion to all shampoo brands. In this context it is worth noting that the final shampoo battery arrived at in this fashion is identical with the Dove battery shown in Table V.4, and for the two other brands only one or two feeling word appear in the joint battery substituting one or two in the direct brand solutions. In the case of Sanex "boring" appears instead of "weary" and in the case of Head and Shoulders "boring" substitutes "doubt". In both cases feeling words gave rise to relatively few answers. Here it should also be emphasized that we do not try to maximize explained variance in the data. Rather we want to isolate the positive-negative emotional dimensions in their own right.

The usefulness of the batteries is further supported by the analysis, which is provided in Table V.6. Here, the number of positive and negative non-zero responses is counted for the 10 general feeling statements in the shampoo category. On line 4, the number of answers to the three (or two) most frequently mentioned other feeling statements are given. Finally, the number of remaining statements is shown.

Table V.6: No. of Statements Answered (No. of Questions) for 3 Brands of Shampoo

10 general statements	Dove	H&S	Sanex
Positive	67 (6)	26 (6)	78 (6)
Negative	12 (4)	18 (4)	4 (4)
Total	**81 (10)**	**44 (10)**	**82 (10)**
Few special statements	16 (2)	14 (3)	19 (2)
Remaining statements	18 (12)	13 (11)	18 (12)
Grand total	**125**	**71**	**119**

It appears that for all brands, 60-80 % of all provided answers are given to those feeling words included in the general 10-item battery. With an addition of the answers given to 2-3 feeling statements specific to either of the three brands, but not included in the general battery, the proportion of the feeling statements included increase further.

A large number of remaining items (12-13) have very few answers associated with them. Thus, in analyzing 'what feeling responses a particular brand gives rise to', we might look only at the 10 common statements plus 2 or 3 additional ones. The addition of the 2-3 items, however does not improve the solution markedly, so in order to make brand comparisons most meaningful we decided to stay with the 10 best statements in this and in other categories.

7. Computing Emotional Response Strength

For the further analysis, an emotional score is computed for each brand for each respondent. For each emotional statement for each respondent the scale value of his answer is multiplied with the weight the statement has with each of the two dimensions. Then these scores are summed up for each respondent as a negative emotional and a positive emotional strength score.

This is done in the example shown in Table V.7. This raw factor score is used since it preserves the magnitude of the response for different brands by avoiding standardization and normalization. Here the Net Emotional Response Strength (NERS) is computed as the difference between the positive and the negative scores.

At this point some may argue that one cannot have positive and negative evaluation on orthogonal axes and then compute the difference. The argument is more linguistic than real. If we think of positive and negative dimension as reflecting approach and avoidance tendencies there is a solid evidence in the psychological literature for the computation of the difference between these. As in so many other cases it is the names of things that disturb over thinking. Not the thing in their own right. Contemporary discussions about "can you feel happy and sad at the same time" (Luce, 1998).

Table V.7: Example of Calculation of Positive and Negative Emotional Response Strength (NERS) Score for a Respondent's answers to the feeling questions for Dove (respondent no. 283)

Emotional Statement	Answer	Factor Loading +Emotions	Positive Score (answer * Loading)	Factor Loading - Emotion	Negative Score A x C	NERS (Pos. Score – Neg. Score)	Numeric sum
	A	B	A x B	C			
Desire	2	0.59	1.17	0.00	0.01		
Stimulating	3	0.74	2.21	0.02	0.06		
Happy	0	0.90	0	0.00	0		
Fine	6	0.68	4.08	-0.03	-0.02		
Fresh	4	0.75	3.01	-0.04	-0.02		
Pretty	2	0.82	1.64	0.01	0.02		
Critical	0	-0.01	0	0.75	0		
Doubt	0	-0.02	0	0.72	0		
Worry	5	0.01	0.04	0.54	2.70		
Irritating	2	-0.01	-0.03	0.90	0.18		
Total			12.12		2.93	9.20	15.05

Similarly as a measure of the involvement with or arousal associated with the brand the numerical sum (NUMS) of the positive and negative scores are computed. The net emotional response strength (NERS) score for the 3 shampoo brands are shown in Table V.8a. Here data are aggregated across subjects. Also in the table, as comparison similar scores are computed for the brands in the high involvement transformational category: perfume. Again, a standard 10 question solution for all the brands in this category is used.

Table V.8a and V.8b: Emotional Response Strength Score, Net Emotional Response Strength (NERS) and Sum Response Scores for Three Shampoo Brands and Four Brands of Perfume

Table V.8a

BRAND	VALID RE-SPONDENTSN	+EMOTION	-EMOTION	DIFFERENCE (NERS-SCORE)	SUM (NUMS-score)
Dove	40	4.981	1.604	3.377	6.585
Head & Shoulders	29	2.376	2.996	-0.620	5.372
Sanex	42	6.833	1.284	5.552	8.117
Average		4.730	1.961	2.770	6.691

Table V.8b

BRAND	Valid respondents N	+Emotion	-Emotion	Difference (NERS-score)	Sum (NUMS-score)
Hugo Boss	45	7.100	1.716	5.383	8.816
Laura Biagotti	17	9.165	0.229	6.663	9.394
Van Gils	16	7.263	2.103	5.160	9.366
Nina Ricci	4	8.813	1.175	6.638	9.983
Average		8.085		5.961	9390

Several things should be observed here. The net emotional response strength (NERS) scores for the shampoo brands are very different. When the NERS is interpreted as a score representing a market standing (reflecting differences in brand value solely ascribable to the brand name) the three brands are ordered Sanex, Dove, Head and Shoulder. Also, negative NERS scores for the Head and Shoulder brand is worth noticing. Since the brand is positioned as a shampoo to be used against dandruff, the explanation for the negative NERS can be assumed to be derived from the negative emotions aroused by dandruff. Since the brand is chosen by a number of consumers, cognitive considerations concerning the usefulness of the brand seem to overrule the negative emotional response.

Finally, NERS for all the shampoo brands are small, and since low involvement information-processing brands are assumed to arouse only limited emotional response, this seems to be the expected result. With high involvement and transformational products, we would expect larger NERS and larger numerical sum scores (NUMS). The data in Table V.8b on perfume confirm this assumption. These scores are more positive, than the shampoo scores. Almost by definition, the brands that consumers know and use must give rise to positive emotions. If it was not so, the brands would most likely disappear from the market.

Table V.8 also exhibit the sum of the numerical values of the scores (NUMS). As discussed in the previous chapter, this score tells "how much" emotion is aroused and may be taken as an indication of arousal or of an involvement with the item rated. In this sense the perfume brands are more involving that the shampoo brands.

The scores for users and others, respectively, are shown for the shampoo brands in Table V.9. Users are here defined as those who use 'only', 'most frequently' and 'on and off'. The differences between users and non-users of the brands are significant. Thus, one may conclude that the emotional differences relate to the respondents' brand choices.

Also it should be noted that the low scores for Head and Shoulders are ascribable to the very low scores among the non users. This further confirms the observation that users choose the brand after cognitive deliberations of its merits against dandruff, whereas non-users – presumably they don't need to use the brand – judge it solely by an emotional reaction aroused by the concept of dandruff.

Table V.9: Emotional Responses for Users and Non-users (All Respondents, n=182) (Here all respondents are included since some of the data cells would otherwise become extremely small)

	Uses N= 23	Do not use N=159
Dove, +Emotion	0.979	1.111
Dove, -Emotion	0.069	0.279
Dove Net Emotional Response Strength (NERS)	**0.91**	**0.832**
	N=23	N=159
H&S +Emotion	2.97	0.256
H&S -Emotion	0.32	0.731
H&S Net Emotional Response Strength (NERS)	**2.65**	**-0.525**
	N=59	N=131
Sanex +Emotion	1.968	1.416
Sanex -Emotion	0.294	0.283
Sanex Net Emotional Response Strength	**1.694**	**1.133**

8. Feeling Statements Dominating the Responses in all 4 Rossiter/Percy Grid Quadrants

So far we have looked almost only at two categories. The same procedure with similar results is used with the remaining categories. In the low involvement, informational grid quadrant, detergent, gasoline, and headache remedies are treated like the shampoo category, and the 10 'best' feeling statements are identified for each of the categories. The best statements in each of the categories appear in Table V.10.

Table V.10: 10 "Best" Emotional Statements Selected for Low Involvement Informational Categories

Feeling	Total	Detergent	Shampoo	Gasoline	Pain killers
Desire	4	X	X	X	X
Sexy					
Exciting					
Stimulating	1		X		
Happy	3	X	X		X
Fine	3	X	X	X	
Calm	1				X
Fresh	2	X	X		
Pretty	2	X	X		
Expectation	3	X		X	X
Pride					
Success	2			X	X
Aggressive	1			X	
Smart	1			X	
Relief	1				X
Critical	3	X	X	X	
Doubt	3	X	X	X	
Boring					
Sad	1				X
Pain	1				X
Loneliness					
Worry	4	X	X	X	X
Irritating	4	X	X	X	X
Fear					
No of Responses	1763	426	526	316	495

As suggested earlier, one might argue for two or three more or fewer statements, but for the sake of simplicity the number of 10 feeling statements is decided upon in this and subsequent categories. Increasing the number of statements does not change the nature of the solutions, but the percentage of explained variance changes. For these low involvement, informational products (Table V.10, first column), it appears that three statements enter into the solutions for all four categories (desire, worry and irritating). Five statements enter into three of the four categories (happy, fine, expectations, critical, doubt).

One can discuss whether one should work with four different sets of statements; one for each category (or maybe even one for each brand), or whether one should try and identify a common set of statements for the entire low involvement informational group. Here we decided to work at the individual category level, since a solution based on the same statements in all three categories would have to include statements of no importance for some of the categories.

Of course, it would be possible to work with less than 10 statements, but doing so gives somewhat lower explained variance for all of the brands. Moreover it would be hazardous to extend the solution based on the three categories to all other categories that fit the "low involvement informational" type of product. Also it appears in the subsequent analysis of the three other quadrants in Figure V.3 that the "best 10 statements" for the categories vary much more between the categories in each of the remaining quadrants than it appears from Table V.10 regarding the low involvement informational category.

The three remaining Rossiter/Percy groups are analyzed, using the same method as described for the low involvement/informational category. Again we find that a meaningful selection of 10 items can be made for each category, and that this selection can be applied for all brands in the category. The statements used for each of the categories, however, vary widely, so that we recommend making separate selections of the 10 statements (feeling words) for each individual category. In Table V.11 is shown the frequency with which each statement appears as one of the 10 statements selected in the four quadrants. A few (2 = desire and happy) statements are present in all of the product categories in all 4 quadrants, so that these can be used for all brands across the quadrants.

Table V.11: No. of times words appear (for Rossiter-Percy Grid categories.)

Feeling	Hi/Transf	Hi/Infor	Low/Inf	Low/Transf
Desire	4	4	4	4
Sexy			1	2
Exciting				
Stimulant	3	2		3
Happy	4	4	4	4
Fine	3	2	2	2
Calm	1	1	1	
Fresh	3		1	2
Pretty	3	2	3	2
Expectant	3	4	4	3
Pride				
Success	2	4	4	2
Aggressive			1	
Smart	3	2		
Relief	3			
Critical			1	2
Doubt		3	1	
Boring		4	2	1
Sad	1		2	2
Pain	1	1	1	3
Loneliness		3	1	1
Worry	4	4	2	1
Annoying	4		3	4
Fear			1	2

The number of statements provided for each quadrant varies dramatically from 1763 for the low involvement informational quadrant to 4444 for the high involvement transformational quadrant. In Table V.11, the most frequently appearing feeling statements for each of the 16 brand quadrants are shown. If one wanted to point at one possible overall feeling battery, it could be derived from this. It would probably include the statements: desire, happy fine, pretty, expectation, success, worrying, annoying, pain and sad.

Now we can compute emotional response scores along the lines previously shown in Table V.7. These scores are reported in Table V.12. Here the brand average is the average scores for the brands. With these, our hypotheses, H1-H4, can be reviewed.

Table V.12: Emotional Response Strength Scores and Net Emotional Response Strength Scores (NERS) for Categories and Brands

	Valid N	Positive strength	Negative strength	NERS	Category average	Grid average
Low Involvement/Informational						
Shampoo Category	63	7.294	1.597	5.697		
Dove	40	4.981	1.604	3.377		
Head & Shoulder	29	2.376	2.996	-		
Sanex	42	6.833	1.281	5.552	2.770	
Gasoline Category	65	4.334	0.283	4.051		
Shell	20	2.842	-0.090	2.933		
Hydro Texaco	35	6.851	0.704	6.148		
OK Benzin	42	3.509	0.682	2.827		
Q8	24	4.484	0.202	4.282	4.047	
Detergent Category	47	4.249	0.653	3.596		
Ariel	25	4.575	0.526	4.049		
Bio Tex	39	4.158	0.945	3.213		
Neutral	30	3.300	0.624	2.677		
Persil	13	2.794	0.560	2.234	3.043	
Pain Killers Category	49	4.562	1.177	3.384		
Panodil	35	4.542	0.784	3.758		
Magnyl	22	4.333	0.836	3.497		
Aspirin	14	3.875	0.757	3.118	3.457	3.360
Low Involvement/Transformational						
Coffee Category	52	8.952	1.199	7.754		
Merrild	52	8.269	1.896	6.374		
Gevalia	44	6.157	0.956	5.201		
BKI	32	4.880	0.805	4.075		
Karat	29	4.534	0.602	3.932	4.895	
Cereal Category	80	8.622	1.146	7.476		
Kellogg's	48	8.452	1.411	7.041		
Guldkorn	32	7.695	1.154	6.541		
Ota	38	7.037	1.057	5.980	6.521	
Bread Category	79	8.398	0.996	7.402		
Wasa	45	6.783	0.843	5.939		
Schulstad	52	6.763	0.835	5.928		
Kohberg	50	7.240	1.081	6.158		
Hatting	43	8.441	1.182	7.259	6.321	
Cosmetic Category	69	11.264	2.215	9.050		
Nivea	39	8.150	1.376	6.774		
Max Factor	28	8.833	1.818	7.014		
Maybelline	18	7.599	1.476	6.123		
Pierre Robert	21	9.282	1.491	7.791	6.926	6.142

	Valid N	Positive strength	Negative strength	NERS	Category average	Grid ave-rage
High Involvement/Transforma-tional						
Perfume Category	78	9,67	1,02	8,65		
Hugo Boss	45	7,10	1,72	5,38		
Laura Biagiotti	17	9,16	2,50	6,66		
Van Gils	16	7,26	2,10	5,16		
Ninna Ricci	4	8,81	2,17	6,64	5,96	
Cars Category		0,82	8,37			
Fiat		3,17	0,07			
Skoda		2,81	0,03			
Toyota		1,45	5,57			
Citroen		1,54	5,37	2,76		
TV-Sets Category		2,74	4,88			
B&O		1,93	13,71			
Philips		1,89	7,07			
Panasonic		2,02	5,37			
Grundig		2,19	4,76	7,73		
Amusement Parks Category		1,19	8,51			
Tivoli		1,25	11,24			
LEGOland		1,18	9,86			
Bon Bon Land		1,76	6,25			
Bakken		1,63	6,27	8,40	6,21	
High Involvement/Informational						
Cell Phone Companies Category		3.75	5.90			
Sonofon		3.76	3.22			
TDC		5.79	1.50			
Orange		5.76	1.30			
Telia		6.24	-0.59	3.74		
Computers Category		2.74	6.68			
Dell		1.23	5.98			
Apple Macintosh		1.77	5.67			
Fujitsu Siemens		2.08	6.00			
Hewlett Packard		2.88	6.57			
IBM		2.86	6.49	6.14		
Airlines Category		2.21	4.34			
Maersk Air		1.71	5.02			
SAS		3.00	3.07			
Sterling Airways		1.40	3.47			
Krone		5.21	1.78	3.34		
Banks Category		3.63	3.77			
Danske Bank		4.64	2.45			
Nordea		4.36	3.54			
BG Bank		3.76	0.00			
Alm. Brand Bank		4.53	3.76	2.44		
Newspapers Category						
Berlingske Tidende		2.36	4.92			
Politiken		2.02	4.96			
Jyllands Posten		1.88	3.50			
BT		2.17	4.03			
Ekstra Bladet		3.85	2.16	3.91	4.89	

C. Testing the Propositions

P1: From the results in Table V.12 it is obvious that consumers generate positive and negative emotional response tendencies and that these differ significantly between brands and categories. In all of the initial brand analyses a solution with two orthogonal dimensions reflecting positive and negative emotional tendencies make sense.

From Table V.13a, where average net emotional response strengths (NERS) scores for brands are computed for the four Rossiter/Percy grid categories, it is evident that:

P2: High involvement gives rise to higher NERS scores, than low involvement does.

P3: Similarly, transformational products give rise to higher NERS scores than do informational categories. However, one might have expected a larger interaction effect resulting in higher NERS scores for transformational/high involvement brands. That this is not so may be seen in the light of the choice of actual product categories to represent this quadrant. Inspecting the categories included it becomes evident, that one of them stands out with very low NERS scores: automobiles.

In the case of the automobiles a possible explanation suggests itself. Two of the brands – FIAT and SKODA – sell well because of low prices, seemingly not because of the emotions they arouse.

We have earlier argued that the numerical sum of positive and negative response strengths (NUMS) reflect the amount of emotion aroused. If we look at the numeric sum of the emotional scores for brands in all categories (Table V.13b), we also find that transformational categories give rise to higher numerical scores than does informational ones, and similarly high involvement provides higher positive numerical scores than low involvement.

Again – for the same reason as for the NERS – the interaction effect does not show up, but in both cases if we delete the automobile category it decreases (see footnotes for tables).

Table V.13a and V.13 b: Average NERS-score for R&P Grid, and Average Numerical Emotional Score (NUMS) for R&P Grid

Table V.13a: NERS scores

	Informational	Transformational	Average
Low Involvement	3.360	6.142	4.751
High Involvement	4.893	6.214*	5.553
Average	4.127	6.178	

*Computed without cars: 7.156

Table V.13b: NUMS scores

	Informational	Transformational	Average
Low Involvement	5.133	8.540	6.836
High Involvement	10.268	10.126*	10.126
Average	7.701	9.333	

* Computed without cars: 12.96

For 6 categories in the fast moving consumer goods area, data are available on frequency of purchase of the various brands. If users are classified as those, who use 'almost always', 'most of the time', and 'sometimes', against those using 'rarely' or 'never', scores in Table V.14 emerge.

Table V.14: Average Numerical Emotional Scores for R&P Grid

	Average NERS Among users of the brand	Average NERS among non users
Bread	6.73 (n=165)	3.23 *) (n=34)
Coffee	5.58 (n=89)	4.35 *) (n=66)
Shampoo	6.16 (n=37)	2.67 *) (n=85)
Cereals	6.20 (n=75)	2.98 *) (n=75)
Detergents	3.68 (n=65)	2.03 *) (n=47)
Head Ache Remedies	0.66 (n=48)	0.25 *) (n=49)

*) Difference significant $P \leq 0.001$

Here it is seen that users generate higher emotional response tendencies than non-users. When similar tabulations are made with regard to durable products, a classification of 'owners', those 'considering to purchase' and 'others', can be applied. Here, the first two categories score significantly higher than the remaining groups.

In subsequent research, we shall look into prices charged for products in different categories, relative to the NERS scores. This is done in order to illustrate the hypothesis that high NERS scores indicate high brand equity – and therefore prices above the average for the category under study. Tentative findings here suggest such correlations. For example with regard to amusement parks, the higher the NERS score is for the park the higher the prices for beer and ice cream in the park.

D. Discussion and Conclusion

The findings give rise to some interesting observations in addition to the confirmation of the propositions tested. It has high face validity in the Danish society that brand names like B&O (Bang & Olufsen Television), LegoLand, and Tivoli, are among those giving rise to the highest NERS. Similarly, it has high face validity that among those with the lowest NERS scores in 2003 are the car brands Fiat and Skoda, the bank BG Bank and Telia – the dominant Swedish telecom operator – which had a hard time trying to gain a market foothold in Denmark.

1. Emotion and Brand Equity

In recent years the management oriented research in marketing has made substantial progress in developing the concept of Brand Equity.

Several scholars, Keller (2003), Aaker (2000), Franzen and Borgmann (2001) to name but a few, have developed systems for building and managing brands, where emphasis is put on the tools that can make a brand great in the sense that consumers form a relationship with the brand.

The concept brand equity is seen as consisting of three different but interlinked constructs: Mental brand equity (or Consumer Based Brand Equity), Behavioural brand equity (or Behavioural brand response) and Financial brand equity (or Market based brand equity). Of these three elements we will limit our discussion to the Mental Brand Equity – or Consumer Based Brand Equity – since that is the type of brand equity construct where emotions play a large role as a component.

The objective of branding efforts – development of a deep, lasting relationship – is seen as the top of a development ladder (or pyramid for that matter), where the bonding of the consumer progresses hierarchically from mere awareness of the brand via a deepened and broadened awareness and understanding of the brand's features to forming clear associations with the brand and eventually end with the consumer "embracing" the brand.

Central to the formation of the attachments between consumer and brand is developing associations, that encompass the product and its attributes but that also rely on emotions – or feelings – so that the attachment is not only based on cognitively stored aspects such as features and performance, but also on emotional relationships.

Figure V.5: Keller's Consumer Based Brand Equity System (Keller, 2003)

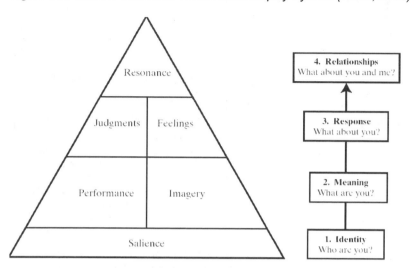

Keller (2003) can be taken as the advocate of this type of thinking that presents product branding as a source of differentiation and thereby a source of influencing consumer choice in the long run – branding is seen as the basis for forming consumer loyalty. Keller's branding system is illustrated in the figure above.

As can be seen, the concept feelings is a part of the bonding process at the last step but one. It is seen as the counterpart to judgments and together the two concepts form the stage "Response", the answer to the question "What about you?".

The authors are rarely very explicit about what type of emotion or feeling that are seen as instrumental in building strong and lasting re-lationships with brands. Basically "feelings" or "emotions" are seen as an affective response as opposed to the primarily cognitive response that forms the basis of Judgment – in Keller's terminology.

However, it stands to reason that there is a strong element of emotion and feeling – in the meaning of the words that the present authors use – in the bonding of a consumer to a brand. The positive emotional response tendency towards a brand, we argue, is a straightforward example of the approach tendency associated with emotional response. The stronger the bonding between consumer and brand, the more the emotional response can be assumed to generate feelings: "I love my Levi's!" and feelings that may grow to a high level of consciousness, the more the consumer is bonded to the brand.

Figure V.6: The Brand Value Chain according to Franzen and Bouwman (2001)

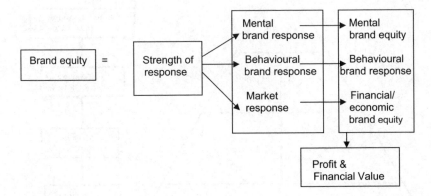

Thus, NERS, net emotional response strength, may be seen as a measure of that unique part of brand equity, which is inherent in the brand name itself, and not ascribable to generic product factors: distribution, price, quality, and similar market factors.

An interesting observation in relation to brand equity considerations has to do with the category scores relative to the brand scores. In the majority of categories, the category score (the score where people chose feeling words, associated with the category per se) is higher than brand scores in the same category (the scores where the respondents chose feeling words relating to the brand names).

This clearly suggests problems to major brands in many product areas. If an individual brand generates NERS at a lower magnitude than the product category, it indicates that basically you are communicating something which is less positive than the category as such. You are certainly not adding value to your specific brand above the value that stems from the basic product or more precisely from the basic product promise expressed by the category. An issue that will be dealt with further in Chapter XI.

With this in mind, it is possible to return to the data in Table V.12 and to look at the different categories to identify brands that actually do score better than the product category, and thus provide some added value to that of the basic product itself.

Such brands exist in the detergent category (Ariel), in the airline company category (Maersk Air), among the amusement parks (Tivoli and LEGOLand), among the television sets (B&O and Phillips), in the bank category (Alm. Brand Bank) and in the painkillers category (Panodil and Magnyl).

The evidence for the hypothesis is of course limited to the selection of categories and brands in the present study. The brands selected do not always include the market leader, which may skew the

observation on individual categories concerning the relationship between brand NERS and category NERS. This is likely to be the case
in the car category since none of the four car brands chosen are
among the market leaders.

However, it is nonetheless remarkable that of the 64 generally
well known brands included in the study, only 9 appear to be 'outstanding' in this sense.

Still another observation relates to the high involvement informational categories, banks and mobile phones, where we find high
negative emotional response scores, and consequently low NERS
scores. A reason for this may be, that when respondents react to individual banks and mobile phone companies, not only the brand itself
comes to mind, but also those many confusing experiences customers in the two areas have had with prices, fees and extra charges,
that has dominated the marketing activities of these companies in recent years. As suggested before, in such a market consumers may
well be more concerned with the concrete offers in forms of prices
and product features and less with the brands themselves.

2. NERS and NUMS

Finally, we look at the numerical value of the response strength as a
sum, not only as the difference between a positive and a negative
score. The amount of emotion (positive as well as negative) conveys
important information in addition to the NERS score. A high emotional
potential suggested by high numeric emotional response scores
(NUMS) may translate into moderate NERS scores if high negative
emotional responses are generated also.

The extent to which the numerical sum score gives separate information in addition to the NERS score is illustrated in Figure V.7.
For most brands high NERS corresponds to high NUMS, however,
this is not at all the case with the high involvement/informational
products where moderate NERS scores often combine with high
NUMS score, suggesting that for these brands overall evaluation to a
high extent is influenced by cognition evaluation also.

Figure V.7: NERS and NUMS scores for brands in the 2003 data

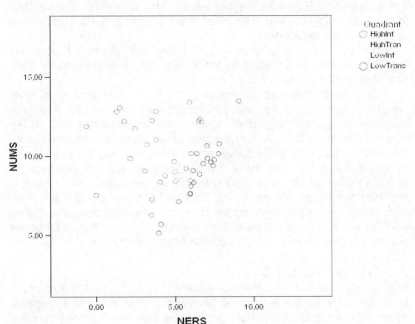

3. Methodological Comments

An important issue is whether the NERS scores as computed here are influenced by cognitive bias (Poels and Dewitte, 2006). Obviously the answers to the single questions are, but the derived underlying factors should not be. Exactly what the answers to the different feeling questions have in common is the emotion underlying the answers to the feeling questions. This does not rule out the influence of some response bias, but the uniform nature of the factors derived suggests, that common underlying emotional response tendencies are reflected in the computed score.

The project reported – being unique in its nature – gives rise to some other methodological considerations. Secondly, when working with randomly selected and moderately motivated respondents the use of extensive rating task, involving such subtle topics as feelings, tires the respondents to an extent that it influences their conscientiousness in completing the task. The questionnaire used is not more extensive than many questionnaires used with students or other more motivated respondents. Forcing the respondents to consider many brands, some of which give no emotional meaning to them at all, and then to relate those brands that do to 24 different feeling words, most of which give no meaning to the brand in question, does reduce the quality of the ratings.

The amount of unexplained variance, even in solutions where as much variance as possible is to be extracted, also suggests this. Still the consistency with such positive and negative emotional response tendencies is emerging without a single exception. This confirms the validity of the approach.

Finally it must be emphasized that a major consequence of these problems combined with the limited size of the sample of 200 for each brand result in computations for some brands being done with very few respondents. In quite a few cases the number of responses upon which the computation of the NERS scores is completed is on the low side. TNS/Gallup who sponsored the data collection showed understanding for these problems and it was decided to carry out a new survey with a modified questionnaire and with a much larger sample.

E. Summary

This chapter provides the basic argument about how consumer an- swers – of a conscious nature – to feeling questions can be used to infer about the underlying emotional responses to brands and catego- ries of brands. Since this book is about consumer behaviour, it is of great importance to establish the possibility of measuring emotional responses with the use of survey methodologies, since this is the only feasible way to measure consumer responses to brands in a way that is useful to a marketing organization. The chapter also pro- vides a detailed walk-through of the steps in research design and data analysis that leads to the conclusions concerning emotional re- sponses. The reader should be able to see the seeming validity and relevance of the measurements from the rich amount of data pre- sented and should also be able to see the way in which measure- ment of emotional responses fit together with theories on the devel- opment and maintaining of brands.

The chapter, in addition to measurement of positive and negative emotional response, presents two summary numbers that express how a consumer is emotionally attached to a brand: the Net Emo- tional Response Strength measurement, which directly indicates the intensity of the attachment or response, and the NUMerical Sum of emotional responses that indicate the total amount of emotional re- sponse or arousal to a brand or category. The two measures are suitable for different purposes and are offered – and compared – as supplementing summary measurements of an emotional consumer attachment to a category or to a brand.

Chapter VI

Further Evidence on Mental Brand Equity

CHAPTER OUTLINE
Chapter VI concludes our presentation of the role of emotions in consumer choice. The chapter describes a replication of the 2003 study that was carried out one year later, the 2004 study. A number of methodological considerations went into the planning of the 2004 study and the chapter deals with these considerations: The 2003 questionnaire was rather long, the contact form – with drop-off questionnaires – was not as efficient as a web based interview, a need for more observations per brand and broader observations per respondent than just in one category and finally a desire to test measurement using fewer feeling words. These considerations are dealt with in detail as a lead-in to the findings. A discussion of differences and the sources of differences between the two studies lead up to a discussion of the results in general and specific observations of differences in emotional responses between users and non-users.

The discussion on brand standing and brand strategy that was opened in Chapter V is continued in more detail in this chapter both as far as outstanding brands is concerned and as far as the implications for brand strategy of various "generic" positions vs. categories and competition go.

The chapter closes with discussions of the NERS measure – or rather the role of emotions as measured by NERS – in choice situations of varying complexity, in the case of choice of spokespersons and more generally in connection with advertising and behaviour.

CHAPTER OBJECTIVE
Our objective with this chapter is to further present arguments that emotional responses exist and can be measured – and that the results of these measurements are not very sensitive to changes in research methodology or questionnaire design, and consequently, that the measurements are valid and reliable. The demonstration and confirmation is based on data from an additional large-scale survey on consumers' responses to brands. We intend to demonstrate the relevance and usefulness of this type of measurement in marketing management contexts, through integration of the emotional theory into branding considerations and a broader field of choice behaviour and marketing applications,.

A. The Background for the Replication

The face validity of the findings of the 2003 project were high, clearly indicating that there is such a phenomenon as emotional response tendencies associated with brands, that such tendencies can be quantified by systematic analyses of answers to questions about feeling words, – and that the response tendency vary with the type of product and brand in question.

Nevertheless, a number of reasons made it natural to consider a replication of the 2003 study, not least of which was the desire to track the emotional response tendencies over time in order to indicate reliability in the measurements and the results. Also, we desired to try to overcome some of the problems of a more practical nature that were encountered in the first study. Those problems primarily had to do with:

- Number of feeling words presented for rating and a rather long questionnaire
- Interview procedure and size of the sample of respondents that evaluated each individual brand
- Selection of relevant feeling words for computation of emotional response tendency
- Context in which brands were rated – each respondent only rated brands from one Rossiter-Percy grid quadrant

B. Procedure

1. Number of Feeling Words

In the first study each respondent was faced with a list of 24 feeling words from which the respondent selected those he/she felt had most meaning in relation to the different brands. Subsequently he/she was asked to express the degree to which the particular feeling word connected with each of the brands.

Also involved were questions on consumption and background criteria. All this made the answering time for the self-administered questionnaire amount to 30-45 minutes.

In the 2004 replication the number of feeling words included was reduced to 16 (the feeling words can be seen in Table VI). This was done by deleting the questions generating the fewest responses in the first round and/or appearing with the lowest frequency in any of the individual selections of 10 statements based upon which the NERS-scores where computed.

Secondly in the questioning procedure the answer to the question about whether the particular feeling word had meaning in connection with the brand was separated from the subsequent rating of the degree of association of the feeling word with the brand name.

Also in the 2004 data collection a few questions making it possible to compute interview-based STAS-scores (Hansen and Christensen,

2003) for the fast moving consumer goods were included. A few measurements making it possible to compute frequency of consumption were maintained from the first questionnaire,

2. Interview Procedure and Size of the Sample Evaluating Each Individual Brand

In the 2003 study, respondents were recruited by asking them in a nationally representative omnibus survey whether they would like to participate in a scientific study of emotions. Among those answering positively to this, a quota sample of 800 respondents was established.

In the first study the total sample of 800 where divided into four sub samples of 200 where each respondent was asked to evaluate one group of 4 brands out of a total of 4 groups of 4 brands each. Each group of four brands held brands from one Percy-Rossiter grid quadrant only. In this way the first 200 respondents evaluated all brands in the low-involvement transformational product category, 200 respondents evaluated all brands in the high-involvement informational categories etc.

In the 2004 study computer based interviewing via the internet was used. This made it possible to steer the respondents in a more straightforward manner through the feeling questions and present them in a random order. The total sample was set at 4000 respondents out of an internet panel database of 30.000. These again were divided into four sub samples, meaning that for each brand 1000 interviews were completed. Each group of 1000 respondents was a quota sample representing the Danish population between 15 and 59.

The total number of brands included was 100 covering 23 categories. The brands and categories appear in Table VI.2. In the questioning the choice of brands to which the respondent responded was determined by random selection from the total number of brands. This procedure meant that the individual respondent no longer only evaluated brands from one quadrant of the Rossiter-Percy grid, but rather evaluated a number of brands selected at random from the total selection of brands.

The rationale of this change in the interview procedure was that, in 2003 each respondent on average answered for 16 brands and 4 product categories and, consequently, on the average ideally was asked to rate a total of 580 feeling words concerning those brands which he was giving answers to.

Ideally, in 2004, one could, for each brand, have limited the questioning further from 16 to those 10 feeling words selected from the 2003 study for the computation of the NERS-score for the brand/product category and thereby further reducing the number of feeling words to which the respondent must respond. The reduction of the 24 statements down only to the same 16 used for all brands was decided in order to give the respondents more room for variation in choosing relevant feeling words in connection with different brands, and to avoid the complicated task of presenting a new chart of feeling words for each brand to which the respondent was to answer questions.

In the 2nd study each respondent was asked to respond to 400 feeling words (against 580 in the first study). He/she gave, on the average, 4.8 responses per brand/category (against approx. 3 in the first study), corresponding to app. 30 rating tasks for each respondent.

Data collection took place in august 2004 whereas data collection in 2003 was completed in June-July. To secure that the data in 2004 again can be illustrated by a two-dimensional solution, a cluster analysis was carried out across all brands and categories. The results are shown in Figure VI.1.

The cluster analysis reflects how frequently the feeling words are being used together across all respondents and all brands and categories. The strong separation between the positive and negative feeling words is evident. The positive feeling words cluster into what could be labelled 3 basic feelings; joy, social accept, and instrumentality (stimulating, fresh, healthy). Similarly the negative feeling words group into; dissatisfaction (critical, annoyed) and sadness. In Chapter XI we shall look more at cognitive feelings as they appear related to the underlying emotions.

Figure VI.1: The hierarchical cluster analysis of the 16 feeling words

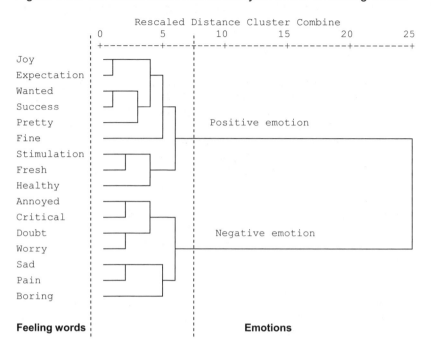

3. Selection of Feeling Words for NERS Computation

The computation of the NERS scores is slightly modified in the second study since the much larger sample made it possible to compute a factor solution for each brand in each category using the 10 feeling words determined for the category.

In brief the procedure is:

First the number of responses given for each brand and category was computed. Subsequently a factor analysis was conducted on all 16 items of the ratings given to the feeling words for each brand and each category. Based on this, 10 feeling words where selected as being particularly salient and relevant for each product category.

As in the first study, there is only little variation in the feeling words used by respondents for different brands within each category – the salient feeling words. The difference between basing the selection on individual brand solutions or one solution for the whole category was not larger than one or two feeling words – and that only in a few cases.

Some words had very low relevance in some categories, as measured by the fact that they were not used at all in these categories. These words were of course excluded from the factor analysis for the particular product categories and brands.

Apart from these remarks, the selection of the 10 items to be used for computation of the NERS-scores for each category was based on the following criteria:

1. The most frequently used feeling words where given priority irrespective of their valence – positive or negative.
2. In all cases six positive and four negative feeling words where selected for the NERS computations. The choice of 6 and 4 was based on the wish to facilitate comparisons between the two studies. In the first study this choice was natural since there where many more positive than negative responses. In the second study relatively more negative responses occurred, still the division in 6 positive and 4 negative statements largely reflect the frequency with which answers where given to positive and negative feeling words.
3. Feeling words loading high on either the positive or the negative emotional dimension where given priority
4. Feeling words either loading on both of the two dimensions or on neither of them were excluded.

In Table VI.1 an example of the computations and procedure underlying the selection of salient feeling words are given. The example is breakfast cereals. Both individual brand figures and figures for the category as a whole are shown.

The procedure is as follows:

1. The frequency tables (1st. part table in the example) demonstrate that almost all feeling words are mentioned with a reasonable frequency – with very few exceptions.
2. The brands factor loading tables (2nd part table in the example) demonstrate that brand specific factor analysis produce almost identical solutions concerning the feeling words that load on the two factors – irrespective of brand.
3. The category and brands factor loading table (3rd part table in the example) demonstrate that the salient feeling words are almost identical, irrespective of the type of analysis: Category, brands or category and brands combined.
4. And finally the last part table (4th part table in the examples) demonstrates how the final 6 positive and 4 negative feeling words are selected for further analysis. For this the joint category and brands factor analysis from 3rd part of the table is used (explained variance 0.58). Here the most frequently used words (last column) and those discriminating the best between positive and negative factors were used (i.e.: in the breakfast cereal example, Fine is selected in spite of Success having a higher loading on the positive factor. However, Success loads also on the negative factor and has a much lower occurrence, 263, than Fine with 1222).

Table VI.1: Selection of category feeling words for cereals

1st part table

# responses	Kellogg's	Quaker	Sum	Category	Total
Joy	101	82	183	498	681
Fresh	160	84	244	787	1031
Stimulating	117	76	193	739	932
Wanted	121	63	184	451	635
Expectation	107	60	167	514	681
Healthy	382	481	863	1742	2605
Success	77	40	117	146	263
Fine	213	168	381	841	1222
Worry	47	21	68	235	303
Sad	15	15	30	95	125
Doubt	58	24	82	258	340
Pain	11	14	25	65	90
Critical	100	30	130	516	646
Annoyed	84	27	111	378	489
Pretty	20	13	33	91	124
Boring	59	102	161	409	570
total	1672	1300	2972	7765	10737

2nd part table

Factor Loadings	Kellogg's		Quaker Oats	
	neg	pos	neg	pos
Joy	-0,033	0,600	0,087	0,569
Fresh	-0,079	0,546	-0,002	0,592
Stimulating	-0,008	0,507	0,057	0,542
Wanted	0,030	0,607	0,060	0,652
Expectation	0,126	0,522	0,116	0,473
Healthy	-0,264	0,474	-0,253	0,445
Success	0,210	0,387	0,200	0,499
Fine	-0,065	0,292	0,008	0,349
Worry	0,575	-0,013	0,670	0,013
Sad	0,703	0,295	0,571	0,167
Doubt	0,566	0,000	0,612	0,062
Pain	0,560	0,352	0,726	0,376
Critical	0,575	-0,119	0,584	-0,048
Annoyed	0,540	-0,181	0,676	0,023
Pretty	0,348	0,432	0,600	0,329
Boring	0,439	-0,034	0,313	-0,177

3rd part table

Factor Loadings	Category		Brands		Category and brands	
	pos	neg	neg	pos	pos	neg
Joy	0,639	-0,004	-0,015	0,593	0,632	-0,003
Fresh	0,604	-0,103	-0,069	0,565	0,597	-0,090
Stimulating	0,610	-0,074	-0,007	0,523	0,596	-0,051
Wanted	0,566	0,109	0,028	0,622	0,584	0,097
Expectation	0,515	0,087	0,109	0,508	0,518	0,099
Healthy	0,557	-0,205	-0,318	0,398	0,513	-0,236
Success	0,454	0,336	0,198	0,440	0,421	0,281
Fine	0,401	-0,034	-0,053	0,320	0,379	-0,038
Worry	0,006	0,601	0,608	0,023	0,012	0,604
Sad	0,146	0,591	0,615	0,278	0,174	0,601
Doubt	-0,024	0,595	0,598	0,048	-0,009	0,601
Pain	0,314	0,607	0,572	0,400	0,331	0,599
Critical	-0,062	0,543	0,589	-0,079	-0,058	0,552
Annoyed	-0,194	0,527	0,578	-0,095	-0,167	0,542
Pretty	0,427	0,451	0,392	0,427	0,421	0,434
Boring	-0,130	0,355	0,352	-0,076	-0,117	0,359

4th part table

Basis for variable choice	Category and brands			Chosen variables
	pos	neg	responses	
Joy	0,632	-0,003	681	Joy
Fresh	0,597	-0,090	1031	Fresh
Stimulating	0,596	-0,051	932	
Wanted	0,584	0,097	635	Wanted
Expectation	0,518	0,099	681	Expectation
Healthy	0,513	-0,236	2605	Healthy
Success	0,421	0,281	263	
Fine	0,379	-0,038	1222	Fine
Worry	0,012	0,604	303	Worry
Sad	0,174	0,601	125	
Doubt	-0,009	0,601	340	Doubt
Pain	0,331	0,599	90	
Critical	-0,058	0,552	646	Critical
Annoyed	-0,167	0,542	489	Annoyed
Pretty	0,421	0,434	124	
Boring	-0,117	0,359	570	

The example in Table VI.1 illustrates the individual judgments that had to be made in the process of selecting the feeling words. In order to obtain enough negative feeling words, some were included even though other negative feeling words exhibited higher loadings on the negative dimension, but since they also loaded significantly on the positive emotional dimension – or were mentioned with a lower frequency than the chosen - they were discarded.

4. Computation of NERS-Scores for Brands and Categories

In the 2003 study the loadings from the joint category analysis were used as weights for computation of NERS-scores. This was done because some of the brands had so few respondents actively associating feeling words with the brand that no meaningful loadings could be calculated. In the 2004 data set the number of responses was much larger, enabling us to establish individual weights for each of the brands in a category - and still using the same 10 feelings words for the computation.

This procedure was compared to the previous procedure - computing the score for the brands using the same category weights in selected categories – by studying how it influenced the NERS-scores.

It was found that using the same weights across brands gave slightly lower NERS scores per brand. The difference however was minute. An observation suggesting that the final NERS-scores are not highly sensitive to minor alterations in the battery of feeling words used, so that meaningful scores can be computed by having respondents rate slightly different feeling words. A conclusion to be verified by subsequent analyses. Comparison over time, however, requires ideally the same battery used again and again.

Table VI.2: Average NERS scores per brand and category, 2004 study

Low involvement informational	NERS	Number of responses
Shampoo	2,26	2643
Sanex	2,23	675
Matas	1,98	698
Dove	1,94	634
Garnier Fructis	0,89	385
Head & Shoulders	-0,17	531
Mobile phones	0,46	2926
Nokia	2,08	799
SonyEricsson	1,72	561
Samsung	1,42	381
Siemens	0,65	359
Butter	0,27	2391
Lurpak	1,59	629
Kærgården	1,13	728
Engholm	1,12	296
Bakkedal	0,66	373
Gasoline	-0,94	2062
OK	1,21	491
Q8	0,83	432
Statoil	0,68	424
Hydro	0,62	401
Shell	-0,19	523
Insurance	-2,63	3308
Tryg	-0,70	552
Topdanmark	-1,01	512
Codan	-1,15	522
Fair forsikring	-1,65	478
Alm. Brand	-1,90	505

Low involvement transformational	NERS	Number of responses
Coffee	4,26	3476
Gevalia	2,30	668
Merrild	2,30	582
Karat	2,25	518
BKI	1,90	498
Bread	3,64	3568
Schulstad	2,82	830
Kohberg	2,62	820
Hatting	1,59	699
Beverages	2,40	3281
Rynkeby	2,52	746
Faxe Kondi	2,46	687
Coca Cola	2,20	906
Fun Saftevand	-0,13	616
Cereals	2,17	2916
Ota	2,41	615
Kellogg's	1,63	734
Candy	2,15	3420
After Eight	2,86	822
Toms	2,81	845
Stimorol	2,45	717
Haribo	2,29	878
SorBits	2,20	706
Malaco	1,83	578
BonBon	1,78	673
Spirits	1,32	3321
Rød Ålborg	1,83	568
Gammel Dansk	1,73	607
Bacardi	1,63	598
Martini	1,30	443
Chips	0,28	2864
Kims	0,89	748
Estrella	0,64	543

High involvement Informational	NERS	Number of responses
Newspapers	2,22	3519
Urban	1,69	440
MetroXpress	1,63	560
Politiken	0,95	674
Berlingske Tidende	0,61	665
Jyllands-Posten	0,48	719
BT	-1,52	789
Ekstra-Bladet	-2,30	892
Glasses	1,26	2683
Thiele	1,28	364
Synoptik	0,86	563
Weekly magazine	-0,44	3259
Femina	0,85	496
Alt for Damerne	0,53	603
Billed Bladet	-1,56	749
Her og nu	-2,05	632
Kig ind	-2,38	613
Se & Hør	-2,60	800
Mortgage credit	-0,56	2693
Nykredit	0,07	578
Realkredit Danmark	-0,13	572
BRF Kredit	-0,50	434
Banks	-0,65	3184
Jyske	0,46	418
BG	-0,98	466
Nordea	-1,11	550
Danske	-1,28	628
Real estate dealers	-2,06	3052
EDC	-0,57	578
Danbolig	-0,59	443
Home	-0,61	580
Nybolig	-0,69	532
Mobile phone companies	-2,28	3466
Telmore	1,13	533
CBB Mobil	0,15	225
Mobil 3	-0,99	375
TDC Mobil	-1,21	797
Sonofon	-1,71	700
Telia	-1,85	705
Orange	-1,87	654
Debitel	-2,08	604

High involvement transformational	NERS	Number of responses
Amusement parks	5,04	3379
Tivoli	5,71	912
Legoland	5,40	861
Bakken	4,56	810
BonBon-land	4,37	639
Toys	3,95	3052
Lego	4,86	904
Brio	3,82	754
Fisher Price	3,19	565
Chater companies	3,41	3082
Spies Rejser	3,36	722
Tjæreborg Rejser	3,35	705
Star Tour	3,12	652
MyTravel	2,95	638
TV stations	0,77	3198
DR 2	2,73	699
Zulu	2,17	590
TV2	1,87	758
DR 1	1,36	704
3+	0,46	507
TV3	0,45	634

It should be noted also that the computations of the NERS scores rests on much the same assumptions that the computation of the total Evaluative Score in the multiattribute models (Formula II.4). Here only the positive and negative evaluations are weighted with the extent to which they associate with the positive and negative factors. A similar score can be obtained by computing the factor scores for each alternative. Since this score however is standardized and normalized, it would make it difficult to make comparisons across different product areas (and brands).

In Table VI.2 average NERS-scores are given per brand and per category. In the same table the number of respondents is included, based upon which computations are made for each brand. Also in the cases where the brands had been included in the 2003 study the scores from that study are included. From this it becomes obvious that the NERS-scores in the second study differ significantly from those in the first. The data suggest a systematic change in the negative direction.

C. Findings

1. Comparison between 2003 and 2004 Scores
In Figure VI.2 the NERS scores for all 42 brands in both the 2003 and 2004 data collections are shown, plotted against each other.

Figure VI.2: 2004 scores and corresponding 2003 scores

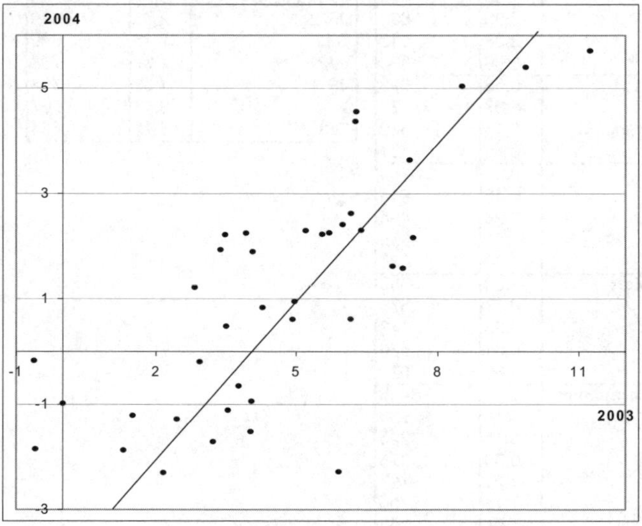

This figure suggests a strong positive correlation between the scores of the two studies. Actually a linear relationship between the two sets and measures is suggested by observing the data in Figure VI.2. This correlation analysis gives the following results (shown in the figure):

Equation VI.1

$NERS_{2003} = 0.914 \cdot NERS_{2004} + 3.692$
$R^2 = 0.619$, $p \leq 0.000$ (0.95 confidence interval)

Attempts with various possible non-linear relationships did not improve the explanatory power of the relationship in Figure VI.2.

A slightly better fit could be obtained by transforming brands alone (Lundsteen and Hansen, 2006). This solution has not been used since this method only can be used on brands and not the overall category itself, and we would like to keep the relationships between product categories.

2. Significant Differences

There may be several reasons for the NERS scores to have changed from the first to the second year. In Chapter X we shall discuss the use of NERS-scores for tracking purpose, and in that connection we shall direct our attention to these differences again.

Fundamentally, the differences have to do with a structural shift in the numerical values of the observations, as illustrated by the intercept value of -3.692 and with variations in scores between the two years as illustrated by the correlation coefficient of the regression of 0.619. However, the slope of the regression equation of 0.914 suggests an almost one to one linear relationship between scores from the two studies.

Below we comment in more depth on the differences in methodology between the two years. This is because we are convinced that the major reasons for the structural differences between the two years have to do with differences in methodology. As will be discussed in Chapter X significant deviations in scores for individual brands can to a large extent be explained by marketing actions and trend developments.

3. Differences Occurring Because of Different Computation Methods

There are systematic differences in the scores from the two years, because,

1. In the first year, because of the size of the sample, NERS is computed using the same weights (the "category weights") for all brands in the same category. In the 2004 data separate weights are established for each brand.
2. Owing to the reduction of the gross list of feeling words from 28 to 16, and because of differences in the frequency of use of single feeling words in the two years, the NERS-scores in the two years are not always computed based on exactly the same feeling words. In a few cases 2 or more feeling words may differ.
3. The loadings (weights) used in the 2nd year tend to be smaller than those in the first year. This reflects that the amount of variance explained by the two first factors is lower in the 2nd year compared with those from the first year.
4. Finally, the artificial recording of the 2003 caused by some respondents' annulling to complete all questions correctly may have influenced also.

As to the first differences it is possible to compute the NERS-scores from the 2nd year using the category weights rather than the individual

brand weights. When this is done, we find that the change in compu-
tational procedure only has a minor effect on the NERS-scores.
Rather, the analysis confirms the observation already made several
times, that the NERS-score for a particular brand is not highly sensitive to minor variations in the choice of otherwise meaningful feeling
words for the computation.

To explore this further an analysis of a random selection of 16
brands is based on a reduced set of feelings words. Only the "best" 3
positive and 2 negative are used. This is done by concentrating on
those for each category with the largest number of observations
and/or the highest loadings.

Again we find only minor variations between the NERS scores
computed based on the 5 "best" feeling words and those based on all
10. This is shown in Figure VI.3

*Figure VI.3: Correlation between NERS scores for 27 randomly se-
lected brands computed with 5 "best" feeling words and
all 10 feeling words.*

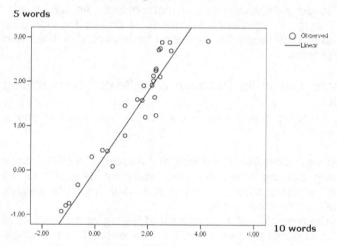

$R = 0.949$, $R^2 = 0.901$, $p < 0.1 \cdot 10^{-19}$

Even with a similar analysis conducted with a random selection of the
feeling words (for each brand every 2nd feeling word was chosen) an
almost as high correlation is observed ($p \le 0.1 \cdot 10^{-14}$ against $p \le 0.1 \cdot 10^{-19}$).

It is possible also to compute new scores from the second year
using (almost) the same feeling words as those used in 2003, with
the reservation that the reduction from 28 to 16 of the gross battery in
a few cases eliminates feeling words used in the computations made
in the first year. When the computation is made for the 42 brands and

categories present in both years we find that the change in the feeling words used for the computation has only little effect on the NERS-scores and it can not explain the systematic differences in the scores in the two years.

Thus the two above observations taken together allows us to conclude that the computation of the NERS-scores is not very sensitive to the precise choice of feeling words, as long as those chosen represent a "random" representation of the entire population of feeling words (500 or more words).

As to the fourth explanation we have recalculated the 2003 data using a procedure similar to that used in 2004, - and as a consequence of that reducing the number of useable responses. When that is done the average 2003 score decreases on the average 10%.

The authors shall save the reader from the cumbersome reading of 100 such cases, but rather discuss the differences between the two data sets in a different way.

Thus, none of the four single factors discussed can explain the systematic deviations between the results of the two data collections. Neither in combination do they do so. Some more factors relating to the data collection method should be had in mind also. The first sample being a sample of individuals participating in a random national interview survey answering positively to completing a self-administered questionnaire may by character be different from the individuals that respond to an internet-based questionnaire.

Apart from the latter all having computer access they may also be different along a number of other criteria (for instance education and income). Also whereas the sample for the 2003 study is a quota sample of adults 15-75 years, the 2004 sample covers only adults 15-59 years.

Another factor, of course, is the different way of presenting the questions as a printed paper-and-pencil questionnaire or on a computer screen. Differences in such results from comparable studies using both methodologies are well known. In the latter version the average respondent also has to respond to a lower number of feeling words, because the computer controls the number of statements for each brand as opposed to the former case where all combinations are pre-printed in the questionnaire.

The use of pre-programmed exclusion of irrelevant combinations of feeling words/brands/categories in the interviewing reduces the actual number of rating tasks with which the respondent is faced to much less than one third of the theoretical number. Thus the rating task in the computer version is much smaller and easier carried out than that in the paper and pencil version of the questionnaire.

One immediate effect of this of course is an increased number of actual responses to feeling words for brands - on average the respondents mentioned 3 words in the 2003 study versus 4.8 in the 2004 version. Also in the internet sample relatively more negative feeling words where rated than in the 2003 sample. Structural differences in sample and in data collection may account for this. It is well established that data collected with a self-administered questionnaire compared with similar data collected by telephone interview differ (Havermans, 2005). We may assume that similar differences exist in results when paper-and-pencil versus web-based data collection is used.

Like in other cases, differences may relate to the respondents in the internet sample having more time to search for relevant answers, being faced with fewer irrelevant questions and possibly some of the social demographic differences between the two samples may have an impact also. From other research it is known, that the better educated respondents tend to be more critical, and since an internet based sample will be slightly biased towards a better educational level, this may in our case account for the slightly larger number of negative responses.

4. Comparing 2003 and 2004 Results

The data for the 32 brands and 9 categories from the 2003 study also included in the 2004 data collection can be transformed to conform with the 2004 study results by using the regression equation VI.1. The resulting two data sets are shown in Table VI.3.

Figure VI.4: A scree plot for Garnier Fructis (shampoo)

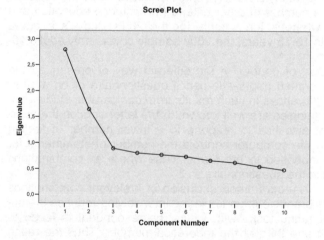

5. Two or more Emotional Dimensions?

The final question to take up here is whether two rather than three or more dimensional solution is appropriate in the 2004 analysis also.

One way of analyzing this is to look at the amount of variance described by 2, 3 or more factors. In essence one can compare the amount of variance explained by looking at diagrams like those in

176

Figure VI.4. Here an example is shown, showing that the amount of variance explained clearly levels off already from the 3rd factor and onwards. Similar diagrams can be shown for all cases in the 2004 data set suggesting that it makes good sense to limit the analysis to two factors. Also the hierarchical clustering shown in Figure VI.1 demonstrates the strong division in a positive and a negative grouping of the feeling words.

Table VI.3: Transformed 2004 study NERS scores and 2003 NERS scores by Rossiter & Percy Grid

Brand/category	2004	2003 transformed	Difference
Low involvement/informational			
Shampoo	2,26	2,19	0,06
Sanex	2,23	2,04	0,19
Dove	1,94	-0,34	2,28*
Head & Shoulders	-0,17	-4,72	4,55*
Gasoline	-0,94	0,39	-1,33*
OK	1,21	-0,95	2,16*
Q8	0,83	0,65	0,19
Hydro	0,62	2,69	-2,07*
Shell	-0,19	-0,83	0,64
Low involvement/transformational			
Bread	3,64	4,06	-0,42
Schulstad	2,82	2,45	0,37
Kohberg	2,62	2,70	-0,07
Hatting	1,59	3,90	-2,31*
Coffee	4,26	4,44	-0,18
Merrild	2,30	2,93	-0,63
Gevalia	2,30	1,65	0,65
Karat	2,25	0,26	1,99*
BKI	1,90	0,42	1,48*
Cereals	2,17	4,14	-1,97*
Ota	2,41	2,50	-0,09
Kellogg's	1,63	3,66	-2,04*
High involvement/informational			
Banks	-0,65	0,09	-0,74
BG	-0,98	-4,04	3,06*
Nordea	-1,11	-0,17	-0,94
Danske	-1,28	-1,36	0,08
Newspapers	2,22	-0,23	2,45*
Politiken	0,95	1,39	-0,44
Berlingske Tidende	0,61	1,34	-0,73
Jyllands-Posten	0,48	-0,21	0,69
BT	-1,52	0,37	-1,89
Ekstra-Bladet	-2,30	-1,68	-0,62
Mobile phone companies	-2,28	2,42	-4,70
TDC Mobil	-1,21	-2,40	1,19
Sonofon	-1,71	-0,52	-1,19*
Telia	-1,85	-4,68	2,83*
Orange	-1,87	-2,62	0,75
High involvement/transformational			
Amusement parks	5,04	5,27	-0,23
Tivoli	5,71	8,26	-2,55*
Legoland	5,40	6,75	-1,35
Bakken	4,56	2,82	1,74*
BonBon-land	4,37	2,80	1,57*

*significant difference (at 0,05 level)

In the table the absolute deviations are computed. To judge which of these can not be ascribed to random variations, one has to consider partly the number of observations based upon which the NERS scores are computed, and partly the magnitude of the difference itself. Using a chi-square test it is possible to identify those cases where the differences are significant. For 14 out of the 32 brands, and for 3 out of the 9 categories, there are significant differences, consisting of either an increase or a decrease in NERS scores. These differences will be analyzed in more detail in Chapter X.

6. General Results

When we compute average NERS-scores for the brands in the four cells of the Rossiter/Percy Grid, we arrive at findings in line with those of the 2003 study. From Table VI.4 it appears that the highest NERS-scores occur for high involvement transformational products and the lowest for low involvement informational products. As shown in Chapter V, much the same pattern was found in the NERS-scores from the 2003 study – although the difference in NERS score between low and high involvement in the transformational category is much more marked in 2004 than in 2003.

Table VI.4a: Average NERS scores by Rossiter and Percy grid category, 2004 study

	Informational	Transformational
Low involvement	-0.36	1.86
High involvement	0.66	3.42

When studying the NUMS scores – Table VI.4b – a pattern appears in 2004 that resembles the pattern from 2003 with one exception: in 2003, the NUMS scores in the two high involvement categories were numerically similar, to some extent due to some of the brands in the 2003 study. In 2004 the NUMS scores follow a pattern which seems intuitively more logical: NUMS in the transformational categories are generally higher than in the informational categories, reflecting that the total emotional activity is higher when self gratification is at stake rather than when problem avoidance is the issue.

Table VI.4b: Average NUMS scores by Rossiter and Percy grid category, 2004 study

	Informational	Transformational
Low involvement	1,78	2,32
High involvement	2,22	3,56

This observation also suggests that the differences between the 2003 and 2004 data are to a large extent ascribable to systematic, methodological differences rather than to anything else – apart of course from differences that are caused by changes in marketing activities or market trends that will be discussed later in Chapter X.

Another indication of such systematic methodological differences appears when one looks at the order in which brands are rated in the nine product categories for which data are available for both years. In practically all cases the rank ordering is identical or deviates only with one position in the ordering. Actually as we can see later, some of the changes in rank ordering observed may be explainable by things happening in the market between the two years.

7. Users and Non-Users
When hypothesizing about the relationship between strength of emotional reaction and usage of a particular brand, one is to expect higher emotional reaction amongst users than amongst non-users. The argument is that because of the higher frequency of exposure to the brand, the stored positive emotional reaction in implicit memory must be much higher amongst users.

For 35 of the FMCG brands in the sample questions are asked about the frequency of use. Users of brands are registered as those who report that they use the brand all the time or regularly. Similarly respondents are asked about the possession and purchasing plans for a number of durables and services, such as mobile phones, cars, amusement parks, insurance companies, real estate dealers, television channels and charter travel companies. Frequency of use is measured also. Here a distinction between those owning/using and planning to purchase on the one hand and the rest is used to identify "users". This makes it possible for all brands to distinguish between users and non-users in a meaningful way. Based upon this it is possible to compute NERS-scores for users and non-users of brands and categories as it appears from Table VI.5.

Table VI.5: NERS-scores for users and non-users, where category differences are not established it is because of lacking data on use. All differences significant $p \leq 0.001$.

Low involvement Informational	Users NERS	Non-users NERS	# resp.	% users
Shampoo	2,26	0,12	2643	100
Sanex	2,99	1,69	674	41
Matas	2,59	1,65	696	34
Garnier Fructis	2,88	0,15	385	27
Dove	2,65	1,74	632	22
Head & Shoulders	2,37	-0,71	530	17
Mobile phones	-	-	-	-
Nokia	2,91	0,69	800	63
Siemens	2,57	0,00	359	25
SonyEricsson	3,43	1,20	561	24
Samsung	-	-	-	-
Butter	0,46	-1,35	2391	89
Kærgården	1,58	-1,00	683	87
Lurpak	2,25	0,95	596	57
Bakkedal	1,63	-0,21	357	49
Engholm	2,27	0,56	282	35
Gasoline	-	-	-	-
OK	1,80	0,14	491	65
Statoil	1,10	0,12	424	57
Q8	1,44	0,09	432	55
Shell	0,48	-0,90	523	51
Hydro	1,24	0,00	401	50
Insurance	-	-	-	-
Tryg	0,36	-1,30	552	36
Topdanmark	0,51	-1,71	512	31
Codan	0,53	-1,56	522	20
Alm. Brand	-1,18	-2,07	505	19
Fair forsikring	0,78	-1,77	478	5

Low involvement Transformational	Users NERS	Non-users NERS	# resp.	% users
Coffee	4,51	0,88	3476	93
Merrild	3,04	1,51	554	55
Gevalia	3,23	1,61	634	46
BKI	2,97	1,35	472	38
Karat	3,43	1,71	488	36
Bread	3,64	1,58	3567	100
Schulstad	3,19	1,33	829	81
Kohberg	3,32	0,38	819	76
Hatting	2,14	0,23	698	71
Beverages	2,89	-1,49	3282	89
Rynkeby	2,70	2,01	709	80
Coca Cola	3,44	-1,36	853	79
Faxe Kondi	3,36	1,43	650	59
Fun Saftevand	3,23	-1,85	565	40
Cereals	2,51	0,45	2916	83
Kellogg's	2,50	0,24	674	68
Ota	3,06	1,92	568	48
Candy	2,31	0,06	3421	93
Haribo	2,62	0,22	858	89
Toms	3,12	1,33	822	85
Malaco	2,35	0,42	572	74
After Eight	3,50	1,83	807	62
Stimorol	3,04	1,60	707	61
BonBon	2,89	0,64	658	53
SorBits	3,01	1,45	698	49
Spirits	1,85	-1,71	3322	85
Bacardi	2,62	0,62	574	55
Rød Alborg	3,16	0,57	540	54
Gammel Dansk	3,13	0,37	575	52
Martini	2,54	0,65	420	44
Chips	0,75	-2,38	2865	85
Kims	1,45	-1,29	710	85
Estrella	1,39	-0,22	519	60

High involvement Informational	Users NERS	Non-users NERS	# resp.	% users
Newspapers	-	-	-	-
MetroXpress	2,55	0,95	560	43
Jyllands-Posten	2,57	-0,84	719	39
Urban	2,66	1,08	440	38
Politiken	3,55	-0,15	674	30
Berlingske Tidende	2,79	-0,06	665	24
BT	1,70	-2,48	789	23
Ekstra-Bladet	0,37	-2,93	892	19
Glasses	-	-	-	-
Synoptik	2,05	0,12	564	38
Thiele	2,79	0,84	364	22
Weekly magazines	-	-	-	-
Femina	3,60	-0,15	496	27
Alt for Damerne	3,66	-0,51	603	25
Billed Bladet	2,32	-2,46	749	19
Her og nu	1,37	-2,65	632	15
Se & Hør	0,89	-3,20	800	15
Kig ind	1,14	-2,84	613	11
Mortgage credit	-	-	-	-
Realkredit Danmark	0,94	-0,56	572	29
Nykredit	1,75	-0,41	578	22
BRF Kredit	0,97	-0,74	434	14
Banks	-	-	-	-
Nordea	0,96	-1,94	549	28
Danske	0,93	-2,13	628	28
BG	2,05	-1,71	466	20
Jyske	3,61	-0,04	418	14
Real estate dealers	-	-	-	-
EDC	0,51	-0,92	579	24
Home	-0,02	-0,80	580	23
Nybolig	-0,14	-0,85	532	22
Danbolig	0,20	-0,71	443	12
Mobile phone comp.	-	-	-	-
TDC Mobil	0,13	-2,22	797	43
Telmore	4,80	-0,88	533	35
Sonofon	-0,01	-2,11	700	19
CBB Mobil	3,76	-0,41	225	13
Orange	0,78	-2,18	654	11
Telia	0,21	-2,07	705	10
Debitel	-0,35	-2,22	604	8
Mobil 3	-0,10	-1,06	376	5

High involvement Transformational	Users NERS	Non-users NERS	# resp.	% users
Amusement parks	-	-	-	-
Tivoli	6,36	5,16	912	46
Bakken	5,23	4,30	810	28
Legoland	6,84	4,98	861	23
BonBon-land	6,61	4,00	639	14
Toys	-	-	-	-
Lego	5,65	4,10	904	49
Fisher Price	4,25	2,50	565	39
Brio	4,82	3,31	754	34
Charter companies	-	-	-	-
MyTravel	4,20	2,70	451	18
Star Tour	3,98	3,17	429	9
Spies Rejser	5,52	3,38	459	8
Tjæreborg Rejser	5,23	3,26	457	6
TV stations	-	-	-	-
TV2	1,95	-0,31	753	97
DR 1	1,54	-2,58	698	96
DR 2	3,60	-0,42	645	82
TV3	1,60	-2,24	543	77
3+	1,49	-1,72	440	76
Zulu	3,43	0,61	472	72

The basic proposition: that higher emotional response tendency is associated with more frequent use and acceptance of the brand, is strongly confirmed. It is remarkable that all NERS-scores are higher among users than among non-users. There is not a single deviation in all the cases in the total data set for which comparisons can be made. When comparing those 13 FMCG that are included in both the 2003 and 2004 sample the same applies to users as well as nonusers in both years. Also in both years the largest differences between users and nonusers are found in the low involvement transformational categories. One may speculate that here the emotional response tendencies play the largest role.

8. Outstanding Brands

Going back to Table VI.2 it can be seen as in the 2003 study that in the 2004 data some brands stand out in the sense that they have a higher NERS-score than the category itself. As outstanding brands in this sense we find some of the same as those from the first study (the small bank: Jyske Bank, Tivoli and Legoland).

One or more outstanding brands in this sense are also found among cereals, candy, soft drinks, toys, magazines, and glasses.

Further examples of this phenomenon are found in the mobile phone company category where – although all brand evaluations are negative - the category as such is even more negatively evaluated than the brands in the study (which are the major ones in the market). The same applies to insurance companies, real estate agencies, real estate financing, mobile phones and petrol companies.

Finally in some categories all brands in the study are rated lower than the category as such. This appears in the categories of charter travel companies, coffee, newspapers, bread, and shampoo. The assumption is that in these categories "generic" consumption of the category has a reasonably high emotional response potential, but the individual brands are perceived as having less emotional appeal.

Thus we may classify the 23 product categories in Table VI.2 as follows:

1. Categories where all brands give rise to higher NERS-scores than the category as such
2. Categories where all brands give rise to lower NERS-scores than the category as such
3. Categories where one or a few brands stand out with higher NERS-scores than the category as such and than their major competitors.

In the first category we find mobile phones, chips, butter, mortgage credit, gasoline, real estate, mobile phone companies and insurance companies. All categories give rise to low or (in 2004) even negative NERS. Here it seems that the major companies (included in the study) have managed to create a slightly more positive response than the category as such. It is worth noticing that the group includes 3 FMCG categories with retailers own brands being common (bread, coffee, and shampoo) and two categories where a very large number of small operators exists, not included in the study.

Turning to the second category we find coffee, bread, shampoo, charter companies, newspapers, real estate dealers, snacks, butter, real estate financing and mobile phones. Here the individual companies rate lower than the product category as such. Thus the product as such is positively evaluated, but none of the marketers (included in the study) have managed to position themselves as outstanding. Or even worse: the low NERS scores for individual brands illustrate that consumers when choosing between alternative brands experience a choice between unsatisfactory alternatives, since no alternative meets the "generic" expectations of the category.

Finally we have the categories where one or more brands are outstanding in the sense that they have higher NERS-scores than the category as such and as their competitors. This applies to banks (Jyske Bank), amusement parks (Tivoli and Legoland), Cereals (Ota), TV-stations (DR and TV2 and their sub-channels), candy (Toms, After Eight, Stimorol), alcoholic beverages (Rød Aalborg, Gammel Dansk, and Bacardi), soft drinks (Faxe Kondi and Rynkeby), toys (Lego), weekly magazines (Alt for Damerne and Femina), and opticians (Thiele).

In all of these categories we find that some of the brands rate higher than the category per se (Table VI.5). In some instances this is more expressed than in others. In such cases we may talk of outstanding brands or brands with very high brand equity.

9. Other Implications of the Findings
Looking at the three categories of markets one realizes that the challenges for the single brand in the various markets are indeed very different.

In the first type of categories, the aim of the individual brands of course must be to maintain the position and possibly look to strengthening it further both in relation to the category as such and in relation to its competitors. In this context the difference between the NERS among users and non-users may be an important factor to look for. The smaller the difference is, the more it seems that activities aimed at gaining new customers may be successful – since an important potential exists amongst non-users who respond relatively positively to the brand already.

Thus looking at the differences between the NERS among users and non-users may provide useful information in its own right. In the petrol market and among TV-stations the difference between users and non-users is much larger than for the charter companies and shampoo companies. In the former markets, companies will probably find it much more difficult to attract new customers form non-users than companies in the latter. In the latter categories, the smaller difference in NERS between users and non-users may indicate potential for attracting new customers from non-users, since they are already "emotionally primed" towards the brands.

An interesting example for this strategy can be taken from the insurance companies where Alm. Brand is the most negatively valuated in terms of NERS, but on the other hand is almost equally negatively valuated among users and non-users. In the same manner in the soft drink category, the market leader Coca-Cola seems to have much more to overcome when trying to convince more new customers about the brand's appeal than one of its major competitors, Faxe Kondi.

In the second category it is mandatory that brands are able to communicate the ability of the brand to satisfy the basic needs that consumers generally associate with the product category. In some cases, brand managers will be well advised to look for and identify the specific reasons why consumers do not experience their brand as a satisfactory alternative with a view to improving these factors to achieve "par for the course". Also, brand managers must look for and activate those feelings that relate to and create positive emotions for the brand, and thereby make the brand one which has a higher appeal than the market as such.

In the third category some major players have managed to establish themselves as providing superior brand quality to that offered by other brands in the market – thereby giving them a high emotional part of the total mental brand equity. For these outstanding brands it is important to understand the basis for the emotional strength among the consumers. This will enable them to continuously elaborate on and demonstrate the uniqueness of the brand relative to its competitors, as experienced by consumers. For the remaining brands in these categories it is important to understand what feelings and emotions form the basis of the strong emotional ties between their competitors and their customers. From this insight they will be able to develop their own strong features that will generate stronger emotional responses from consumers.

It has been demonstrated – albeit briefly - that the data give meaningful insight in the structure of the brand's mental brand equity. Also the type of data studied provides information about emotional strength among users and non-users that can guide in developing marketing objectives and strategies.

For a soft drink brand like Rynkeby for instance, with very little difference in NERS-scores between users and non-users, and with a relatively high score compared with the market as such, efforts simply to increase brand awareness may more easily result in attracting more users and generally increasing usage than the same strategy would for some of its competitors with different values of NERS over-all and between users and non-users.

We shall return to the speculation regarding brand strategy de-parting in the NERS structure of the different markets in a later chap-ter (Chapter XII). Here let it only be repeated, that we have convinc-ingly demonstrated that one can measure, the immaterial or emo-tional aspect of brand equity meaningfully in terms of Net Emotional Response Strength (NERS). It can be done with a relative simple procedure which is not extremely sensitive to the specific choice of test items used. And the method provides results that can be repro-duced even with some modification in the data collection procedure. We therefore conclude that the NERS-score and the structure of the NERS-scores in various markets reflect important aspects of the competitive situation and individual brand positions, and thereby pro-vide insight useful in planning future marketing strategies.

D. The Role of Emotion Revisited

In the preceding pages we have documented that we can quantify Net Emotional Response Strength (NERS) in a reliable and in a valid manner. We have discussed some of the implications of the NERS-scores for brands and product categories, and we shall return to these issues in the last part of the book, dealing with Advertising and Communication effects. Before doing this, we want to review briefly, some of the ways we think emotions play a role in consumer behav-iour.

1. NERS in Straight Emotional Choices

Anything that appears to us, such as a picture being perceived through the eyes, or a name through the ears or as a form felt with our fingers, have some emotional response tendency, weak or strong, associated with it.

But not only things in our environment give rise to emotional re-sponse tendencies. Thoughts we have, associations we make or fearful dreams we experience have related emotional response ten-dencies.

To non-humans this probably represents all the brain activity con-trolling behaviour and the individual's interaction with its environment.

Such emotional associations may be sheer unconscious corre-lates shaping our relationship with the environment. Sometimes they may give rise to unconscious cognitive counterparts that we label feelings and perceptions and which enter into our way of solving the problems inherent in coping with our environment.

It is questionable but not completely unlikely that some higher animals may have the ability to establish such unconscious cognitive counterparts entering into their solving of problems presented to them by their environment. But only humans have the ability to become conscious of feelings and cognitive elements of various kinds representing aspects of our environment and the relationship among them. Since we have this ability to perceive these and manipulate them in problem solving, when we do so, we tend to suppress the importance of the more immediate, more frequent and more original pure emotional response tendencies associated with things we encounter in our environment or in our mind.

On the other hand, as contemporary neuro-economics show, the ability to lean towards faster and more easily made emotionally guided choices may be quite useful when faced with many trivial cases.

But again we have positive and negative emotional response tendencies to everything, our home, our job, our wife, our car, our different shirts, all the brands we know, all the stores we know, all the people we know. These emotions influence how we choose among them. Elements in our environment such as pictures or other representations of the alternatives or pictorial or symbolic representations emerging from our memory may activate these basic emotional tendencies. We may disregard them, suppress them, substitute them with cognitive considerations and alternatives but at the onset they are there. If they do not have the power directly to influence our choice they may still play a role in arousing feelings, cognitions and evaluations of what alternatives will be chosen. Since many consumer alternatives are of limited importance, NERS may be weak but some positive and some negative elements deriving from inherited tendencies modified by later experiences will always be there.

If we were not humans, emotions most likely would control our behaviour directly. From very early in the origin of the species we have learned that snakes are dangerous and we may intuitively without much consideration avoid a snake appearing in front of us. Our development as more advanced species however has taught us that some snakes found in a particular environment are not that dangerous at all.

In addition to modifying an innate human emotion: "lions are dangerous", we may add knowledge to this in terms of modified emotional response tendencies: "lions with kids are extremely aggressive and dangerous". This expanded information storage may or may not be a cognitive phenomenon. In some instances what Damasio has labelled somatic markers may be at work, but our ability as humans to use cognitive processing gives us an enormous advantage over animals. It is far from always that we need or use this cognitive ability, however.

The routinized processes, of which much consumer behaviour is composed, may be completely emotionally controlled and also many instances of impulsive behaviour may be partly or completely emotionally governed. On the other end of the scale we may make complex, multi stage, multi attribute choices when we buy a new winter coat or a home entertainment centre. Still some emotional response tendencies associated with materials, colour, style, brands etc. enter into the final choice.

It is a paradox that we label that of what we are not aware as unconscious, deriving the definition from what we somehow can become aware of. In the light of human development it would be a more natural way of perceiving the unconscious emotional processes as the primary guiding element to our behaviour and look at what we become aware of as emotions perceived as feelings and cognitions and something additional to the primary and elementary emotions.

Our culture has taught us, the church, philosophers and others have preached that our immediate emotional responses may contain elements of bad and should be controlled and governed by our ability to apply cognitive reasoning to the impressions and cognitive elements activated in our minds. This is true in many important aspects of our lives; our relationships with friends and families, our relationships with important material possessions and our relationships with the way in which we spend our time.

But in the limited sphere of human behaviour that constitutes consumers' choices among mostly trivial alternatives this way of looking upon things may be to assume that our lives are much more complicated than they actually are.

It is a good thing that people concerned with consumer policy work to set up rules about how things may be offered for our consumption, and how information should be conveyed about them, and this in its own right is an important element making it possible for us to act meaningfully in the extremely complex world the contemporary society presents to the consumer.

In most cases of consumer behaviour, it is a choice among available and more or less trivial alternatives, and the consumer may in his choice rely on the unreflected immediate NERS associated with the alternatives.

The choice between coffee brands in the store, between salad dressings for the salad in the restaurant or between stockings to wear on a particular day, may most easily and conveniently be made as mechanical NERS based responses.

Sometimes the choices may contain a little more conflict. The choice between coffee and tea after dinner may involve some cognitive, maybe unconscious, processes, where elements in addition to the immediate response potentials aroused by the alternatives enter the considerations. Unconsciously we may reflect on having difficulties falling asleep after coffee late in the evening or preferring the coffee because it does better with the brandy we may eventually decide to order also.

Most commonly, however, consumer choices give rise to little cognition and are basically NERS guided. The routinized choices of a detergent, shampoo or toothpaste brand that we normally label loyalty behaviour are such cases. Many so-called impulse purchases made in the store, triggered by the mere presence of the particular alternative of candy, paper tissue or razor blades may be governed only by Net Emotional Response Strength of the alternatives. A straight emotional choice may be made or a somatic marker may influence what will occur.

Mostly, when disturbing elements enter into the choice situation some cognitions, conscious or unconscious, will come into action. The choice between the beer brands in the bar may a completely Net Emotional Response Strength governed choice, but the fact that the beautiful person at the neighbouring table is observing our behaviour may give rise to some cognitions resulting in a choice of a more expensive export luxury brand.

NERS is the governing factor when the alternatives are given and no disturbing factors enter. The NERS that a brand elicits may be the most important asset that the brand owner has. It may not always determine that his brand is bought, but on the whole in most situations a high NERS makes the choice of his brand more likely.

In the consumer's daily environment, however, disturbing factors may be many. Offers in the store, information communicated on displays, the influence of other people present in the purchase situation, the lack of availability of the normally purchased brand or some recently conveyed information about unpleasant aspects of the brand normally chosen, may be examples of such factors creating situations, where not only the NERS but also cognitions and even conscious cognitions may be activated and guide the choice.

Thus, cognitive decision making may lead to other results than the most immediate alternative being chosen – which is what a purely NERS-guided choice process would lead to. But it does not hurt the chances that our favourite brand is chosen when it enters into the conflicting situation with a high NERS relative to that of the alternatives under consideration.

At the outset, brand X may be the one with the highest NERS, but the consumer is constantly bombarded with market stimuli, observing other consumers, being exposed to advertising or discussions with friends, so that in the next actual purchasing situation, some cognitive activity may be activated and overrule the immediate NERS guided choice.

On the whole, however, most consumer choices are guided by NERS built up by past communication, repeated purchases and satisfied use; but sometimes, cognitive elements enter into the equation. The woman buying a lipstick may, without really thinking about it, be inspired by a new shade of colour from a different brand and pick this in spite of her, in the beginning of the shopping trip, positive NERS towards her traditional choice. Experiences with the new lipstick may be positive and next time it may be chosen again. This time NERS of the new brand has been adjusted and the choice occurs completely automatically again – but with a new outcome.

2. NERS in Extended Emotional Choices

So far, we have centred on examples from fast moving consumer goods and similar product areas. However, major purchases such as cars, refrigerators, computers, televisions etc. may be seen in the light of the NERS associated with the different brands also.

The purchase process itself may be extended in time and may involve multi-attribute evaluation of many aspects of the alternatives considered. But still somewhere in the process a NERS towards the different alternatives is there, and may in the marginal case be the determining factor guiding the choice.

The NERS associated with durables may be important in another way also. Early in the process, the choice alternatives are narrowed down to a range of acceptable ones, and in this process the NERS associated with the brand may be one of the determining factors making a certain brand included among the alternatives for final consideration.

Also in many choice situations of this nature, the optimal solution is rarely a clear-cut one. Some alternatives may have advantages on some dimensions, other on others. Again here, the NERS may enter and become a factor tipping the balance of the total evaluation of the alternatives. In many instances, the emotional mechanism may then be a help that guides the consumer through otherwise complicated evaluation processes.

NERS may be associated with corporate brands also. Here NERS may be a factor in the way in which brand extensions are accepted or rejected and corporate NERS may influence many situations such as job choice, choice of financial supplier etc.

The choice of bank may be the one located closest by, but when more, alternative services from the bank are entering into consideration, the choices often become complex and no clear-cut best choice emerge. Again here, NERS may be a factor determining the final choice of the consumer, making him cut through the underworld of complicated comparisons.

To summarise, if it was not that we as humans were equipped with the intellectual power of carrying out conscious or unconscious cognitive evaluations, simple NERS would guide all our behaviour. To some basic items in our lives simple inherited emotional response tendencies may alone be at work, but in most instances NERS may have been modified by past experiences, something which may also happen without any conscious or unconscious cognitive activity involved.

In his book "The origin of consciousness in the breakdown of the bicameral mind", Jaynes (1976) argues that human behaviour originally has been governed by a kind of inner voice much like that experienced by the schizophrenic patients having unknown voices dictating his or hers behaviour. The NERS, as we are measuring it, may reflect these basic action tendencies controlling behaviour before the ability to consider other factors gave rise to cognitive reflections and more complex choices. When such instances of cognitive reflections and complex choices occur, their outcome may be somewhat reflected in adjusted emotional response potentials in future situations, just as relevant information attended to with more or less concentration and more or less consciously may have impact on NERS for future choice situations.

People have emotional response tendencies towards companies, organisations, associations, persons and the like. They of cause rarely make choices directly involving these elements but in many instances when cognitions are involved, they are aroused and the emotional response potential associated with them come into play.

The choice of a new car is of course not directly guided by the emotional response potential associated with the company name of a Detroit-based carmaker. Similarly, the decision about supporting one or the other "public" organisation is not directly controlled by the emotional response potential aroused by the name of the association, but this among other factors may influence the more or less complex multi attribute choice processes preceding the final decision. Often, also choices among important items involving extended decision-making may be complex and there will be no simple outstanding winner among the alternatives. In such instances, NERS becomes the factor, which also plays a role in the process.

Even in simple routinized choice processes the emotional response potential may be adjusted by such factors as noise in the choice situation, newness in forms of displays or effective packaging, special offers etc. – and without much cognitive activity occurring. Here, no complex process is initiated but the noise from children demanding a particular cereal brand, or simply pressures from other people present in the store may abrupt the immediate, unconscious emotional choice and some conscious or unconscious adjustments occur, but also here the "noise" from the children and similar disturbing elements may be eliminated by an emotional response of "picking up the candy".

Still, NERS is the basic stock of brand equity. It reflects that part of what the company has managed to build up as an asset in the market normally referred to as "emotional attachment to the brand". An asset that in many different ways becomes important when consumers make choices.

To some it may seem the straightforward and simple solution to predict purchases plainly by asking about the preferences for different brands. In surveys using a seven-point scale it is, however, well established that such expressed preferences often reflect wishful thinking on behalf of the respondent, attempts to impress the interviewer and many other disturbing factors discussed in the preceding chapter on attitude and consumer choice may be at work.

NERS as we are measuring it has the advantage of forcing re-spondents to become conscious about feeling words that otherwise in appropriate situations might have become activated in connection with brands, product categories, corporations, sponsors etc. By treat-ing these responses systematically we arrive at a much more neutral and unambiguous expression of the emotional response tendency that the brand, the product category, the company, the sponsored party, the organisation etc. may give rise to.

Thus NERS as being estimated here differently from straight for-ward preferences is one of the basic elements of mental brand eq-uity. However the brand equity that the stock market values and puts a price on not only consists of the mental brand equity, it also is influ-enced by the distribution that the brand builds on, the price level that has made it acceptable for the consumers, and the technical quality that makes the brand perform well and reinforce the consumers' sat-isfaction and thereby also their emotional response strength to the brand.

Emotional response potential may differ significantly between product categories. And as we have seen, the emotional response potential for coffee, detergents or soft drinks are not necessarily the same as the average emotional response strength generated by all brands in the market. The consumer has his own perception of the product category and in some instances he may have emotional re-sponse tendencies associated with one or more or brands in the market higher than that associated with the product category itself. Such brands we have labelled outstanding.

Here the marketers have been able to build a brand equity ex-tending above the natural evaluation and emotional responses aroused by the product category itself. In other instances the product category per se gives rise to more positive emotional response strength than any of the brands in the category. The important ser-vices provided by products such as mobile phones may be recog-nised by the consumers in general, but the confusing pricing policy, low experienced service quality and constantly changing offers in the market may make the emotional response tendency associated with any single brand less than that associated with the product category per se.

In some instances one might argue that the emotional response strength is of only hypothetical value since the choice among the al-ternatives in the market is to such an extent guided by deliberate cognitive conscious considerations that the influence of NERS is ruled out entirely. The choice of the bank to provide the loan for the new car may to such an extent rely upon nearness of the bank, inter-est offers, perceived service quality from the bank etc. that the NERS associated with different alternative banks may be of only theoretical importance. On the other hand, the NERS associated with the pre-ferred bank, and built up over a number of satisfactory encounters with that bank may very well far exceed the NERS associated with any alternative bank – and as long as this remains the case, it may keep the consumer loyal to the presently preferred bank even when meeting tempting alternative being promoted by competition.

Also, cases arise where the cognitive choice process is so complex that the multi-attributes evaluations provide no clear-cut answer and the consumer is left in a conflict which at the end of the day may be solved by simply choosing the bank alternative with the largest NERS.

3. NERS of Individuals

As suggested earlier, we have NERS tendencies to everything in our environment and to everything we cognitively may bring into our attention from our internal storage of information and experiences. One particular category deserves special mentioning here. Individuals have NERS associated with them. Individuals may be important in a marketing context in many different ways. The public spokesperson of the company is important and the higher the NERS associated with him, the more confidence it is likely that the messages he brings on behalf of the company are received with. The company with public spokespersons judged positively by media agents may have an advantage also, if they are chosen when particular issues arise to whole industries or when media are in need of point of views expressed professionally in their covering of upcoming headline issues.

Individual artists or sport heroes may gain high salaries for recommending specific products or companies and undoubtedly in choosing among alternatives. The company investing large sums in such communications would be well advised by choosing sport persons, artists or other public person with a view to the NERS, their names give rise to

The reader may be left in this stage with the impression that we are imposing upon him the view that simply the more NERS associated with brand, individual, companies etc. the better and automatically the more profit will be generated on the bottom line for the company. This of course is a crude oversimplification that it is important to modify.

The bottom line provided by the brand is the function of the functional qualities of the brand itself, the taste of the ice cream, the tenderness and smell of the tea, the refreshing qualities of the beer etc. The consumer's accumulated experiences with these product qualities however have a strong impact on the NERS he is associating with the brand. The ability of the company to make its brand available in all stores and maintain a high distribution level is important also. Each time the consumer is faced with a situation where he cannot chose the preferred, highest NERS scoring brand, the company runs the risk of the consumer modifying the relative strengths of the normally chosen brand as compared with the one forced upon him in the situation with insufficient distribution.

Deals, special displays, personal communication from friends, recommendations by sales persons in the store and the whole list of marketing activities found in the standard marketing textbook represent factors that may counteract the immediate emotional response strength determination of the choice, and in turn modify the emotional response strength the consumer brings forward to the next situation where a choice among brands in a category is to be made.

But also with major services and durables, NERS is important. The airline company or the insurance company with the highest NERS may get away with less convenient flying times or a higher rate offered to the potential customer.

In the political world, NERS plays a special role, as we shall see in a subsequent case. NERS may vary widely among political candidates and may change in the course of election campaigning. Here, as in other instances of emotional appeal of individuals, the loyal adherers to particular parties tend to have strong NERS for their political leaders. More interesting is the way in which they are looked upon among the voters for other parties.

As we shall see in a subsequent example the political leader of a particular party has the strongest positive NERS scores of all candidates among those planning to vote on her/him. But he/she also has the lowest NERS score among those not considering her party as an alternative. In contrast the political leader of the leading (and winning) party has high NERS scores both among committed voters as well as among potential voters (Chapter X).

Moreover, as the NERS scores of the political leaders change in the course of the campaign, so do the voting behaviour. Major blunders by this or that political leader may destroy his NERS score among potential voters and have impact on the final election. In contrast, a consistent flawless and error free positioning of himself may make the political leader a winner in the final election.

In summary, NERS may be seen as formed by positive experiences, positive communication, positive observation in ones social environment and positive experiences in stores and other places where the product is present. NERS thus can be seen as a cognitive-free preference or abstract attraction that the individual carries with him much like he carries emotional response tendencies with him to guide his actions against dangers or attractive alternatives in his environment. In the language of some authors this is labelled somatic markers (Bechara and Damasio, 2005).

4. NERS in Consumption

Consumer behaviour is also consuming. What we wear, what we eat, what we read, what we drink etc. are in many instances strongly emotionally influenced.

Our choice of the cantina's standard sandwich for lunch may be a completely mechanical process and the one we choose may be the one with the strongest net emotional response tendency. Again, all the alternatives that appear in front of us in consumption situations have emotional response tendencies associated with them and in turn they may influence cognition and thereby become factors in the determination of our consumer behaviour.

In other situations without any conscious but still some cognitive activity we may choose which of three possible shirts to wear on a particular day. Still, another example of unconsciously guided choice completed without any cognitions may be our choice of orange juice for breakfast rather than milk or tomato juice from the refrigerator.

5. Marketing Communication and NERS

The processes through which mass communication, displays and opinion from others influences our emotional response tendencies are not well understood. The talented creative may with a special approach to communication about a brand change its NERS completely in the target group. Another advertiser may spend millions of Euros on ingenious messages without accomplishing much.

We may speculate that when relevant information is provided in an attention-getting fashion, effects will occur. Much experimental work is needed to teach us more about how these processes function and fulfil our gap of understanding of how mass communication works. However, recent experimental research also seems to point to the fact that even unfocused exposure can lead to formation of positive emotional reaction through mere repetition (Janiszewski, 1993).

Emotions may be strong as when we see our child being hurt or they may be weak like the emotion aroused by a candy bar near the cash register in the supermarket. In consumer behaviour emotions are generally weak but so are the cognitions that can be caused by the emotions also.

It is not that emotions are something new thrown into our modeling of consumer behaviour. It was there before cognitions in the survival of the species. It is only later in our development as humans that the ability to cognitively cope with problems has come into being. With that ability we tend to look back at the more elementary unconscious emotional processes as less important and as a little disgraceful. Maybe we should revise our view and depart in emotional processes in understanding how relatively simple and not too consequential consumer behaviour occurs.

6. Emotions and Behaviour in General

In their origin many emotions, the sparrow's flight from the hawk, the mice hiding from the cat, are learned through millions of years. Those sparrows and those mice that did not learn it, did not survive. The descendents of those first sparrows and mice became millennium by millennium more and more likely to be born with the proper defensive behaviour programmes built into their genes and the emotionally controlled proper responses ready when needed.

In this way the majority of mice and sparrows came into life with the pre-programmed defensive mechanism. In a similar manner the smell of cheese to the mice tied in with positive emotional responses. Unfortunately to some mice the smell might occur together with the presence of a cat and the outcome was catastrophic. Eventually some more fortunate mice might be able to programme a proper defensive reaction in the case of combination of the smell of the cheese and presence of cat. This response might eventually be programmed into the very basic emotional responses with their location centred in the amygdale.

In humans these elementary response tendencies are still there, but our predecessors have through millions of years modified the elementary responses to a repertoire of more appropriate, innate emotional impulses. Different smells of cheese may attract our attention and generate different emotional responses. Even the adjusted, innate emotional responses may be modified by cognitive processes into cognitive markers acquired through experience. We may have learned to know that the strong smell that some cheeses have does not necessarily mean that they have a bad taste.

The human emotional behaviour is adjusted through millenniums of years and culture has taught us that some naturally inherited responses may not be that good at all. After all this is what human culture is all about. The Ten Commandments contain the essence of cognitive learning to be superimposed on elementary emotional impulsive responses. It is the essence of what our culture, church or faith with which we have grown up is all about. Our head tells us what to do but still in some instances our heart may know better. We may risk our lives to save our drowning child or we may offer a kidney to save the life of a dying brother. In many of those instances where our heart overrides our brain emotional processes may play an important part.

The impulses we feel towards behaviour or physical elements in our environment may have positive as well as negative sides to them. If we follow the impulse the net positive or net negative strengths are likely to be governing our behaviour. Both positive and negative emotional responses tendencies may be weak or strong. When they both are strong we experience conflict and are more likely to come to use cognitive processes to solve the conflicts. We talk about more involvement, more arousal being activated. When both negative and positive emotional response tendencies are weak - as in the case of many choices of consumer goods - we may use our net emotional response tendency as a behavioural guide and thereby solve the problem. Or maybe let a few unconscious, cognitive elements enter into the process and let them make a fast, easy decision for us.

We may not always automatically choose the emotionally most attractive alternative though. In the store, the net emotional response tendency for plain coffee may be stronger than that for caffeine free coffee but knowing that our mother in law will be present for coffee in the evening may adjust our immediate choice to a decaffeinated variant since it is what we know she prefers.

We can do this even without reflecting consciously about it but still we have modified our initial choice from what it would have been had the sheer emotional response tendency been allowed to dominate.

In contemporary life most strong emotional responses are inappropriate. It is not really a good idea to yell bad words after the driver of the car in the traffic who takes our place in the line for the next exit. And it is certainly not appropriate when a 13 year-old schoolboy takes his father's gun and shoots the teacher and the schoolmates that mob him. It may be an important issue in contemporary society to develop educational programmes that teach us to control such socially damaging, primitive impulsive behaviours.

In most consumer behaviour such unfitting emotional responses are less consequential. The one cigarette more, that one should not take, is – in the short run at least – not highly consequential. The last drink before you drive home may be more harmful in the short run. Also and hopefully most drivers have developed cognitive controls that annul these hazards.

It may be a common phenomenon in connection with some consumer behaviour that the unreflected impulse emotional response may not be so harmful in its own right but its accumulated effects may be very damaging. The first pancake with syrup for breakfast may be activated by million of years old cravings for food when it is there on the plate, but in a contemporary society with abundance of food in front of the individual again and again in the course of the day the consequences may be extremely unhealthy. The preserved meal that may be far too large seen in light of our physical needs may still be completed and the plate left empty, because of elementary emotional mechanisms that govern our eating behaviour.

The increasingly worrying consumption of drugs and pills of all kinds are other points in case. The lifestyle containing these opportunities has developed with increasing speed within relatively few centuries. Much fewer than it takes nature to modify genetic built-in emotional response repertoires appropriately. All these genetic adjustments that time has not made possible for us to develop, the contemporary individual has to substitute with cognitive reflections built on top of our inherited emotional response tendencies.

Our environment has changed far too fast for us to keep up with the many scary aspects of contemporary life. Important issues arise for research, teaching, doctors and others. Advice is needed to help the individual through the complex myriad of impulsive repertoire of possible behaviours. However, in everyday life most of what is going on is less dramatic. The continuous sequence of choices the individual is making as he buys, stores, consumes, and discharges consumer goods occur with little or no conflict and acquired or modified emotional response tendencies do most of the job perfectly.

Important, however, is it that most of those net emotional response tendencies that enter into our consumer choice are not the originally inherited basic ones but rather in the form of somatic markers modified and refined by past experiences. They are formed by what we have learned, what we have met in advertising etc. It is the culturally adjusted NERS that we bring with us into choice situations and that we modify by experience and sometimes adjust cognitively.

E. Summary

The chapter basically addresses three broad issues: the question of methodology, the integration of emotional response tendency into branding strategy and brand challenges and a broader integration of the theory of emotional response into general reflections on consumer behaviour. Concerning the first issue, the chapter demonstrates a certain sensitivity to change in contact procedure and interview setting, however the sensitivity tends to be in the form of a linear transformation of results ascribable to web contact instead of drop-off, self-administered questionnaires. Also some testing as to the sensitivity to number of words used for measuring the response tendencies is carried out. This demonstrates a substantial robustness – again confirming the validity of the measures. Based on the much larger sample in 2004 compared to 2003, a test of solution as to two (positive/negative) or more underlying dimensions is carried out.

The second issue of branding and branding strategy deals with the challenges that can be identified, depending on what emotional responses are registered for the brand amongst users and non-users and compared both to category averages and competitors' positions. A basic framework of generic challenges is developed, depending on the brand NERS compared to the category NERS.

The third issue is discussed at length in order to demonstrate the general usefulness of the emotional theory and the type of measurements proposed in this book for marketing management decisions.

Part II

Marketing Communication
– and Emotions

In part one we have looked at models of consumer choice with special emphasis on the role emotions may play in such a context. We have also proposed a way in which the marketer may measure the emotional appeal in his brand by judging positive and negative emotional reactions and eventually estimating the net emotional response strength (NERS) associated with his brand.

We have done that with inspiration from contemporary neurology. Before returning to the implications of this approach to the study of brands and other topics for marketing communication we shall take a closer look at ways in which the effect of marketing communication traditionally is being decomposed and measured. We shall do this with particular weight placed upon advertising. Neither because this is the only, nor the single form in which marketing communication influences brand equity, but because it is the most studied area.

More explicitly, we shall look into the role of advertising, how it is optimized, how it is budgeted in practice. We shall also review findings from others and by ourselves regarding the effects of advertising and how such effects generally have been measured. In doing so we shall return to some behaviourally and some cognitively based views on marketing communication. In doing so we also highlight some of the shortcomings of such approaches and thereby emphasize when a better understanding of underlying emotional processes may help us get more insight.

Finally we shall return to the issue of emotions and discuss how measurement of these can improve the short as well as the long term planning of advertising and other aspects of marketing communication. In this connection we shall also improve our understanding of the way in which immaterial elements of brand equity may be studied using the NERS measures developed in part I.

Chapter VII

The Role of Advertising

CHAPTER OUTLINE

This chapter forms the entry point to our discussion of how advertising works. The chapter discusses the formal conditions for determining optimal levels of spending on various promotional items, particularly advertising. The concept of elasticity is treated in detail, particularly because this concept has had a tendency to disappear from textbooks – particularly advertising textbooks – and a number of formal conditions for optimal spending levels depend on relations between various elasticities and sales response functions. Although not used to any great extent in daily operations, these fundamental arguments do merit more attention in the authors' opinion, not least because today's data-rich marketing environment in many instances lend themselves to attempts at estimating advertising and price elasticities. With such estimates, better decisions are a clear possibility with a view to optimising the return on marketing investments. The chapter also deals in detail with the fundamental arguments about advertising's functions in relation to novelty and innovation and in relation to competition and competitive spending – again, because these arguments really are fundamental and tend to be forgotten in a modern marketing environment.

The second part of the chapter discusses practical approaches to advertising planning, looking at budgeting, allocating spending across media and planning considerations in campaign execution and timing of campaigns.

CHAPTER OBJECTIVE

The chapter provides a classical framework for analysing and determining optimal efforts with respect to the promotional parameters, particularly advertising. Our aim in doing this is to inspire today's marketers with ample access to data to take a new look at modeling from the classical formulae in order to arrive at decisions that make more profit as regards advertising than what is possible basing decisions on intuition or past experience.

SETTING THE SCENE

Marketing can be characterised as "decommoditizing brands". Without marketing it is products, which are bought by the consumers, without any special preference for one or the other and under no circumstances at a premium price. By means of effective marketing activities brands are created to which the consumers are connected and for which they pay more. A brand therefore has a higher (inherent) value than a product.

In the discussion of company value, "Brand Equity" does play an increasing role compared to the value of fixed equipment, inventories etc. Attempts at estimating the immaterial values of a company previously centred on assets such as: human resources, know-how, capacity for innovation etc. In recent years, however, the concept of Brand Equity – seen as a composite of mental brand equity, behavioural or market brand equity and financial brand equity – has moved to the forefront of attempts at estimating the "true" value of branded goods companies.

Research on acquisitions of branded goods enterprises shows that the brands of the enterprise are the assets that persist in the long term. Production equipment may be changed – or production outsourced - human resources are moved around and changed and stocks are consumed. Since this trend is increasingly general amongst western industrial companies, control of the brand value is a central company management problem.

In an earlier chapter we looked at the Brand Equity concept in the sense of the Consumer Based Brand Equity – or the mental brand equity. Here, and in the following chapters of Part II of our treatise we shall focus on the dynamics of brand equity. How it is developed, built, maintained and managed. Here advertising and communication in a broader sense play major roles.

Advertising in this connection plays two fundamental roles. It helps establishing brands by introducing them to the consumers, but advertising and communication also is used to substantiate the attraction in the brand and thereby increasing the brand's value. The role and ability of marketing communication to build and maintain brands is generally well known and accepted. For this reason major amounts of money are spent on advertising by branded goods companies. It is also well known that marketing communication alone does not make a strong brand. Only those companies who manage to integrate the essence of their brands in all operations and communications with both consumers and other stakeholders, who consistently deliver quality over time, really create brand equity.

Decisions on the big advertising budgets are often made on very vague assumptions. Tactics and actual decisions are often based on individual know how, "many years of experience", and specialists' advice. Strategic decisions on board and management level are made based on information of a much more general and intuitive nature, compared to decisions made on investment in production equipment, human resources, IT and other management areas. The need for better decision information and decision models in the advertising budgeting process is obvious.

Large corporations reportedly are developing Marketing Mix Modeling (Kuijten and Foekema, 2005) as a way of utilizing historical experience in simulating effects of future actions. Also several attempts at linking levels of advertising expenditure to sales effects have been carried out under the broad heading of Sales Modeling. Modeling approaches provide promising results, however the approaches are still far away from providing decision makers with optimization models, primarily since the modeling approaches rely heavily on fitting models to historical data – to a large extent without regard for future changes in exogenous variables that may affect the model parameters dramatically, or for changes in effects as modeling results are extrapolated outside of the small intervals where historical data may have a high forecasting power.

A. Optimal Marketing Strategy

In marketing theory, as suggested in Chapter I, we distinguish between 4 categories of tools that marketers can use. McCarthy (1968) elegantly labels them price promotion product and place. Similar groupings are proposed by the Danish authors Rasmussen (1977) and Kjær Hansen (1960). They talk about the action parameters price, advertising and product quality later expanded with the fourth parameter distribution (Rasmussen, 1977). It is this formulation, which is fundamental for most presentations of marketing theory, not the least for the classical Kotler "Marketing" 4 P's (1980 and later).

It is possible at the theoretical level to specify how the marketer should optimize his combined use of the 4 parameters price, promotion, product and place.

If q_1 is the amount sold in period 1, if P_1 is the price charged for the product in the period, if K_1 is a measure of the quality characteristics of the product, if D_1 is the cost spent on distribution, and if A_1 is the amount of promotional effort, then in a dynamic situation, including the activities of the competitors $(q_2 - q_n,)$ this can be expressed as follows:

$$\text{(I)} \qquad q_1 = q_1(P_1, K_1, D_1, A_1)$$
$$q_2 = q_2(P_1, K_1, D_1, A_1,$$
$$P_2, K_2, D_2, A_2)$$

$$\cdots$$
$$\cdots$$

$$q_n = q_n(P_1, K_1, D_1, A_1$$
$$\cdots\cdots$$
$$P_n, K_n, D_n, A_n)$$

(Palda 1964, p.18 after Brems 1951)

(In this form the authors neglect the loyalty phenomenon: that q_n may in itself be influenced by q_{n-1}, that is by past purchases.)

If we like traditional economists introduce a Coop-Douglas production (Wiens 2005) function we arrive at the optimal overall mix of the enterprise resources. For the multi-period planning horizon it is the one that will yield the highest positive value of the difference between the sum of the discounted future values of revenues (that is, the present value of future revenues) and the sum of the discounted future values of net purchases (that is, the present value of future net purchases, of advertising, distribution, product quality, basic raw materials etc. (Palda, 1964).

This very complex rule is not easy to apply. Thus most marketing theory is concerned with partial analysis of price decisions, quality decisions, distribution decisions and promotion decisions.

When looking upon these partial decisions, however, the complexity increases dramatically when one is forced to consider also the extent to which interaction occurs between the action parameters (The four P's) when they are changed simultaneously – and even more complexity is added when other factors influencing demand are changed.

Each of the four action parameters must be seen as composed of several individual parameters and each one of these must be studied in its own right. An approach underscoring the extreme complexity of having to deal with all decision variables simultaneously.

Price, quality, product development, distribution and distribution channels are not the topic of this treatise. Our concern is with the promotion element, and in particular with advertising.

Under the term marketing communication, Ottesen (1973) considers all the different kinds of information that may be provided from the enterprise to the market.

Basically he introduces a distinction between individual and mass communication on the one hand and a distinction between personal and impersonal communication on the other hand.

Table VII.1: 4 kinds of communication used by the company in its marketing effort (Ottesen, 1969)

	Sender appears:	In person	Impersonally
Approach to target group as:	Individual	Personal selling	Phone, sms, Direct response, websites, etc.
	Mass	Sales meetings, presentation	Advertising, sponsoring, PR etc.

In Table VII.1 the four kinds of communication are illustrated with some examples listed in each category.

Individual communication is dominated by personal selling either person to person or with the use of a media such as the telephone or the Internet. In the latter cases it becomes impersonal individual communication. The company that uses SMS in mobile marketing actually applies thousands of impersonal individual communication encounters. Website marketing, similarly, can be classified as impersonal and individual communication – and the reliance on the effect of website communication and opportunities for individually adapted transactions stem from this fact.

Individual mass communication may take the form of meetings, lecturing and the like. Impersonal mass communication is traditional advertising but also other uses of mass media such as some forms of sponsoring, PR, and product placements are points in case.

In the following we shall limit our discussion not only to the promotional parameter but by and large also to the use of impersonal mass communication in the form of advertising and the like. This is not so much because of the other terms being unimportant, but rather because much of what is published relates to the effects of that kind of communication.

Again here, it must be remembered that this very partial point of view gives rise to important considerations as to the interaction between the different promotional activities (substitution versus complementarity between the different elements in the marketing mix used by the company).

In defence of this partial approach to the problem we may argue that the different promotion activities have a number of things in common, so that some of the generalisations derived relating to advertising can with more or less ease be adapted to other promotional activities.

They must all in most common cases be expected to have positive elasticity, which is true of any promotional activity, that is, they are generally believed to have more sales as the primary effect.

In theory, they may all be varied almost continuously. That is the advertising budget, the sales budget, the sponsoring budget etc. may be increased or decreased with any amount of money.

In the real world there may be some minor limitations to this. To choose to advertise on Television requires a certain minimum budget for the activity to be meaningful at all, and at least for smaller companies additions to the sale force comes in jumps. Here one more sales person is a dramatic discontinuous increase. Similarly signing a particular sponsoring contract may represent an expense of such a magnitude that the decision in its own right has the character of an investment decision.

In the following we shall take up some of the basic issues relating to advertising decision making. We shall start with some basic questions about the determination of optimal advertising. From there we shall turn to the procedures dominating practice today, and we shall do so in the light of our more basic rules concerning the optimisation of advertising.

Also we shall look at the elements that the advertising decision making process often is broken down to: budgeting, media group choice, creative execution and timing.

1. Optimal Decision Making

It is a basic rule in economic theory that the optimal solution is found where marginal costs involved in increasing the activity equals the marginal income or marginal revenue generated. This rule applies as well in the short as in the long run. Albeit, exactly what cost and what revenue are marginal may differ, but the basic rule holds in all cases.

Marketing decisions as to the use of price, distribution, product quality and communication is governed by the same principle. Any marginal changes in marketing costs should result in at least a similar change in marginal revenue – or larger. In most cases, as we shall see, this - since measured activity in most cases results in marginally decreasing effects – implies that the enterprise should continue to increase its efforts until the resulting revenue equals the last increase in effort. This consideration of marketing as an independent activity that may be optimised with all other factors of the company remaining unchanged is however often somewhat removed from reality.

To decompose marketing communication further into personal sales, formation of corporate identity, sponsoring, advertising etc. is even more questionable. Advertising works in positive (complementary) and negative (substitution) ways with all other marketing activities. Nevertheless in the following we shall attempt to adhere to a partial view.

2. The Dorfman-Steiner/Barfod Theorem

It is well established that with regard to price in the optimal situation (Rasmussen, 1977)

$$\text{(II)} \qquad p/(p-c) <= - (dq/q)/(dp/p) = -e_p$$

Where p = price
                  c = (estimated) variable costs
                  q = quantity sold
                  dp = small (marginal) increase in price
                  dq = small (from dp resulting) increase in quantity sold
                  e_p = price elasticity

To put it differently the price elasticity in the optimal situation must be equal to or greater than the ratio between the price per unit and contribution per unit. Since the contribution $(p-c)$ always will be smaller than p, in the optimal situation the numerical value of e_p must always be greater than 1, and the larger the contribution the lower the price elasticity is required in the optimal situation. A similar rule applies to advertising and promotion.

Looking at any group of promotional activities, being it sales promotion, personal selling or advertising, the general rule still applies that the marginal effect of additional spending should be at least equal to the marginal increase in revenue derived from the spending.

This basic rule, however general that it is, has been formulated into the more informative "Dorfman-Steiner" theorem for promotional activities. What might be less known is that this theorem was actually first formulated in Danish by Barfod (1944).

In the process of formulation of the Dorfman-Steiner theorem we again need to define price elasticity as:

$$e_p = (dq/q)/(dp/p)$$

Similarly promotional or advertising elasticity can be defined as:

$$e_a = (dq/q)/(da/a) \quad \text{where,}$$
a = promotional spending
da = increment in promotional spending

And finally the elasticity of increased unit costs, corresponding to increases in product quality can be defined as:

$$e_k = (dq/q)/(dk/k) \quad \text{where,}$$
k = unit quality cost
dk = increment in quality cost

In its original formulation, distribution costs were not considered as a separate entity, but they can easily be seen as following rules similar to the elasticity of advertising or the elasticity of unit cost.

Dorfman-Steiner (1954) realised that in a world of differentiation and less than perfect competition the optimal situation for the company must rely not only on marginal production cost being equal to marginal contribution obtained from sales. Promotion efforts and among these advertising and the quality differentiation of the product must be considered also. With advertising elasticity defined as e_a and quality elasticity as e_k (as above), the theorem reads (for a derivation see Palda 1969, pp. 9-12)

(III) $\qquad |e_p| = (p/(p-c)) * e_a = e_k$

In words, the theorem states that if the single-product firm can manipulate price, quality and advertising, it will find itself at the profit-maximising point where the numerical value of price elasticity of demand equals the quality elasticity of demand and the numerical value of marginal effects of advertising on sales. Since price and other elasticities rarely remain constant with varying q, this means that the theory only describes conditions that must be met in the optimal situation. It does not allow us to solve for either of the included variables.

In more common terms the theory says that in the optimal situations the numerical sensitivity of the price must equal the sensitivity of quality and again this must equal the sensitivity of promotion multiplied with the ratio between prices and costs (profit ratio).

From this it is again obvious that the optimisation problem of advertising can not be looked upon partially. When this is still dominating, however, it is frequently attributed to the difficulties in getting relevant data concerning a real total optimisation of the total effort. With a partial view on advertising effects, one has again to consider what Rasmussen (1977) called complementarity and substitution between parameters of action.

With complementarity one thinks of the phenomenon that the parameter of action when applied creates synergistic effects of other parameters of action, e.g. with an improvement in quality, the use of advertising has an increased effect by informing of the improved product. Similarly with price changes, deals or offers the total effect will increase if advertisement of the price reduction is made at the same time.

Substitution is seen to occur where the use of one tool (i.e. price) substitutes for the competitor's use of another parameter of action (i.e. quality), a quality improvement in the competitor's product may in the short term be counteracted by price reduction or by an increased advertising effort. In the same way a competitor's special advertising lucky punch (creatively or through innovative media choice) can partially be met with a price reduction.

Also within each category of action parameters one can speak of complementarity as well as substitution. It might be appropriate in many cases to complement a TV campaign with campaigns in daily newspapers and magazines allowing more detailed information of the product to be provided to the consumers. When in the following the communication and especially advertising parameters are discussed, these considerations have to be remembered.

Also the communication parameter includes, as said before, both the sales effort and advertising. To a large extent one can speak as well of substitution and complementarities between the use of these two varieties of the communication parameter. This has led to the classic distinguishing between "push" and "pull" marketing strategies – closely mirrored in marketing parlance by above- and below-the-line activities.

Push strategies presuppose that the basic approach to selling products is putting constant pressure on the distribution stages, wholesale as well as retail, and in business-to-business marketing selling efforts directed towards to the final buyer. One can speak of the use of sales force against all stages in the distribution system, and of advertisement towards these with some special offers intended to improve sell-in and distribution (merchandising).

Pull strategies presuppose that the enterprise first and foremost tries to build its sales by creating demand from the final consumers.

Product quality and consequent customer satisfaction, advertising and special offers to consumers belong to this category.

3. Optimal Advertising

The partial equilibrium conditions for optimal advertising effort have its base in the Dorfman-Steiner theorem. However, it is also possible directly to formulate the conditions for optimality.

In the optimal situation the increased expense in advertising should be less than or equal to the gain (contribution) achieved.

We assume that sales are a continuous positive function q (A) of advertising spending (A).

$$q = q(A)$$

The condition to be fulfilled for an increase in advertising to be profitable then is:

Loss Gain
dA   <= dq(p-c)

Where p-c is contribution per unit: i.e. sales price less variable costs. From this it can be derived (Rasmussen, 1977 pp. 220-21) that in the optimal condition:

(IV) $A/(p-c)q <= (dq/q)/(dA/A) = e_a$

That is, for it to be worthwhile to increase advertising, the ratio between the total advertising budget for the product and the total contribution from the product must be smaller than or equal to the advertising elasticity.

As long as sales are a positive function of advertising, e_a will always be positive. As long as one assumes a decreasing response (sales) function as in Figure VII.1, e_a will be decreasing, and as long as contribution per unit is assumed to be constant, a point will always exist where e_a becomes smaller than the critical ratio in Equation VIII.4.

Figure VII.1: Decreasing advertising response function

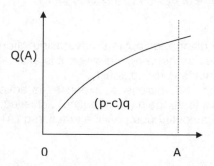

Further, as long as it is worthwhile to keep the product in the market (the price exceeds the unit contribution), the critical ratio (p/p-c) is always larger than zero. Also the larger this ratio, the higher the amount of advertising is to be expected.

In general the larger the contribution ((p-c) relative to p) the smaller the advertising elasticity required for an increase in advertising to be profitable. Thus it is no wonder that many fast moving consumer goods (FMCG) with relatively high margins can run large advertising budgets profitably.

Figure VII.2: S-shaped advertising response function (Rasmussen, 1977, p.217)

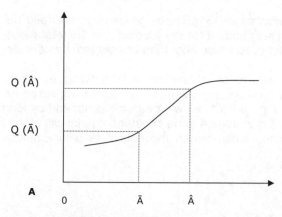

In some instances an S-shaped advertising demand function is assumed (Figure VII.2).

The occurrence of s-shaped or decreasing response functions is a major – unsettled – issue in the advertising literature (Simon and Arndt, 1980). In case of a s-shaped relationship, advertising may in some cases not be worthwhile at all, or only at quite high levels. If the turning point in Figure VII.2 is at such a low level of advertising that the revenue generated up to the turning point is smaller than the advertising budget corresponding to this point, then advertising at this, or any lower level, will not be worthwhile. Advertising though, may still be profitable if a point $\hat{A}$ exist on the decreasing part of the response curve, so that the total $(p-c)q_{\hat{a}}$ exceed $\hat{A}$.

This point will always be to the right of the turning point and implies that if an S-shaped advertising response function is assumed, and in such cases a certain minimum amount of advertising must be administered for advertising to be worthwhile at all. Conditions where this is not worthwhile may very well exist in cases with high initial investments in the advertising as with high production cost for TV-advertising.

With these considerations for optimality we must remember that (IV) represent a condition which has to be met in the optimal situation it is not a function which can be solved for different values for A.

Secondly we have to bear in mind that q – that is the total sales - either takes place in the same period as the one in which advertising is spent or includes some discounted value reflecting effects of advertising carried out in this period occurring in later periods – the carry-over effects.

We shall subsequently come back to this fundamental problem in connection with advertising planning and advertising research, but to summarise:

One observation is that the advertising elasticity is positive and in the optimal situation always smaller than 1, since the total amount of money spent on advertising must be smaller than the total revenue in the same period (given that no possible effects in future periods are assumed).

The larger the contribution (p - c) the smaller we will require the advertising elasticity to be in the optimal situation. Therefore, in practice we will find that more advertising is recommendable when the profit rate is high.

A third observation is the following:

The larger the number of units sold (in the optimal situation) the smaller the required advertising elasticity. This can also be put differently: In markets with relatively few transactions you need a higher response probability to each unit of promotional activity to make it profitable. Thus in markets with costly or expensive – big ticket items - transactions as is often the case in business-to-business markets or with major consumer products such as durables, homes etc., companies will tend to use promotional forms providing higher response probabilities per unit of effort. In such markets personal selling will often dominate over the use of mass advertising.

If the advertising elasticity can be assumed to be constant, an optimal advertising level can be determined as $A = q(p-c) * e_a$. Under these conditions we see that the advertising elasticity defines the constant proportion of total revenue to be allocated to advertising.

Such a condition may not always be unrealistic. In the special case when the advertising response function can be described as

(VI) $q = L*A \exp(e_a)$
Where L is any constant

The advertising elasticity remains constant. Even if such a relationship does not apply to the entire advertising response function it may still be valid in some interval around the actual and/or optimal spending level.

Consider, as it will be discussed subsequently, that a not uncommon advertising budgeting procedure is to allocate a fixed percentage of total revenue to advertising, it can be seen that such a policy could be optimal only if the advertising elasticity is (relatively) constant, and if the initial proportion of advertising is optimal in the first place. It is indeed rare that either of these conditions is fulfilled completely and consequently determining optimal advertising in this way may be a dangerous procedure.

As mentioned an S-shaped demand function for advertising implies that very low levels of advertising have no or little effect. But still, if advertising is worthwhile at all, the effectiveness (e_a) increases until a certain level, after which it starts to decrease.

This observation supports the commonly held belief among promoters of advertising that a certain minimum of advertising has to be allocated for it to be worthwhile at all and inversely, at a certain level the returns to advertising are diminishing and may even become negative. In this discussion the term wear-out often appears.

In this sense wear-out relates to the effect of a total campaign, but wear-out may also be discussed in relation to particular campaign elements such as individual executions etc. Here repetition of the same advertising may face decreasing returns and sooner or later become unprofitable.

4. Optimal Advertising in a Dynamic World

Advertising planning always has to consider future effects, since its effects will only be observed in coming periods. This will be discussed subsequently. But not only must advertising planning try to factor in the effects of advertising on sales as such, the planning of advertising must take into account expectations about the future activities of competitors, since their marketing activities may very well have effects on the company's performance.

Here one can speak of three ways of acting, "conjectural" versus "autonomous" versus "monopolistic" behaviour. The conjectural reactions appear when each enterprise plans its advertising considering what is expected from the competitors and expecting the competitive reactions to originate from the company's actions and to have effect on the company's sales volume. This is a situation that occurs in oligopolistic markets with relatively few competitors and where product differentiation is not extreme.

This is characteristic of the situation for most fast moving consumer goods. But also for many durables and other goods the oligopolistic market form is dominating, and the use of parameters of actions such as advertising will typically be planned conjecturally. That is, the competitor's possible reactions and their effects on the company's performance are taken into consideration.

The other case is autonomous behaviour, where each supplier determines the action parameters, the price, the advertising, the quality etc. with an assumption that the effects of competitive actions will have an effect on the company's performance – in the form of a general limitation of the market accessible to the company – however, the competitive actions are not expected to take the company's own actions into account, they are planned by competitors for other reasons, such as a general planning methodology, fixed percentage of sales allocated to advertising etc.

This type of behaviour is often found in markets characterized by perfect or almost perfect competition and/or where the number of suppliers is large. Here the possibilities for making decisions about advertising and product quality are limited and prices are more or less seen as being enforced by the market.

A lot of agricultural enterprises act under these assumptions, transport markets typically function under the autonomous competitive behaviour assumptions, and so do a lot of international raw material markets. Markets with one large supplier and any number of very small suppliers may also exhibit autonomous behaviour on the part of the large supplier – and on the part of the small suppliers as well. Neither party assumes their particular actions to produce specific reactions: the large supplier does not expect the small suppliers to do anything in particular as reactions since they are perceived as too small or too insignificant; the small suppliers do not expect the large supplier to react to their actions in particular, since they believe that the large supplier does not see it as profitable to react to their marketing actions as long as they result in status quo in market share distribution.

A special case of autonomous behaviour is referred to as monopolistic competitive behaviour. This can be seen in monopolies or almost monopolistic markets, where a company simply does not reckon at all with competitive actions, since they are not seen as having any effect on company performance. But not only near-monopolies or extremely differentiated companies exhibit traits of monopolistic behaviour, often also companies introducing new products – new innovations or major new improvements to existing products - exhibit clear traits of monopolistic behaviour.

When conjectural behaviour exists, we find mutually interdependent adaptation of the action parameters by each competitor. This situation can be described by a so-called kinked demand curve. In the case of advertising this is illustrated in fig. 5 (Rasmussen, 1977, p. 240).

Figure VII.3: The kinked advertising demand curve

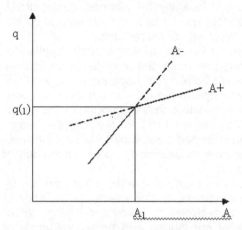

A- represents the demand curve as it will be if the competitor does not increase advertising when the company changes its advertising from the starting level, A_1. A+ is the curve showing what happens when the competitor matches the company's changes in advertising.

At any given level of advertising the resulting sales volume has to be read on the vertical axis. When considering a reduction of the advertising level, the company will not expect the competitors to match or follow the reduction. Therefore the company will expect a more sensitive advertising demand function (The A- line in the Figure VII.3).

On the other hand, if the enterprise increases the advertising effort, it will expect the competitors to do the same. The resulting sales increase will therefore be less than it would have been had the company been allowed to expand its advertising budget alone. In this situation the company will expect the demand to follow the less steep curve in Figure VII.3 (A+1).

The total advertising demand curve considering the reactions of the market to the company's changes in advertising can be characterised by the full drawn kinked curve in Figure VII.3. If the company plans to decrease the advertising budget, it will expect a relatively larger sales reduction because it will not expect its competitors to do the same.

On the other hand when considering increasing its advertising level, the company must expect that competitors will do the same and consequently it will have a relatively much smaller increase in sales as a result.

Figure VII.4: *The kinked price demand curve under conjectural behaviour (A. Rasmussen, p. 240) (E$_p$ price demand curve with computation following price changes by the company. E$_p$: Price demand curve when computation does not follow changes made by the company. EM$_n$ and EM$_p$: corresponding marginal income curves. MC: marginal cost curve)*

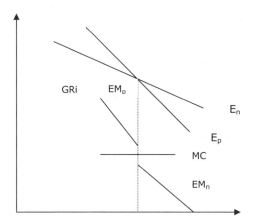

A similar situation exists in connection with price considerations. For comparison these are illustrated here. The kinked price demand curve is shown in Figure VII.5. The jump that will appear in the marginal revenue curve under these circumstances is illustrated. There is a vertical jump in the intersection of the autonomic and conjecturally based demand function, i.e. no matter where marginal costs are as long as they stay in this interval it is uninteresting to consider price changes. Thus only if significant cost changes appear, price activities would be considered.

This argument is particularly relevant when it comes to price. Immediately when the competitor learns about a price reduction, he may follow with a similar price reduction. Based on these considerations, price reductions are more interesting when they take a form which the competitor cannot follow immediately or when it is signalled that it is only of temporary nature.

This may be the case with deals and offers such as two for one, special discounts, etc. The discounts can be hard to match immediately for the competitor and as the offer will come to an end the competitor may feel less impelled to respond immediately. Another thing is that in contemporary merchandising such price promotion activity is so frequently executed, that a reciprocal neutralisation of its effects may result anyway, and the significance of the kinked price demand phenomenon is to some extent reduced.

With regard to advertising the situation is somewhat different. From the point in time where the competitor observes a new advertising initiative – typically as the campaign is aired or inserted - some time will pass before an effective counter effort can be made.

First, it may take some time before the competitor realizes or can measure that the new advertising activity actually has impact on the market. Secondly, it takes time to create the campaign to be initiated as a counter move. Thirdly deadlines for booking media time may increase the time lag from when a campaign is planned to when the insertions can actually be made.

In the situation of advertising activity in contrast to price activity, the company has an advantage from having a new advertising initiative alone in some period in time until the competitors can react with a similar action.

The total time lag from a marketing action such as a new advertising campaign – the response time - may be seen as constituting of several parts: The first part is the time lag before the competitor realizes that an action has taken place and that it has effect on the market. The second part is the decision time lag, the time it takes for the competitor to decide on a suitable response. The third part is the technical implementation time lag, the time it takes the competitor to develop and execute the response.

In Figure VII.5 we have illustrated the principal pattern of sales as a result of a delayed competitive reaction due to reaction time lag.

Figure VII.5: Sales before and after a competitor reacts

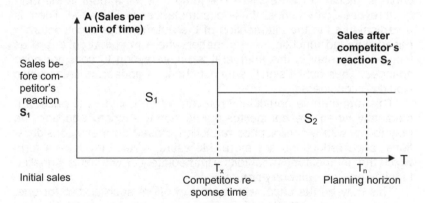

Here the company reaps the benefits of the full revenue resulting from the advertising increase in accordance with the less steep demand function in Figure VII.4, until the competitor reacts. This is illustrated by the area "S_1" in Figure VII.5. The elasticity corresponding to this we denote e_{a1}.

After the competitor has reacted to the increased advertising volume, the company will only enjoy the limited increase in sales that is derived from the more steep demand function (this is S_2 in Figure

VII.5). The elasticity corresponding to this we may denote e_{a2}. This is smaller than the elasticity before competitors react.

The revenue in this later period can be seen as the square"S_2", where T_x is the time lag from initiation of the campaign until the competition reacts. T_n is the time horizon for the planning of the advertising. In such a situation the condition under which increased advertising is profitable can be stated as (Rasmussen, 1972, p. 245.):

(VII) $(A/q \, (p\text{-}c)) * T_n <= e_{a1} * T_x + e_{a2} * T_{n\text{-}x}$

Here it follows that the ratio between advertising spending and total revenue in the time period considered must be smaller than or equal to the elasticity applying until competitors react, $e_{a1,}$ weighted by the length of this period (T_x) plus the elasticity following that, e_{a2} , weighted by the length of time from the reaction of the competitors to the end of the time horizon.

From this formulation it appears, that the larger the difference in advertising elasticity in the two time periods, and the longer the time it takes for the competitor to react, the more profitable an increase in advertising spending will be to the company. Again, we find that the ratio of total advertising to total revenue is critical, but what is important is also how long it takes before the competitor reacts.

One more thing to be observed is that if the advertising elasticity following the competitors' reaction (e_{a2}) is large enough, then the critical rates will always warrant an increase in advertising. Similarly if the elasticity prior to competitors' reaction (ea_1) is too small, an increase in advertising will not be worthwhile at all.

Since advertising effects are always larger when new products are introduced or new product features can be claimed (because of the complementary effects between "newness" and advertising), the ability of the advertiser to create newness, change and variety will make increased advertising spending more attractive.

On the other hand, when products are stable and similar across competitors due to lack of innovation, it may be difficult to bring down the advertising level of the brand since this will produce a relatively much larger decrease in sales if the competitors do not match the reduction in advertising spending.

5. A Word on Elasticities

For the theoretical treatment of optimal advertising the demand elasticity with respect to advertising is critical. If we know this advertising elasticity we can much better determine optimal advertising spending. In the real world, advertising elasticities have not been easy to estimate. There are many reasons for this, some of which will be outlined here.

For the discussion, a fundamental distinction must be made between issues relating to the determination of the amount of advertising effort (A and dA) and issues relating to estimating the effect of advertising (estimating the related q and dq) since both measures are critical in determining the "true" advertising elasticity.

So far we have assumed that the amount of advertising under consideration can be quantified meaningfully and unequivocally. This, however, is not an easy task, and it encompasses amongst other issues the following:

A. Comparison of advertising in different media types. How much is a full colour page in a major magazine worth compared with a 30 seconds advertising spot in prime time on a particular television channel? There is no real answer to this question and it is the reason for some of the major problems with which we are faced in advertising planning, as we shall see in a later section.

B. Comparison of advertising in varying time periods across a week, month or year. For seasonal goods, such as fashion, home improvements and a number of foodstuffs, the value of advertising in the beginning or right before the appropriate season is much larger than later in the selling period – the elasticity of advertising varies across time, however, the price of advertising usually is less variable over the year for a comparable unit of advertising.

C. Estimation of the amount of advertising in terms of the advertising budget or the amount of money spent. To the extent that the price paid for different media reflects the different effectiveness of these, such a measure could have some merit. However, different media with different prices have different values to different advertisers. Moreover prices may vary widely between advertisers. The large companies with many products lines to be advertised may pay much lower prices for the same amount of advertising (no. of pages, no. of spots etc.) than the smaller company with only a minor brand to advertise. Thus it cannot be assumed that summing up the amount spent on different media for a brand automatically provides a meaningful quantitative measure of the total amount of advertising.

D. Advertising campaigns may have different themes or different creative executions and they may function very differently in the market – corresponding to widely varying money values of the advertising. So, when using advertising spending, as a measure of the amount of advertising one must assume that the advertiser is always spending his money optimally. As anyone in the real advertising world would realise, this is rarely the case.

As it can be seen, the simple task of quantifying the amount of advertising in reality is a complicated one. However, attempts have to be made and in applied advertising planning some of the problems indicated here are treated in different ways that we shall look into subsequently.

Even with a reliable measure of the amount of advertising at stake it is not easy to quantify the effect of this advertising. Here some of the major difficulties are the following:

a) Advertising functions over time. It is commonly believed that advertising that has appeared way back in time may still influence the behaviour of contemporary consumers. Exactly how long the effect of advertising may extend in time is a problem in its own right. In common advertising planning a distinction is made between short term, medium term and long-term effects of advertising. The short-term effects are seen as those that can be identified immediately after - and related to a particular exposure to advertising. The medium term effects are those within the planning horizon (normally the year) that can be related to the advertising spending in the same period of time. The long-term effects are those that can be identified in subsequent planning periods or time intervals. In the next chapter we shall look at different ways of analysing these effects.

b) The most obvious approach to the study of the effect of advertising is to look at sales and advertising over time and see how they relate. In this approach one problem is the choice of the length of the time intervals to be studied. If the unit for analysis is a year, we have eliminated seasonal variations and made it possible to introduce other independent variables also available on a yearly basis (such as personal or household income). In the market place, however, things normally change so fast that you rarely have more than a small number of years available with comparable observations of advertising and sales for the same brand. During the period of analysis many other factors may also have changed, such as the competitive situation, income, consumers' age distributions etc. In an attempt to overcome this problem, marketers sometimes analyse shorter time intervals, such as quarterly, monthly, weekly or even daily data. Although some of the shortcomings mentioned above are eliminated by using shorter time intervals, other factors, however, may begin to influence the sales unpredictably. Seasonality is one such factor, but also special events in stores such as deals, promotions, competitive activity or unexpected positive or negative press coverage may make the data unfit for analysis.

c) A major problem in studying the relationship between advertising and sales is to keep other factors under control. Either you have to have data where other factors have little or no influence or you must be able to quantify all other important factors, such as prices, distribution, competitors' prices, income distributions, offers, trends etc. This as will be discussed in connection with advertising modeling is a problem in its own right.

For these reasons real life estimates of advertising elasticities are rare, and the advertising planner is forced to use approaches circumventing the direct estimation of the advertising elasticity.

Still various attempts have been made (for a discussion see Broadbent, 1999) to estimate advertising elasticities for different products, and in the future, with access to so-called single source data, such estimates may become much more widely used in connection with internal company data, enabling more precise Marketing Mix Modeling or sales modeling, models that in reality are mandatory for any advertising planner who wants to arrive at near-optimal advertising budget size estimation and allocation across products and markets.

B. Different Ways in which Advertising Functions

We shall now try to gain a little more insight into the way in which advertising works in different situations.

An important distinction is between advertising in high and low involvement situations.

In the low involvement situation the consumer is not particularly interested in the product in question, the information provided about it, or the overall situation in which the advertising is experienced. Here we may expect emotional processes to dominate – and we may also expect the processing of advertising information to take place at a very low level of consciousness. Examples are many exposures to television commercials for FMCGs or to print advertising where consumers completely ignore or pass by the advertising more or less without attention. Still in such situations advertising has documented effects and we shall later return to the nature of these.

In the high involvement situation the consumer in contrast is interested in the product, the information provided about it, and possibly in the situation in which it is made available. It may be when studying a brochure for a new car in detail, watching a commercial for a headache remedy claimed to provide relief exactly for the ailment the consumer thinks he is suffering from etc. Cognitive information processing is here much more likely than in the low involvement situation, and we will also expect the information processing to take place at a higher level of consciousness.

Another distinction is between informational versus emotional advertising or as some have it: informational versus transformational (Rossiter and Percy, 1998) or informational advertising versus story telling (Peter and Olsen, 1996). In Chapter V and VI we saw how emotional response varies with these criteria. The key distinction is between providing information that is more product relevant and convincing of product features on one hand and information that is more emotionally appealing and less concerned with distinct product features on the other hand.

When the product, its use, its advantages etc. are in focus we talk about informational advertising. When immaterial aspects of the product, values associated with it, or users linked with it are in focus, we talk about emotional advertising, which when dramatised may take the form of story telling.

1. Advertising of Changes and Novelty

In the real world we may distinguish between two kinds of situations where advertising works very differently. Of course all kinds of intermediate combinations may appear between the two extremes described in the following, but to understand the nature of advertising it may be advantageous to "consider strong cases" or extremes.

On the one hand we have the situation where the advertising conveys new information to the consumer. This appears where new products are introduced, but it is also apparent when new features are added to already existing products. It is difficult to estimate how much of total advertising can be classified as such, but it is evident that this advertising is important. It is so because it is attended to with much greater care by the consumers and because it may generate new behaviour to the extent that the consumer chooses to try whatever new is introduced.

In a dynamic society this unique function of advertising is very often related to inventions, innovations, new product introductions, new public services or other governmental initiatives. Advertising in this role is an important factor in the diffusing of innovations and thereby plays an important part in the dynamics and development of societies.

A majority of consumer spending today takes place in product areas that did not exist or at least functionally were basically different not too many years ago. Such major innovations are the telephone, the car, the radio, the households' wide range of white goods, colour television, IT products etc. They have all relied heavily on advertising for their acceptance.

Basic food products such as pasta and rice barley used in the Nordic countries earlier are now every day ingredients in household consumption and the same applies to a number of other food products. Also here advertising has accelerated the changes in consumer behaviour. In these situations the social role of advertising is primarily to help society develop and adapt dynamically.

From the point of view of a company introducing a new product, advertising has a very special role. The success of a new product depends on a number of factors. Fundamental are the distribution coverage that can be reached, the consumer's willingness to try the new product when it becomes known, the willingness to repeat buy the new product, the price of the product and the extent to which

consumers become aware of the new product. Advertising is important in all of these respects.

Advertising may however also function in more stable societies
simply by introducing what already exists to new consumers. This
applies in much advertising to children and young consumers and it
applies to consumers who move between countries or regions where
they face new stores, new products, new brands etc.

It also applies when consumers enter into new situations in their
lives – as illustrated by the basic family life cycle, where at least 4 or
5 distinctly different household types have been identified with very
different needs and consumption patterns - and thereby become
aware of and interested in products they so far have fully neglected.
For instance marriage, having a child, changing jobs, all may generate new interest in products related to housing, childcare, transporta-
tion etc.

The advantage of advertising of changes and novelty is, that it is
in itself is a factor motivating product improvement, the adding of new
features etc. – precisely because of the realization of the larger elasticities of advertising inherent in such situations.

In a quantitative sense focus is on generation of awareness for
the new product, the new brand etc. In a more qualitative sense emphasis is on generating knowledge of important features, advantages,
possible uses etc. of the new or renewed product. Here the communication task of the advertising is to provide useful information and it
has much in common with that which is described in the classical effect hierarchy model discussed in the chapter on cognitive consumer
models. It also is in close parallel to the central information processing – the central route to persuasion - by Petty and Cacioppo (1986a)
in their work on elaboration likelihood. The more elaboration, the
more information is processed and stored ready to retrieval. The central information process works much like a decision process and is in
the focus of many cognitive models of consumer psychology.

Apart from advertising functioning by generating knowledge about
the brand or product in its own right, through the process perceptions
and images relating to the brand or product are formed. In contemporary society and in many product areas these are not only about the
basic aspects of the product, but also about how it is perceived by
other consumers, and how it provides social value etc. Thus, the
emerging image of the product in the mind of the consumer is the totality of associations that the consumer has with the brand or product
in question, including its usability, technical advantages and how it is
seen in a social context.

For newly introduced products the total sales volume of the new
product in any given period can be seen as the number of first time
purchases made by new consumers who try the product for the first
time, plus the number of repeat purchases made by consumers who
have tried the product earlier.

The number of initial purchasers depends on the number of consumers becoming aware of the product, size and nature of the distribution of the product and the willingness or probability to buy the product when the consumer is becoming aware of it and is able to find it in the stores. Repeat purchases in turn are basically dependent on satisfaction with the initial purchases. A model describing this process is suggested in Urban and Hauser (1983). Here the role of advertising first and foremost is to inform about the new features and to generate awareness of the new product. The validity of this line of thinking has been documented in numerous studies pre-testing new product introductions (Urban and Hauser, 1980). Also attempts have been made to relate advertising pressure to brand recall in product introduction situations (Blackburn et al., 1984).

2. Advertising in Competitive Markets

As opposed to advertising of changes or product novelties, advertising in established and competitive markets first and foremost has as its purpose to help competitors to maintain their shares of consumers' awareness and preferences in an otherwise stable market.

A large proportion of contemporary consumer spending takes place in areas where many different alternatives - brands - exist that functionally are more or less identical, and who all serve the same basic needs. In these areas few or no new consumers arrive and the struggle between the competitors is one of maintaining or gaining market shares in a more or less stable market. The conditions are such that The Kinked Advertising Response Function must be assumed to be at work here.

In established, mature and competitive markets, advertising is often more subject to criticism from a social point of view than in markets where advertising is used to inform about innovations. However, also here the role of advertising may be seen in the light of the function of a liberal economy.

In such markets, over time a certain level of advertising is established and advertising spending may stabilize there. Because advertisers tend to relate their advertising spending to the revenues they obtain, they look at share of voice (i.e. share of total advertising in the market) versus share of market, and as a consequence, budgets are maintained around the same level over time. Changing economic conditions may lower or raise the level, but the competitors attempt to maintain the balance between them in terms of advertising spending. Of course stability does not last forever. In many FMCG categories, major advertisers have been shifting marketing spending from advertising to merchandising (Mela et al., 1997).

This appears to be more common in markets where prices are stabilised and where all products have reached more or less the same level of quality and further, real, improvements are difficult to realize. Here a tendency for competition to switch the focus away from advertising and towards distribution initiatives and activities is frequently observed. Special offers, short time price reductions etc. are popular tools.

When the communication effort primarily consists of promotional and price oriented communication because the focus is on distribution activities, brand equity is generally believed – and even in cases documented – to deteriorate. In an attempt to avoid the deterioration of brand equity following from this, advertisers must try to put emphasis on brand values, in which connection emotional effects of communication becomes important.

In competitive FMCG markets with brands that are perceived by consumers as being fundamentally similar, advertising is more likely to work through peripheral informational processing – through the peripheral route to persuasion. The peripheral information processing in its extreme form can be seen as a process where consumers' perception and attention is concerned with the advertising itself, its story, its execution, its use of pictures, its creative impression etc. In its extreme form it has no immediate effect upon how the brand or product is perceived or evaluated. The only information stored are impressions from the advertising itself, impressions that may be linked with positive or negative emotions and that may be reactivated in terms of evaluations of the liking or attitude towards the advertising perceived. This perception of advertising may be very brief and very sporadic. In many cases it is actually dubious whether the consumer has any focus at all on the advertising it is perceived so to speak at the fringe of consciousness.

In markets of this competitive kind with advertising stabilized at a very high level, one may question whether it would not be to the advantage of all of the marketers (and even to the consumers) to reduce the total level of advertising spending and maintaining the shares of voices of the different advertisers. Unfortunately, the lessons from The Kinked Advertising Demand Curve illustrate that this will not happen as a result of individual company action, only as a result of competitors agreeing to reduce spending levels or as a result of government interference or advertising bans. In most countries agreements of such a kind between competitors would be illegal. And in most western countries government bans on advertising come only after much debate and only in areas where the public safety or health is definitively determined to be at stake.

Another way to look at the competitive market with stable shares of voices and high advertising spending may lead to a different conclusion, namely that advertising is not so bad after all for the consumers.

In the competitive game with advertising being a major factor in competition, some manufacturers loose, others win. It is a sensible assumption that the winners are – also in other aspects than advertising – the more efficient companies. Therefore the competitive game in stable markets with few product improvements still has a positive impact on the efficiency of society as such.

It is not the place here to take a stand on when advertising is good, and when it is bad – in reality advertising may very well be simultaneously good to some, bad to others and even simultaneously good and bad to the same stakeholders. It all depends on the individual's situation in life, his political viewpoints and the general frame of reference of the individual.

In the view of the present authors, however, some forms of advertising may very well be negative to society. Such advertising forms probably are more apparent with new types of media or with new advertising opportunities made possible by technology. The reasons have to do with factors such as: Low level of voluntary regulation on how to employ the media or technologies as opposed to established media forms; low visibility for regulating bodies, whether voluntary or compulsory, of new media or technologies limits or delays initiatives to regulate their use; a general lack of understanding and knowledge of how the media or technologies function in the market and how they may play with consumers' perceptions make them more susceptible to misuse – both intended and unintended.

In the preceding pages we have described 2 different ways in which advertising works. Prior to that we have pointed at ways to determine at least theoretically optimal conditions for an advertiser's spending. Now we shall look at the way in which advertisers actually go about planning and executing advertising.

C. Practical Approaches to Advertising Planning

The models discussed earlier applying to optimal advertising do not leave themselves easily to practical application.

The practitioner will normally divide the complete decision problem about advertising into 4 sub problems, each of which he will then attempt to optimise individually.

The 4 part decisions are related to

1. Determination of the size of the budget
2. Determination of the media groups and individual media to be used
3. Determination of the message of the advertising and its creative execution
4. Determination of the scheduling of the exposures within the period of analysis.

From a theoretical point of view neither of these decisions can be made without considering consequences on the other 3 decisions. If certain media categories are chosen they influence the creative process and it may have implications for the budget. Also the scheduling of the exposures will vary with the media chosen. Television commercials can be placed daily, magazine advertising only periodically and some kind of outdoor promotion only at larger time intervals.

Similarly, deciding on a certain budget size may put limits to the media categories that meaningfully can be applied and to the timing which is feasible – for instance TV campaigns, apart from having fairly high CPM also require costly development of creative ideas and actual shooting of spots. Also different creative solutions lend themselves more or less easily to different kinds of media and may demand more or less extensive production budgets.

In spite of this obvious need for simultaneous consideration of the 4 part decisions in the advertising planning process, the practice of approaching these one by one is widespread.

1. Advertising Budgeting

The division of the complex advertising planning process may be seen partly to arise out of a need for defining more manageable problems, and partly as a result of the organisational structure in the advertising world.

Advertising budgeting is normally tied in with the total budgeting process of the company and it is seen partly in light of the profitability of the actual product and other company activities, partly simply as a component in the total cost structure of the company, competing for funds with other components of the total cost structure.

2. Budgeting with a Fixed Share of Revenue or Profit

Looking at the product's share of voice relative to the share of market may lead to advertising budgeting, where the size of the budget is a fixed share of total revenue or total profit. To arrive at a budget frame as a fixed proportion of total sales is probably the most used practice among advertisers in stable, well-established markets.

As suggested earlier this only results in optimal spending if the initial advertising percentage is already optimal and if advertising elasticity is constant. In stable markets where the percentage spent on advertising has been established through many years of practice, this may not be that bad at all.

However, in declining markets with high advertising elasticity it is likely to move the advertising spending away from the optimal proportion in a negative direction – corresponding to a situation where underspending on advertising increases the downward sales curve. Similarly in a growing market with high advertising elasticity, the fixed percentage procedure will have the opposite effect – that is hurting sales growth through starving the product or brand of advertising funds.

To determine the size of the advertising budget in relation to contribution – whether gross or net contribution - functions in very much the same way. Here the $(p-c)*(q)$ term rather than total sales is the critical factor.

In this connection the company may also make reserve allowances for advertising to be used if conditions in the market change or new opportunities arise; typical examples of changing conditions that companies tend to make reserve allowances for are changes in the competitive situation. Realising that the time lag from a decision to introduce new products is taken until the time they are ready for launch is considerable, some companies will attempt to have one or more alternative brands or campaigns ready in the case that competitors should take a move making it necessary to counteract.

The rationale behind this behaviour, however, may be dubious: If the reserve product or campaign is excellent, then why not introduce the product or use the campaign? And inversely, if either product or campaign is of a quality that does not readily lend itself to market introduction, then why use either in the case of competitive attack, when you would expect any company to field its strongest weapons? The procedure is reportedly employed by FMCG companies with dominating market shares in any given product category. The reserve products then serve as frontal attacks against any competitor entering the category with a niche product. The procedure may be strategically sound if the costs incurred in launching such counterattacks are smaller than the discounted profit loss arising from loss of market share due to the competitive actions, should they remain unchallenged. Probably not many companies engaging in "reserve product" strategies attempt to make that calculation.

3. Marginal Budgeting

In many real life situations the advertising budgeting process reduces itself to consideration of whether it is worth to increase or to decrease the advertising spending in the year to come. This may be a meaningful procedure provided the advertising to sales ratio is well determined in the first place. Here emphasis will be on such factors as the expected development of the total market, changes in consumer income and spending, increasing needs for merchandising activities, shift of marketing resources to E-marketing activities, changes in the competitive situation and in this process, comparisons are made with competing brands and with other brands in the company's portfolio.

Particularly competitive considerations may be important here. Assuming a company has made improvements in its product and want to capitalize on that, it may call for additional advertising.

The possible reactions of competitors may also enter into such considerations. In many stable consumer goods markets this competitive situation can be characterised as the "prisoner's dilemma". The essence of that dilemma consists of two prisoners sitting in separate cells and being asked to tell the truth about the joint crime in which they have been involved. The situation is so that if both tell the truth they will get a moderate punishment. If both lie the punishment will be less severe, but if one tells the truth and the other lies, he would get a mild sentence, but the liar would get the most severe punishment.

To the marketer the situation is often very similar. In a stable market with a few dominant companies where all decide to increase advertising spending, the market may increase slightly and everybody gains a little from doing so – possibly with no significant effect on profits. However if one decides to increase spending and the others maintain their spending the one with the increased budget will gain market share from the other – and possibly making his investment profitable. Finally if none of them invest in additional advertising, they will all make more profit than if they all increased their advertising spending.

It is the problem of conjectural behaviour and the mechanism of the kinked demand curve with respect to advertising, discussed earlier, seen from a different point of view. It is not uncommon in such situations seeing "signals" being sent from the category "statesman" that: I do not want to increase my advertising, but if you do, I will do so too", in the hope to stabilise advertising at the present levels for everybody in the category.

4. Communication Goals

It has been argued that since it is so difficult to establish a reliable relationship between sales and advertising (Colley, 1961), it makes sense, rather than formulating goals in terms of sales with dubious measurability or causality, to the advertiser to look for other goals for the advertising activities that may be more easily quantified and where stronger causal links can be established between advertising and the resulting measurement variables.

This brings us back to the two basic advertising situations; the growing and the constant market cases. In the growing market it would be natural to employ brand awareness and awareness or understanding of important features of the newly introduced product or of the changes introduced in the already existing product as goals to be achieved by advertising. To the extent that brand awareness is an obvious function primarily of advertising, this may be a useful measurement to follow to see whether the amount and type of advertising spent is achieving the desired outcome.

In the stable market situation brand awareness is not very sensitive to advertising pressure, since for most brands it is already high and we may have to look for other variables as yardsticks for the quality of the communication planning – and through whose measurement we can determine how well we are doing. Depending upon the degree of central versus peripheral processing we expect, we would work with intervening variables such as advertising awareness, attitude toward the brand, attitudes toward the advertising, emotional responses, liking, purchase intentions etc.

Most commonly however, advertisers tend to focus on advertising awareness, since this awareness in the short run is the most sensitive to the amount spent on advertising, and since changes in the other effect variables are not easily measured in the short run. Still measures such as ad-liking, brand attributes and the like, are commonly used in the planning process.

Here the budgeting question becomes: how much money do we have to spend to achieve a certain brand recall, a certain advertising awareness, a certain amount of liking, or some specific attitudes towards the brand. Working with advertising budgeting along these lines, accompanied by appropriate tracking of the development in the key variables, the company may accumulate considerable insight into the mechanisms generating recall, liking, attitude changes etc., and into the role they may play for the subsequent sales.

When budgeting in terms of communication goals one also brings the creative process more directly into the budgeting considerations. This appears when goals are measured in terms of how many consumers in the potential market exhibit changes in attitudes, perceptions or even dispositions to act – and to what extent these changes must be present. Such measures may more easily lend themselves to the specifications of what and how to communicate as a part of the creative process, resembling the teaching process where certain changes from initial to terminal behaviour are expected to arise from teaching and learning efforts. This type of goal formulation are closely tied to the cognitive view of information processing inherent in classical hierarchy of effects thinking or in central route to persuasion modeling of information processing.

5. Dynamic Budgeting

As it has become evident there is no obvious single way to determine the optimal advertising budget for the period – or periods - to come. In reality most advertisers rely upon different combinations of the kind of thinking, which has been described in the previous pages.

To structure such a process Broadbent (1989) has proposed that a dynamic view of the budget is recommended. Here it is suggested that the price aspect and promotion budgeting is done simultaneously and departing from this an expected volume is estimated and following this, contribution is calculated depending upon fixed production costs and advertising and promotional costs. This process is repeated in an iterative process until an acceptable and "believable" budget is arrived at.

D. Media Group Comparisons

The choice of media groups to be used may partly be determined by overall considerations made in the budgeting process where the need for different kinds of support for other marketing activities may call for advertising towards retailers or in retailers' free newsletters, or for political or habitual reasons may call for the choice of media more or less linked with the advertiser.

In other situations the media group choice is made or guided by specialists in a media agency. In some instances the choice between media groups may be a simple: "TV or not TV?". However, with the increase in media agency involvement in strategic advertising planning, considerations as to how to reach different target groups or – even more complicated – different parts of the same target groups through different media are becoming increasingly common. And also a number of more qualitative factors play an important role in media group selection.

We shall discuss briefly 3 factors:

1. exposure situation for the medium
2. physical characteristics of the medium
3. qualitative media characteristics

The exposure situation differs widely between the different media. With television the consumer is more or less forced to be exposed on the condition that he is having the opportunity to see. He may still react defensively, reorienting his attention, zap away, leave the room or in other ways overlook the commercial. Thus the interaction between the commercial and the consumer in many cases is likely to be characterised by low attention perception and peripheral information processing and only rarely would we expect more extensive information processing to occur.

With radio listening the same applies though to an even larger extent. Most radio listening is a secondary activity and attention in the first place is low. Primary radio listening concentrate on news breaks, informative programmes, culture programmes etc. Here advertising occurs less frequently than in the combined talk- and music programmes that dominate radio used as a background factor.

With print the exposure situation is basically different. The amount of attention to give to any particular advertising is determined solely by the reader with access to the medium. He may choose to read the full ad with high attention, or he may choose to skip the page and maybe only observe enough of the advertising to decide to go on without paying more attention. Even here, however, some peripheral information processing occurs. When the reader does pay attention to the advertising, chances are that more central information processing results.

The basic problem in media group comparison remains that the value of an exposure is not the same across media groups and that value of exposures therefore are difficult to compare with an objective of allocating media spending rationally across media groups. In spite of this, the concept "Opportunity To See" (OTS) is critical in practical media planning, and is used together with GRP (or its target group equivalent: TRP) as an expression that conveys a sort of meaningful impression of, what a specific media group can produce in terms of reaching a consumer group.

The prime reason why it is impossible to compare media exposures across media groups have to do with the fact that the different media differ physically in many ways.

Television provides live pictures in colour with accompanying sound. Radio provides auditive stimuli alone – however visually suggestive they may be with clever use of the medium - print media visual stimuli alone. Then again print media present visual stimuli in very different manners. The production quality in a four colour exclusive magazine is very different from the reproduction in black and white in inexpensive retailers' free sheets.

When it comes to print, a very important decision to make when an advertiser chooses between different types of print media has to do with production cost versus the production quality. Particularly with freely distributed advertising this is a complex problem. The full range of reproduction techniques are used ranging from the multi colour product brochure printed on high quality paper for cars, and other durables, to simple black and white newspaper print, local news papers or retailers free sheets.

Some qualitative media characteristics relate to the environment in which the exposure occurs. Presence of noise and disturbing factors may vary widely. The concentrated newspaper reader is putting more mental energy into his reading than a relaxed television viewer, who is engaged in conversation simultaneously with watching the television; and the person passing by an outdoor poster seated in a city bus or driving a car may be even less concentrated in his attention.

Other qualitative media factors may reflect different values associated with different media, carrying over to the advertising effect of the media. The prestigious colour home magazines may provide a much better environment for the stylish furniture ad than the more chaotic environment of the daily tabloid newspaper.

The amount of time the publisher can document that the reader of the magazine spends on his publication is important, and so is the number of times it is taken up again for continued reading, and the length of time it stays in the household. Another important factor is the number of different individual readers a single issue accumulates. For daily newspapers it may be 2-3 individuals. For some expensive magazines the number may be as high as 8 to 10. With the copy moving from household to household the average number of individuals reading the issue increases. The same mechanism is at work with magazines that are the stock of waiting rooms or in hairdressing salons.

In practical media planning the choice of media group or media groups is usually made early in the process. Increasingly media planning is turning into a task of determining which parts of an overall target group may be reached by this medium and which part by that. Therefore the task of covering the target group appropriately consists in uncovering all relevant media touch points where the advertiser can place his message to reach consumers. Today these touch points are much more varied than 25 years ago, partly because of a proliferation of TV and radio channels, a proliferation of magazine titles, partly because of the basic trend towards more individualization amongst consumers and a corresponding explosive growth in the use of personalized media such as web sites and e-mail marketing. It would not make much sense to start with the creative work and then have that work guide the media strategy when the reality is, that developing a media strategy is in itself a crucial and complex exercise that may wind up with a plan consisting of the use of 5 different media groups, each requiring specific creative executions for the campaign to work in an integrated way. Assuming that an S shaped response function applies to the amount of money spent on each media group a certain minimum level of advertising in each particular media group chosen has to be allocated for it to be effective. Also there are fixed costs involved with and particular to each media group. The television production and creative costs are high, but also magazines and other print media will require some investments in creative work, and technical production of the material.

If we disregard the fixed cost involved in adding any particular media group to the media plan, we can apply the Dorfman-Steiner theorem to the solution of the problem.

This theorem suggests that in the optimal situation the elasticity of each of the different media in use should be equal to each other, and again should be equal to the ratio between contribution per unit and the price per unit.

The theoretically correct optimal plan for allocating a given budget between different media groups would entail starting with the media group providing the largest revenue per EURO spent and, assuming diminishing returns, continue to spend money on this medium until a level is reached where the response becomes lower than what could be obtained by allocating money to the second best media group. Continuing in this matter one should end up with the media plan with a budget divided between different media categories so that the return from additional spending on any one of these media groups is equal to that of the other media categories.

This relatively simple procedure, however disregards the two elements introduced earlier: There are initial fixed costs associated with selecting a media group and there may be increasing returns to increased spending with the first insertions in any given media group. That is they may exhibit an S-shaped response function.

So in addition to the rule of equal marginal return from each media group, one must also for each media group ask the question: Is it worthwhile to start spending on this group at all, considering the fixed cost involved and the minimum level of spending to be obtained before diminishing returns set in?

Another modifying factor relates to the previously discussed substitution and complementarity between different marketing activities. Just as we may discuss substitution and complementarity between advertising and price, we may do so in connection with the different media groups. Complementarity effects would mean that combining two media groups in one plan gives a larger effect than would be obtained by using the one group alone. This is often referred to as media synergy effects.

The television campaign may gain from the use of print because print enables the advertiser to convey other and more detailed information to the target group. Also print reaches different target groups and simply the effect of seeing the message in two different executions may have an added value in its own right.

Depending upon the way in which the measurement of the opportunity to see is operationalized in connection with different media, the actual time spent with the media may vary.

With television what has been measured is who are able to watch the television in the time interval where the commercial is being broadcasted. At the particular moment where the spot is on, other activities may occur. Actually it is not uncommon to find that 30% or more of those having opportunity to see actually do not for various reasons see a particular commercial.

They may be zapping, other temporary action in the room may have their attention or other tasks may be performed. The extent to which this occurs will vary with the number of factors such as availability of alternative channels, access to zapping facilities, the location of the commercials in or between the programmes, the length of commercial blocks, etc.

With print media, reading time is an important factor. Between different magazines the average number of minutes spent with the medium differs widely. Similar differences exist in other print media. More time is spent on daily newspapers than on the free local advertising newspapers, which again attract more time than the retailers' free sheets.

Another important factor to consider in evaluating different kinds of media is the number of exposures provided. The way in which opportunities to see are being measured in television means that each exposure event provides one and only one opportunity to see. In print media however the possibility exists to returning to the magazine and to read it on different occasions. Again here wide differences exist. For different magazines the average figure ranges from 1.5 numbers of readings to 3.0.

Another technically related aspect of the media effect has to do with the environment in which the exposure takes place. In principle exposure may take place at home, at work, with friends and at other locations than these. Television for any practical purpose always takes place at home, newspaper reading to a very large extent also, whereas radio listening, reading of many magazines and exposure to posters predominantly occur out of home, that is at work, with friends etc.

E. Campaign Execution

In the process of building the campaign 3 important steps can be identified:

- Message choice
- Basic campaign theme
- Individual executions

In all steps, a number of decisions are made of importance for the effect for the final campaign. It is not the purpose here to discuss this whole process. Rather we shall limit ourselves to some aspects that relate to the overall budgeting and campaign planning process.

As suggested earlier, in practice the 4 partial advertising decisions are made stepwise: Budget, media group choice, creative execution and campaign timing and scheduling are dealt with more or less independently. Important interactions however exist particularly between the campaign and its execution, the media group choice and the timing of the campaign. When media groups have been decided upon, major creative decisions are made by the same token.

If TV is chosen as part of the media mix, it almost turns the campaign planning into one centred on feasible TV executions first, and then campaigns in other media that may meaningfully be executed to relate to the TV campaign.

The ability to provide real full colour moving pictures with sound gives some unique creative possibilities that cannot be implemented with other media. If these are important for the particular message to be conveyed, this may in it self dictate the selection of television as the main media group of the campaign.

Other creative considerations may put emphasis on other media. When the need for reproduction in print of high technical quality is required, more expensive brochures or high quality magazines become obvious candidate choices. When the ability to relate the timing of the advertising clearly to the time of purchase, the choice of media that may reflect this are likely to be made: newspapers, free sheets, free distributed, local newspapers etc.

As we shall see in a later section the choice of creative strategy must be made in the light of the emotional meaning of the product and its competitive situation.

All in all, however, the creative decisions must be made with major attention directed to the media to be used so that the creative solutions play on the particularities inherent in each individual media group and media option.

F. Timing of Campaign or Scheduling

The media scheduling problem has to do with how the advertising budget is spread over time and single media within the same media group. Given the budget, the campaign itself and media group choices made the remaining but not least complicated part of the advertising budgeting process relates to timing or scheduling of insertions.

In the timing of the campaign (and in securing that it actually runs in accordance with the schedule) the specialized media agency in later years has become an important player. Seasonal patterns in demand, variations in media prices over the year, the need for specific advertising pressures in different sub periods are all factors considered.

In any given planning period two things have to be considered. Partly what effect does advertising carried out in the past have for the present situation, and partly what effect will the advertising we are paying for in this period have in subsequent periods – the carry-over effect.

A common way to cope with this problem in theory and in some practical applications is to assume that the effect of advertising in a given period deteriorates with a certain percentage, for instance the effect in a subsequent period is only 30% of that in the initial period. Eventually the effect in a third period may then be assumed to be 30% of that in the second etc. For computation of total advertising effect based upon this assumption a model – ADSTOCK – has been proposed by Broadbent (1999). This will be dealt with in more detail in the following chapter on ad effects.

One may use this way of thinking when looking upon daily, weekly, monthly, quarterly or annual advertising. Obviously the rate of forgetting is smaller, the shorter the time interval. If 98% of the effect on a particular day is maintained until the second day then we can calculate – with a constant rate of deterioration of the remaining advertising effect - that after a week only 80 % of the effect remains, and after a month it is reduced to 33 %. A common figure used to express this phenomenon is the advertising half-life. The half-life is the time that has to pass before half of the effect of the advertising has disappeared. We shall look into more of these concepts and their use in the next chapter.

With TV, consideration of half-life leads to a question about whether spots should be broadcasted continuously or in blocks and then in how many and how large blocks. It leads to a question about whether or not to concentrate in one TV channel or to spread the budget over more channels and it is a question of how to cope with seasonality, varying media prices, and over the year consideration of special events such as special offers, introductions of new features added to the product, Christmas etc. The same problems exist in connection with scheduling advertising in print media, in display media (posters, traffic signs etc.) radio, internet banners etc.

A basic issue in media planning is the trade-off between reach and frequency. This trade-off is essential, since reach has a cost and increasing reach increases the cost. Frequency similarly carries a cost and increasing frequency therefore also increases costs. With a fixed budget only certain combinations of reach and frequency are feasible because of the cost associated with each factor.

In media planning reach denotes the coverage of a population or a specified target group and which the campaign tries to impress. This is measured as a percentage of population or target group within the campaign period. Formally, reach is defined as the number of consumers exposed at least once in the campaign period as a percentage of all consumers. If only reach in a target group context is relevant, then target group reach becomes the percentage of target group members that are exposed at least once during the campaign period.

Frequency refers to the number of exposures or opportunities to see the consumer has in the campaign. Exposure frequency can be described either through a frequency distribution or as an average number of exposures for all consumers (in the target group). Both the frequency distribution and the average number of exposures are relevant to study in order to determine the effectiveness of a given media plan.

The frequency distribution, as shown in Figure VII.6, illustrates the dispersion of consumers across numbers of exposures – this is crucial, if it is believed that a certain minimum level of exposures (so-called effective frequency) is necessary for the campaign to achieve anything at all. The figures exemplify a situation where 20% of the population is not exposed, 15% is exposed once, 10% is exposed three times and so on. Furthermore the figure illustrates the assumption that frequencies below 3 and above 8 are ineffective and that the effective frequency lies between 3 and 8 exposures. Above that is regarded as excessive.

Figure VII.6: Example frequency distribution illustrating ineffective, effective and excessive frequencies

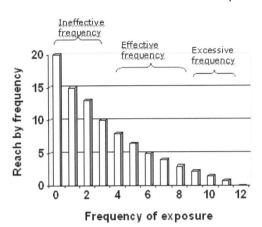

The average number of exposures yields easy information on how successful the trade-off between reach and frequency has been, particularly when comparing different media plans designed for the same target audience.

However, if effective frequency is an issue, the average number of exposures can be a very misleading metric – since a high average may be achieved by having 75% of the target group not being exposed or being exposed with less frequency than the effective frequency, and the remaining 25% being exposed with an extraordinarily high frequency. In Figure VII.6, for instance, the numbers illustrate that the plan has an average frequency of 2.93. However, only 36.5% are exposed with the effective frequency of between 3 and 8, so the illustrated plan does not seem frightfully efficient.

A frequently used measure is Gross Rating Point (GRP), where 1 gross rating point represents 1 percentage of the population being exposed once. Precisely the same metric can be applied in a target group context, where Target Group Rating Point (TRP) denotes 1 percentage of the target group being exposed once. Thus 150 GRP may mean that on the average all consumers have been exposed 1.5 times. GRP – or its equivalent TRP – function very well as a media planning metric that illustrates the power of alternative plans to deliver reach and frequency. The metric, however, does not say anything about how many are exposed at all. Any combination of numbers for reach and frequency that produce 150 as the result when they are multiplied will produce 150 GRPs. The reach may be only 50%, meaning that all exposed consumers are exposed on the average 3 times. The reach may be 75% with the average exposed person being exposed 2.

Both with regard to reach and frequency campaign planning becomes more complicated when more media groups are in use. The concern should then be to compare the reach and frequency properties of different media groups with each other in order to make meaningful allocation decisions. For instance print and TV may be compared by comparing GRP – or TRP – and their associated prices.

This, however, again raises the problem of media group comparisons, already introduced. There is no obvious way of comparing GRP's in different media groups, although computing the metric is deceptively simple, and just depends on a proper definition of what is perceived as an OTS. But in reality, the dilemma remains unsolved: Is a full page in four colours in a magazine equal to 60 or 30 seconds television exposure? Does effective frequency vary across media groups depending on the perceived instrumentality of the media options – reading a special interest magazine to one consumer may be a high-involvement pursuit meaning that one OTS automatically produces a frequency of one and that frequency is effective because of the high-involvement nature of the reading situation. The same consumer when exposed to the same message on a game-show TV channel may need a frequency of 8 for the exposure to be effective.

Assuming that in the market place prices tend to adjust to a competitive level, one might argue that the comparison should be made between the number of GRPs or TRPs delivered by say 50.000 Euros spent on television exposure with 50.000 Euros spent on print media exposure. The difference in delivery power as measured by GRPs between the two media groups would then be illustrative of the different efficiencies associated with the media groups' ability to deliver the message and to create an effect.

Gross Rating Points or Target Rating Points are used as a summary measure of the exposure weight that a given campaign has within the population or within the target group. The metrics may even be used as a measurement unit of what the advertiser wants to buy from a specific media option, for instance a TV channel. Rather than paying for a specific selection of spots at specific times (the way most TV advertising is sold in Denmark and also in some instances in international contexts, such as Super Bowl, FIFA World Championship transmissions, etc.), the advertiser may simply buy a certain number of gross or net rating points (the internationally most used way of selling air time on TV).

For GRPs or TRPs to be an accepted currency in media purchasing, the exact measurement of viewing of television programmes and commercials or reading of print media or radio listening becomes an important instrument in the media planning process. With television this may be done with electronic meters attached to the TV sets in a representative sample of households. With print media the traditional measurements are self-reported reading measurements one week – or in the case of magazines even longer – back. For radio self-reported measurements on what the individual remembers to have heard is the most commonly used measurement. But electronic measurements of radio listening are just around the corner.

For TV viewing, it stands to reason that an electronic meter – although it may report falsely: it may be on, but nobody is watching because they went to the kitchen or to the bathroom - is basically more precise as a measurement tool as a reliance on consumers' memory stretching 1 week or more back. In the case of radio, reliance on recall of programmes listened to certainly is inferior to some form of electronic measurements of, whether the car radio was turned on and what station it was tuned to.

In print readership surveys, it has been attempted (Randrup, 2004) to use SMS and mobile phones for questioning readers about their daily readership. The results are promising, providing print media with the same type of measurements of who and how many have been exposed today to a given commercial message that are known from the TV world. When thoroughly developed, this type of measurements of print media will enable advertisers to buy GRPs or TRPs from the publishers in more or less the same way that GRPs are bought from TV stations.

To illustrate the basic problems involved in media scheduling we shall look into an example of media planning. We have chosen to look upon a TV campaign. For many major advertisers this is the primary medium and in terms of available media planning data, the coverage data are available. The considerations applied here, however, apply as well with print and other media also.

Figure VII.7: Different TV media planning schedules

	Frontloaded	Balanced	Backloaded
Continuity			
Flighting / Bursting			
Pulsing			

Figure VII.7 illustrates the two dimensions in media scheduling, namely degree of continuity and placement of the media purchase across the planning period. With full continuity, the same amount of GRPs is bought in each small time period through the planning period. The advertiser's message is exposed every day – but maybe only to a small proportion of the audience, with a small reach. However, after the end of the planning period the assumption is that the necessary reach has been accumulated.

With full bursting, a number of GRPs are bought in a short period of time, then after a pause a similar number is bought again. This way, the advertiser attempts to ensure, that a high reach can be achieved during the periods, where he is active. Since budgets are limited, he has determined that he will not be able to achieve a continuous high reach, so he has to limit himself to on-off high reach.

The other dimension illustrates the model for concentration of effort across the planning period that the advertiser uses. With a balanced approach, the weight in the continuous or bursted spending is evenly spread across the whole planning period. With a frontloaded approach, more of the budget is spent at the beginning of the planning period and less at the end. The opposite solution is backloading as shown.

In campaign planning three major questions arises.

1. How large should the total advertising pressure be?
2. How should it be distributed over time particularly to what extent should burst or continuity be used?
3. Assuming that one exposure not always is enough for the campaign to have effect upon sales then exactly what is the optimal level of exposure for particular campaigns

Often the total campaign pressure largely has been determined in the stage where the total budget has been decided upon, and the actual is then concerned with maximizing the number of exposures, the reach or both within a given budget.

However, in some cases campaign goals may be formulated in terms of how much ad or brand awareness should be obtained or in terms of other communication variables. The basic question then becomes how much pressure is needed to assure that the goal is reached.

Also, in some instances when the possible effect of the particular scheduling is estimated, it may lead to reconsiderations on the budget with the purpose of increasing or reducing it.

The optimal exposure level, - optimal frequency – is a classical issue in media and advertising planning. A number of studies summarised by Napels (1997) suggest that often around three exposures between each purchase – or prior to each purchase - are needed to obtain the best results. The reasoning behind this argument can be illustrated as it is done in fig. VII.8

•

Figure VII.8: Response and exposure frequency distribution: X_1 – X_2 level of optimal frequency.

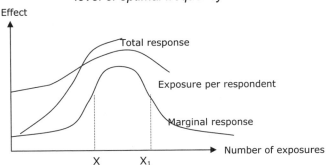

Here an inverted S-shaped response function for a particular product is illustrated. As long as the response function is progressively increasing with the value of each additional exposure the response increases – and more exposures should be added. When the response function begins to decrease, the opposite becomes the case.

The total effect of the campaign can be seen as a multiplication of the response and the exposure function. That is, one exposure gives the effect of the first exposure two exposures produce two times the effect of the second exposure etc. After a certain point the total effect decreases because the addition of more frequency does not offset the loss in effect of the additional frequency. The total effect of the campaign, as stated, can be seen as the product of the response effect curve and the exposure distribution. In a specific decision situation, the media planning problem is to determine that media plan and scheduling which maximises this product for a given budget.

To maximise the effect of exposures consists in creating a schedule where as many consumers as possible are being exposed within the interval where the response is the largest, and as few as possible are exposed either with very few (ineffective frequency) or with extremely many exposures (excessive frequency). (2-5 exposures in the diagram). This level defines the optimal level of exposures.

Here two considerations should be made. First the meaning of this whole argument depends very much upon what response is being measured. Often in practical media planning ad recall is measured, however in reality sales or sales contribution should be in focus. Maybe the optimal exposure level, when looking at ad recall, may be as low as 3-4, but when it comes to actual short-term sales effect, the level might be much higher.

Secondly, with a campaign with balanced continuity, a rather low exposure (Reach) level results. When campaigns using burst are chosen a higher reach results at the price of the average number of exposure per customer across the planning period. In the extreme a very high reach will result in campaigns being concentrated in very few periods. This leads us to the standing debate of reach versus frequency.

Some researchers have argued (Ephron, 1988) that advertising exposure should always be as close in time to the following purchase. The so-called recency principle of exposure. In reality this in many instances leads to scheduling coming close to a continuous plan. This is particularly the case with FMCGs, which can be assumed to be bought regularly and with short intervals. For this reason, the recency principle would lead the advertiser to advertise continuously, since there are always consumers close to a purchase incident. Other researchers (Jones 1995, Broadbent, 1999) have argued that the effect of the additional exposures following the first (within a one week planning period) decreases so much that one should rarely plan for more than one exposure prior to each purchase.

Much frequency planning rests upon opportunities to see or GRPs. Here it should be remembered however, that exposure in terms of opportunity to see is not the same as the kind of exposure used in many effect studies, where the response may be ad recall or even actual sales. To obtain ad recall corresponding to a certain optimal frequency may require more than one OTS because not all opportunities to see in reality mature into actual exposure, thereby generating ad recall. In the same way the kind of exposure needed for generating a short-term sales effect may be even higher in terms of average exposure frequency.

This whole debate has been on a general level and often with primarily fast moving consuming goods in mind. Thus whatever conclusions one may favour, they have to be modified by considerations that are relevant to the actual products or services being advertised. With campaigns where newness is introduced some studies show (Waring, 2005) that a much lower effective frequency is necessary than when an advertiser seeks to achieve a sales increase of an established product in a mature market.

A number of confounding matters may also influence the straightforward effective frequency planning. There may be a high campaign complexity, with interaction between media groups and between marketing mix elements such as advertising and promotions, both retailer and consumer, and the target group's viewing pattern in general (it is generally believed that heavy viewers require more exposures for the same effect to occur).

Also variations in media prices over the year may enter into the final planning, since advertising for non-seasonal goods may take advantage of cheaper media prices, typically during high summer or in February, where conventional wisdom has it, that no consumers will react to advertising. Either because they are busy lying on the beach or because they are depressed after Christmas and January sale periods and have no money left to spend.

This complexity, which unfortunately is the rule in practical advertising rather than the exception, requires either very astute decision makers with highly developed intuitions or sophisticated planning systems and modeling of advertising effects. The profile of the most efficient media planners at the media agencies tends to combine these two sets of skills. For the remaining readers, a detailed account of how to approach this very complex process can be found in Broadbent (1999).

G. Summary
The chapter illustrates that most decisions taken in connection with advertising – and in a broader scope, all promotional and marketing – planning, may rest on mathematically formulated conditions of optimality when it comes to determining the amount of spending. In practical life, this is rarely done, and the reason most often cited for this is lack of reliable data. However, more and more companies have the possibility of accessing large amounts of data that might be used for modeling and the optimisation discussion in the chapter should serve as an inspiration to such modeling to arrive at better decisions. In practical advertising planning, the four sets of decisions outlined in the chapter are usually decided upon individually, since that more or less is the only way to go about such planning, but unless the decision maker has excellent intuition or access to extensive and well structured past experience, the resulting decisions in all likelihood are suboptimal. Knowledge about what is known of advertising's effects will provide good guidance – and that is the topic of the next two chapters.

Chapter VIII

Econometric Modeling and Short Term Effects of Advertising

CHAPTER OUTLINE
This chapter deals with empirical evidence on how advertising works – in the meaning: what types of sales effects can be expected from a given advertising effort. The chapter covers three basic approaches to estimating advertising effects: econometric modeling, estimation of advertising elasticities and response modeling based on interview data.

The second part of the chapter deals primarily with estimating short term effects of advertising on sales and does so primarily through studies employing single-source data, where simultaneous data are available on individuals' media exposure (primarily TV) and brand purchases. This part deals with various aspects of short term effects, such as effects of promotions together with advertising, measurement of advertising retention rates and estimation of advertising elasticities through measurement of half-lives of advertising.

The last part of the chapter deals with an interview-based approach to generating data that are similar in form to single-source data in markets where single-source data are unavailable.

CHAPTER OBJECTIVE
Our objective with this chapter is to provide the reader with empirical evidence as to several advertising effects that have been determined in elaborate studies under varying conditions. When an advertiser is aware of the size and nature of these effects, he can employ them in decision situations as supporting arguments for budget determination in the absence of the his own numbers. It is our aim to supply the decision maker with a frame of reference as to short term effects of advertising that can be expected as well as with inspiration as to how he can develop his own measurements.

A. Approaches to the Study of Advertising Effects
In the preceding chapter we have tried to summarize the conditions for optimal advertising as it appears in economic theory. Following this we have briefly outlined the procedures that companies generally apply in the process of budgeting advertising. Throughout this discussion it has become evident that much is not understood about the effects of advertising and an increased knowledge of this is mandatory for better advertising management.

Particularly the effect of advertising upon sales has been difficult to estimate. However in more recent years, the availability of single source data has created a renewed interest in these relationships. In this chapter we shall present some of the findings published. In more recent literature on advertising effects it has become common to make a distinction between short, medium and long-term effects. We shall adhere to this practice here.

1. Econometric Modeling at the Aggregate Level

As suggested earlier, the success in quantifying the effect of advertising upon sales with the use of econometric modeling has been limited. Time series of such a length that meaningful estimates can be made are rarely available and when cross-geographical data is used it is hard to find enough comparable regions. Among published studies the few available where either the role of other factors than advertising have been limited or where the number of observations has been large enough to allow for more variables to be included in the study have been made.

The classical long-term study is based upon the Lydia Pinkham data (Palda, 1964). The company's sales of a non-prescription medical product and advertising expenditures have been made available from 1907-1960. The data is illustrated in Figure VIII.1.

Figure VIII.1:   Sales and Advertising for Lydia Pinkham 1907-60 (Palda, 1964).

The market situation has been characterized by the limited importance of other action parameters than advertising and by limited competitive activities. The model describing the relationship appears as follows:

Equation VIII.1 $S_t = 396 + 39 S_{t-1} + 27 A_t + 16 A_{t-1} + 16 A_{t-2}$

S_t is Sales in periods and A_t is "Advertising" in period "t". Advertising is estimated to influence sales together with actual sales in the preceding period and it does so for three periods with a diminishing effect. It is noteworthy in this case that if long-term effects are seen as those appearing after the first year, this effect (2nd + 3rd years) is (16+16) larger than the combined short (one month) and medium term (the following 11 months) (27). Also effects after the third year are not traceable in the data. This is in contrast with the observation that advertising for brands no longer in existence may still work and can be exploited – the cases of so-called petrified demand. Other academic findings are reviewed in Assmus et al. (1984).

Even though internal applications are made in larger companies with good statistics available on sales, advertising, pricing, competitor activities etc., few findings are published. Exceptions can be found however, for instance (Assmus et al., 1984) shows how short time changes in prices advertising and promotion has long term effects on advertising. In such studies, the number of periods to be analysed is increased by using periods shorter than a year (quarters, months, weeks or days), but the seasonality (yearly, monthly, weekly) must be considered. One such case is published by Croone and Horsfall (1983) for Kellogg's Super Noodles in the UK using 4-weeks data from February 1980 to February 1982. They suggested a model to explain sales that works as follows:

Equation VIII.2   Sales = $\beta0 + \beta1$ (adstock) + $\beta2$ (price) + $\beta3$ (distribution)

The Adstock is the computed aggregate effect of past advertising (see Equation VIII.6). The last two variables are obtained from retail audit data, and the advertising effect is introduced through the ad stock variable (expressing the carry-over effect of advertising in previous periods). With the three variables ad stock, price and distribution, 84% of the variation in sales is explained.

Considering that the model does not include competitive activities or other disturbing factors in the market, the result is good. One may wonder that loyalty in terms influence of last years sale does not appear among the explaining variables. Maybe at the appropriate level these effects, known from other studies (first and foremost Palda's described above) is picked up by advertising and distribution effects, since these variables may in themselves be correlated with last year's sales.

Nilsson and Olsen (1993) used a similar model for a Danish brand of cereal. Here season, trend, relative price, advertising, distribution and in-store promotion were among the independent variables. A further development of this model is found in Olsen and Hansen (2002). A number of cases of this nature appear in the "Advertising Works" series. Unfortunately attempts to generalise findings from these several hundred British cases has never been published. With fewer, but Danish cases, a similar attempt is being made within the Center for Marketing Communication at the Copenhagen Business School in cooperation with The Danish Advertising Agency Association.

In line with these findings are results from experiments testing the effect of advertising. An early version of this is published by Ackoff and Emshoff (1975). For Anheuser-Busch in the US they carried out a number of experiments testing effects of varying advertising pressure. They tested the effect of increasing advertising expenditures up to 3 times and down to zero from current level. For the beer brand in question they found that advertising could be reduced by almost two thirds when a flighting schedule approach was used. When advertising was completely eliminated some long term effects (after one year) appeared. Similar findings are reported by Aaker and Carman (1982). They experimented on frequently advertised fast moving goods. Also they found that for the brands studied some reduction in advertising spending was warranted, and only half of that increasing advertising found stimulated sales sufficiently to warrant the added spending. Other early experimental results from studies varying the advertising pressure are reported in Eastlack and Rao (1989) who conducted 19 experiments for Campbell soup. Again here the results were ambiguous and only in one third of the cases there were significant sales increases resulting from added spending. Of interest is also the result that on the whole variations in advertising executions had greater effects than variations in advertising scheduling. Undoubtedly their results should be seen in the light that they relate to an existing fmcg in stable markets. As discussed in Chapter VII advertising when used with new products or containing new product features work differently.

2. Estimating Advertising Elasticities

As discussed earlier estimation of advertising elasticities are rare, but with increased access to single source data such estimates become feasible. In a study by Assmus et al. (1984) reviewing 128 econometric models they find average elasticities around 0.2 with higher sensitivity for food as compared to other products. In a meta analyses of advertising elasticities from 260 studies Sethuraman and Tellis (1991) find an average elasticity across all cases of 0.11. These authors also found differences between durables and non-durables with highest sensitivity for non-durables.

Both Assmus et al. (1984) and Sethuraman and Tellis (1991) report higher elasticities in Europe as compared with US.

Interesting findings are also reported by Abraham and Lodish (1999). Based on Behaviour Scan US electronic single source data effects of different campaigns are reported for up to two years after the campaign start. The Behaviour Scan technology provides continuous registration of recent purchases and TV exposure data in different test cities. As with STAS and similar data they find from 360 Behaviour Scan cases that not more than 50% of the cases show a significant change in the sales. Moreover, the difference between established and new brands is found again with 59% of the new products' campaign showing an impact on sales against 45% among established brands. 76% of this effect is still found in the second year and very little is found in the third year. Other findings from the same source are reported in Lodish et al. (1995). Here average advertising elasticities are computed for 141 brands. Again, we find the different average effect for new vs. established products. The results are illustrated in Table VIII.1.

Table VIII.1: Average percent measure in sales across 15 cases (Lodish et al., 1995)

	N	Average elasticity	Std. Deviation	Std. Deviation of the average
All tests	141	.13**	.40	.03
New products	52	.26**	.49	.07
Established products	89	.05	.32	.03

** significantly different from zero

More general discussions of quantitative models and their application in connection with advertising and other marketing variables are available in Lillien et al. (1992) and Hanssen and Parsons (1993).

Published findings derived from econometric data rarely relate to single campaigns or short period advertising planning. Rather, they help the company throw light on more basic strategic decisions regarding the balancing of the different action parameters or marketing mix variables, such as price, assortment, advertising, promotion and distribution. A review of published studies is found in Tellis (2003).

The econometric modeling normally works with aggregate data and time series that are fairly long. For these reasons, econometric modeling rarely provides support for tactical decisions. Information to support the tactical decisions has to come from advertising response modeling. Here individual companies model sales for shorter time intervals. Specific findings from such approaches are rarely published but considered proprietary for the company or its advisers. Companies specialising in advising on such modeling are emerging. For descriptions of these works, see Ambach (2005).

3. Advertising Response Modeling with Interview Data at the Individual Level

In contrast to analysis based upon aggregated data, data collected at the individual level provide information that is much more sensitive to changes in advertising spending and in advertising content. Such data lend themselves easily to modeling. The methods used for such approaches normally cover 1-3 or more years of data repeated on weekly or monthly basis. Sales may come from the company's own files or from Nielsen Retail Panel data. Other data included are Advertising Spending from own data and/or specialised agencies generating advertising data on media and brands like TNS, Media Intelligence. Also prices and distribution are covered and other product relevant data such as temperature, seasonality etc. may be included. Public reporting of these attempts is practically always only concerned with methodology and only shows illustrative examples of findings. Single cases can occasionally be found in the Advertising Works publications mentioned earlier.

Sometimes, the validity of measures such as ad recall, ad evaluation, message understanding, self-reported purchases etc is low. Sometimes they are uncertain as indicators of the overall effect of advertising.

Brand preferences and brand awareness are probably more closely related to long-term market behaviour than attitudes towards the ad, ad awareness or ability to recall specific elements from the advertising message. But on the other hand, these latter measures are generally more sensitive to short term changes in advertising, so post-test data of this kind are attractive for tracking modeling.

In advertising response tracking, the dependent variable must be seen as an intervening variable between sales and exposure. The sales effect itself can rarely be used. Most frequently, ad-recall or recall of specific campaign elements is used. When this is the case, the critical assumption is that the ad-awareness somehow relates to sales.

Evidence to suggest that this may be the case is available. Hollis (1992) demonstrated a relationship between Millward Brown's awareness index (a measure established individually for each campaign reflecting its ability to generate awareness) and subsequent sales. For 70 US brands and 235 executions, Hollis found a significant short-term sales effect in 54% of the cases.

When the data is averaged for brands, when the focus is upon fast-moving consumer goods and when new introductions are excluded, some relationships between ad awareness and sales are demonstrated. Early such evidence was reported by Broadbent (1984). Here, ad-stock rather than ad-awareness is related to subsequent sales. Haley and Baldinger (1991), using pre-test data, also demonstrated such an effect – but they also repeat that this is not always found and it only explains variations in sales moderately well. Other variables such as liking and persuasion have a similar impact on the sales results in their controlled experiments. Later, Jones and Blair (1996) and Jones (1998) show similar evidence. On the whole, it is safe to assume that various pre-tests and tracking measures of intervening advertising effects somehow relate to subsequent sales, but much more knowledge about the specific nature of these relationships and their limitations is required. Particularly data on the role of variables reflecting peripheral information processing are lagging such as measures of changes in emotions.

Systematic studies of the relationship between variables intervening between advertising exposure and sales on the one hand, and tracking of the exposure on the other have found widespread use. Many syndicated tracking services that have developed since the 1970s provide such modeling opportunities. It is beyond the scope of the present chapter to cover all the different versions of models applied in detail. Rather, a thorough treatment is found in Broadbent (1999). Here, we limit ourselves to a brief description of the type of modeling going on, illustrated with a few selected examples.

Many ad response models are derived from the adstock concept, introduced by Broadbent (1979). These models stem from earlier response models such as the one used to describe the Lydia Pinkham data (Palda, 1969).

In this formulation, one assumes a decreasing influence from advertising in earlier periods, which can be described as a distributed lag model. A common version of this the geometrical lag structure model is formulated by Koyck (1954):

Equation VIII.3   RESPONSE$_t$ = $\beta_0{}^*$ + r (response$_{t-1}$)+ β_1Ad$_t$

where $\beta_0{}^* = \beta_0(1-r)$ and r is the Retention Rate and β_0 is the effect of the advertising (Ad)

In this way, the response in period t is described as a function of the accumulated effect in the previous periods and the advertising in the period t. In any period, the effect retained from previous periods is r. Therefore, the parameter r has been named the advertising retention rate, and the converse (1-r), the advertising forgetting rate. β reflects the effect of advertising. For a discussion of its estimation, see Hanssen and Parsons (1993).

In the above formula, the relationship between advertising and effect is linear. Many authors have argued for a diminishing return function or an S shaped response function (McDonald, 1995, 1997b; Napels, 1997; Gullen and Johnson, 1986; Jones, 1995). Empirical studies (Waring, 2005) indicate that the form of the response function varies depending on the type of product being advertised.

In advertising response studies, the independent variable, advertising, may be measured in terms of budget, gross rating points, adstock, or other meaningful expressions for the amount of advertising.

Many ad-tracking systems work with such models. Important contributions have been reported from Millward Brown International (Hollis, 1992; Dyson et al., 1996). Here, the effect most frequently measured is ad awareness, but brand awareness and claimed recall of specific advertising elements are also used. These variables, more sensitive to advertising exposure, are used where the final effect upon sales is difficult to trace. In commercial applications, model specifications are often not given, rather findings are reported in terms of plots of actual and predicted variables. Many such examples have been published. They may take on the same form as shown in Figure VIII.2.

Figure VIII.2: Millward Brown's modeling case using ad awareness as the dependent variable, and Gross Rating Points (GRP) as the independent variable with pure level and awareness in dexes as parameters (Martensen et al., 2001, p. 196)

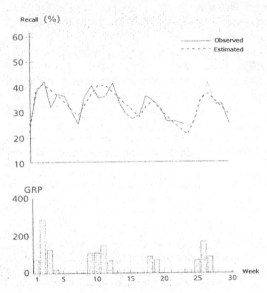

Also working with advertising recall as the dependent variable, Rice and Davis (1993) showed findings based upon a model for a diminishing return response function. A generalized version of this model using other variables than recall as the dependent variables has been tested on Danish television campaigns by Grønholdt (1996).

B. Short Term Effects

1. Modeling at the Level of the Individual Respondent with Single Source Data

The attempts to quantify the effect of advertising using different kinds of marketing research data described so far have not worked well with purchase and media exposure data, either because the data have been too aggregate to build meaningful models or because the data have not been causally linked, that is exposure data and sales data have been collected independently of each other. Also the absence of variables that may reflect peripheral information processing is a drawback.

When sales have been considered, it has been at the aggregate level. When sales data are available at the individual level, more sensitive data analyses can be carried out. Single source data can be used for this. Again, published studies are scarce, but experience is building up among major advertisers. McDonald (1969) reported a classical study. Here, information about media exposure was collected from respondents for whom regular consumer panel data was also available. This made it possible to study the relationship between one purchase and media exposure since the previous purchase.

The propensity of panel members to switch to another brand, or not to switch away (i.e. stay `loyal'), was found to be related to whether or not there had been opportunities to see advertising for the brand (OTS) since the previous purchase. In this analysis, McDonald found different effects in different product categories and a tendency towards diminishing returns in general resulting from an increasing number of OTS.

Later, Gullen and Johnson (1986) have replicated these findings and also observe considerable effects of sales promotions. Similarly Tellis (1988a) in a study of toilet tissue find only small effects of advertising as compared with effects of sales promotion. Moreover he also found loyalty to play a role and the return to be decreasing with increased advertising pressure. Similar relationships appear in more recent studies based upon more contemporary single source data (Jones, 1995, McDonald, 1995, and Hansen et al., 2002). In this connection Jones' (1995) Short Term Advertising Strength concept (STAS) is important. The STAS measure of advertising effect expresses the short-term effect of advertising by comparing purchase response among people exposed to advertising within the last seven days with the purchase response among those not exposed. The higher this ratio, the larger the short term effect.

Equation VIII.4

STAS =   <u>Market share among those exposed * 100</u>
              Market share among those not exposed

Working with Nielsen U.S.- Household Panel Data combining bar code scanned purchase data and people's media exposure, measured as registered television viewing, Jones analysed brands in twelve categories over twelve months. For these twelve categories for 78 brands, the STAS scores are shown in Table VIII.2.

Table VIII.2: STAS scores from Jones (1995) and other sources by quintile.

	US	UK	Germany
Top	236	184	154
Ninth	164	129	127
Eight	139	119	116
Seventh	121	114	108
Sixth	116	110	106
Fifth	108	107	101
Fourth	103	102	100
Third	97	98	98
Second	89	93	92
Bottom	73	73	83

Similar findings were also reported for the UK by McDonald (1995 and 1996) with data for 9 product categories based upon a JWT panel (see again Figure VIII.3) and for 68 brands in 5 categories based on Ad lab panel data from Taylor-Nelson. Later, Jagger (1998) also shows the same distribution based on German GfK-data (Table VIII.2). Finally in Germany Wildner and Kindelmann (1997) find STAS effects to be larger with medium size households and to diminish with the extent of competing advertising.

Since STAS scores significantly higher than 100 reflect effect of advertising on sales, the overall picture derived from this is that in only around half or a little more of the cases a significant short term effect is found, and quite a few negative effects are documented. The old saying springs to mind: *"Half of our advertising works, half is wasted. If only we knew which half is wasted!"*(Quoted to Lord Liverholme, Unilever in the 1920'ies).

One problem with these data (Naples, 1997) is that nothing is known about the number of exposures in the period preceding purchase. However, using data from a J. Walter Thomson panel covering nine categories (the data originally analysed by McDonald), Jones and Blair (1996) published findings showing STAS calculations for 0,1,2,3, and 4 OTS in the four days preceding the purchase. The findings suggest a relatively small contribution by the second and following OTS compared to the first. Similar data published by Roberts (1998) show the same. These findings are shown in Figure VIII.3 and similar results are reported by Pedrick and Zufryden (1991) in a study of 3 years of single source data for yoghurt.

Figure VIII.3: Effects of 1, 2+ exposures within a 4-day period (Roberts, 1998, exhibit 4)

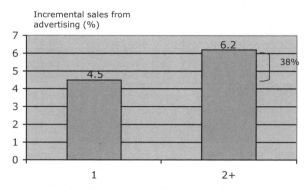

Incremental sales from advertising (%)

Number of exposures in 3-days period prior to purchase

Two aspects of the STAS measure in particular have been discussed. First, using a constant period of seven days for the analysis may provide different results for products with varying purchase cycles. That is, brands purchased very frequently may respond very differently to weekly exposures as compared with brands purchased much less frequently. Secondly, it has been argued that by only taking exposures in a single week prior to the purchase into consideration, you ignore all influence from earlier exposures, such as done by the adstock effects discussed earlier.

As previously mentioned, McDonald (1996) basically confirmed the usefulness of the STAS measure with the British Adlab data, but also pointed out the importance of other factors that may influence this effect measure. Thus, using the British Adlab panel, McDonald (1997b) shows evidence that the STAS is affected by "purchase-viewing bias" in cases where a brand is bought more by heavy than by light TV viewers or vice versa. This point of view has also been put forward by Broadbent (1998), but is found to have only moderate effects in Hansen et al. (2002).

In an attempt to look into some of the problems discussed with the STAS measure, Schroeder et al. (1997) report findings for seven brands tested with Behaviour Scan, each in two or more test markets. Here, the time of exposure was fixed and STAS for purchases on subsequent days were computed. The STAS score naturally decreases with extended time lags between exposure and purchase, but still after 4 days significant effects are found. Their study also focused on the complexity of the STAS data. Thus, it is suggested that the inclusion of more variables into the explanation of STAS effect scores makes sense. In contrast with Jones' "one exposure is enough" claim, they found that reach is rather negatively related to the STAS measure, and in particular they found important interactions with promotions and a need for more complex modeling with data on the individual level.

Similar data reported by Roberts (1998) are shown in Figure VIII.4 giving a detailed picture of the effects following exposure. They also demonstrate the sensitivity of the STAS measures to the length of the period with exposure prior to the purchase analyzed.

Figure VIII.4:   STAS measures following exposure on a particular day (Roberts, 1998)

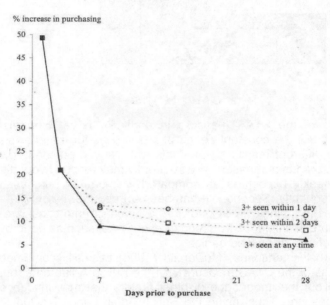

More general modeling of single source data is discussed by Broadbent et al. (1997), who points to the importance of factors such as relative price, competitive activities, quality of own ads etc. In concluding his discussion, he writes: "it is a tragedy that the richness of the information in single source has seldom been tapped, there is so much more in the panels than brand last purchased and saw in last week... So the application of response functions and effective frequencies seems to us to be only part of scheduling decisions for media campaign... We suggest that we spend less time reanalysing and reinventing a media construct developed before single-source data were available, and more time exploring the dynamics of how advertising works under the spotlight of single-source analyses". This view is supported by Ehrenberg and Barnard (1994).

Findings inspired by these and similar observations are provided by Roberts (1997) and Roberts (1999). Using Taylor Nelson Super panel data combined with viewing data from Meridian Television, they studied the relationship between share of purchases and the number of exposures prior to purchase. While they confirmed the overall picture emerging from other studies with somewhat longer lasting effects, they also documented the influence of promotional activities, competitive advertising, scheduling and viewer habits. These data come from 750 super panel homes equipped with TV-meters providing single source data from 1995 to 1999, where 113 brands in 10 FMCG categories were analysed. The idea underlying this analysis is shown in Figure VIII.5.

Figure VIII.5: Contingency table analysis (Roberts, 1998, exhibit 1)

The author writes:

> *"The number of brand purchases made by households who saw advertising is tested against their expected number of purchases. This expectation is derived from the share of brand purchases made when no advertising had been seen within the last 28 days. If advertising has no effect, then, all other things being equal, we should expect the share of brand purchases to be the same for both those who saw advertising and those who did not. Any positive difference, which is statistically significant, can then be considered as the incremental purchasing generated by advertising."*

In the analysis described above, "the percentage difference in brand purchasing was calculated for all market purchases where the household had seen at least one advertisement in a defined 'window' of time prior to purchase, compared with purchases that occurred when advertising had not been seen for at least 28 days."

The analysis was repeated by extending the definition of the time window to cover 1, 3, 7, 14 and 28 days prior to the market purchase occasion. Figure VIII.6 shows the results.

Figure VIII.6: Duration of short-term effects (Roberts, 1998, Exhibit 3)

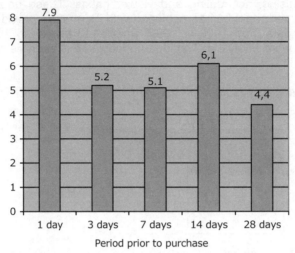

Incremental sales
from advertising (%)

Period prior to purchase

Not surprisingly, the greatest increase (7.9 %) is associated with pur-chases when the household was exposed to advertising within the previous day. However, as the window of the prior period is ex-tended, there is only a relatively small decline in the percentage in-crease, and those purchases associated with seeing advertising at some time within the last 28 days show an increase of 5.2 %.

Another way of looking at this is to calculate how much effect can be documented resulting from exposures in different time intervals. Roberts writes:

"Clearly advertising does continue to influence consumers' purchasing for some time after the last exposure was seen. The data here are best fitted by an exponential curve that de-cays at a rate of 4.4 % per day, indicating a half-life of about 16 days. This of course implies that advertising will continue to influence consumers' purchases in the short term beyond the 28-day limit imposed by the contingency table analyses. At a decay rate of 4.4 % per day only 72 % of the full effect of ad-vertising will occur within the first 28 days."

The nature of short term advertising effects is also spelled out clearly when the length of the exposure interval and the number of expo-sures are varied simultaneously (Figure VIII.7)

Figure VIII.7: Effect of frequency of exposure

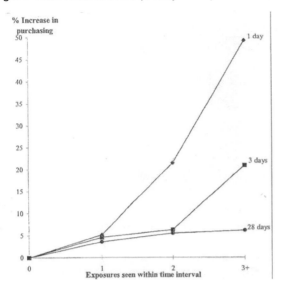

The classical (Napels, 1997) observation derived from studies of op-timal exposure frequency is brought out again. The second and the third exposure within a short time interval have more effect than the first. One may speculate, that what happens is, that the message does not get across with a majority of the audience until the 2nd ad 3rd exposure within the short time interval. With only one or two expo-sures, many do not really get to pay sufficient attention to the ad – or the message does not imprint itself sufficiently on memory for action to take place. These early findings are replicated in a later study based on more than 5 million purchases reported in the TNS Super-panel single source data from 2001-2003. Beaumont (2003) reports findings from this enlarged sample which largely confirms the findings already reported by Roberts (1998), but because of the larger sample and more brands included she and later Waring (2005) are able to add important insight into the short-term effects of advertising.

They are able to look for differences in the effects in different product categories. They find the low-loyals to be by far the most in-fluenced by advertising (Figure VIII.8). An observation made earlier by Deighton et al. (1994) and later replicated by Hansen et al. (2006a).

Figure VIII.8: Low loyal purchasers are more responsive to adverti-sing (Beaumont, 2003)

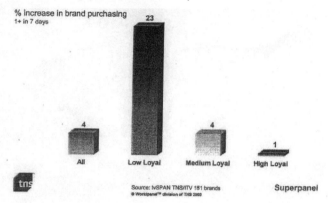

They also look at companies divided into "Launch", "Innova-tion/newness" and "Maintenance" – or in our terminology, competitive advertising. Her findings are impressive and strongly confirm our ear-lier suggestion, that central and more effective information processing occurs more often depending on the degree of newness in the cam-paign (Figure VIII.9). An observation which is also in line with the re-sult regarding elasticities computed from econometric analysis re-viewed earlier in this chapter.

Figure VIII.9: Wide variation on sales uplifts attributable to TV adver-tising for individual brands (Waring, 2005)

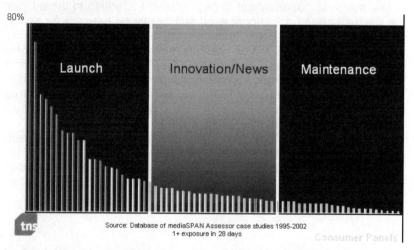

In line with this Beaumont reports findings on optimal frequency. Fewer exposures are needed to obtain the same effects with an in-creased degree of newness in the campaign (Figure VIII.10).

Figure VIII.10: Effects of first and subsequent exposures for different kinds of campaigns (Waring, 2005)

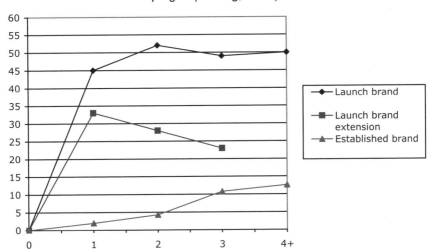

An important issue in contemporary media planning was touched upon in Chapter VII (Figure VII.X), namely the issue of the relative advantages and disadvantages of burst, continuity and pulsing as a media scheduling strategies. Here Waring (2005) finds very different results for companies in the grocery category. The results are shown in Table VIII.3. On average, the pulsing strategy seems preferable. But other factors should be considered also in the planning. Among these are the degree of newness as discussed before, seasonality in demand and in media prices, the nature of the target group as loyals or not, heavy viewers or not, etc.

As an added thought, pulsing does combine the advantages of continuity that is exposure close to the actual purchase, with burst, where high visibility is ensured through a short-term increase in share-of-voice. This might be the reason why pulsing seemingly is the most efficient strategy: It actually consists of elements of the two basic strategies simultaneously.

Table VIII.3: Schedule delivery for Grocery category – no seasonality (Beaumont, 2003)

% market purchase covered by:	(a) Continuous	(b) Bursts	(c) Pulsing
1+ exposures in prior 28 days	70.0	45.2	71.3
Concentrated exposures	1.0	4.4	8.6
Recent & concentrated exposure	.8	2.3	2.8

2. Purchase-Viewing Bias

Broadbent (1999, pp. 149-153) and McDonald (1997b) have worked with the idea that there is a relationship between media usage and purchase behaviour: a so-called Purchase-Viewing bias (P-V bias). McDonald writes (1997b, p. 24):

"A Purchase-Viewing bias occurs if a brand is bought more (or less) heavily by heavy television viewers than by light television viewers, so that occasions preceded by advertising come from one group more than they do from the other group"

The P-V index is computed as the share of purchases with prior advertising among the heavy media users, divided by the share of purchases with prior advertising among the low media users.

If the P-V index is greater than 100, the brand's share of purchase occasions among the heavy media users is larger than among the low media users. However, if the index is smaller than 100, this indicates that the brand-share purchase is larger among the low media users. Broadbent (1999, p. 150) has illustrated these scenarios by an example:

"Take Bird's Mild Coffee, and compare this with Nestlé's Gold Blend, a rather bitter 'coffee-lovers' brand. Because of the demographics of buyers of these brands – and of television viewers – it happens that the Purchase/Viewing index for Mild coffee is above one, or positive. People who prefer Bird's Mild Coffee are older, downgrade and watch more commercial television than average. But the index for Gold Blend is below one (negative). That is, people who prefer the bitter coffee are younger, more upgrade and watch less commercial TV."

It is interesting to learn that a P-V index smaller than 100 can be explained by studying the demographics of the purchasers of the two coffee brands. This example therefore suggests that simply monitoring the media-usage is not enough; it is necessary either to include other variables in the analysis or to get a more detailed description of the situation at the time of purchase or to seek explanations for unexpected results.

Broadbent et al. (1997) have also studied the P-V bias situation and found that in every case they had looked at, an explanation for the bias could be found in the demographics of the respondents. From their study, they concluded that the weight of viewing should not be neglected as a factor that influences the result of the STAS calculations.

Some preliminary studies of a P-V bias with the datasets from the Adlab database have been done (Hansen and Hansen, 2001b). Here, it was found that the P-V bias plays a minor role in influencing the effect scores. More important for explaining the effect is the occurrence of deals, offers and other promotion activities.

Based on French and German data, Jagger (1998) points out that exposed people basically differ from unexposed people in terms of usage pattern, media, exposure and values. This, in turn, may account for some of the differences in effect ascribed to the advertising exposure per se. Also, Jagger emphasizes the importance of interaction with in-store activities, suggesting very strong effect measures for campaigns appearing simultaneously with deals and the like. And he emphasizes the importance of competition and suggests the use of some measure of share of advertising (or share of exposure) rather than exposure per se.

3. Promotion and other Effects

Roberts (1998) reports evidence for FMCG brands confirming the importance of looking at the data in relation to other marketing activities, particularly in-store activities, competitive advertising and user and media habits. In contrast with Ehrenberg and Scriven's (1997) emphasis on reinforcement, he found stronger short-term effects among low loyals than among high loyals. He also found stronger effects among heavy users than among light users, and he found stronger effects from peak hour exposures than from off peak hour advertising.

Finally, Roberts digs into the duration over time of the effects, and suggests that the 7-day interval used in the STAS measure may be quite meaningful, but that a 3-day or a 2-week interval could have been used yielding the same results. Similarly, he looks into the effect of more exposures, and in contrast to the simple STAS findings, he suggests an additional effect from two or more exposures within 3 days or less prior to the purchase.

There has been some debate (Lodish et al., 1995) as to whether or not the STAS measure is a realistic way of describing the effects of advertising. It can be argued that STAS is too simple in its current form, and takes too few variables into consideration, for example it does not consider promotion, pricing, competing activities or prior advertising.

Lodish et al. (1995) argues the importance of correcting the data for biases due to e.g. the promotion activity being different in different shops, pricing and competing activities. Another argument by Lodish et al. (1995) is, that one may question the fairness of giving all of the one week advertising similar weight in estimating the effect of advertising and disregarding all previous advertising. A third point Lodish et al. (1995) brings up is the loyalty-question. If a household is loyal to a particular brand, how large an effect will the advertising for this brand really have – the household would most likely have purchased the brand anyway.

4. STAS and Logit Modeling

A study looking for ways alternative to the STAS to measure short-term advertising effects a study is reported by Hansen et al. (2002b). Their analysis is based on the British Adlab single source database. This study is reported here in some detail.

Adlab is a diary-based, single source panel, which was set up by Central Independent Television in September 1985 and ran through to March 1990. The panel was set up with the intent to perform in-depth study of the relationship between advertising and purchase (Moseley and Parfitt, 1987). The panel had about 1000 respondents reporting in a diary their radio usage, TV viewing, reading of newspapers and magazines and daily purchases across 48 product categories with numerous brands in each category (McDonald, 1997b). In addition to the media-usage data, there exists a file with information on where and when advertisements for the various brands did occur. Finally, each individual respondent is described using 40 demographic variables.

By combining the above-mentioned data, it is possible to determine whether or not the individual respondent has had an Opportunity-To-See (OTS) advertisements for the brand studied. In the data, it is also possible to see whether or not the purchase was made in connection with a promotion activity.

The number of Opportunities-To-See (OTS) for ads was used to indicate the media pressure. The number was determined by combining the media-usage file with the advertisement record file. In the present discussion, only the effects of television advertising are reported.

Even though the data set is quite old, it can still be used to establish basic connections between purchases and related ad exposures. It is rare to have access to a single-source database such as Adlab with continuous observations over a 5-year period for academic research.

For the data special analyses were conducted for 89 brands. Those brands were selected, for which most advertising and purchasing occurred. The data sets represent 18 product categories. For each brand a file was constructed giving the current purchase; which brand was bought, was there a promotion activity, and how many pence were spent? There is also information about when the last purchase within that specific category took place, and which brand was purchased on this last occasion. Also the number of ads the respondent has seen for the brand on each of the 28-day period prior to each purchase was registered.

From these data, first the STAS index is calculated as the ratio between the brand's share of purchase occasions among those respondents who have been exposed to advertising during a seven-day period prior to purchase, p_1, and the brand's share of purchase occasions among those respondents who have not been exposed to advertising during a seven-day period prior to purchase, p_2.

It is important to be able to determine the significance of the STAS measure (Hansen and Olsen, 2001). If the p_1 and p_2 in the STAS score is thought of as two independent binomial distributions, it is possible to calculate whether or not the two proportions

$$p_1 = \frac{Y_1}{n_1} \text{ and } p_2 = \frac{Y_2}{n_2}$$

are significantly different from each other. The significance is determined by a z-test. If the z-test value is greater than 1.96, it is significant on the level 0.05. If this is not the case, p_1 and p_2 cannot be said to be significantly different from each other, meaning that the proportion of people who have purchased brands with prior advertising cannot be separated from the group of people that purchased without prior advertising.

As the second method for estimating the effects of advertising a logistic regression model is used. The logit model estimates the probability of a household purchasing a particular brand given the explanatory variables. The dependent variable is binary, i.e. it takes on two values: "0" if the brand is not purchased and "1" if the brand is purchased. Using a linear regression model when the dependent variable is binary results in problems with the error function. A logit model has the advantage that it takes these issues into account. Furthermore, it also ensures that the response function is curvilinear with asymptotes at both zero and one, which naturally meets the original constraints when the dependent variable is binary (Neter et al., 1989). Another advantage of working with a logit model is the possibility of including numerous explanatory variables, so that it is possible to make a more varied analysis taking into account e.g. a P-V bias, promotion activities and so forth. The general logit model formulation is given by Equation VIII.5:

Equation VIII.5 $$E\{Y\} = \frac{\exp(\beta_0 + \beta_1 X_1 + \ldots + \beta_n X_n)}{1 + \exp(\beta_0 + \beta_1 X_1 + \ldots + \beta_n X_n)}$$

where $E\{Y\}$ is the expected outcome, i.e. the probability of purchase. $X_1 \ldots X_n$ are the various explanatory variables, β_0 is the base level of sales and $\beta_1 \ldots \beta_n$ are the parameter estimates for the various explanatory variables. The sign of these parameter estimates indicates whether an increase in the explanatory variable will have a positive or a negative influence on the purchase probability. The β's indicate the increase/decrease of a unit increase in the respective explanatory variables. However, since the model has undergone a logistic transformation, it is necessary to calculate $\exp(\beta)$ to find the sensitivity value of the respective explanatory variables.

For this work, two logit-models have been estimated. In the first model, advertising information was included as the only explanatory variable, while in the second logit model both the advertising and information on promotion at the time of purchase were included as explanatory variables. An inclusion of a purchase/viewing bias had no results on the effects.

The ad-effect was quantified by use of adstock calculations. The adstock values were calculated on the basis of advertising information in a 28-day period prior to each individual purchase.

As will be recalled, $Adstock_t$ denotes the value of the current ad-pressure as a function of prior advertising (OTS) and the retention rate. The crucial issue in the adstock calculation is the determination of the retention rate. In order to choose the retention rate, we tried different values ranging from 0.5, 0.6,..., 0.9, 0.95, 0.96,..., 0.99. The value that suited the data best was chosen. In this analysis, we chose to work with a retention rate of 0.97. It is important to remember that we were working with daily data, and a daily retention rate of 0.97 is equivalent to a weekly retention rate of 0.80. This rate is equivalent to a half-life of 22.8 days or 3.1 week, respectively.

Adstock is here computed as:

Equation VIII.6 $\quad ADSTOCK_t = r(adstock_{t-1}) + (1-r)GRP_t$

where r is the retention rate.

5. Comparing STAS and Logit Results

The following results are based on calculations for the 89 FMCG brands distributed across 18 product categories. The media pressure was determined by studying the number of OTS for each respondent. The STAS calculations were done on the basis of the OTS 7 days prior to each purchase, whereas the adstock calculation, as explained, was done using a retention rate of 0.97 to describe advertising pressures today as a function of advertising 28 days prior to each purchase.

The choice of .97 as a daily retention rate was supported that this was the one of several tested that gave the best estimates. The effects of varying the retention rate are discussed subsequently. Two versions of the Logit model were used. One with prior advertising for the brand as the single independent variable. The 2nd including also the occurrence of special offer as an independent variable.

Table VIII.4: Results from the STAS and logit model analyses. Logit model 1 with only Adstock as independent variable. Logit model 2 includes also the occurrence of promotion as an independent variable.

Brand	STAS-Index	Significance of STAS-index [1]	Advertising parameter estimate (b1) [2]	Significance of b1 from logit model 1, the Chi-square value [3]	Advertising parameter estimate (b1) [4]	Significance of b1 from logit model 2, the Chi-square value [5]	Promotion parameter estimate (b2) [4]	Significance of b2 from logit model 2, the Chi-square value [3]
Kellogg's Cornflakes	105.6	3.89	b1: 0.0377	99.50	b1: 0.0383	102.66	b2: 0.0124	9.69
Kellogg's Rice Krispies	105.5	2.17	b1: 0.0193	23.42	b1: 0.0206	26.60	bb2: 0.0216	80.50
Kellogg's Bran Flakes	111.7	3.82	b1: 0.0162	39.70	b1: 0.0173	45.44	b2: 0.0201	98.45
Kellogg's All Bran	109.8	2.81	b1: 0.0178	54.63	b1: 0.0181	55.83	b2: 0.0037	4.15
Kellogg's Special K	117.3	4.46	b1: 0.0197	58.76	b1: 0.0195	57.89	b2: -0.0084	19.73
Kellogg's Frosties	84.2	6.13	b1: -0.0232	42.34	b1: -0.0227	40.60	b2: 0.0088	15.78
Other Kellogg's	136.1	15.60	b1: 0.0204	118.26	b1: 0.0208	121.74	b2: 0.0105	12.78
Nabisco Shredded Wheat	105.5	1.78	b1: 0.0098	2.70	b1: 0.0091	2.31	b2: -0.0092	16.59
Nabisco Shreddies	91.6	1.59	b1: -0.0131	8.42	b1: -0.0118	6.90	b2: 0.0229	214.20
Quaker Sugar Puffs	108.6	2.08	b1: 0.0176	18.35	b1: 0.0177	18.75	b2: 0.0057	9.49
Weetabix	102.8	1.83	b1: 0.0198	12.95	b1: 0.0177	10.30	b2: -0.0314	77.43

[1]: critical value: 1.96 [2]: from logit model 1 [3]: critical value: 3.84 [4]: from logit model 2

[5]: critical value: 3.84

As an example of the STAS measure and both logit models, data for breakfast cereals are shown in Table VIII.4. The results for all data can be found in Hansen and Hansen (2001b). The first column indicates the product category, while the second column specifies the brand name within the categories. Column 3 shows the STAS indices and the calculated significance of the indices is shown in column 4. In column 5 the results from logit model 1 are shown, where "b1" is the parameter estimate for the effect of the adstock value. The significance of the b1 values are given in column 6. Results from the second logit model with two explanatory variables are listed in column 7. Here, "b_1" is the parameter estimate for the adstock effect on sales correlated for the influence of deals.

The "b_2" indicate the change in the purchase probability of a one unit change in the respective explanatory variable. However, because of the logarithmic transformation, it is necessary to calculate exp(b) to get the percentage value. The "b_2" can be said to indicate the sensitivity of the promotion variable.

6. STAS Results

The STAS-index has been calculated for all the brands. Furthermore, the significance (Hansen et al., 2001) of this index has been calculated to decide its accuracy.

63 percent of the 89 brands had a positive STAS index, indicating, if it is significant, that there is a positive effect from advertising, while the remaining 37 percent proved to be negative. A total of 51 percent of the indices were found to be significant and positive. In total, 67% of the parameter estimates were significant. The range of the STAS indices is from 73.4 till 140.0.

7. Logit Model Results

In the first logit model, an adstock calculation of the OTS in a 28-day period prior to purchase is the only explanatory variable. As mentioned, we used a daily retention rate of 0.97 in our adstock calculation. In this model, we did not correct for any promotion activity at the time of purchase.

Equation VIII.7 gives the general logit model formulation. For logit model 1, we can calculate the estimated b-values for a specific brand, for instance Kellogg's Cornflakes. This gives us the following expression:

Equation VIII.7 $$E\{Y\} = \frac{\exp(0.1539 + 0.0377 \cdot X_1)}{1 + \exp(0.1539 + 0.0377 \cdot X_1)}$$

X_1 is the explanatory variable, the adstock calculation, and for any given value the purchase probability of this specific product can be calculated. The b1 value is in this case 0.0377, and the corresponding sensitivity value is exp(0.0337) = 0.034, which means that a one unit increase in the adstock gives a 3.4 percent increase in the purchase probability of Kellogg's Cornflakes, or an advertising elasticity of 0.034.

In the second of the two logit models, we included promotion as an explanatory variable alongside the adstock calculation of the OTS. This was done to see whether or not promotion could be a helpful factor in explaining some of the negative adstock parameter estimates from the first logit model, or simply contribute to generating a better level of general explanation.

The promotion activity information is included as a binary variable, i.e. either there was a promotion activity associated with the purchase or there was not. From the 89 brands, we found that 64 percent of the adstock parameters were positive, while the remaining 36 percent were negative, and a total of 67 percent of the adstock parameter estimates were significant. Focusing on the parameter estimates "b2", a total of 89 percent of the promotion effect estimates are significant.

To explain why some of the brands in STAS as well as the two logit model exhibit negative adstock parameter estimates, one could speculate:

1) The brands with negative adstock parameter estimates have positive promotion parameter estimates. In other words, the purchases of these brands are made more on the basis of promotion than on the basis of advertising and since promotion and advertising may be correlated, promotion may pick up on the effect of advertising as well and thus overrule the effect of advertising. Half of the brands that had negative adstock parameter estimates had a significant positive promotion parameter estimate. On average, 13.6 percent of all purchases made for these brands were made in connection with a promotion activity. On an overall average 11.7 percent of all purchases were made in connection with a promotion activity. For the brands with positive adstock and no significant promotion parameter, only 5.5 percent of the purchases were made in connection with a promotion activity. Thus, promotion account for some of the negative advertising effect.

2) The brands with negative adstock parameter estimates can be explained on the basis of studies of the market situation for most of the FMCG in the analyses. These can be characterised as a zero sum game where somebody else must lose if another player wins. In this context it is remarkable that the brands where the negative ad effect is not explained by promotion represent 8 different product categories. This is a strong indication of a connection between the shares of the different brands. Within each product category, there will be some winners and since we are studying the brands in each category with the highest number of purchases and most advertising, among the brands studied there are also likely to be losers. In a zero sum game,

there will be brands that lose market share on account of other brands winning market share.

3) Poor ad campaigns may generate negative results. We do not have access to the actual advertisements themselves, nor do we have any other material indicating whether the different ads or campaigns were good or bad. A genuine confirmation of this explanation is therefore not possible. However we find that it is relevant to remind ourselves as marketers, that campaigns actually occur that do not further the sales of the advertised products either through a misdirected media strategy or through misdirected creative work.

When we compare the logit parameter estimate for adstock found in Model 2 with the STAS indices, another interesting result appears. The summary of the results is shown in Table VIII.5:

Table VIII.5: Comparison of STAS and logit adstock parameter esti-
mates

	Positive adstock parameter estimate	Negative adstock parameter estimate
Positive STAS	40	6
Negative STAS	7	20

It is the immediate conclusion that the two models to a large extent give corresponding results.

It is interesting to observe that in the cases where a positive adstock parameter estimate was found, a corresponding positive STAS index was also found and vice versa for the negative estimates. Only a total of 13 cases had opposite STAS indices and logit parameter estimates. And among these none of the STAS scores deviated significantly from 100, indicating that the campaigns in question were without effect on sales.

This means that in spite of the fact that not all STAS effects are significant, they still give a good indication of whether the group exposed to ads in a 7-day period prior to purchase is more likely to purchase the brand or not. We do not propose that the two methods yield the same results we are simply suggesting that the general trend in the results from the two methods is the same.

8. Estimating Retention Rates and Advertising Elasticities

In a subsequent study the focus was on choosing the optimal retention rate to learn whether it is reasonable to assume that there is an overall retention rate for all brands within each of the different product categories, or whether it is better to work with different retention rates for each brand. Again, data from the Adlab, diary-based single-source panel, was used.

Initially, all 18 product categories with a total of 89 brands were included in the study. The focus again was on major brands with medium or heavy advertising and with a high number of purchases. Only TV-advertising was considered. To conduct the analysis it was necessary to obtain a minimum number of observations, and brands that did not meet this requirement were excluded from the analysis.

To estimate the relationship between advertising and purchasing, we once again used the logistic regression model. In our initial work, we learned that we could improve the parameter estimates significantly by including not only advertising as an explanatory variable but also promotion at time of purchase.

Therefore, the analysis we will discuss here is based on a logit model with two explanatory variables, namely the advertising pressure expressed by an adstock calculation and promotion information at the time of purchase, here termed offer. The focus of the study was to determine advertising half-lives for the different brands that were included in the study.

In our initial analyses we assumed the same retention rate (97 per day) and thus we worked with advertising half-life of 23 days for all brands.

The equation used to calculate the adstock value was given in Equation VIII.4. To determine the optimal retention rate, we estimated the logistic regression model with a selection of different retention rates, and we then defined the criteria for the optimal retention rate as being the case where the largest significance of the corresponding parameter estimate was found.

The retention rate is an expression of how much the consumer remembers from the past. When used in our case, it denotes how much the consumer remembers of the advertising that has taken place in previous periods. However, the retention rate can be a difficult figure to estimate because the interpretation is somewhat difficult. Therefore, it is often useful to study the term "Advertising half-life".

As will be recalled, Advertising half-life expresses the number of days before advertising has had half its total effect. The formula for calculating this factor is given by the equation below, in which r denotes the retention rate (Broadbent, 1979).

Equation VIII.8
$$Half - life = \frac{\log 0.5}{\log r}$$

Similarly a crude estimate of the advertising elasticity can be computed from

Equation VIII.9
$$e_A = +\beta(1-\theta)$$

Where θ is the market share, and β the parameter in the logit model. Which for the most common cases in Figure VIII.11 correspond to elasticies ranging between -0.1 to 0.3. Here the findings reported by Tellis (2003) are worth recalling that the overall mean for advertising elasticities for all the cases he reviews is around 0.1. He also finds that elasticities in US are about half the size of those estimated in Europe.

The larger the retention rate used, the more memory the consumer has of previous advertising and the longer the half-life of advertising is. Some examples of this are given in Table VIII.6. Also, by using retention rates it is possible to calculate the corresponding elasticity:

Table VIII.6: Connection between the daily retention rate and the half-life of advertising.

Retention rate	Half-life in periods (days)
0.50	1
0.70	2
0.90	7
0.95	14
0.99	69
0.999	693

For the 89 brands studied, we have tried to estimate the optimal retention rate by studying the significance of the corresponding parameter estimate, with the optimal retention rate being the most significant one. We experienced a very large variation among the different brands. Not even within the different product categories can the retention rate be said to be constant.

In Table VIII.7 the results are shown for each product category. The product category is given in Column 1. The retention rate interval is shown in Column 2 while the average product-category retention rate is stated in Column 3. The category half-life calculated on the basis of the average product-category retention rate is stated in Column 4.

Table VIII.7: Optimal average retention rates and the corresponding half-life of advertising

Product category	Daily retention rate interval	Average daily product category retention rate	Average product category half-life (days)
Deodorants	0.010 – 0.999	0.657	1.7
Shampoo	0.015 – 0.999	0.772	2.7
Biscuits & wafers	0.055 – 0.999	0.777	2.8
Dairy Spreads	0.360 – 0.999	0.786	2.9
Savoury Spreads	0.605 – 0.970	0.788	2.9
Gravy Makers	0.825 – 0.999	0.938	10.8
Dog Food	0.695 – 0.999	0.944	12.0
Instant Coffee	0.885 – 0.999	0.962	17.9
Toothpaste	0.875 – 0.999	0.962	17.9
Washing Powder	0.825 – 0.999	0.966	20.0
Tub Margarine	0.920 – 0.999	0.979	32.7
Tea Bags	0.970 – 0.993	0.981	36.1
Cat Food	0.930 – 0.999	0.982	38.2
Breakfast Cereals	0.960 – 0.999	0.986	49.2
Toilet Rolls	0.980 – 0.999	0.986	49.2
Chocolate Bars	0.905 – 0.999	0.986	49.2
Butter	0.975 – 0.999	0.993	98.7

With relatively few observations for several brands, some extreme observations can be expected. Still it is interesting to see how large differences that are found within the individual product categories and between the different product categories. Between categories the advertising half life varies 1.7-49.2 days, if one disregards the category with the highest advertising half life. For the entire database we find an overall average daily retention rate of all brands of 0.91 with a corresponding half-life of 7.4 days.

The fact that there are these large variations both within and across the product categories suggests that it is a rather uncertain and approximate measure when the same overall retention rate is used. Therefore, a more precise analysis would result from estimating an optimal retention rate per brand rather than assume the same overall retention rate for all brands.

Still, when the different average retention rates for categories are used in the logit model rather than the same 0.97 for all only minor changes in the advertising effect estimates result. Thus, the logit does not seem to be that sensitive to differences in retention rate assumptions. A quality with the model since retention rate information is rarely available. When the individual product categories are studied it is, in most cases, found that there exist brands with high retention rates and brands with low retention rates. Thus, the hypothesis applying to each category is again confirmed. That is, there are product category winners and product category losers also in the sense that some brands have long advertising half-lives and some brands have short advertising half-lives.

9. Implications

In this analysis, we have estimated the optimal retention rate for 89 brands. We found that there was a very large variation among the different product categories. We also found this variation within the individual product categories, which indicates that there is no general overall retention rate rather we are dealing with a brand specific variable, which should be estimated individually in each single case.

However, one of the questions that remain is whether or not it makes sense to have a retention rate less than 0.5 where the advertising half-life is 1 day, or a retention rate greater than 0.99 where the advertising half-life is 69 days.

Without really explaining these large differences, a comparison of the findings with other published advertising half-life results (Goerlich, 2001) may serve as a form of validation. Their findings are shown in Figure VIII.11.

Figure VIII.11: Distribution of half-lives. Source: Regrouped from Goerlich (2001).

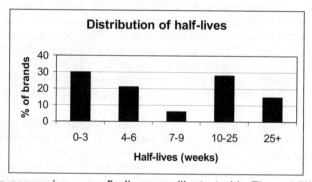

In comparison, our findings are illustrated in Figure VIII.12. These are divided into the same intervals as those used by Goerlich. In both data-sets, the "u" shaped form appears even though the data in Figure VIII.12 is more skewed toward the right than Goerlich's data. An observation which is even more expressed in still earlier data from Clarke (1976). It would be interesting to study the extent to which this is a result of the ten years' time difference between the collections of data, the differences in modeling or the differences in the way the data were collected since Goerlich's and Clarke's data are based upon aggregated econometric analyses of sales data, while ours are based on single source data.

Figure VIII.12:   Distribution of half-lives for FMCG brands (Hansen and Hansen, 2001b)

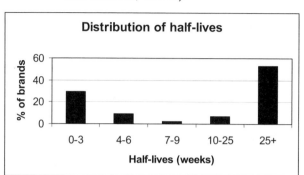

Another factor that can influence the estimation of the retention rates is the degree of loyalty among the consumers towards brands. The loyal consumer would probably have bought the particular brand whether or not they saw advertising for the brand prior to the purchase. Work on expanding the model (Birch, 2003), with an explanatory variable that describes individual differences, not the least in consumers' loyalty towards the brands studied, suggests that loyalty as reflected by past purchasing behaviour diminishes the advertising effect estimates, but does in no way overrule them.

In spite of all moderations that can be found in relation to the procedures, the unquestionable conclusion stands out: Many companies spend large amounts of money on advertising that is either inefficient or that simply does not work. Whether this is due to faulty creative executions, misguided media strategies or to the simple fact that advertising elasticities for the advertised products are close to zero, one cannot say from these studies. So, in that sense, much still remains to be explained about how advertising works in the mind of the consumer.

C. STAS Measured Through Personal Interviewing

As we discussed earlier, Short-term advertising strengths (STAS) represented one of the first attempts to analyse single source data systematically. It is possible to obtain STAS-like information without having access to electronic single-source data, using personal interviewing (Hansen, 2000; Olsen and Hansen, 2002 and Hansen et al., 2006a).

This can be done by measuring:

1. The number of respondents who recall that they have been ex posed to television advertising for the brand within the last week, and
2. The number of respondents who claim to have bought the brand within the last three days.

This measure of "attitudinal" STAS effects – ASTAS - of different campaigns, brands and media has promising qualities as an approximation, when electronic single source data are not available, be it in smaller countries, for products that have long purchasing cycles, such as durables and many services, or product markets of such limited size that panel data simply do not exist.

In the first study reported here, questions have been asked of a total sample of 12,022 respondents. Data was collected continuously from January to December 1999 by TNS-Gallup Denmark. CAPI was used and 23 major fast moving consumer goods were included in the study. The 23 brands were selected based on the total advertising expenditure in the last half year prior to 1999.

The most obvious way of analysing the data was to make the same computations as those upon which Jones' STAS-measure is based. When this was done, the STAS-scores for 23 brands were numerically much larger than those known from other studies. This effect is almost certainly caused by the attitudinal effect of the AS-TAS-measure.

Another problem, which also relates to the scores computed directly from personal interviews, consists of the following: One would expect STAS-scores for weeks with campaigns to be higher than STAS-scores for weeks without. This, however, is not always so. For some brands, STAS-scores computed, in campaign-periods[x]) are lower than in periods without regular campaigns.

This phenomenon can be explained by making two separate observations. When moving from a period without campaigns into a period with campaigns, ad-awareness increases. This is a well-established fact from many tracking studies. When moving from a non-campaign period to a campaign-period, reported purchasing may also increase. We confirmed this from our data. However, in most cases, the increase in ad recall is larger than the increase in the reported purchasing. When this is the case, you may find a lower STAS-score in campaign-periods than in non-campaign periods.

In all events, our STAS scores are higher than STAS-scores normally reported from electronic single source data. As mentioned previously, this is a consequence of the "attitudinal" nature of ad recall and self-reported purchases.

For the above reasons, the data-analyses are broken down into two steps:

1. Awareness-effect and
2. Short-term purchasing effect

---

[x]) *Campaign-periods are here defined as weeks where significant spending has been observed and one week following the last week with spending.*

1. Awareness Effect

The attention, or awareness effect, is analysed in Table VIII.8, where the observations are broken down into those made in weeks with campaigns and those made in weeks without campaigns.

Table VIII.8: Ad-recall in Weeks with and without Advertising and the Recall Index

Brand	TV-ad recall % with campaign (A)	TV-ad recall % without campaign (B)	Recall index (A/B)
Tuborg Squash	44	13	338
Jolly Cola	32	12	273
Høng cheese	30	11	270
Ekstra bladet	16	6	247
Twist chocolate	16	7	236
Omo detergent	16	9	170
Vel detergent	6	4	170
Merrild coffee	14	8	169
Riberhus cheese	19	13	151
Kohberg rye bread	34	23	149
BT	16	11	145
Stimorol chewing gum	11	7	145
Pickwick tea	(3)	2	144
Respons shampoo	9	6	142
Estrella snacks	16	11	138
Colgate toothpaste	16	12	136
Femina	8	6	134
Whiskas	30	24	123
Se & Hør	33	27	121
Aquafresh toothpaste	7	6	114
Gevalia coffee	15	13	114
Schulstad rye bread	17	16	109
Kellogg's cornflakes	30	30	102
Total	**19**	**12**	**167**

In this analysis, the most difficult problem arises in connection with respondents who claim to have seen advertising in weeks without advertising. This problem is known as "false recall". False recall may be due to errors made by the respondent in the answering process or to advertising seen in other media than TV.

But it is probably also caused by "the long-term effect of advertising" as discussed by Stapel (2000). It is, therefore, interesting to look at the frequency of this phenomenon for different brands. This is done in column 2 of Table VIII.8. The different magnitude of this long term effect of past advertising is staggering. Furthermore, the proportion recalling ads when campaigns are on is shown in column 1. Finally, a Recall Index is shown in column 3. It is remarkable that effect vary greatly between brands.

From a theoretical point of view, one would, as mentioned above, expect campaign recall to be zero in weeks without campaigns. It is, however, a well-established fact that this is not so. The recall index in Table VIII.8 however shows the magnitude of the real recall effect of the campaign, because the effect of people claiming to have seen campaigns they cannot have seen are eliminated by forming the ratio of the two key figures in column 1 and 2.

The data in Table VIII.8 is presented in a descending order of the recall index, the average of which is 167 for all 23 brands. The index is larger than 100 for all brands, suggesting a positive recall-effect in campaign periods. For the best performing, the index is almost three times as large as that for the lowest scoring brand.

These variations reveal important things about the brands and the campaigns in question. With knowledge of the actual brands studied, the position of the highest and the lowest scoring brands is not surprising. Tuborg Squash (Index 338) was a much talked about brand and the campaign was highly rated at the time of the data collection, whereas the campaign behind Kellogg's (Index 102) is a very traditional one, also aimed at children (who are excluded from the sample).

Also ad-recall in periods without campaigns provides meaningful information. Among the brands with the highest recall in non-campaign periods, you find the big spenders of the past, headed by Kellogg's. Therefore, ad-recall in periods without campaigns also reflects long-term effects of past advertising and probably also other marketing activities.

We can therefore conclude that advertising awareness measured as it is done using ASTAS measurements and analysed in campaign- and non-campaign-periods reveals important information about the campaign effects in its own right.

2. Short-term Sales Effect

For most of the brands studied here, the TV-advertising budget represents an important part of total advertising spending. With a given brand, one will expect purchases caused by other factors – such as habit, loyalty, offers - besides TV-advertising to occur at a rate unaffected by current TV-spending. In contrast to this, purchases generated by TV-advertising will occur mostly when TV-advertising is being broadcast.

The crucial question, however, is whether an effect on sales can be found. Here, purchase-rates during campaign periods compared with purchase-rates in non-campaign periods may point towards such effects. Purchases made in weeks with and without campaigns are therefore measured for all 23 brands, and the respondents are divided into those claiming exposure, and those claiming no exposure to the ad.

The result of this analysis is that there is a much higher purchasing-rate among consumers claiming to have been exposed to the ad than among non-exposed consumers. The crucial problem is, of course, what to do with those respondents who claim to have seen the ad in periods where no TV-advertising was broadcast. These people may refer to advertising seen earlier, to advertising seen in other media besides TV or they may simply be mistaken.

With the purpose of measuring the short-term sales effect of TV-advertising, we have developed a special measure - ASTAS or "Attitudinal STAS" - that resembles the traditional STAS score. The definition and graphical and mathematical development of this measure is found in Hansen and Olsen (2001). The formula for the computation of ASTAS is

Equation VIII.10

$$ASTAS = \frac{p_1 q_{11}}{p_2 q_{21} + (p_1 - p_2) q_{22}}$$

where

$p_1 =$ The proportion of the respondents claiming recall in weeks with spending.

$p_2 =$ The proportion of the respondents claiming recall in weeks without spending.

$q_{11} =$ The proportion of the respondents having bought the brand in weeks with spending given recall.

$q_{12} =$ The proportion of the respondents having bought the brand in weeks with spending given no recall.

$q_{21} =$ The proportion of the respondents having bought the brand in weeks without spending given recall.

$q_{22} =$ The proportion of the respondents having bought the brand in weeks without spending given no recall.

In the study reported here data are available so that the ASTAS scores can be computed for 18 of the 23 brands in the analysis (in five cases some of the cells used for computing pq's are empty).

In Table VIII.9, the brands are presented in descending order of the ASTAS index together with their recall index. As one can see, there are important deviations even though there is a tendency for the better-recalled brands to have higher ASTAS-scores. This shows that the ASTAS measure provides additional information, relative to the advertising awareness-score.

For a brand like Riberhus cheese, advertising awareness is in the higher end of the scale, whereas the ASTAS-score is among the lowest. Contrary to this, the brand Kellogg's has a low recall index, but a rather high ASTAS-score. The most extreme brand is Jolly Cola, with a recall index of 273 and an ASTAS-index of 102. Based on Table VIII.9, we can therefore conclude that TV-campaigns for the different brands function very differently.

Table VIII.9: ASTAS Index and Recall Index for the 23 Brands.

Brand	ASTAS Index	Recall Index
Høng cheese	137	270
Twist chocolate	129	236
Tuborg Squash	123	338
Kohberg rye bread	119	149
Merrild coffee	118	169
Gevalia coffee	116	114
Kellogg's cornflakes	111	102
BT	108	145
Femina	103	134
Jolly Cola	102	273
Vel detergent	101	170
Se & Hør	101	121
Riberhus cheese	100	151
Schulstad rye bread	97	109
Aquafresh toothpaste	96	114
Stimorol chewing gum	90	145
Estrella snacks	88	138
Whiskas	84	123

When looked upon together, the two scores confirm that campaigns function very differently. In Table VIII.9, we see some campaigns doing very well with both high recall and sales scores. Others are doing poorly across both dimensions, whereas still others either do well on the ASTAS or on the recall scores but not on the other. These observations should give rise to serious consideration on behalf of the advertisers.

For the reasons discussed earlier, the ASTAS-score reflects attitudes as well as behaviour. This means that one should treat the scores in Table VIII.9 with caution. However, obvious applications are comparisons of the same brand over time, and particularly comparisons between different campaign-periods. Similarly, comparisons can be made between competing brands and between product areas, provided that each of the different product areas are thoroughly represented in the data material. Also, comparisons between media (i.e. Print and TV) can be carried out.

In a later study also print advertising was explored (Hansen et al., 2006a). Here, data collection took place on TNS Gallup, Denmark's internet panel. 4000 interviews were conducted with a target group of 15-59 years. Data included 34 FMCG with up to 6 brands in 10 different categories.

On the average in the half year preceding the data collection (spring 2004) each brand spent EURO 280.000 on television and EURO 320.000 on print. Advertising comprises magazines, newspapers and retailers' free sheets with the last category being by far the largest (270.000 per brand). With the use of coupons and free gifts being restricted by Danish law and with the availability of TV advertising appearing very late (in the later 80'ies) retailers' free sheets have become the major merchandising media for manufactures allowing price reduction and "one for two" and similar offers. Thus, the print advertising apart from reflecting exposure close in time prior to many purchases also reflects the degree to which merchandising was an important element for the brand.

A major observation from the study was the significance of print advertising for the brands studied. For 15 out of the 24 brands AS-TAS scores are higher for print than for television. The score together with awareness scores and spending data are shown in Table VIII.10.

Table VIII.10:   Average ASTAS, ad awareness and spending for 34 brands in 10 categories (Hansen et al., 2006a)

| | N | Average ASTAS | | | Average aware-ness | Average spending (mill. DKK) | | | |
		Print	TV	Diff.		Print	Free sheets only	TV	Diff.
With print ASTAS advantage	15	197	121	76	86%	2.773	2.320	1.300	1.473
With TV ASTAS advantage	19	157	260	-103	152%	2.066	1.610	2.644	- 0.578
Averages	34	174	200			2.369	1.890	2.068	

An overall impression of the findings is given in Table VIII.10. Here it appears that for brands with the highest print ASTAS scores print average spending per brand is also much larger than television spending (more than two times). For brands with the highest television AS-TAS scores we find higher television spending per brand than print spending. Looking at the ad awareness data, one might speculate that somehow television campaigns survive longer in the memory of the consumer than do print campaigns. An observation being confirmed when we look at ad awareness for products with little or no TV or print spending in the preceding years. Here, we find the percentage recalling TV advertising within the last week even though no television advertising has been broadcasted in the half year preceding the data collection to be quite high (7.6%) but still higher for those with TV spending (15.2%). For those with very little print spending (less than 80.000 EURO for the half year preceding the data collection) the print ad awareness is 3.1 % against 8.6 % for those with print spending. Thus, for both kinds of advertising, the media have long run effects in terms of recall long after the termination of the campaign. This effect is much larger for TV than for print though suggesting the stronger brand building effect of TV as compared with predominantly merchandising offers commercialised through retailers' free sheets. Better insight into the emotional impact of the two kinds of campaigning would throw more light on the nature of these different effects. Another interesting effect can be observed when reported TV ad awareness and ASTAS scores for the same brands are compared. This is done in Figure VIII.13.

Figure VIII.13:   TV awareness (Recall Index) and ASTAS for 34 TV
campaigns (Hansen et al., 2006a)

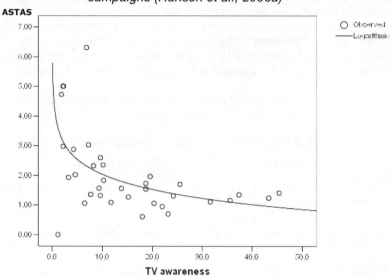

TV campaigns tend to give either high awareness or high ASTAS. A phenomenon, which is less experienced with the print campaigns. An observation reflecting a problem with much advertising is that you can easily create awareness by being entertaining, exciting, surprising and the like but you accomplish this on the expense of the major communication goal: "Go out and purchase" the brand. Reversibly, by emphasising product features, advantages or use of the product for FMCG you may loose part of the audience in the process. In essence it has to do with central versus peripheral information processing with TV ads. Thus, to understand the functioning of most TV advertising you must look at peripheral processing, - and in particular emotional processing.

In this connection interesting findings are reported by Waring (2005). Using the 15.000 household large TNC super panel she analyses print campaign effects research like it has been done for TV by Roberts (1998) and Beaumont (2003). Here print campaigns are in magazines and newspapers, but she finds short-term (and medium-term) sales effects much in line with the Danish findings. She finds 11% more purchases among exposed consumers than among unexposed consumers for brands with heavy print advertising. A result only slightly lower than for similar findings for TV advertising.

On the whole ASTAS measures give "indications" of advertising effects. Real understanding of what is going on, however, requires better insight into the emotional processes underlying the attitudinal reasons to recall purchases and advertising exposure and into how emotionally based brand equity contributes to shaping buying behaviour .

D. Summary

In this chapter we have reviewed recent attempts to study the relationship between advertising and sales. This has been done particularly by looking at short term effects.

Short-term effects are studied as the purchases made from 1 to 28 days following the exposure. Several studies reporting short term advertising strength (STAS) and Attitudinal STAS suggest that on the average for FMCG a STAS-score between 110 and 120 is likely. This corresponds to overall advertising elasticities of 0.1 to 0.2.

However individual deviations are large and between a third and half of all advertising has negative or no short-term effects. This is important since it is doubtful whether any longer run effects can exist without an initial short-term effect (Charlton-Jones, 2005). To this comes that advertising with an elasticity of 0.1 to 0.2 requires very high margins to be economical. Thus the essence of the findings in this chapter is that many advertisers should take a very careful look at their advertising to ensure that it is indeed profitable in the short run – or that it generates effects that persist in longer runs, the topic of the next chapter.

Finally, we have shown how interview based ASTAS measures as an alternative to single-source panel data may also reveal important aspects of campaigns' ability to get across (get awareness) and convince (reproduce claimed purchases).

Both these data and the data on short term effects show the importance of gaining more insight into the unconscious, largely emotional responses that govern people's responses to brand names and the like – since it remains documented that loyal consumers tend to remain loyal and for other reasons than current advertising.

Chapter IX

Medium and Long Term Effects of Advertising

CHAPTER OUTLINE
The ending note of the preceding chapter was that many advertisers probably will have difficulties documenting the profitability – in the short term – of their advertising spending, due to the generally low level of advertising elasticity demonstrated and to the generally large proportion of brand advertising with no or even negative short term effects. What may make the advertising effort profitable is effects in the longer run to add to the short term. This chapter takes a look at some of the evidence for advertising's medium and long run effects.

The first part deals with empirical evidence that documents a marked medium term effectiveness of advertising and actually a much larger effect than the short term effects dealt with in the preceding chapter.

The second part deals with empirical evidence that documents long term effects of advertising, part of it documenting awareness levels staying high after several years of advertising effort and part of it discussing findings that relate share-of-market to share-of-voice, another way of documenting longer-term effects of advertising.

CHAPTER OBJECTIVE
Our objective in introducing medium and long term effects of advertising is to provide the reader with the inspiration to think and plan advertising efforts not only for short term effects but also for the added benefits – that seem to be much larger than the short term benefits – that can be reaped by consistent and innovative use of advertising. We aim to support this argument by providing empirical evidence that advertising does have a significant effect on sales in medium and longer runs.

A. Medium Term Effectiveness
Jones' (1995) (Short Term Advertising Strength) look at effects within a week after exposure. Other authors look at short term effects up to 30 days after the exposure (Roberts, 1997, McDonald, 1971 and Hansen, 2002b). In any event medium term effects are seen as those – in addition to the short term effects – that occur within the first year.

A distinction between short, medium and long-term effects has previously been introduced (Roberts, 1997, but also Jones 2003 and Beaumont 2003). All these authors suggest that the magnitude of medium term effects by far exceed that of the short-term effect, and thus should be considered in all advertising modeling. The exact size of this effect is difficult to pinpoint, but that it is important is certain. We shall review some of the evidence presented by Roberts (2000).

Roberts works with the Taylor-Nielson Super Panel TV-Scan based on electronic single source data. He selects 113 brands for analysis based on their different volumes of advertising. He also concentrates on the larger brands. Thus his results are not representative for all of FMCGs, but merely illustrative, and primarily indicative for the major brands – which incidentally tend to be the brands with the largest advertising budgets. Even so, they are remarkable and should be kept in mind by any advertising planner.

The analysis starts by dividing (brand by brand) into purchases made with advertising exposure and purchases made without advertising exposure in the preceding 28 days. Roberts writes (p. 77):

> *"On average, a brand purchase was followed by a further 22 purchases of the product category in the ensuing 12 months, of which the brand itself was repurchased on 9.6 occasions. Thus the subsequent brand loyalty was 43.8 %." This statistic underlines the fundamental importance of repeat buying for established FMCG brands."*

Moreover the brand loyalty of the original brand buyers only declines very slowly over time, as Figure IX.1 shows. Moreover he finds the same effect for brands bought with and without promotion (Figure IX.2)

Figure IX.1: Brand loyalty over time (Roberts, 2000, p. 4, fig. 2)

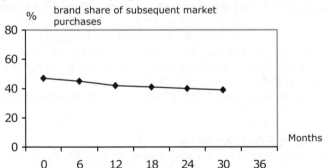

For all the 113 brands, he reports an average increase in consumer purchases of 5.2% (Figure IX.2). As it can be seen from the figure marked differences exist depending on whether purchases are made at regular prices or whether the brands have been on sale. The average result can be shown to correspond to 9.6 times the short term purchasing effect. In a later reporting Waring (2005), based on data from a larger single source base from TNS, confirm these data and also show similar results for print. Here the medium-term effect runs about three times the short-term effect.

Figure IX.2:   Subsequent brand loyalty (12 months) by condition under which brand was originally purchased (Roberts, 2000)

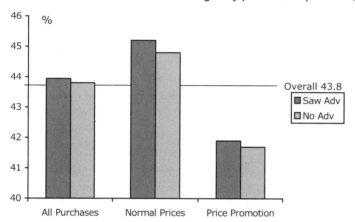

Interesting findings are also reported by Abraham and Lodish (1989) based on Behaviour Scan US electronic single source data. They find significant medium-term effects, for those about 50% of the cases where they found significant positive effects of advertising. The total first year effect is +22.4 %. Some effect is still found in the second year but very little effect is found in the third year. Findings that are in line with these based on two product cases have been reported by Tellis (1998a+b).

The data in the Adlab database do not lend themselves easily to the same kind of medium-term effect analysis, as do the super panel data. However it has been attempted with a few selected product categories with many purchases and heavy advertising (cereals and coffee). Here 4 to 6 additional purchases are found in the medium term period relative to the initial first purchase.

Also French single source data have been used for this kind of analysis (Jagger, 1998). With a somewhat different procedure, these studies, report similar results. It would be an overstatement to claim that one always should expect medium term effects of a magnitude of 3 to 10 times the short-term effect. Even though, many major FMCG manufactures with access to single source data have insight into the extent of medium term effects for their brands, none of this is available in published form. The issue is however so important that more published data are eagerly awaited.

One may in this context remind the reader, that STAS scores alone, such as these that are known from published studies, (Figure VIII.3), rarely warrant the very large advertising expenditures that are actually spent. With an added medium term effect of the magnitude discussed here, the size of many advertising budgets becomes much more understandable − although our fundamental conclusion from the STAS studies still stand: A significant proportion of advertising spending in the FMCG sector is wasted money, if only short term effects are considered. To this can be added that medium term effects are found if a short term effect appears. Thus the 15 to 25 percent of the cases in Table VIII.2 where a STAS score is lower than 100 is found must be expected to be inefficient if only sales result within a year are considered.

All in all much more needs to be understood about medium-term effects and it is unlikely that full understanding can be gained without more insight into peripheral emotional information processing of advertising material, also.

B. Long-Term Effects

Long term effects are seen here as those effects on sales that can be proved to occur a year or more after the short and medium term effects. That long term effects on sales occur is evident from recent work by Tellis (2003). In his review of 450 US tracking studies he found that when advertising efforts are maintained over a period of years, its' effect can be found to last for two or more years. In this case the combined effects in the 2nd and 3rd year can be as large as that of the first year.

In a different context Mela et al. (1997) finds as well medium and long terms effects of advertising and promotion. Particularly they find that from 1984 to 1991 consumers become more sensitive to prices and promotions in areas with decreased advertising and increased promotion.

Finally the results from Clarke (1976) should be kept in mind, who finds that a little less than 50% of the advertising effect is to be found in the 2nd years or later. But he also finds that if there is no short and medium term effect then there is no long term effect either. A finding also supported by Jones (1995) and by Lodish et al. (1995). The latter find that if there is a medium term effect, 76% of that carries over into the 2nd year, but only little into the third.

It is a well-established fact that we all remember brands that have not been advertised nor sold for decades. Long-term effects may be almost everlasting. In contemporary marketing, the concern with brand equity focuses on this. Brand equity reflects on the brand's ability to maintain sales or prices at higher levels in the long run. Building and growing brand equity results from the use of all marketing mix variables over a long period of time. Advertising is only one of these.

The stability of the NERS scores for brands (Figure VI.2) also suggest that emotional response tendencies reveal important aspects of long term advertising effects; an issue to be analyzed in more detail in Chapter XI.

To the extent that advertising contributes to brand equity beyond its immediate sales effects, it must be ascribed to the long-term effects of advertising. This is even more difficult to pinpoint than the short- and medium-term effects, but the advertising planner must also consider the economic value of these effects.

To look at the relationship between share of market and share of voice has been a way of getting insight into longer lasting effects of advertising (Figure IX.3). When it is found, that more successful and larger brands may get away with relatively lower advertising spending than their competitors, it is assumed to show that they reap the benefits of past advertising. Departing in published findings of share of voice/share of market relationships, we shall try to understand this relationship by analysing the Adlab data already introduced.

Figure IX.3: The Advertising Intensiveness Curve (Jones, 1990)

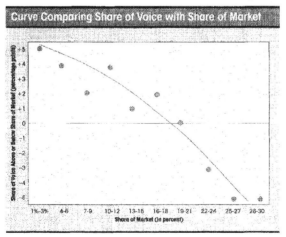

We depart in the Advertising Intensiveness Curve, developed by John Philip Jones (1990) and confirmed by Buck (2001), to assess how brand-marketing strategies are applied with respect to advertising (Broadbent, 1999).

Brands that are small in market share will have a positive ratio Share of Voice to Share of Market, as it is illustrated in Figure IX.3, while brands that have large shares of market will have a negative ratio Share of Voice to Share of Market.

Using the Adlab database we have studied, how different types of markets affect the Advertising Intensiveness Curve. Thus the existence of a negatively shaped advertising effectiveness curve documents the existence of long term effects. This is reported in detail in Hansen and Christensen (2005). Some of the main findings are given in the following.

1. Method

In order to establish the connection between Share of Voice and Share of Market, it is necessary to find valid measures for this relationship based on what is available in the Adlab database (see Chapter VIII). Because we dealt with FMCG product categories we have chosen TV advertising as the advertising spending area where the Share of Voice has been measured. This was justified by the fact that the overwhelming part of the spending on advertising in FMCG brand categories in the late 80's was done on TV, hence making the number of TV spots a valid indicator of the total spending on ads.

When using single-source data, the straightforward thing to do is to use the actual number of purchases of a particular brand, divide this by the total number of purchases in the product category, and let this be the measure of the Share of Market for the brand. Similarly, share of voice is computed as the number of exposures to the brand divided with the total number of exposure within the category. This computation, however, constitutes a serious problem, because quite a large number of brands – on average around 60 % – in all the examined categories did not advertise.

The fact that this is the case makes these particular brands of little or no use in the analyses, keeping in mind, that what wanted is to examine the relationship between positive Shares of Voice and positive Shares of Market. Therefore, the data we use are adjusted by removing brands that have "no voice" and constellations of brands that did not have their own brand name in the purchase diary ("other brands"), and subsequently an adjusted Share of Market is calculated, where "the market" now consists only of those brands that have positive Shares of Voice. Since growing or declining market shares of those brands that were excluded might distort the analysis, a few product areas were deleted where such tendencies were found. The excluded areas all are such that had a growing share of unadvertised retailer brands.

2. Analysis and Results

Of the total number of 844 brands in the 48 categories, 314 brands in 45 categories were selected, representing a total number of purchases of 1,017,798, and a total of 154,784 TV ads broadcast in the period 1986-1989.

Each brand's Share of Market was calculated, relative to the other advertised brands in the same product category. Figure IX.4 shows the plot of these 314 brands, and the linear regression best fit of these data. The linear regression model explains 34.7 % of the total variance in the data (R=.589).

The sensitivity of one unit change in share of market on share of voice is .582. This indicates that an increase of share of market with 1 percentage point should correspond to an increase in share of voice of 0.582 percentage points in order to keep up with the rest of the market.

The regression analysis show that the relationship between Share of Market and Share of Voice, proposed by John Philip Jones, also existed in these FMCG products. Based on the UK Adlab single source data on average, brands with smaller market shares evidently keep a share of voice above their share of market, while brands with larger shares of market in general have relatively smaller shares of voice. This is interpreted as a long term effect of previous advertising (Jones, 1999)

Figure IX.4: All brands with Share of Voice > 0. Advertising Inten-
siveness Curve found with linear regression analyses
(Hansen and Christensen, 2005)

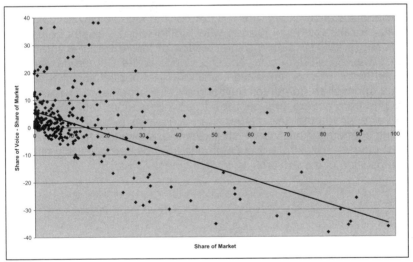

Admittedly, with 34.7% explained variance by the model, the relationship does not come across as strongly as in John Philip Jones' original work. But here data were over 10% fractiles, not reported individually. As we shall see in the following many factors operating in the markets may cause deviations from the general pattern.

3. High Voice and Low Voice Product Categories

Our hypothesis is that the level of advertising in a certain product category will influence both the slope and the constant of the Advertising Intensiveness Curve. Therefore we divided the data into two categories depending upon whether a high level of voice or low level of voice was predominant.

Among the 45 examined brand categories, the level of voice varied from category to category – the highest level was found in the "breakfast cereal" category, with a total number of TV advertisements of 24,468 in the 4-year period. At the other end of the scale was the product category "packaged soup". In this category only 146 TV ads were reported in the total 4-year period.

The average number of TV ads in the categories was 3,400. This was used as the separation value between high and low voice categories. Then we did a standard linear regression on the two new datasets – the results are shown in Figure IX.5. Both correlations are significant with:

$R = .515$ for high voice brands
$R = .634$ for low voice brands

Also there were significant differences between the slopes of the Advertising Intensiveness Curves in data from each of the two different voice levels. The slopes are – 0.586 for the high voice brands and – 0.402 for the low level brands with a difference in slopes being significant ($p = 0.01$). Both the intersection of the Advertising Intensiveness Curves with the axis, and the slopes of the Curves depend on, whether the market has a high or a low level of total voice. What the data themselves do not tell anything about is whether the relationship results from advertisers' decision to advertise more with lower share of voice, or whether the market share follows as a result of the advertising spending. An issue we shall return to subsequently.

Figure IX.5 illustrates how high and low voice respectively alters the position of the Advertising Intensiveness Curve.

Figure IX.5: All brands with pos. Share of Voice. Advertising Inten-
siveness Curves for all brands, high voice, and low
voice markets. (Hansen and Christensen. 2005)

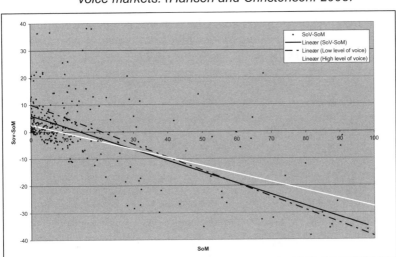

It shows that brands that operated in high voice markets did not have
to have quite as high SoV relative to their market share, as the
brands with lower share of market. Jones (1995) found that larger
brands may get away with underspending around 5-6%, whereas the
small brands had to advertise more.

4. Oligopoly and Competitive Markets
Turning the focus to the type of competition in markets, we have
separated the data into two different categories of markets, oligopoly
type of markets and competitive type of markets. In the analysis the
brand categories were separated in such a way that an almost equal
number of brands fall into each of the two categories. The selection
rule for the oligopoly category was, that the two leading brands combined should hold more than 45 % of the total market, including those
brands with no voice. This resulted in 27 product categories with a total of 146 brands being classified as oligopoly markets, while the remaining 18 product categories, with a total of 168 brands, were classified as competitive.

Linear regression analyses were carried out on these two new
sub-groups of the Adlab database. The result of the analyses is
shown below in Figure IX.6.

Also in this case both models explained significant amounts of the
variance, 32.6 % and 44.7 % respectively. Since there are no significant differences in the slopes of the two models, the two Advertising
Intensiveness Curves could be said to be parallel. The difference be-

tween the two market types appeared in the level of the curves. The Advertising Intensiveness Curve for oligopoly markets was above the one for the competitive markets.

Figure IX.6: All brands with pos. Share of Voice. Advertising Intensiveness Curves for oligopoly and competitive markets (Hansen and Christensen, 2005)

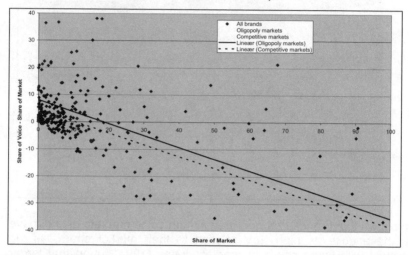

This has some important implications for brands in oligopoly type of markets. First of all, when new brands are introduced into an oligopoly market they need to hold a higher share of voice than new brands introduced into more competitive type of markets. Secondly, smaller brands in oligopoly markets also need to keep relatively higher shares of voice, perhaps forced to do so in order to compete with the dominating market leaders.

The effect of this is illustrated when an analysis like the one in Figure IX.5 is carried out for each of the two categories. In oligopoly markets on average a brand hold a market share of 18.5 % before the share of voice was equal to the share of market, while in competitive markets this occurred at a market share of 10.7 %.

The "Kinked demand curve" affect discussed in Chapter VII may be ascribable to this.

In oligopolistic markets companies tend to act conjecturally – that is they make marketing decisions considering what effect they may have on competitors. Yoo and Mandhachitara (2003) demonstrate how this can be built into sales modeling for two brands simultaneously. With data on whisky brands in Thailand they show how a carryover effect model in competition can be used for identifying proper strategies considering the reactions of the competitors. This mechanism seems to result in relatively higher advertising spending in oligopoly dominated markets than in more competitive markets.

5. Share of Voice and Share of Market in Individual Markets

The many and often large deviations found in the relationships reported so far makes it natural to look at individual markets and try to explain what exactly is going on.

To carry out more detailed analyses on how individual categories have developed, and particularly to focus on related changes in share of voice and share of market, it was necessary to concentrate on markets with at least three advertised brands and on markets where the total share of market held by the advertised brands was relatively stable over the period of analysis. This last issue implied, as discussed earlier, that markets with penetrating retailer or other new brands are excluded from the analysis.

Based upon these criteria, the following analysis was carried out on 34 product categories, covering approximately 314 brands. Of the 34 markets, 29 markets showed a clear, positive correlation between share of voice and share of market. Among these, 26 had an advertising intensiveness curve with a negative slope. Of the 29 markets, where data for more than one year exist, 15 markets showed a positive correlation between changes in share of voice and changes in share of market. Thus, in at least half of the markets changes in SoV drive changes in SoM.

We have here selected 5 markets to illustrate the most common patterns found for the individual markets.

a) Breakfast Cereals

The first category to be illustrated is the breakfast cereal category, where data exist on the purchasing of and advertising for 26 brands over a 4-year period. One single producer of different kinds of cereals, the Kellogg Company, heavily dominated the category. This producer alone holds a total market share of more than 60 % in the UK market.

The dominating brand is Kellogg's Cornflakes, with a market share in 1986 of around 24 %. The second largest brand is Weetabix, produced by the leading British producer of breakfast cereals, Weetabix Ltd. At the beginning of the 4-year period, this brand held a share of market of around 19 %.

An analysis of the data showed that both leading brands underspent on advertising every year in the 4-year period – meaning that their share of voice is lower than their share of market. This is illustrated in Figure IX.7. Whereas smaller brands in the breakfast cereal category were forced to advertise more than their share of market would suggest, these large established brands are able to sustain their dominating positions in the market with a relatively small investment in advertising.

The Kellogg Company in the 4-year period introduced a number of new brands into the UK market. In order to get a foothold in the market, the producer was forced to invest significantly in advertising spending for these brands. This overspending on advertising both in 1988 and 1989 is shown in Figure IX.7. The overall result for the producer is an increase in total market share, from 64.2 % in 1986 to 66.6 % in 1989. At the same time, an increase in share of advertising can be found. In 1986, the Kellogg share of total TV advertising in the breakfast cereal category was 73 %. This compares to 77.5 % in 1989.

Figure IX.7: Breakfast cereals. Under-spending on advertising for leading brands (Hansen and Christensen, 2005)

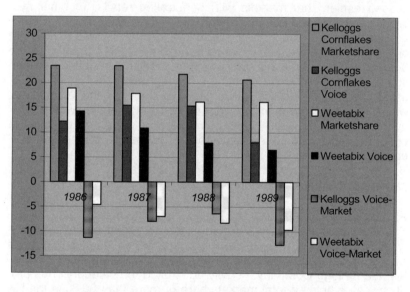

Figure IX.8: Breakfast cereals. Overspending on advertising for new Kellogg's brands (Hansen and Christensen, 2005)

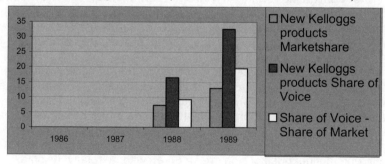

Overall, although the Kellogg company was spending more on advertising in the 4-years, relative to the total share of market of the Kellogg brands, large differences exist between brands, and our analysis suggests that the larger, established brands of the company are in a sense paying for the introduction of new brands into the market, simply by being able to sustain significant, large market shares with relatively small advertising budgets.

By redirecting advertising spending to new products, the Kellogg Company was able to broaden the market and the customer base, and to increase total market share of their brands, without significantly increasing the total spending on advertising.

This ability of the old brands to maintain a strong market position must undoubtedly be seen in the light of their ability to sustain strong emotional response tendencies like NERS or other emotional responses.

The complete picture of the breakfast cereal category is shown in Figure IX.9. The figure shows the Advertising Intensiveness Curve for the category. In spite of the overall correlation being significant there are important deviations – but still the curve supports the theory that smaller brands need to overspend on advertising, while larger, well-established brands can afford to under-spend while still maintaining their dominating positions in the market.

Figure IX.9: Advertising Intensiveness Curve, breakfast cereals (Hansen and Christensen, 2005)

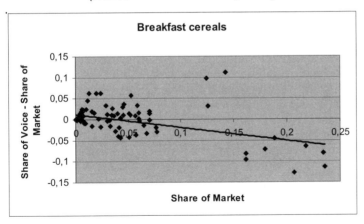

Figure IX.10 shows that advertising in general seems to work in the product category. The positive relationship between changes in share of voice and share of market indicates that an increase in the spending on advertising, relative to total advertising spending in the product category, will in general lead to an increase in market share.

*Figure IX.10: Changes in share of voice and share of market, break-
fast cereals (Hansen and Christensen, 2005)*

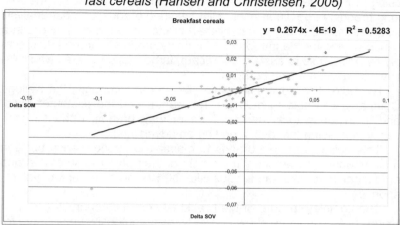

b) Chocolate Bars

The same picture of a positive relationship between changes in share
of voice and share of market can be found in the data on a number of
other product categories. Although the magnitude of advertising effectiveness varies from category to category, they all seem to indicate that on some level advertising works. Such relationships are
prevalent in the majority of the cases analyzed. Chocolate bars is another example.

The chocolate bar category is dominated by one large brand,
Mars, which holds an around 30 % market share. An analysis of data
from a 3-year period, depicted in Figure IX.11, shows the positive relationship between changes in share of voice and share of market,
but as it appears, the relationship is not as clear as in the breakfast
cereal category.

Figure IX.11: Chocolate bars. Changes in share of voice and share of market (Hansen and Christensen, 2005)

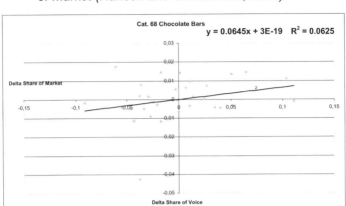

Again, the Advertising Intensiveness Curve drawn from data in this particular category shows that, in general, smaller brands need to overspend on advertising in order to maintain their market shares, while larger brands (in this category particularly Mars) can profit from being large, and maintain their leading position in the market while, relatively speaking, under-spending on advertising (Figure IX.12). The ability of Mars to maintain their strong position undoubtedly reflects the brand's character as outstanding would most likely have shown up in NERS scores had they been available.

Figure IX.12: Advertising Intensiveness Curve, chocolate bar category (Hansen and Christensen, 2005)

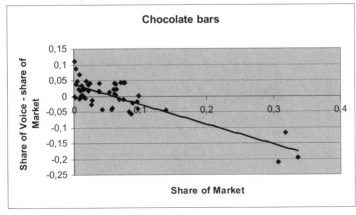

c) Automatic Washing Powder

Another example of significant advertising effects is found in the automatic washing powder category. In this case, the positive connection between changes in share of voice and share of market seems clearer than in previous examples, indicated by the steepness of the line in Figure IX.13.

Again, the category is dominated by one large brand, Persil Automatic, which holds around 30 % of the market. There is some indication that this brand under-spend too much during in 4-year period, since it loses significant market shares from 1986 to 1989 (Figure IX.14.)

Figure IX.13: *Changes in share of voice and share of market, automatic washing powder (Hansen and Christensen, 2005)*

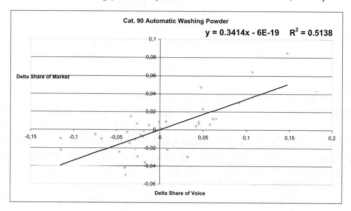

Figure IX.14: Advertising Intensiveness Curve, automatic washing powder (Hansen and Christensen, 2005). Figures with indication of year are for Persil automatic

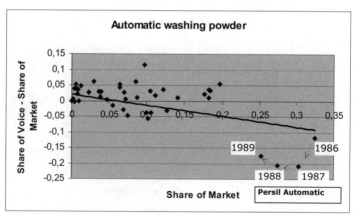

This category gives an example of the fact that it is important to get an accurate estimate of how much it is possible for a producer to under-spend without losing market shares. To track the NERS score of the brand may provide warnings of such negative developments. As it appears in 1987 and 1988 and partly in 1989 Persil went too far in underspending and lost market share by doing so. Among the categories analysed the majority showed results in line with those two reported so far, but there are exceptions. The next category analysed is an example of this.

d) Canned Soup
Figure IX.15 shows the relationship between changes in share of voice and share of market in the canned soup product category. That the relationship is a different one in this category as can be seen from the negative slope of this curve. This indicates that, in general, increasing the relative share of advertising for a brand in this category would lead to a loss of market share for that particular brand. However, the explanation for this seemingly negative relationship lay in the development of the market in the years analysed. At the beginning of the period, the brand Heinz Standard held a market share of nearly 90 %, and was therefore completely dominating this product category.

Figure IX.15:Changes in share of voice and share of market, canned soup category (Hansen and Christensen, 2005)

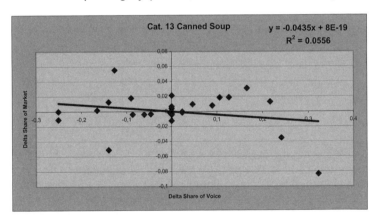

Then, Heinz started to innovate the category, and introduced a number of more specific brands with particular tastes, appealing to particular target audiences. These new products were heavily advertised for a short period of time, but as they quickly became popular and gained significant market shares, advertising for these new products almost stopped. Still, they continued to grow in market share. This result was that the leading brand, Heinz Standard, lost market shares, even though Heinz continued to advertise their leading brand to the consumers. This is the explanation for the negative relationship between changes in share of voice and share of market, which can be observed in Figure IX.15. Obviously the new varieties had soon established positive NERS on which they could capitalize after their introduction.

The lesson to be learned from this is that although in most cases there seems to be a positive relationship between changes in share of voice and share of market over time, some markets may show different, market-specific patterns of behaviour. Particularly the introduction of new successful brands has this effect.

e) Household Cleaners
This product category gives yet another example of how product innovation in a particular market can significantly alter the relationship between changes in share of voice and share of market (Figure IX.16).

Figure IX.16:Changes in share of voice and share of market, house hold cleaners (Hansen and Christensen, 2005)

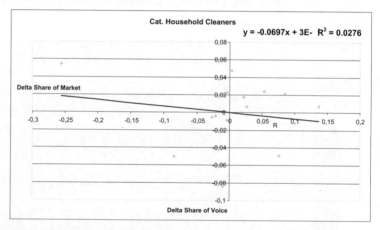

In the period of time covered by the data, a significant change from powder cleaning products to liquid cleaners occurred in the UK. The fast growing popularity of this new, innovative line of products resulted in liquid cleaners increasing in market shares faster than their share of voice increased. At the same time, advertising for the leading powder cleaner was almost doubled, and still it lost almost a third of its market share, not being able to advertise its way out of trouble.

f) Margarine
Finally, in analysing the data, we found an example of how great advertising can influence the Advertising Intensiveness Curve in a product category. In the margarine product category, only two products where advertised, Stork and Krona.

In the mid 1980s, Stork was very successfully promoted with a long running and award-winning advertising campaign, the result of which can be seen in Figure IX.17. Although the smaller of the two leading brands, Stork was still able to cash in on a very successful, prize-winning advertising campaign, by under-spending on advertising, and still raise the market share from 26.6 % in 1986 to 38.4 % in 1989. The question then is, would it have been possible for Stork to achieve an even better market share with more advertising? And how did the successful campaign rate in terms of NERS? Being a low involvement product category more information on peripheral information processing effects would possibly have thrown more light on this category.

Figure IX.17: Advertising Intensiveness Curve, packet margarine (Hansen and Christensen, 2005). Data to the left relate to the Stork brand.

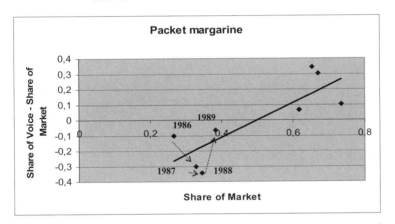

C. Summary
The chapter documents that advertising, when successful, does have an effect beyond the first year. It is also demonstrated in general, that larger brands can get away with a smaller share of voice relative to their share of market than smaller brands. This effect can be ascribed to long term effects of previous advertising.

Analysis of data separated into markets with high and low TV spending suggests, that brands that operate in high voice markets cannot afford to underspend in advertising to the same extent as products that operate in low voice markets. This is particularly true, if they aim to increase their market shares.

Given the empirical data that show that larger brands can maintain their market position with slightly smaller than average share of voice, the effect may be ascribable to the strength of the brand as reflected in the mental brand equity – or in the terms of this book: in the emotional response tendency towards the brand.

In examining the effects of oligopoly versus competitive markets we found, that in oligopoly markets there was a general tendency that the smaller brands in the market overspend more on advertising than the smaller brands in more competitive markets. In these markets there are often one or two well-established brands that make it much more difficult for smaller brands to establish themselves, hence smaller brands are forced to overspend to a greater extent than smaller brands that operate in more competitive markets.

When it comes to specific product markets, there are vast differences across product types, but larger brands generally tend to be able to underspend on advertising without losing market power and dominance. Still, as several examples show, larger brands cannot underspend too much without being punished on market share. Combined with the documented effect that outstanding advertising has on market share, the issue of the consumer's attachment to the brand as reflected in the emotional response seems to be a key measurement to understand how advertising may work in longer runs with established brands.

Chapter X

Measuring Advertising's Effects

CHAPTER OUTLINE

This chapter presents an overview and review of advertising testing, both from an optimisation viewpoint, from a historical and evolutionary viewpoint and from a purely how-to-do-it viewpoint. The topic is treated intensively in the book because the authors believe that there has been a tendency to letting thinking about testing advertising lead to theories of advertising's effects – instead of the other way around, having the theories of advertising effects drive development of the measurement instruments to apply.

The chapter opens with optimisation considerations and presents some of the classic arguments on testing – or not testing – advertising. A couple of important distinctions are discussed, such as how testing fits in with the development process of advertising, sensitivity and validity of effect measures, qualitative or quantitative methods and finally a confirmation that effect measures are the focus of advertising research, not exposure measures which belong in the realm of audience research.

From these introductory parts of the chapter it continues with the three main parts:

1. Historic evolution of advertising testing and an overview of the contemporary views on advertising testing; this part covers a number of ongoing debates such as the relevance of recall or recognition measures, using liking as a key performance measure for advertising, how to cope with central or peripheral information processing in testing and the role of feelings as effect measures
2. Considerations on measurement in effect testing; in this part the discussion is centered around the various types of measurement instruments: Mechanical, advertising or brand recall measured, various types of scaled measurements and using market based measures as effect measures for advertising.
3. Data collection techniques in effect testing. This part discusses what types of stimuli are available as test instruments: concepts, animatics, sketches and it discusses when to test: before, during or after a given campaign. This part ends with comments on modeling the effects of advertising, primarily awareness as a function of advertising pressure

CHAPTER OBJECTIVE

With this chapter on advertising testing we aim to raise a debate about how theories in advertising testing have had a function of shaping the thinking about how advertising works. This aim is fulfilled by an overview in its own right of the large body of existing testing procedures that fundamentally build on a cognitive view of advertising effects – and that have had a tendency to shape thinking about how advertising should be developed. Since this book is about a new paradigm in how consumers arrive at making choices, we argue that the small but growing body of testing solutions and ideas that build on views of the role of emotions in consumer choice and information processing probably will be more relevant as tools for assessing the effectiveness of advertising executions.

SETTING THE SCENE

Measuring advertising's effects is often referred to as advertising testing – and advertising testing is more often than not perceived as being a minor part of that larger support discipline to the marketing profession, market and marketing research. However, the discipline: Testing how advertising works and whether it does work has touch points that greatly transcend the activities of the company market researcher or some specialist at a research agency.

Advertising testing has traditionally relied heavily on cognitive models of effect, but in later years more concern can be observed with feelings, often in terms of their effect on cognitive processing of advertising material.

The key objective of advertising testing is – as stated above – to shed light on communication problems that are very central to planning, budgeting and executing advertising in order to appeal to consumers:

- The explorative question: How do specific advertising executions work?
- The descriptive question: To what extent does advertising work?
- The normative question: How can we make advertising that will work?

The first question really is the one addressed by most commercial applications of advertising testing: Testing a suggested execution to support a decision as to whether it can run or needs to be developed further.

The second question is the one addressed in the two preceding chapters concerned with measuring short term, medium and long term effects on sales of advertising.

And the third question is at the core of works such as this book in the sense that only through studying carefully how the brain actually works when processing information and when making consumption choices will we be able to proscribe how advertising should be made in order to work – either on developing mental brand equity or on sales, or on both.

Under the broad heading of advertising testing – an activity that is meant to provide information in order to improve the quality of advertising decisions – we usually refer to a number of broad research categories, such as:

- Pre-testing: Determining which executions will with the greatest probability produce the desired results, to a large extent an explorative question
- Post-testing: Determining what effects – out of either the traditional advertising effects or of the desired and intended effects – materialize as the campaign unfolds and how many persons in - and outside the target group have noticed the campaign and have experienced the effects, to a large extent a descriptive question
- Lifestyle and psychographic research, which really is not advertising testing but rather audience research that will help advertisers to develop more meaningful target group descriptions or provide a deeper insight into target consumers' behaviour or simply describe readers/watchers/listeners of individual media options in a   more facetted way
- Basic communication research and behaviour research that will pro vide advertisers with insight into how consumers process commercial communication and how processed information is used by consumers in reaching consumption decisions, this is the true, normative question as referred to above.

As one can well imagine, measuring advertising's effects requires a solid understanding of, how advertising works as part of the total marketing mix that the company brings to bear on the market. The larger part of this book attempts to build such and understanding by analyzing consumers' behaviour and how advertising and other forms of communication might influence that behaviour.

This chapter primarily deals with the discipline of measuring market communication, but it will draw extensively on theories and models of consumer behaviour and information processing by consumers put forward in other chapters of the book.

A. The Economic Argument for Testing Advertising and Monitoring its Effects

There are good economic reasons for spending a certain percentage of one's total advertising budget on testing at different stages in the advertising development process. The Dorfman-Steiner (1954) theorem, of course, applies here. The theorem basically states that investments in various activities that may support each other should be balanced in such a way that the elasticities of each activity with respect to a marginal increase are numerically equal.

For the purpose of advertising testing, we should therefore refrain from thinking in terms of one general advertising elasticity, we should separate advertising spending into its component parts:

- spending on testing
- spending on creative development and production
- spending on media insertions

Corresponding to these component parts, we may define "test spending", "advertising media" and "advertising production" elasticities. The meaning of these elasticities would be:

- Testing elasticity – increasing spending on testing will produce advertising that is better at achieving the desired objectives. The elasticity is positive, and may very well have an S-shape, since taking the first step from pure intuitive judgment to a crude consumer probe might actually not produce any added insight. At the other end of the function, from some point of spending it has a diminishing returns form, meaning that additional spending on testing will improve quality, but not by very much (the testing to death syndrome).
- Creative and production elasticity – actually this might very well be divided into two elasticities, one for each part. Again, the elasticity must be assumed to be positive, the form is probably of the degressive variety, indicating that the first investments in creative work and production work produce the biggest increases in effect. After a certain point of spending, additional effect is indeed very hard to come by (the advertising as art syndrome).
- Media elasticity – the media elasticity must be assumed to be positive (but under certain circumstances it can become negative) and have an either S-shaped or degressive form. Both situations have been argued, S-shape as indicative of advertising of innovation or newness, degressive as indicative of advertising of established brands in competitive markets. The assumption is that from some point in spending, returns will be almost nil and they might actually become negative, if consumers will stop buying a brand because they think they have seen too much advertising for the brand.

Just as is the case with other marketing action parameters in the optimal situation, these elasticities should be equal. In other words, spending on testing should be increased until the test elasticity equals the media and the production elasticities. In the real world, however, one will almost always find companies operating with much larger testing elasticities than the media and production elasticities.

Also adhering to the classic theorem, it should be noted that the budget for media and creative production should be aimed at making these two elasticities equal. This rule of thumb is very rarely met in practice. With the increasing importance of the "media agencies", this tendency may be gradually changing, but in our experience, the trend is primarily in the direction of collecting data central to the work of the media agencies (i.e., monitoring and tracking studies to document effect after the advertising has run).

Advertising pre-testing is being done to a much lesser extent than one would expect – since the elasticity can be expected to be very high. Compared with the amount of money and time spent on evaluating and comparing different media plans, the total amount of money spent on advertising pre-testing is minimal. There are a number of reasons for this state of affairs, and it may be useful to review some of these.

1. Financial Responsibility

In media research, it is the norm that audience research is paid for primarily by the media corporations. They pay because they gain an economic advantage from providing data about their audiences, and since the marginal utility of slightly better data compared to that of the competitor is considerable, the media spend enormous sums of money on research. However, at the end of the day, media research is paid for by the advertisers via advertising prices.

With regard to advertising pre-testing, it is somewhat more uncertain who initiates and pays for the research. Some advertisers claim that this kind of research is part of the service that the advertising agency should provide. When this is the case, the advertising agency may be tempted to avoid testing entirely, or to do so at very low costs. Also they may prefer to do so qualitatively, leaving as much leeway as possible to the interpretation of the findings.

In some cases, the advertiser undertakes to pay for the pre-testing activities. In such cases it can be expected – and it is indeed wise to do so – that the advertiser will agree beforehand with the agency as to what methods of testing will be applied, what key performance indicators will be measured and what benchmarks should be achieved. This way the only possible outstanding issue between agency and advertiser is who gets to pay for the possible reworking of the campaign material – in itself not a small issue to debate.

Quite apart form the economic discussion arising out of the testing activity, another aspect of the advertising agency's role in the advertising pre-testing process has to do with the agency's possibly limited motivation – for professional and/or emotional reasons - to participate in an evaluation, which may eventually result in the cancelling or modifying of the campaign suggested in the first place.

2. Costs of Testing

In looking for appropriate advertising pre-testing approaches, the agency or the advertiser will be mindful of the expenses involved in carrying out the test. The major part of the total costs is not really the test itself. The costs associated with the production of the test material are high, particularly those associated with changing or redesigning the campaign in accordance with the test results. The earlier the test is conducted, the less severe the added creative costs will be for the agency, but the lower the validity of the test results will also be.

Another argument that one comes across is, that the costs of the test could be put to better use buying one or two more insertions! This is only true if the increased effectiveness of the execution is less than that of the test costs as a percentage of the total communication budget. This percentage is likely to be very small. So pragmatically, the argument says that any execution inserted additional times will be more efficient than making sure the execution does, what it is supposed to do. And if that is so, one may wonder why so many advertisers spend money on advertising agencies instead of producing the ads themselves!

The elasticities discussed above are, of course, not easy to quantify, but in the long run, the company should aim at equalizing them. Since only marginal revenues can be expected in relation to each of them, it will be useful to discuss this issue further. Here, the concept of expected future revenue is crucial (Miller and Starr, 1960).

Consider the costs of pre-testing advertising assuming that the costs of a wrong decision are high. The wrong decision may imply a failed introduction, lost market shares, high costs associated with storage, changed production planning, wasted media spending, etc. If experience has shown that with testing, the chances of choosing the right alternative increases from P_1 to P_2, then the costs of pre-testing will be well worth the while, if $P_2 - P_1$ times the loss resulting from a wrong decision (c_w) is larger than the test costs.

A discussion of possible values of P_1 and P_2 can be found in Urban and Hauser (1980). Obviously, with a certain difference between P_1 and P_2 for a particular test design, the relation between the cost of test and the potential gains from more successful market introduction is critical.

Unfortunately – for marketers in small national markets - the test costs (C) are more or less identical in all population size markets. Thus, one would expect more testing in major markets and, more importantly, more radical campaign changes. Furthermore, the relationship between costs to test and the increase: $(P_2 - P_1)$ is important. Generally speaking, tests with larger $(P_2 - P_1)$ values can be expected to have higher costs. So, when more is at stake, higher test costs are obviously warranted, regardless of whether these result from more testing or more elaborate tests. Therefore one would expect large population size markets to exhibit more activity with pre-testing and particularly more sophisticated and therefore costly pre-testing.

3. Timing

Another important issue is that a test resulting in changes or re-planning of a particular campaign also delays the start of the campaign. Often, overall campaign planning leaves no room for changes and adjustments in the execution following testing. In such cases testing may therefore be avoided simply to save time. In the economic terms used here, this means that the value of the lost time must be added to the test costs. Proper planning could minimize this cost element.

4. Test Validity

The creative people in advertising agencies quite often complain that tests do not focus on the important aspects of advertising creation. Over the years, and as recently as in Caroll (2005), business journals have carried articles by creative people arguing that testing is great but that they can't seem to get tests that support their work. This whole debate may gain a new perspective when the emotional role of advertising becomes better understood and testing adjusted appropriately.

From a different standpoint some advertisers also, implicitly, argue against testing with the viewpoint: "it doesn't matter whether the target group likes the advertisements as long as they sell". And in heated discussions between advertisers clamouring for attention-grabbing advertising and creative people advocating the soft sell approach, any points about testing – and what to test for – also seem to get lost.

The simple answers are that advertising should indeed be intended to produce something, very often also something of a communicative nature, which functions as an intervening variable between advertising and sales. And that these types of objectives should be clearly stated and agreed on between advertiser and agency.

This argument is clearly formulated and contained in the title of the publication by Colley (1961): `Defining Advertising Goals for Measured Advertising Results'. Here, Colley and many others later (e.g. Rossitter and Percy, 1997 and Belch and Belch, 2004) argue that one must define what an advertising campaign should bring about, and then design the test so that it controls the extent to which these goals are fulfilled through the recommended creative work.

Yet another obscuring argument has been put forward by testing organisations claiming to have "the one and only" valid measure of advertising effects upon sales. These measures will be reviewed subsequently, but the basic argument is twofold: a) the general – or specific -knowledge about how consumers decide and how advertising interacts in that process is not that far advanced that it seems likely that one "universal" set of measurements is superior to all other sets, and b) that no particular scale or a particular "buying intention change measure" so far is so closely related to later sales that it can be used as the one and only ultimate measure of advertising effectiveness.

5. The Communication Gap Between Researchers and the Creative People

Yet another argument is that even though good and valid advertising pre-testing can be done, the results are presented in such a form that they make no sense to the creative people.

To learn that the arguments used in the ad are less persuasive does not provide any clues as to how the arguments could be changed to become more persuasive. In the media research world, life style and value studies have provided some information to help bridge this gap as they describe target groups in very minute behavioural and attitudinal terms. In advertising testing, a similar information bridge is lacking. Here learning about emotional responses, what creates them and how they can be built, may be useful.

6. Interpretation

An extension of the issue just discussed could be labelled "the interpretation issue". This can be exemplified by the questions such as: "Is it good or bad that a certain percentage of the population, after having been exposed to the advertisement, know our brand to have this or that property? Should it not rather have been twice as many?" The real issue here, of course, is that most measurements of advertising effects are, at best, interval scaled. On such scales, there is no objective zero points. Therefore, results make sense only when compared with something.

One may compare effects in different groups, with different executions, or with effects measured in past tests. The latter alternative, in particular, has led to considerable concern with norms, which may sometimes trigger the counter argument that "the norms do not apply to my product, my campaign, my agency, my choice of media etc".

In practical advertising, however, several testing systems with carefully established benchmark bases, do show impressive results in predicting the performance of a particular execution of a spot or an ad on the system's predetermined key measurement variables – also when the number of benchmark observations in the particular category are few, probably because, irrespective of category, a TV-spot has to work on TV in competition with other spots and programming and those surroundings are the same irrespective of category.

B. Some Important Distinctions

One may wonder why advertising testing is being done at all, given the foregoing arguments against it. But the need for feedback from consumers to the creative bodies is nevertheless overwhelming. Similarly, advertisers' demand for comparative evaluations of differ-

ent campaigns, at different times and in different areas also necessi-
tates advertising testing.

In the following, we shall look at how advertising testing has developed, the measurements applied, the data collection techniques
used, and the evaluation of the results. Finally, we shall speculate as
to the future of the whole area. Before we proceed to discuss the
above-mentioned issues, however, it would be useful to highlight
some important distinctions.

1. The Advertising Development Process
An advertising campaign passes through a number of stages, including

1. target group formulation
2. communication goal formulation
3. creative idea identification
4. evaluation of alternative concepts
5. early tests of unfinished executions
6. tests of finished executions prior to first insertion
7. tests of finished executions in early or first applications
8. tracking of campaign effect
9. tracking of sales effect

Even though all these steps are concerned with the same underlying
advertising objective, the research methodology, and the variables
measured, interpretations etc. change in the course of the process.

In early stages, strategic and problem identification research is
carried out. In the later stages, evaluative and problem solving research is conducted. The present chapter focuses on the latter aspect of communication testing.

Pre-testing may take place at different stages. Generally three
stages are involved, depending on the degree of finality of the creative product:

1. Concept testing.
2. Draft/storyboard testing.
3. Test of final execution.

The last two stages are more likely to be quantitative in character,
whereas the early concept testing may be wholly or partly qualitative.
Furthermore, the variables measured in the different steps vary.

With pre-testing as a concept, most marketing professionals will
assume a test that is carried out before the execution is actually aired
or inserted. However, market-based pre-testing as a special variety of
pre-testing is carried out with actual insertion of an ad or airing of a
spot. It usually takes the form of single tests immediately after the in-

troduction of the campaign, such as 'day after' recall of television ads or page traffic studies of print advertising. But it can also take the form of experimental insertions in a controlled test design.

2. Quantitative versus Qualitative Approaches

Most qualitative research methodologies can be and have been used in advertising testing. Some argue that they are useful only in the early stages of the process (Percy, 1997), others may use them in the testing of final executions as well. Usually, however, the later in the advertising development process the test is carried out, the more quantitatively it is designed.

The major advantage of the qualitative techniques lie in their flexibility, in their ability to provide soft data, and in the relatively limited demand put on the quality and degree of finalization of the tested executions. The latter restriction is rapidly diminishing in importance, since the use of computers for production of advertising dummies and the existence of comprehensive banks of stock photos enable agencies to simulate finished ads with looks and feels as if they were the "real" product. Qualitative test data are discussed in more detail in section D.1 in this chapter

3. Sensitivity versus Validity

Most traditional advertising testing builds on an information-processing model of the individual, best described as the effect hierarchy.

Wärneryd (1959) described the process as composed of

1. attention
2. information processing
3. evaluation
4. preference formation
5. and resulting behaviour

This kind of cognitive thinking has underpinned most of the development of advertising testing since the early days.

Measurements reflecting processes early in the effect hierarchy are generally quite sensitive to changes in the variables causing them. Advertising awareness changes quite easily in response to changes in the creative strategy, in advertising spending and in media choice etc. Purchase intentions, on the other hand, are often quite stable and unaffected by changes in communication variables, just as very few people change their favourite tooth paste brand because of a single exposure to a tooth paste advertisement.

On the other hand, the validity of the measure is generally greater, the later in the sequence it is obtained. Purchase intentions are more closely related to subsequent purchasing behaviour than advertising awareness.

Similarly, we may find that measures at intermediate levels in the effect hierarchy are also characterised by intermediate levels of sensitivity and validity. For instance, brand awareness may be crucial for penetration in new markets, but for predicting market shares of major brands in existing markets it is of very low importance.

In the same way, changes in specific beliefs held about brands may be better (more valid) estimates of subsequent sales than brand awareness. Here, however, changes may be difficult to quantify following a single or a few exposures. In communication research and in advertising testing, attempts are often made to overcome this by the use of so-called "forced exposure", i.e. by designing tests where the respondents' attention is directed towards the communication to an artificially high degree compared to a real market situation. Through this procedure, sensitivity is increased, but it is questionable to what extent this occurs at the expense of the validity of the measurement.

4. Exposure versus Effect Measures

Measuring advertising exposure may be seen as an early step in the advertising effect hierarchy. As discussed in the last chapter it is often referred to as opportunity to see (OTS). It is normally dealt with in media and audience research. Here, the purpose is to compare different media and different combinations of media in terms of readership (print) and amount of exposure (TV and radio).

C. Modeling the Advertising Effectiveness Process

1. The Age of Recognition versus Recall, 1930-70

In the history of quantitative approaches to advertising testing, the first age begins with the recall methodology, developed in the late 20s (Dubow, 1994).

In its original version, respondents were asked what they remembered having seen in a particular publication: yesterday's newspaper, last week's magazine etc. The technique may involve different levels of memory aid. Particularly with the aided recall versions, it has been emphasised that the respondent should recall at least some positively correct information from the advertisement for the measurement to be judged reliable and discriminating.

A major criticism of this method is that people tend to exaggerate how much they recall. In response to this criticism, the so-called proven recall technique was developed by the Starch organization in the 30s (Lipstein, 1985).

Another early approach was the recognition test. Here, the respondent is shown the advertising material before being asked what is read fully, noted or just looked at. It can be used to study what happens to material that appears in publications, or it can be used to evaluate selected material in an experimental setting. In any event, the basic measurement is the level of recognition of what was seen.

Until very recently, the use of recognition data for advertising testing was decreasing. In academic research, however, it has survived and in later years an understanding of the structurally different psychological processes underlying recognition and recall has generated renewed interest in this measure. It has been suggested that whereas recall relies upon activating "coded" information-structures of processed attitudinal and informational items (some would say information stored in the left side of the brain), the recognition process relies to a much larger extent on regeneration of holistic impressions stored very differently in the brain (Du Plessis, 1994b). Thus recognition without recall may indicate the occurrence of emotional information processing.

With the advent of television and the increasing importance of television advertising, the recall technique lent itself easily to adoption to the "day after recall" measure. This was originally developed by Gallup-Robinson and put into extensive use by Procter and Gamble in the 1950s. Eventually, Burke obtained the rights to the Procter and Gamble test and one of the largest advertising testing organisations of the 1960s and 1970s emerged. Part of the usefulness of this measure is that it can easily be combined with audience measures obtained from diaries or with meters. Via audience research and from "day after recall" measures, respectively, it is then possible to both know how many viewers have seen the programme and to estimate how many of those viewers have seen and recall the commercial. The method has been heavily criticised though. In particular, advertising professionals have claimed that recall does not necessarily relate to sales.

It has been argued also that TV day after recall measures of ads has been disastrous to print advertising since no similar technique emerged focused on print. Re-analysing print recognition data suggests that the relative efficiency of TV advertising has been overrated (Jones, 2003 and Hansen et al., 2006a).

More recently contemporary neuromarketing developments have been suggested to "be peace brokers in the recall war" (Penn, 2005, p. 23).

2. Qualitative Research

Parallel with this development, a growing use of qualitative techniques occurred. These are not a major topic in this chapter, but a few remarks should be made on the subject. Starting in the 1950s with traditional motivation research, the standard in-depth and group discussion (focus group) interview techniques developed and they have subsequently dominated the scene until recently. In later years, semiotic approaches have also become popular (Mick, 1986).

The Dichter (1964) motivation research tradition was an American development of the early 1950s. However, in reaction to the somewhat controversial findings, great emphasis was later put upon developing more qualitative advertising evaluation techniques. Nevertheless, when more quantitative techniques (i.e. the Schwerin-test) became available in London in the 60s, they were met with severe criticism because of the lack of sensitivity to the creative process and its elements. Consequently, focus group interviews and in-depth interviews were the preferred advertising testing methods in many places in Europe.

Later, however, quantitative testing became dominant in Europe as well, but the need for qualitative information related to more quantitative tests was obvious and today a number of measurements are built into nearly all test systems, enabling an isolation of the elements of the tested advertisement that have a positive or negative effect. Such semi qualitative ingredients in otherwise more quantitative tests are often referred to as "diagnostics".

3. The Age of Advertising Evaluation, 1940-65

The whole debate led to a quest for other measures of advertising effects. A number of judgmental procedures came into use. "Advertising evaluation" was the critical term. Here, the respondents judged the advertisement according to a number of dimensions such as:

Is it convincing?
Do you like it?
Is it interesting?
Which one (of these) do you prefer?

Respondents are asked to evaluate aspects of the advertisement themselves. Once again, this was met with strong criticism from many practitioners. It was claimed to be of no importance whether the respondent liked the ad or not. The critics assumed that ad liking had no direct effect on subsequent purchases. Nevertheless in the 1980's such measures were reinvented under the title Attitudes towards the Ad (A-Ad) (see D.4 in this chapter)

4. The Persuasion Age, 1960 - to Date

Other researchers looked for measurements related to sales. A measure of change in attitudes, intentions, or preferences was what was needed. Such measures have become known as "persuasion" measures. Basically, two kinds of persuasion measures exist: pre and post exposure measurements of changes in attitudes, preferences, purchase intentions, or the like, and various kinds of scaled preferences. In several instances, persuasion measures have been shown to relate to subsequent sales.

However, a major problem is that most of these measurements require very large samples to produce statistically significant results. Changes in purchase intentions for fast moving consumer goods are generally small. Therefore, the measurements tend to be insensitive. The artificial exposure situation may also create unpredictable effects. On the whole, it seems that if a relationship can be established, it varies greatly between product areas and between situations (Fothergill and Ehrenberg, 1965).

5. Contemporary Views

a) Revival of Multi-Attribute Modeling

The effect hierarchy thinking is still dominant in advertising testing, in spite of also more recent critique (Weilbacher, 2001).

Much communication research takes its point of departure in classical social psychology. The Yale-Hovland School has been very influential in this respect (Hovland and Janis, 1959). The multi-attribute models (as discussed in Chapter II) of consumer choice, 'Fishbein modeling' (Fishbein and Ajzen, 1975), have also been influential.

In later years, with software making it easy to handle the more than standard tabulations needed for computing and reporting the variables in the model (I), commercial applications have also become more frequent.

$$\text{I} \quad A_{1j} = \sum_i a_1 b_{1j}$$

where a_1 = perceived importance of attribute i
and b_{1j} = belief about brand j on attribute i

The normative beliefs and the perceived content models have also been taken into use (Hansen et al., 2004). Lately, proponents of the effect hierarchy of thinking, however, have been arguing for a revival of the classic multi-attribute formulation. Fishbein and Middlestadt (1995, 1997) in reviewing the more important evidence against the multi-attribute model suggest that practically all of the reported findings can be explained by methodological flaws in design, by measurement errors or by erroneous interpretation of the results. Opposing views are put forward by Miniard and Barone (1997) and by Schwarz (1997). At the time of writing, this argument is still in progress and as late as 1997, Martin Fishbein himself claims "as long as no other interpretation has been proven, I shall adhere to the classic one" (personal conversation).

b) Feelings in Response to Advertising

A number of researchers in the 1980's have pointed to the importance of feelings in understanding the effects of advertising (Goldberg and Gorn, 1987). For a review of the various approaches used in the study of feeling effects, see Chapter III. As we shall see in the next chapter contemporary theories on emotions may bring important insights into the process of understanding how advertising is processed and how its effects should be measured.

In the extreme, these authors see the advertising communication process primarily as one that generates feelings or that appeals to feelings that already exist. "These feeling reactions include not only liking and disliking but also love, hate, fear, anger, joy, sadness, and so on (Holbrook and Hirschman, 1982).

It is suggested that feelings may influence attitudes towards the ad as well as beliefs about the brand and thereby the total attitude towards the brand. This occurs in interaction with other information processing activities and, in extreme cases, these effects are dominant. This is much in line with the views put forward earlier in this book. However, the reader should – as always when feelings and emotions are discussed – distinguish between the basic emotions (Chapter V and VI), and the feelings derived from these. In much discussion about feelings in advertising, emotional appeals of advertising and so forth, it is rarely very clear, what connections or relations between emotions and feelings are believed to be relevant.

c) Central vs. Peripheral Information Processing

In the ELAM model introduced in Chapter II the central processing route is very similar to the traditional information processing model's picture of the way in which consumers treat information (see Figure II.14). The peripheral processing, however, is different. Here, information is received and stored more or less unprocessed, and traces can be found in terms of recall or recognition of the advertisement rather than brand recall or changes in attitude towards the brand. If the stored advertising information is eventually aroused in a subsequent purchasing situation and if it is linked to the brand advertised, it may at this time influence purchasing behaviour. Also, emotional responses are in focus when the concern is with the effects of peripheral communication.

The extent to which either of the two ways of processing information dominates is reflected in the reporting of brand- and product-related recall versus story or ad/commercial-related recall. The first reflects central processing, the latter peripheral processing. Such a measure can be based on the coding of open-ended responses. In Chapter II we saw that in most fast moving consumer goods advertising, peripheral processing dominates.

The ELAM advertising pre-test systems are based on a set of measures covering various types of effects like those described in Table.X.1.

Table X.1: The measurements reflecting central and peripheral infor-
mation processing effects in the ELAM model

Variable	Ad-level (peripheral processing)	Brand level (central processing)
Attention	Ad Recall/ Ad Recognition	Brand Recall/Brand Recognition
Processing	Ad-processing	Brand Processing
Association	Emotions towards Ad	"Linking" Brand/Ad
Persuasion	Total Ad evaluation	Purchase intention and self-reported changes in purchase intention

As determinants of the frequency with which central vs. peripheral processes is dominating we find product area involvement, loyal versus non-loyal target group, new versus established product, change versus reinforcement strategy, type of target groups and type of campaign (for instance storytelling, informational or emotional).

Here, involvement reflects the consumers' motivation towards the ad determined by interest in the product area, by alertness in the exposure situation or by individual differences. Loyalty reflects the consumers' usage of the brand. New introductions (product, brand or feature) may be more or less extreme, but easily detectable. The nature of the target group may be reflected in age, sex, values etc.

The nature of the campaign is somewhat more difficult to deal with. Frequently used tools are naive distinctions such as informational, emotional, celebrity, testimonial, anonymous, spokesperson, slice of life/product/use, animated versus real people etc. A classification with some evidence of different processing results is proposed by Peter and Olson (1987). They talk about storytelling versus image versus informational ads.

In connection with a weak/strong communication distinction, an attempt to arrive at a systematic classification based upon emotional content is proposed (Ehrenberg et al., 1997). In the future, however, more systematic procedures for classifying types of campaigns are badly needed for us to gain more insight into communication effects (Andersen, 2004).

d) Testing with Multiple Variables
Parallel with the academic research, the Advertising Research Foundation with its "Copy Research Validity Project" (Haley and Baldinger, 1991) presented findings very much in line with the views held here.

In the persuasion age of the 1970s and 1980s, advertising research, especially in the USA, was dominated by a number of suppliers of specialised advertising effect measurements that were introduced as the only right answer to the advertiser's need for information about advertising effects. These tests mainly used persuasion measures, but recall/recognition techniques were used as well. In this situation, the Advertising Research Foundation decided to start a project with the purpose of clarifying which test relevance and validity claims were true and which were not.

In the "Copy Research Validation Project", the basic idea was simple: Find a number of cases where two campaigns are tested in two different geographical areas, and where the sales results are known. It was decided beforehand to limit the study to fast moving consumer goods. For each of these pairs of commercials, effects were measured with the various effect measures used by the suppliers of advertising pre-tests. By observing how well the various tests predicted the sales difference between the two different campaigns in each pair, it was hoped to identify the most discriminating effect measures.

In the project a total of 15,000 interviews were carried out. A wide selection of effect measures was included in the tests.

- Persuasion (i.e. brand choice, purchase intention etc.)
- Salience (of brand)
- Recall of ad and brand
- Liking of and commercial reactions to the ads

A total of 32 variables were measured. Beyond the above variables, various "diagnostic" measures etc. were also included. Listed in order of importance, the test concluded that the best measures were

- Liking
- Ad Recall/Ad Recognition
- Persuasion

In spite of some methodological criticism (Rossiter and Eagleson, 1994), these conclusions are still valid, but it is important to note that all of the three measures are correlated with the recorded sales and they are correlated with each other. In some instances some may contribute more than others, but there is always a considerable correlation between the three measures. Finally, when evaluating the results, it is important to recall that only FMCG were included in the study.

At the time the somewhat surprising importance of Liking gave rise to discussions. Walker and Dubitsky (1994) wrote: "Are likeable TV commercials more effective? Is liking a useful measure for evaluative pre-testing? Previous research shows liking can work in more than one way to influence viewer response, and some studies suggest that liking may be a valid indicator of relative sales performance. Analysis of a major copy-testing database demonstrate that liking is moderately, but significantly correlated to other validated measures of effectiveness. Used in conjunction with other appropriate measures, liking measures add substantial value to the assessment and optimisation of advertising effectiveness".

The overall practical conclusion is that a single measure cannot be expected to give a complete answer to all questions about the communication effect of any single campaign. It is more likely that different effect measures are relevant in relation to different campaigns and that, in any case, more effect measures are necessary in order to evaluate entire campaigns.

Haley and Baldinger (1991) write: "The study also confirms that advertising works on a number of levels, and, therefore, that no single measure is adequate to measure the effectiveness of copy seems to receive strong confirmation here. Multiple measurements are necessary for a full evaluation of copy effectiveness".

More recently, Ehrenberg et al. (1997) have pointed at a distinction between what they call "strong force" persuasion ($\approx$ central processing) and "weak force" persuasion ($\approx$ peripheral processing). The strong persuasion theory may apply when high involvement occurs and when the purpose of the advertisement is to create change (in connection with introductions), convincing non-loyals, informing about new features etc. In contrast, the weak "salience" theory may be more relevant with low involvement purchases among loyal and partly loyal consumers with little inclination to change, i.e. where reinforcement is important.

A development away from fully standardized tests towards what one could label "semi-standardized tests" makes the use of benchmark data considerably more complicated and relies more on the skilled interpretation of the test results. Moreover, the choice of test design relies heavily upon the researcher's ability to judge the campaign along the important dimensions discussed. In the extreme, a campaign introducing a new product with many new features may take much more advantage of measures of central processing variables in the effect testing than would be the case when testing a "maintenance" campaign for a well-established brand in an FMCG category.

A campaign for a FMCG with no real differences from its major competitors may expect peripheral information processing and consequently rely on measuring their effects. In many product cases, however, the advertiser may have to use both kinds of measures, since different segments in the market may use combinations of peripheral and central processes to varying degrees.

D. Measurements of Advertising Effects

Regardless of their theoretical conviction, researchers make use of a variety of different measures in an attempt to quantify the effects of advertising exposure. Broadly speaking, they may be classified as:

1. qualitative responses
2. mechanical registrations
3. ad and brand recall and recognition
4. scaled responses
5. market related data

1. Qualitative Data

Qualitative information results from group discussions (focus groups), in depth interviews and the like. The use of these methodologies may be based on any or all of the theoretical foundations described in the preceding section.

Qualitative responses, however, also appear in pre- as well as in post-testing in the form of answers to open-ended questions, which are subsequently coded and analysed more or less systematically. Such questions may appear in many different forms. Examples of such questions are: "What in particular did you like/dislike about the advertisement you just saw?", "what do you think you would tell others if asked about the advertisement you just saw?", "what do you think the advertisement tried to convey about the product?" The number of possible questions is legion and most respondents are able to provide one to five meaningful statements in reply to questions of this kind.

Although specific wording of the questions does influence what items are brought up and the order in which they appear, the same things are generally repeated. It would seem that with the use of a sufficient variety of questions and proper probing, there is a maximum amount of meaningful verbal responses that can be elicited. A listing of this complete verbal response could be - and often is - treated as qualitative information. It is, however, also possible to systematize the information to various degrees. A coding of verbal responses to an advertisement is almost always standard. Coded statements may be classified depending on whether they are positive or negative in nature, and whether they primarily relate to the product or reflect aspects of the advertisement itself and the story contained in this. Such codings may be useful in their own right, but particularly when seen in connection with other meaningful dependent variables such as an overall effect score. They may give important insight into what aspects of the advertisement generate the effects in the study. Such analyses are frequently called diagnostics.

Another qualitative approach used is laddering; the study of means and links between the product and underlying values and motives (Reynolds et al., 1997 and Rasmussen, 2000). The use of semiotic approaches represents a newer trend in qualitative research. The 1980s witnessed an increasing interest in humanistic research within consumer behaviour and marketing research (Belk, 1988). Some of this found its way into advertising research, particularly phenomenological, semiotic or linguistic methodologies.

Here, the content of the advertisement is in focus, not so much for its immediate meaning, but rather as an indicator of underlying cultural values and norms. The focus is on the way in which the receiver of the advertisement interprets and internalises the message.

Commercial applications have been reported. A structured method of reporting, including a suggested framework (Figure X.1), is found in Mick and Buhl (1992). Here, it is suggested that the meaning that the individual consumer ascribes to advertising must be seen in the light of the life stories, acquired values, and interpretation of the person himself. Such an approach, however, is time consuming and expensive.

Figure X.1: Meaning based model of advertising experiences (Mick and Buhl, 1992)

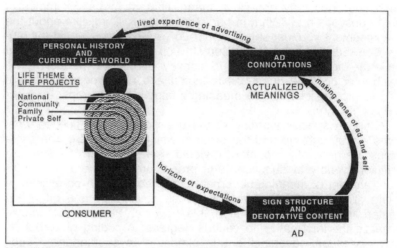

National Life Projects involve meanings associated with nationalities and internationality.
Community Life Projects involve meanings associated with residential areas, peer groups and careers.
Family Life Projects involve meanings associated with family members, including parents, siblings, spouse, and children.
The *Private Self Life Project* involves meanings associated with being an individuated human being, including personal activities and interests.

A pervasive *Life Theme* such as being active versus being passive.

Because of the cost, few studies work with a large enough number of respondents to warrant generalisations. The content of TV programmes and advertising has been interpreted systematically in a more operational form (Hirschman, 1990). When this is done for a brand and its competing brands, it throws light on the basic themes or meanings based on which the product functions.

Semiotic interpretations of advertising perceptions assume that when processing information the consumer looks upon advertising and its content as reality itself rather than applying a hierarchical information theory approach. Particularly with advertising such as dramas or story telling semiotic analyses may be useful. Grayson and Vehill (1997) analyse the likelihood of the different information process styles. With low involvement FMCGs, they find most support for the drama (peripheral) interpretation.

In many ways, the clear boundary between quantitative and qualitative data is blurring. Some of the attempts discussed here illustrate this. Emotional response measures as discussed in Chapter V and VI and again in Chapter X and XI are points in case. Also, new techniques for computer analysis of qualitative data are emerging. Even though the software available today is not perfect, the future may show important developments (Fielding and Lee, 1991).

Apart from the recent tendency to combine quantitative and qualitative approaches, the whole area of communication research may be seen as continuously stretching from pure qualitative research supporting judgmental decisions to quantitative research aimed at prediction of the effect with few judgmental elements in the application (Feldwich, 1998).

2. Mechanical Measures of Effect

Over the years, various mechanical responses to advertising exposure have been registered and interpreted in terms of effect (Ray and Olsen, 1982; Stewart and Furse, 1982; and Stewart, 1984). Many of these have been tried also in attempt to quantify advertising responses. Among the more prominent technologies are:

1. eye movement (von Keitz, 1988)
2. lateral eye movements (Ehrlichmann et al. 1978)
3. tachistoscope (Wexler and Heninger, 1981)
4. dichotic listening (Hansen, 1981)
5. galvanic skin response (La Barbera and Tucciarone, 1995)
6. pulse rate (Ray and Olsen, 1982)
7. pupilometric (Hess, 1972)
8. lever pressing (Kroeber-Riel, 1987)

The use of other more advanced and more complicated techniques can be found also:

- EEG (Electro Encephalo Gram) (Rothschild et al.(1984); Krugman(1977); Appel et al. (1979) and Weinstein et al.(1984)
- Emission Tomography (Lassen et al., 1978) and others.

Most of these latter methodologies have been used in highly experimental settings with very small samples only. Concern for respondent safety, complexity, and difficulties in interpretation of findings have largely ruled out commercial applications of these techniques. To an unknown extent the measures may in reality reflect emotional rather than cognitive responses to communication. And discussed earlier, several of these response measures have been used also in quantifying emotional responses (Chapter V)

The study of eye movements dates back to the late 1950s. With the use of special equipment mounted on the head of the respondent (or in front of the respondent), the movement of the pupils is followed while the test item is being studied. The technique is best used with print advertising, but adaptations to television commercials have also occurred. In the early years, the measurement equipment was complex and expensive and it undoubtedly greatly influenced the respondent's way of observing. In later years, more flexible and less expensive equipment has become available, but its commercial use is still relatively limited.

Basically the findings indicate that any copy or combined material such as an advertisement is perceived by the eye of the respondent focusing on particular items for a very short duration, followed by a move to a new location (Heath, 2001). Thus, what the eye movement study reveals is where the attention is directed, in what order and to what extent. In contrast with many other mechanical registrations of response, this lends itself easily to interpretation. Suggestions as to what to emphasise and what to modify in the creative execution are rather obvious, provided the observations reflect what will happen in a normal media exposure situation (Rosbergen et al., 1997).

Galvanic skin response, pulse rate, lateral eye movements, pupilometric, lever pressure, EEG and related measures reflect arousal, tension and alertness in the respondent in contrast with relaxation (Detenber et al., Link) Such measures require adaptation of electrodes or other measurement devices. For example, galvanic skin response requires the application of two electrodes in different locations of the hand, enabling a registration of the amount of current passing through the sweaty surface of the hand. All of these measures are highly sensitive and strong reactions can be seen to elements in the advertisement or the commercial.

The methodologies have been used in the study of responses to television commercials to register reactions over time. Novelty, surprise, and change in the course of a 30 second commercial led to strong responses. Interpretation, however, is difficult. It is obvious that one can identify what elements create reactions, but it is more difficult to understand the nature of these reactions. Does a change in heart rate following a sudden change on the screen reflect happiness or fear? What is the significance of a response that is twice as large as another response? Even though these and similar questions may be tentatively answered when the techniques are used in conjunction with other measures, the artificial measurement situation, the relatively high cost per observation, and the uncertainty as to the interpretation of results have greatly limited the use of these methodologies.

The last two mechanical measures to be mentioned, tachistoscope and dichotic listening, do not really rely upon mechanical response registration. Rather, the presentation of the test item is mechanically controlled. In dichotic listening, different messages are presented simultaneously to the left and to the right ear, so that any dominating tendency of a message (slogan, piece of music, brand name etc.) is registered. To control ear differences, the presentation of the two messages tested must be randomised with regard to presentation to the left and right ear.

The tachistoscope is a device for providing very brief presentations of messages, down to 1/1000 of a second. This technique is used to measure how early different messages are recognised or recalled. Particularly in the study of picture perception (Sheikhian, 1982 and Kroeber-Riel 1993), the remarkable ability of humans to store pictorial information for extended periods even after very brief exposures has been proven. Contemporary concerns with "peripheral" processing should make the use of the methodology interesting. The role of recognition in connection with ad liking will also be interesting to study.

Finally, facial emotional responses have been measured electronically. Hazlett and Hazlett (1999) show meaningful positive/negative facial exposure changes related to advertising exposure.

On the whole, however, mechanical measures' downfall is their complexity; the complexity of the artificial exposure situation they generate and because of the difficulties associated with interpreting scores. Not until such measures become integrated parts of more holistic advertising test designs can they be expected to pay off in the commercial sense of the word.

Recently, a new wave of research is beginning to appear. As discussed in the first part of this book one of the major reasons for the breakthrough in our understanding of emotional and related choice guiding processes is the insight new hospital equipment for brain scanning gives in the functioning of the human brain. This has primarily come from PET and FMRI scanning. These techniques are now also appearing in studies of the effects of marketing communication. Particularly, findings from FMRI scanning are beginning to appear in the advertising literature (Plassmann et al., 2005, Deppe et al. 2005, McClure et al. 2004 and Plassmann et al. 2005).

Electronic measurements applied in media research are also undergoing rapid development. It is predictable that traditional TV meters will be replaced with monitor devices that the individual is carrying with him. And similar development is ongoing for radio listening, and for the measurement of the exposure to posters and of the outdoor advertising materials.

3.A. Advertising Recall
The extent to which advertising is recalled reflects its attention value, and is measured with aided and unaided recall questions. The levels of recall found vary according to the amount of aid given in the measurement situation. Unaided recall scores for TV commercials in day-after recall designs normally range from 0-20%. Aided recall may approach 100% for impressive commercials.

The amount of recall may be varied by mentioning the name of the TV-programme or magazine in which the advertisement was exposed. The product area may be mentioned ("Did you see any advertisements for cereals yesterday?") or even the brand name. Table X.2 gives an overview of the different kinds of aid given in recall questions.

Table X.2: Memory dredging techniques (Plessis, 1994b)

Technique	Description
Full recognition	Show ad to respondents. It dredges memory with a complete cue and establishes the presence of the ad in memory. A few may lie about having seen it.
Masked recognition	Show ad taking out all brand references. When they say they have seen it, ask them the brand. Those who say they have seen it can be taken as the ad being 'in memory' and the second lot as 'having made the brand-ad link'- The latter interpretation is probably wishful thinking – people might have made the connection at the time of interview. A 'masked' ad is never just another ad. Then it is unlikely that a Mercedes ad looks like a Nissan ad. By simple elimination, many respondents will get to the answer – one will not know how many got there due to the link existing, or by a process of elimination
Full description	If you lack material, or the opportunity to show the ad, you can describe the ad in the name of the brand. You will have to give the results of this method the same interpretation as for 'full recognition', but generally your measure will be lower due to the cueing material being less comprehensive
Masked description	You can try to achieve the same effect as what you strive fro under 'masked recognition' by describing the ad without giving the brand, and if the respondent then claims to remember it, you can ask the brand.
Brand prompted recall	You can give the brand name and ask whether the respondent can remember seeing an ad – then you can ask for a description. Obviously this presents just about the lowest level of richness in cueing material and will get the lowest results.

As shown in Table X.2, recognition may be interpreted as recall with an extreme amount of aid. Structurally, however, recognition is different from recall and in its extreme form it may reflect pictorial holistic information storage in the memory rather than processed and evaluated information. Recognition of print may be measured with the use of "page traffic" questioning or with the use of folders. With ads, storyboards or selected pictures are most frequently used.

When studying ad-awareness, the length of time preceeding the time where recall is measured should be specified. A frequently used approach is to ask: "Have you seen any advertisements recently?"

Here, as with other questions tapping the memory of the respondent, the shorter the time lag between the exposure and the questioning, the more precise - and sensitive - the answer. Therefore, asking about yesterday or last week gives more sensitive measures than asking: "Have you seen any advertisements at all?" With low levels of ad-recall, however, the "yesterday" procedure gives very few responses and the researcher will have to balance the wish for sensitive measures against the need for a reasonable number of observations.

3.B. Brand Recall

Brand awareness is a dominant factor when it comes to deciding which brand the consumer will consider at the time of purchasing. As such, brand awareness reflects deliberation sets, aroused alternatives or similar groupings of those alternatives consumers actually consider.

Thus, brand recall may be an important measure of effect. The more advertising is able to generate brand awareness, the better it works. For established brands, however, brand recall is not very sensitive. With new introductions and with less known brands, the sensitivity is much greater.

As with ad recall, varying degrees of aid may be used. Listing brand names in front of the respondent increases recall dramatically. Apart from its importance in connection with small and new brands, brand recall may also be meaningful in connection with more established brands. In a highly competitive world, it is not possible for the consumer to have high recall of very many brands in any particular market.

In this connection, the structure in brand recall in different markets may be of interest. Laurent and Kapferer (1989) have presented findings on this. They show that in many markets a few brands account for a very high percentage of the total aided recall. The typical relationship is illustrated in Figure X.2. The limited intellectual ability of the individual to store brand names is suggested as an explanation for this phenomenon.

Brand recall is generally not very sensitive when testing ads for established brands in stable markets. In dynamic markets in contrast with new products and brands and the introduction of new features etc., brand recall may be a sensitive and useful effect measure. Of course, with new brands, brand recall relies heavily on distribution also. Blackburn et al. (1984) proposes a model "LITMUS" to estimate brand recall for new introductions based upon rating points, and distribution.

Another important use of brand awareness appears in connection with the concept of salience. In any given branded area, the consumer may have a limited number of alternatives that can be considered. These are likely to be those recalled first; that is, the most "salient" alternatives. Salience in this sense is included in the ARF Copy Research Validity Project (Haley and Baldinger, 1991) and discussed among others by Ehrenberg et al. (1997) and by Keller (2003).

Figure X.2: The relationship between aided and unaided brand recall (Laurent and Kapferer, 1989).

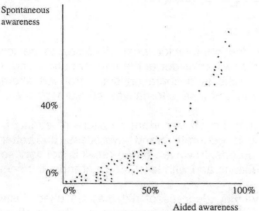

4. Scaled Measures

a) Attitudes towards the Ad (A-Ad)

A-Ad reflects the way in which consumers evaluate specific advertisements and it has been studied since the early days of advertising research. In a way, the concept of attitude toward the ad (A-Ad) may be seen as being parallel with attitudes towards the brand (A-brand). The relationship between the two is well established (Braun and Stayman, (1992)). Early studies were of a more qualitative character and people were asked to express their evaluation of a specific advertisement.

Early findings are reported in Schlinger (1979) who departing in 600 potential items arrived at 8 general dimensions not unlike those shown below. Later more standardized measures were developed, often based on qualitative pre-studies. In a review of more than ten different studies of A-ad (Holbrook and Batra, 1987), more than 100 different wordings of scaled statements appeared: "I learned from this ad", "I find this ad artistic", "this ad doesn't give any facts, just creates an image" etc. To structure the large variety of statements, a few authors have factor-analysed responses to a large number of scaled statements and found six basic dimensions:

1. Emotional ("strong feeling", "try to create a mood" etc.)
2. Threatening ("suggested a solution to a problem", "try to arouse fear and anxiety" etc.)
3. Entertaining ("low level of novelty", "amusing" etc.)
4. Sexy ("sex appeal", "beauty appeal" etc.)
5. Cognitive ("company image", "week", "hot" etc.)

6. Personal (informational), ("uses product claims", "relevant to me", "had information of interest to me" etc.)

The overlap between some of the dimensions in the measurement of A-AD and more feeling/emotional aspects is obvious.

Walker and Dubitsky (1994), using commercial data, found five A-AD factors: entertainment, relevance, information, irritation and confusion. Fewer dimensions are used by Gallup and Robinson (Greene, 1991). Based upon factor analysis of 18 positive adjectives, they found two factors that accounted for more than two thirds of the common variance: 1. "believable", "convincing", "trustworthy" etc.; 2. "entertaining", "amusing" etc. Additionally, they included a dimension combining negative views on the advertisement.

Goldberg and Gorn (1987) asked respondents to classify advertisements and found three categories, namely: feeling based, informative and factual. Haley and Baldinger (1991), reporting on the ARF copy research validity project, found similar dimensions in A-Ad.

Finally, du Plessis (1994a) reviews different authors' proposed A-Ad variables as shown in Table X.3.

Table X.3: A-Ad variables used by different authors (du Plessis,1994b)

Schlinger	Wells, Leavitt and McConville	Aaker and Bruzzone	Muldovan	Aaker and Stayman
Entertaining	Humorous	Entertaining		Amusing/lively Clever/(dull)
Relevant	Relevant	Relevant	Clear	Informative/effective
Alienating	Irritating	Irritating	Tasteless (credible)	Irritating Silly/(believable)
Empathetic	Sensual	Warm	Empathetic/ self-involving	Warm
Familiar	(Unique)			Familiar
Confusing				Confusing
Brand reinforcing				

Obviously, the specific dimensions along which the attitude towards the ad has to be quantified vary with the ad as well as with the nature of the target group. However, more systematic work might result in more standardised measures, which would be useful in comparing findings across studies, campaigns, and cultures.

b) Feelings

Feelings (emotions) sometimes appear as a dimension in A-Ad. Like attitudes towards the ad, feelings are measured with a variety of scaled items. In relation to advertising, feelings may be important in two different contexts. One may be concerned with the feelings generated by the environment of the advertisement and the way in which such feelings influence the perception of the specific advertisement. Such studies are also looked upon as studies of the effects of moods. They may, however, also be studied in terms of the feelings generated by viewing the advertisement. In the latter case, the concern is with the way in which such feelings influence the ultimate goal of the advertisement positively or negatively, i.e. the creation of persuasion, positive liking and brand preferences.

As discussed in Chapter V and VI, feeling words may also be used in attempts to quantify more basic underlying emotions, - an issue to be taken up again in Chapter XI and XII. Particularly the debate relating to the PANA versus the PAD models should be kept in mind.

In advertising research, simpler, reduced batteries of feelings are often used. Franzen (1994) suggests and extended PAD model covering four categories of feeling:

- upbeat (cheerful, playful)
- warm (affectionate, hopeful, calm)
- uneasy (anxious, uncomfortable, tense)
- negative (bored, disgusted, dubious, disinterested)

Feelings can be scaled responses with the respondent indicating to what degree she or he experiences the feeling in question, or they can be indicated by the respondent pointing at feeling words or other stimuli.

Feelings and attitudes towards separate entities, each of which influence liking, preferences and the perceptual process as such, and both are influenced by more basic underlying emotions.

c) Liking

In the ACR copy test validation project (Haley and Baldinger, 1991) liking came out as an important factor. Liking is generally perceived as a one-dimensional overall evaluation of the advertisement. In this sense, it parallels the concept of the preferences towards the brand. Thorson (1991) has reviewed a number of different studies, showing the importance of ad liking to brand attitude, and du Plessis (1994c) has come to the same conclusion, but also points at some conceptual weaknesses of the concept, particularly the unspecified extent to which liking is a function of the message components solely or also of executional components.

Generally, a five-point liking scale is agreed upon and used in many studies. For instance, Madden et al. (1988) report average scores, derived from a large number of tests, on such a scale. The scores are shown below:

- Like it very much 25%
- Like it somewhat 33%
- Felt that it was neutral 30%
- Disliked it somewhat 8%
- Disliked it very much 4%

In the ARF copy research validity project, two different measures are used: "one of the best seen lately" (top box or average) and scaled scores of like/dislike. Among these, the average liking score performed the best.

Table X.4: Liking and Awareness in Day after Recall for 23 TV Ads (Hansen, 1997)

TV	Average Liking (on 10 Points Scale)	Awareness % (Aided Recall)
Yellow Pages	40	32
Coca Cola	35	65
SAS Jackpot	23	52
Tele Danmark Mobile telephone	19	60
Lotto	18	51
Suzuki	16	25
TV 1000	16	33
Super Brugsen (cooperative retailer)	9	74
Knorr Mix	7	35
Whiskas Cat Food	6	36
McDonalds	4	42
BG Bank	3	37
Matas (pharmacy stores)	2	54
Lätta Minarine (margarine)	-3	20
Ekstra Bladet (newspaper)	-5	60
Pedigree Pal Dog Food	-5	55
Neophos Detergent	-11	31
Ferrero Rocher	-12	46
Nivea Visage Optimale	-16	21
Omo Total	-18	33
Studioline Styling (L'Oréal)	-18	38
Organics Shampoo	-19	43
Ferrero Kinder	-44	28

In Danish applications (Hansen, 1997), a similar five-point scale has been used. Table X.4 shows scores for 23 ads together with day-after-recall scores for the same ad. As other findings have shown, liking of ads is not closely related to attention.

d) Attitudes towards the Brand (A-Brand)

A-Brand are important measures of advertising effects. Such attitudes also depend upon past experiences with the product, and the ability of a specific campaign to create measurable changes varies widely. Attitudes towards the brand reflect the way in which the consumer perceives the brand (its image or the beliefs held about it), and the extent to which it can be shown that the advertisement triggers or generates such beliefs; it reflects the advertisement's ability to link in with the brand and not only create interest, entertainment and ad liking.

Attitudes or beliefs about the brand vary dramatically with the nature of the brand and, in contrast to attitudes towards the ad, it is not likely that any standard battery can be found. Rather, in a specific test, the important aspects of the consumer's perception of the brand should be included in the battery, and particularly the beliefs that the ad is trying to influence should be in focus.

The measurement of image and attitudes is not discussed further here (see Chapter II). However, it should be added that to the extent that such measures reflect what has been referred to as "linking" (Brown, 1989), it may be possible to use generalised linking scores to make comparisons across tests possible. Such standardized measures can be developed either with the use of questions that measure linking at the general level ("I think the advertisement says a lot about the brand", "I think the information in the advertisement about the brand is useful to me" etc.) or with the use of brand specific beliefs ("coca-cola is refreshing", "coca-cola is for young people", "Zendium cleans better than any other toothpaste", "Zendium has a pleasant taste").

A-Brand, or brand evaluation, may range from subjective judgments (such as brand "A" is more "in" than others) to a pure understanding of the brand and its nature (knowing about the frequency of departures for trains, of calories in food, about material of fabrics etc). The extent to which communication results in knowledge being acquired, may be measured with the use of simple exam questions such as "true/false" or multiple-choice questions. With the introduction of the Intercity Train concept in Denmark in the 70s, the success of the introductory campaign was measured by tracking with true/false questions such as "trains depart every hour", "coffee is not being served in the train" etc. (Bache and Hansen, 1975). With less tangible product features such as taste, looks, durability, "high class" etc., image type measures are applied. Measures of A-brand, or attitudes towards the brand, may be seen as being parallel to the A-Ad discussed earlier.

As campaigns are meant to reinforce A-Brand, before/after measures may be in focus. With campaigns meant to change understanding or image (such as with new introductions), the ability of the campaign to generate the desired knowledge is central.

e) Brand Preferences

By nature, these are uni-dimensional. Measurement scales used in other consumer studies may be as diverse as lottery measures, +5 -5 rating scales, constant sum scales, paired comparisons, forced switching, first and second choices etc. Basically, all of these and other measures reflect the overall evaluation of the brand or that which is being advertised.

They vary in sensitivity, validity and reliability. Axelrod (1966) found "first brand awareness", "forced switching" and "constant sum scales" the most predictive and sensitive measures. However, differences do exist, and in order to arrive at more stable measures, sometimes more than one scale is used.

f) Persuasion Scores

These scores are meant to be the most predictive of subsequent purchasing behaviour over the years. Much documentation has been published in the Journal of Advertising Research on the validity of different commercial persuasion measures.

In the ARF copy research validity project, persuasion is quantified in terms of pre-post changes in brand choice, constant sum ratings, purchase interest, consideration frame and (top box) brand rating.

In other studies with one-dimensional scales, attempts to quantify persuasion have been made. In the Buy Test (Hansen and Andersen, 1993), a Gutman-scaled buying predictive intention is used. In other studies, the respondents' own ratings of buying intention are preferred. Particularly with durables and services and with less well-established brands, new introductions and with major changes in brand strategy, such measures can be sensitive and relate to other aspects of ad exposure.

The degree of agreement between purchasing intentions and actual purchases may also provide meaning in its own right (Ehrenberg et al., 1997). Intentions exceeding purchase share may be interpreted as a measure of the dominance of pull versus push mechanisms in the market. When a consumer in a particular market expresses higher intentions of purchasing a brand than the degree to which the same consumer actually does purchase the brand, it suggests the presence of an unexplored "pull" potential in the market. Here, advertising preferences, past experiences and other factors have generated a larger intention to buy the brand than its distribution and other factors in the market supports.

On the other hand, when consumers buy brands to a larger extent than their intentions suggest, a push-dominated market situation exists. Here, people actually buy the brands to a larger extent than one would expect from their preferences, because of the brands' availability, promotion, deals and other market-related factors.

With better-established products and brands, self-rated changes in intentions can be used. Such an attempt is reported by Hansen (1997), who worked with self-rated changes in buying intention. These self-rated scores may reveal changes in intentions for up to 50% of the respondents. Typical scores for such a measure are shown in Figure X.3.

Figure X.3: Typical self-rated change in buying intention score after forced exposure in a monadic test situation (Hansen,1997)

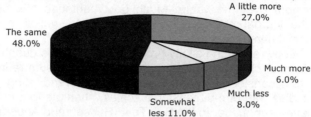

Attempts with commitment as an overall persuasion effect measure are also found. Here a conversion scale is proposed (Hofmeyr and Rice, 2000). This is an 8 category scale dividing consumers in groups from "extremely secure users "over "vulnerable users" to "strongly unavailable non-users". The cases shown by the authors suggest the sensitivity of such a scale as an advertising effect measure. In Chapter XI we shall see how such measures relate to NERS-scores.

Many studies have pointed to an overall effect score. This score may be one-dimensional such as in the case of persuasion scores, or it may comprise scores from different dimensions.

A popular view held in many advertising agencies is that a good campaign must create attention – "a communication portal must be created" – and the ad must be persuasive – "carry the product across". This calls for a combined attention and persuasion score in line with the "commitment" score used by Camphorn (1996) as a summary measure of attention and effect, here termed "bonding". For this score, meaningful sensitivity is documented and together with awareness scores, data is analysed for a two-way classification of ads. The recall index and persuasion index scores discussed in Chapter VIII may be seen in the same light.

A summary measure can also be a combination of the Liking and Awareness Scores. This is done with TV ad data from 'day after recall' testing (du Plessis, 1994a). A Danish report for newspapers is shown in Figure X.4 (Hansen, 1997). Compared to similar data for TV-spots some, although far from perfect, correlations can be observed. The slight correlation for print ads is most likely to be explained by the more selective nature of newspaper reading.

Figure X.4: Liking and Ad-Recall for Newspaper Ads in a major Danish newspaper (Berlingske Tidende) 1994-95 (Berlingske X-Ray Effect Base – Gallup)

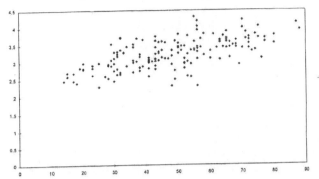

More complex scores take all of the three elements found in the ARF study into consideration. The correspondence between the three measures is far from perfect, but close enough to suggest a mutual relationship to a common fourth factor that could be labelled "campaign effect". Such a score was introduced by Hansen (1997).

Figure X.5: Correlation between attention, liking and persuasion in 18 pre-tests (Hansen, 1997)

	Recall	Liking	Self rated buying Intention
Recall	–	0.63	0.23
Liking		–	0.44
Self rated Buying intention			–

Here recall, liking, and self-rated change in buying intention are measured following exposure to a complete commercial block in a hall test design. For each of these three scores, a figure is computed for the tested ad dividing the score for the ad by the average of all tested relevant ads for comparison. Following this, a geometrical average (multiplying the three scores with each other) is computed. To the extent that each of the scores is larger than one, it shows that in the test ad it is slightly better than average. Similarly, to the extent that the average score is larger than one, the advertisement tested is better than average as a whole. The computation is shown in Figure X.6.

Figure X.6: *Computation of combined Elaboration Likelihood Ad-effect Measure (ELAM) (Hansen, 1997)*

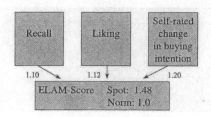

In interpreting these findings, it is important to remember that for some ads liking or self-rated buying intention may be the most important objective, for others it may be attention. This should be kept in mind when judging the total score. However, the score gives a summary measure that enables the researcher to compare the advertisement tested with other advertisements/commercials and with relevant groups of advertisements/commercials.

It also provides a score that can be used as an indicator of creative strength in media planning. Results from tests of six are shown in Table X.5 where the score from one of the same ads shown on television is also included (Tuborg Squash). As shown in the table, the difference between the total effectiveness score (the ELAM score) can be ascribed to the different attention value (recall) generated by the two media, whereas the differences in the cinema spot also depend upon liking and persuasion. An observation also made by Gullen (1998) who shows how pre-test recall scores are poor predictors of similar post-test scores. Again, here the difference in the nature of the exposure situation shows up in the recall of the ad.

Table X.5: *Elaboration Likelihood Advertising Model (ELAM) effect scores for five cinema spots and one TV spot (Hansen, 1997)*

		Recall %	Liking Scale 1 to 5	Self-rated Buying Intention	ELAM Effect Score
C	Tele Danmark	0.38	0.62	(2.5)*	0.70
I	Adidas (shoes)	0.55	0.71	2.61	0.91
N	Statoil (gasoline)	0.51	0.98	2.33	0.80
E	Evers (candy)	0.75	0.85	2.45	1.15
M	Carlsberg (Beer)	0.78	1.33	2.60	1.40
A	Tuborg Squash (soft drink)	0.84	1.62	2.72	1.78
TV	Tuborg Squash (soft drink)	0.29	1.62	2.86	0.62

*not measured across all respondents

Other integrated effect measures have also been attempted. One such effect measure is reported by Deighton et al. (1989) and used by Grayson and Vehill (1997). In the application reported by the latter, an overall effect measure was used, integrating three measures for the expression of belief, three measures for the expression of feeling and two measures each for counter argumentation, attitudes towards the advertisement, attitudes towards the product and attitudes towards the campaign.

Rather than developing a single summary measure, one could attempt to study the overall relationship between the different measures reflecting various aspects of the way in which the advertising communication is being received. Such an attempt is reported by Metha (1994) and later by Hansen (1997). Here, the technique used is a linear structural equation analysis (LISREL). Here the relationships between the different variables are estimated simultaneously relative to a model postulating the direction in which the cause and effect works in each of the relationships. Moreover, the model allows for taking into consideration a larger number of questions used for estimating each of the critical variables in the model.

5. Market Measures

To all advertisers the most valuable measure of the effect of advertising is the sales generated by it. In post-testing, measurements of the market and its reactions are therefore important. Recent developments in research methodology are in a direction where such measures become mandatory for all major advertisers, although the direct causal relationship between advertising exposure and sales is still a vague one. (See Chapter VIII)

Here, market responses will be discussed in terms of

1. sales figures
2. aggregated market data
3. individual purchase data
4. related market responses

a) Sales Data

Advertising would never have come into general use had it not been for some early advertisers being convinced that their sales results could be seen in light of their advertising activities. Actually, in some instances such a relationship is not too difficult to establish. For many retailers, the specific offers advertised weekly result in different sales and by accumulating the experiences, information can be provided that may guide future selection of items to promote as well as creative executions and media choice.

With coupon advertising, at least some of the immediate effect of the advertisement is registered directly through the return of the coupon. Such measures are frequent in connection with direct marketing programs. In some markets, where the influence on sales of factors other than advertising is of limited importance, the study of the direct relationship between advertising spending and sales results may make sense. The Lydia Pinkham data represents a classical case in point (see Figure VIII.1). This approach is discussed in Chapter VIII.

For most advertisers, however, sales figures are not easily related to advertising efforts. There are the two basic reasons for this: First, sales depend upon a number of other factors besides advertising, which is often a relatively minor factor. This effect cannot be isolated and the lack of data further accentuates this problem.

Second, advertising may have an effect not only in the period in which it occurs, but also in subsequent periods. This time lag phenomenon has to be included in any modeling of advertising effects, and this is not easily done. The advertising agency faced with the client's criticism that 'we didn't sell more because of the campaign we just ran', may retort with 'this may be the case, but in the long run the brand has improved its position significantly'.

b) Aggregated Consumer Data
Aggregated market behaviour measures may come from retail audit panels, consumer panels, or continuous ad hoc research. In all instances, market share is most frequently the variable studied. This may be based on sales volume or consumer expenditures in the form of retail auditing data or data from consumer panels. It may also be based on share of purchases or share of items purchased as is the case with some consumer panel data and with consumer ad hoc continuous studies. Also such measures were discussed in Chapter VIII.

Nevertheless, most major manufacturers of consumer goods do track market shares in one or more of the ways here. They do so not only to study effects of advertising, but also to follow the effects of the total marketing activities of the company. They may have varying degrees of success in singling out the significance of the various individual factors influencing the market share over time, but this activity is an important part of their market monitoring.

c) Behavioural Data at the Individual Level
With consumer panel data and with continuous ad hoc work, looking upon behaviour at the individual level is possible; that is, the behaviour of each single respondent may be studied in relation to things such as the same individual's advertising exposure, product availability in the store the individual frequents, purchase of products by deals etc. The growing availability of single source data has increased the interest in this area. Such attempts were discussed in Chapter VIII.

d) Other Market Related Behavioural Data
In some instances, other kinds of consumer behaviour besides purchases may be useful in evaluating advertising effectiveness.

In many instances, advertising is used to generate contacts or leads. The effectiveness of real estate advertising is more easily evaluated by the number of contacts established than by the number of houses sold. Similarly, car advertising is frequently geared to generate "traffic in the store" and can be evaluated by its ability to do so. Many large format retailers use electronic monitoring to accurately count the number of persons entering the store and by correlating these observations with sales of individual items or sales within specific categories they can – to some extent – establish best practice on what products and categories to promote.

In the expanding market for internet advertising the number of "clicks" the advertisement (banner or otherwise) generates, is a frequently used measure (click rate).

Some advertisers may not have increased sales as their primary objective rather they strive for a change in attitude or general behaviour. Environmental campaigns, disease preventing campaigns etc. are cases in point. Here, such related measures as the number of brochures picked up, the number of people talking about the topic or changes in actual behaviour may provide useful effect information.

E. Data Collection Techniques in Advertising Effectiveness Studies

To the advertiser, the choice of data collection methodology is a primary concern of his advertising testing decision. Based upon this choice, his level of expenditure is more or less determined, and the type of data that will be made available to him for decision-making purposes is closely tied in with the methodology used for the data collection.

Testing may be carried out at different stages in the advertising development process. Typical stages where research is done are

1) at the concept level
2) pre-testing
   a) at the storyboard or draft level
   b) at the animation or layout level
   c) at the (almost) final production level
3) test marketing
   a) after first market exposure as test marketing
   b) full scale
   c) single source split cable tests
   d) sponsoring
4) post-testing
   a) with aggregated data
   b) with individual level data

1. Concept Testing

Qualitative concept testing in terms of in-depth interviews, focus group discussions and the like are discussed elsewhere in this book. More quantitatively oriented approaches may also be used in concept testing. A typical procedure available from many research institutes is a quick evaluation of a reasonably large number of alternative concepts by the use of simple measures such as A-Ad liking, positive/negative aspects of the concept, understanding etc. These tests may be carried out in connection with omnibus surveys or in special hall or personal interview settings.

2. Pre-testing: Tests of Art Work at Varying Stages
In later stages of the pre-testing procedure hall, home or cinema designs dominate, but combinations including CAPI interviewing also occur.

In the hall-test design, respondents are interviewed in test centres that are frequently located in shopping malls or in downtown shopping areas. Respondents are invited in sufficient numbers to make up a meaningful quota sample relative to the product in question and the target group for the particular campaign. They are then experimentally exposed to the advertisement being tested.

This exposure may take several forms. With television it may be as a storyboard, an animation or a more or less final production; prints drafts, semi-final versions or finished prints may be used.

Part of the exposure will almost always be a "forced exposure" in the sense that the respondent is more or less forced to spend time in front of the material being tested. Various forms of disguises and distractions may also be introduced. This is done partly to divert the attention of the respondent from the particular test item, partly to create a competitive media environment. In television, a block of five to ten ads may be shown while one or more test spots are introduced. Similarly with print, a folder with a number of advertisements from competing or unrelated product areas can be shown (folder test).

Sometimes, in an attempt to make the exposure situation more natural, the test item is presented as part of a "natural" environment. In the case of television or radio spots, the item to be tested is introduced 15-30 minutes into regular programming. With print advertising, dummy magazines or newspapers may be used.

A special version of the hall test design is the cinema design used for testing of television ads. Here, a reasonably large number of respondents are invited to a cinema where a programme, a movie or some other material is shown. The items to be tested are introduced into the programme as part of "natural commercial blocks".

The rationale behind the cinema design is the creation of a natural situation where the respondent is not likely to realize that anything is being tested during the exposure. Whereas quotas can be maintained in the hall test, the total audience in the cinema test represents a rather haphazardly collected sample. A focus is introduced by inviting pre-selected respondents or by concentrating on those sub-segments of the total audience relevant to the target group of the particular ad. However, the desire for a large sample size and the degree of precision with which the target group is matched will always be a balancing act.

Another aspect of the cinema test, compared with the hall test, is that - at the same cost level - it is possible to work with a significantly larger sample. This has its advantages when less sensitive measures such as changes in purchase intentions, in attitudes etc. are to be studied. Moreover, the ability to produce large samples at competitive prices improves when more than one ad can be tested in each viewing. This is an important feature in, for example, the McCollum-Spielman test design (Spielman, 1988).

More realistic exposure situations are generated when measurements are obtained after "natural" exposure has occurred at home. In strict pre-testing, this can be achieved for television by mailing out videotapes or print test issues of the publication containing the material to be tested. A special procedure for testing outdoor advertising should also be mentioned (Copage, 1998). Here, the test items are manipulated into a TV-presentation of a typical "from home to work" trip.

Regardless of whether data collection takes place in halls, cinemas or at home, practically all of the variables discussed in the preceding section may come into use. However, some designs go better with certain measures than others.

Meaningful measures of ad recall and ad recognition normally require a less intensive exposure than that generated by forced exposure. Therefore, only when competitive advertising or program material is included in the test situation do such measures make sense. That is, the more realistic the test situation, the more meaningful the ad recall/recognition measures become.

Brand related measures such as brand awareness, brand image, perception of brand attributes and brand preferences are influenced by many factors other than the single advertising exposure: brand familiarity, past purchase experiences, previous advertising exposure and shopping expenses all play a major role for variables of this kind. Therefore, in order for them to make sense as measures of advertising effects, they somehow require a benchmark for comparison. This can be provided by norms, by accumulated experience or by the use of a pre/post design. In this particular area, norms nearly always have to be brand specific. To the extent that the advertiser knows what the brand preferences, brand awareness and perception of brand attributes would normally be, he may judge deviations (as they are measured in an advertising test situation) as an effect of the advertising exposure.

However, norms of this nature are difficult to develop. They require many observations and limited as they are to the single brand, the opportunity for accumulating these are few. These problems are particularly important with well-established brands where brand recall and brand preferences are high and stable.

Semi-qualitative data or diagnostics can be and are used in most advertising testing. Because of the coding involved with these questions, they may increase the cost of the individual test in proportion to the number of open questions asked, as well as the number of respondents in the test. They are also more expensive with personal CAPI or CATI interviews compared to the completion of pre-coded questions. However, the usefulness of the diagnostic information in explaining why various ad elements indicate an effect makes them almost unavoidable in most test situations.

3. "Day-After Tests"
The day after design, which has been especially developed for the measurement of ad recall for TV and radio, provides an opportunity for testing the campaign material when final, but before major media investments are made. In these tests, measures other than recall are also normally taken. Most of the variables described in section 5 can be used.

A major problem with day after and similar tests are the high costs involved in identifying respondents who have actually seen the advertisement/commercial. Extensive screening may be needed to find the relatively limited proportion of the population that has been exposed. Alternatively, exposure may be secured by mailing respondents the test material in advance, as is done with some forms of "page traffic"/"through the book" studies, or respondents may be found close to where exposure takes place, as is done with some kinds of poster testing and testing of cinema ads.

4. Split Cable and Similar Test Designs
Rather than doing full-scale test marketing, campaign testing can be conducted if purchase information can be obtained from respondents who are exposed to the campaign in a controlled manner. BehaviorScan (from IRI) and others provide such a system (licensed in Europe to GfK).

In a geographical area, consumers' purchases can be registered in-store or at home using bar-code data, and television ad exposure can be controlled via split cabling and can be measured with TV-meters. Similarly, direct mail advertising can be controlled and exposure to other media may be registered. In this way, the purchasing behaviour of consumers can be compared with that of other consumers by administering controlled exposure to the campaign.

By eliminating a large number of possible disturbing factors, relatively clear-cut answers appear about the advertising effect in the particular geographical area and with a particular media combination used in the controlled setting. Tests of this kind are quite expensive and the operating of standardised systems of this kind requires a research agency with a considerable turnover in order for it to be profitable. Therefore, they primarily exist in major markets.

5. Test Marketing

Test marketing, in connection with advertising testing, normally requires two or more comparable market areas with controlled media exposure, so that campaigns can be run in natural media with coverage limited to the areas involved.

Test marketing is extremely expensive and rarely used for the testing of advertising campaigns alone. Rather, companies will use test marketing in situations where major and different strategic options are available, and where the company wants to test these strategically different approaches and marketing mixes thoroughly. However, with the testing of new products, product innovations and the like, the testing of the advertising element of the campaign is an important ingredient. In smaller markets, test marketing may become so expensive that full-scale introductions are preferred instead.

6. Post-Testing

Advanced tracking based on market behaviour and considerations of the competition relies upon data gathered through retail auditing, consumer panels, continuous omnibus, or similar services. This was discussed in Chapter VIII.

Consumer panel data provides information at the individual level over time. They can be used in different kinds of data analyses in an attempt to understand how advertising influences sales. In this connection, emphasis is frequently placed on brand loyalty and switching.

What measures should be chosen for continuous tracking is a decision to be made by the individual advertiser taking into consideration the market he is working in, his competitors, the nature of his brand etc. For some advertisers brand recall may be very useful. For others, advertising recall is more useful and for others still, awareness of specific elements of the campaign is preferred. The functioning of advertising as a provider of information or as a rigid, reinforcing factor in mature markets is important for the choice of tracking variables. As we shall see in Chapter XI NERS score provides an interesting possibility for tracking emotional effects of communication.

7. Advertising Modeling

Over the years, researchers have searched for a single variable that reveals all about advertising effectiveness. However, it has become increasingly evident that advertising is a much more complex phenomenon and that it works in many different ways for different advertisers in different situations. In the discussion of advertising effects in Chapter VIII A, such models were introduced.

Consequently, a variety of variables have to be incorporated, and relationships among the different variables need to be studied. In this sense, one might say that advertising research is moving towards a generation of advertising modeling.

F. Summary

In the testing of advertising a wide variety of measures and data collection techniques are being used. The majority of these relate to effect hierarchy thinking and to concepts resembling central information processing (Petty and Cacioppo (1986)). Neither when it comes to pre-testing nor with regard to post-testing have results been convincing: Contemporary studies have been able to indicate increased liking of brands where the exposure is carefully controlled to ensure that the respondent does not focus on the brand – counter to theories of awareness preceding interest. Other studies have pointed at recognition without recall and preference increases amongst individuals who recognise an ad (but do not recall it) whereas no preference increase could be registered amongst those who recalled the ad. This fact is probably due to a number of reasons, but chief among them is, that - as we are becoming increasingly aware - advertising works on more levels of consciousness and cognition, and in more complicated ways than those that are modelled by the classic cognitive effect hierarchies, such as AIDA.

For advertising testing to progress, much further development is needed to build a better understanding of how the consumer processes information of a commercial nature and how that information plays into consumer choice. Through this understanding, better measurements of advertising effects can be developed, just as new developments in advertising testing are beginning to demonstrate.

Chapter XI

The Dynamics of NERS Scores: Tracking and Testing

CHAPTER OUTLINE

The discussion in Chapter VII-IX on advertising planning and advertising effect has demonstrated that our insight in how advertising works based on studies of purchase effects and effect-hierarchical thinking is much less than perfect. The demonstration of the feasibility of measuring underlying, unconscious emotional response tendencies, in Chapter V-VI, makes it natural to look for additional insight into how marketing communication works by studying emotional responses, particularly since observation of consumer choices and processing of marketing communication clearly indicate that other mechanisms than the traditional ones must be active.

Given the measurements of our emotional response tendencies, the obvious question is: how stable are NERS scores over time? And when NERS scores change in value over time, can this can be attributed to or does it reflect changes in the consumer environment, such as in changing market conditions, or changes in marketing communication activities.

In this chapter we will review what our own studies and other findings can document in terms of changes in NERS and other emotional scores and relate those to changing market situations, marketing communication or other marketing determinants. That is, we shall evaluate the usefulness of NERS scores for tracking: uncovering changes in brands' standing in the market or in the brand equity. Among other things, we shall concern ourselves with the sensitivity of emotional responses to campaign changes and in communication pre-testing. The above we shall try to accomplish by looking into:

Significant changes in NERS scores between 2003-2004
A. Other systematic changes between 2003-2004
B. NERS scores as predictors of usage frequency
C. The dynamics of NERS scores for leading political candidates in the 2005 Danish Parliamentary Election
D. The sensitivity of feeling-words used in ELAM pre-testing 1997-1999 and other pre-testing with feeling words and advertising with pictorial emotional measures of feelings/emotions. Sensitivity of responses in testing of design and colour of logos
E. Sponsor effects measured by emotional responses
F. NERS and its relation to brand conversion scores

CHAPTER OBJECTIVE
Our objective with this chapter is to develop understanding of how emotional responses are changing with changing environmental conditions and how such changes seem to contribute towards explaining buying behaviour. We attempt to demonstrate the broader role that emotions play in human decision making with – admittedly - a few illustrations outside of classic consumer behaviour: the political landscape and sponsorship effects. In line with the new paradigm that we aim to establish we document the potential value of applying NERS as a tracking measurement of a brand's health, since it is more sensitive to changing consumer perceptions than much image research which typically taps into conscious cognition – since such cognition probably has less relevance in guiding actual consumer choices.

A. Changes in NERS Scores from 2003-2004
The changes in the computed NERS scores between the two years are shown in Table VI.3 and Figure VI.1. As discussed there, the different measurement procedures applied explain the different levels of the scores in the two years. Apart from these, comparing the adjusted 2003 scores with the 2004 scores makes it possible to divide the 41 scores into 14 for which a significant difference can be found and 27 for which differences most likely are ascribable to random variations in the data.

It should be remembered that even though the 27 cases do not show significant differences, systematic changes between the two years may still be present and we shall look for this following the discussion of the individual cases.

1. Cereals
In the cereal category there are two significant differences. The category as such shows a significant negative change in the NERS score and so does the score for one of the two brands measured: Kellogg's. Data are shown in Table XI.1

Table XI.1: Changing NERS scores for cereals between 2003 and 2005

Brand/category	2004	2003	Difference
Cereals	2.17	4.14	-1.97*
Ota	2.41	2.50	-0.09
Kellogg's	1.63	3.66	-2.04*

* significant difference (at 0.05 level)

Two factors account for this, according to the marketing management of Kellogg's. First, in the year 2003-2004 the media have been dominated by the obesity debate. Here, one of the major scapegoats in the debate has been cereals with high sugar content. In Denmark particularly Kellogg's brands are regarded as having a high sugar content (the traditional oat flake market is dominated by Ota from Quaker Oat).

The other important influence on the position of Kellogg's has been the development in the distribution. Kellogg's withdrew from the Coop stores in 2003 – Coop controls about 1/3 of Danish fast moving consumer goods retailing – since Kellogg's was not able to agree with the Coop stores about marketing conditions. The products did not become distributed in the stores again until after the last data collection.

The obesity issue undoubtedly explain the development in the category as such.

Taken together, these two factors undoubtedly explain the development in emotional response patterns for Kellogg's.

2. Amusement Parks

The famous Copenhagen amusement park Tivoli shows a significant negative change and Legoland a similar development, although it is not statistically significant. This can be explained as a result of the timing of the data collection in the two years. Tivoli and Legoland are amusement parks with relatively short seasons. In such seasonal markets response measures - and also NERS - depend upon when in the year the data collection takes place.

In 2003 data collection was completed late August at a time where a majority of the consumers had visited Tivoli and Legoland. In 2004 it was completed mid June, at a time when relatively few consumers have any recent experience with Tivoli or Legoland since the season has just started. Looking into advertising spending and other possible determinants no other obvious significant changes have occurred, apart from some negative press particularly about the financial results of LEGO, which may further diminish the positive response tendency.

Two other amusement parks in the sample Bakken and BonBon-land have a much earlier season start.

3. Banks

In the bank category (Table XI.2), one bank stands out with a very large positive change in net emotional response: BG Bank. To understand this, we have to look a little more upon the bank situation as such.

Table XI.2: Changing NERS scores for banks between 2003 and 2004

Brand/category	2004	2003	Difference
Banks	-0.65	0.09	-0.74
BG Bank	-0.98	-4.04	3.06*
Nordea	-1.11	-0.17	-0.94
Danske Bank	-1.28	-1.36	0.08

* significant difference (at 0.05 level)

Table XI.2 gives the development results for the three major banks in the Danish bank market: Danske Bank, Nordea and BG Bank. The overall perception of the bank category is probably shaped by the perception of the major banks that all generate negative NERS scores in both years.

In 2003 a smaller bank "Lån og Spar Bank" and in 2004 another less dominant bank "Jyske Bank" was included. Both of these smaller bank show positive NERS, corresponding to their positioning as being closer to the customer, more maverick in their marketing approach. Other studies of bank images in Denmark give similar results, and it is generally accepted in the banking business that the major banks have difficulties developing as strong and positive images as those of the smaller banks.

The dramatic change in the evaluation of BG Bank must be seen on this background. It takes a little Danish bank history account for this. BG Bank was acquired by Den Danske Bank in 2000 and became a subsidiary of this bank. Around 2002-2003 it was decided that BG Bank, with a considerable part of its background in the traditional "sparebank" (small rural banks) clientele and among non-business private consumers should be relaunched in order to capitalize on this traditional position. The relaunch was implemented from early 2004 with a number of changes involving increased emphasis on personal counselling, maintaining and improvement of bank office facilities and a strong communication effort (in the spring of 2004 BG Bank spent about the same amount on advertising as did the two much larger Danske Bank and Nordea). In addition to this strong media effort, a strong promotion strategy aiming at cultural sponsoring was initiated. The change in NERS scores suggests that this concentrated effort has been successful.

4. Gasoline

In the later years gasoline retailing in Denmark has been characterised by a steadily increasing price competition with prices varying up to 20 per cent within the same day as competing gas stations tried to build market share through deep price cuts. Whatever category affinity existed in the gasoline market, this diminished in this process. Thus, the total evaluation of gasoline stations in terms of NERS scores has decreased significantly. (Table XI.3)

Table XI.3: Changing NERS scores in the gasoline market between 2003 and 2004

Brand/category	2004	2003	Difference
Gasoline	-0.94	0.39	-1.33*
OK	1.21	-0.95	2.16*
Q8	0.83	0.65	0.19
Hydro	0.62	2.69	-2.07
Shell	-0.19	-0.83	0.64

* significant difference (at 0.05 level)

This overall development however, covers different trends for different brands. The NERS score for OK from 2003 to 2004 – OK being a traditional price competitive brand actually improves. This is however the only one for which a concentrated marketing effort has taken place, and new stations collocated with Coop retail stores opening up in a period when other gasoline companies have closed down many stations.

At the other extreme Hydro changes in a negative direction, although the change is only significant at the 0.10 level. A phenomenon that maybe is ascribable to this brand's weak position of its new brand Hydro/Texaco after Hydro's acquisition of the Danish chain of Texaco stations. In later years the Hydro/Texaco stations have been marketed under the somewhat anonymous name, YT.

When studying the figures for the gasoline category, it must be remembered that only three or four brands are included in each category, and the category response potential is collected separately, so that it does not constitute the average of the brands included in the study.

5. Newspapers

The scores for the newspaper market are shown in Table XI.4. Here it appears that the category as such improves significantly from the one year to the other whereas all but one of the leading national newspapers have stable or decreasing NERS scores.

The overall development in this category in the early part of the new decennium has been a decreasing circulation for local as well as national paid-for newspapers. In contrast, a number of freely distributed newspapers such as Metro Express and a Danish competitor, Urban have gained market share. Whereas the total circulation of all newspapers on weekdays decreases from 1,440 million in 2001 to 1.294 million in 2004, the circulation of the two free dailies increases from 427.000 to 509.000.

The NERS scores for Metro and Urban are only available for 2004 but they actually have significantly ($p > 0.05$) higher emotional response scores than the tabloid, national newspapers with which they compete for readers. The most likely explanation for the systematic changes in the newspaper market is the fact that these free newspapers to a large extent are picking up younger readers that otherwise have dropped out or would drop out of the newspaper market, and that they in content are more informative and less "sensation hunting" than the tabloids from which they take readers.

Table XI.4: Changing NERS scores for newspapers between 2003 and 2004

Brand/category	2004	2003	Difference
Newspapers	2.22	-0.23	2.45*
Politiken	0.95	1.39	-0.44
Berlingske Tidende	0.61	1.34	-0.73
Jyllands-Posten	0.48	-0.21	0.69
BT	-1.52	0.37	-1.89
Ekstra Bladet	-2.30	-1.68	-0.62

* significant difference (at 0.05 level)

6. Mobile Phone Companies

Here too, significant changes have occurred. On the one hand, Telia has increased its NERS score (but still overall negative), and Sonofon has had a decreasing NERS score. In the period around which the measurements were made, major concentration in the market occurred.

Particularly, Telia in Denmark has acquired Orange and some other, minor companies. Together with this, Telia has made a publicly announced, concentrated effort to improve on its lacklustre customer service. Both factors may account for the positive development of Telia's scores. Telia is simply getting more and more satisfied users.

The opposite may account for Sonofon's negative development. Sonofon has had a decreasing market share and has after a period of very strong marketing efforts reduced its level of activities significantly.

It is remarkable that the category as such as well as the major contestants have negative NERS scores. Strong price competition combined with not always obvious price structures and attempts to bind the customers have hurt the industry markedly. This is a phenomenon that has characterized the market structure in most European markets.

7. Shampoo

For the shampoos we find an overall weak positive tendency and significantly for Head and Shoulders.

Total media spending in the second half year prior to the 2004 measurement is available for the evaluation of the marketing activities for the brands. The spending is available in the two major media groups: television and retail free sheets.

Retailers' free sheets are extremely important as media in the Danish market, and they represent the largest media for most FMCG manufacturers. Advertising in free sheets is usually dominated by special offers in terms of lower prices, three for two etc.

Table XI.5: Changing NERS scores for shampoo brands between 2003 (adjusted) and 2004

Brand/category	2004	2003	Difference
Shampoo	2.26	2.19	0.06
Sanex	2.23	2.04	0.19
Dove	1.94	-0.34	2.28
Head & Shoulders	-0.17	-4.72	4.55*

* significant difference (at 0.05 level)

So, in general terms, spending on television represents the manufacturers' emphasis on brand building, spending on free sheets reflect merchandising activities. Seen in this light, the shampoo figures are interesting. Head and Shoulders has by far the most positive change in net emotional response strength. It is also the brand with the largest spending on television whereas Sanex and Dove in the half year prior to the measurement have concentrated their efforts on merchandising. It seems that this has resulted in a strong improvement of the NERS score for Head and Shoulders as compared with that of the other brands.

8. The Bread Category

In the bread category a single brand stands out with a significant negative change in NERS: Hatting (Table XI.6). When we look upon the marketing activities in the half year preceding the measurement, we note that two major competitors have been spending significantly more than Hatting and particularly so on television, a media group which has not been used at all by Hatting. The spending on retailers' free sheets is proportional to the relative importance of the brands in the market place thus, the real difference in marketing activity lies in the use of television advertising on behalf of Schulstad and Kohberg. Their combination of merchandising and brand building activity seems to have kept them in place in contrast with Hatting, which registers a decreasing NERS score.

Whereas the overall evaluation of the individual brands is positive, the evaluation of the category is even higher. Seemingly, bread baked and sold by real baker shops, which compose a significant proportion of the Danish bread consumption, influences the overall evaluation of bread positively.

Table XI.6: Changing NERS scores for bread between 2003 and 2004

Brand/category	2004	2003	Difference
Bread	3.64	4.06	-0.42
Schulstad	2.82	2.45	0.37
Kohberg	2.62	2.70	-0.07
Hatting	1.59	3.90	-2.31*

* significant difference (at 0.05 level)

9. Conclusion

Looking at all the significant changes observed in the NERS score we have been able to point to important factors shaping and creating the changes. Several of these causes can be characterised as major differences in the markets between the time of the two measurements and several of these have been confirmed by the marketing people of the companies involved.

Still, changes in advertising spending, merchandising and the brand building of the companies may have influenced the NERS scores between 2003 and 2004. When we study these at the level of the individual brand, these changes have not been significant at the 0.05 level. However, they may still be systematic. This is the topic for the next section.

B. Systematic Changes between 2003 and 2004

For all of the brands advertising expenditures are available for 2003 and 2004. These are provided by TNS-Gallup Adfacts and cover expenditures on television, magazines, daily newspapers, local newspapers, outdoor and radio.

Moreover, for some of the fast moving consumer goods brands data are available on merchandising activities in terms of an estimated value of millimetres of advertising space in retailers' free sheets, where special offers, free deals etc. are announced. Finally, ASTAS and advertising awareness data are available for some of the fast moving consumer goods included in the samples. These data were discussed in Chapter VIII and are based on measurements obtained from the same respondents as those providing data for the NERS scores in 2004. The data cover brand purchases within the last three days and recall of advertising thought to have occurred within the last week. NERS and spending data are available for 12 brands in 4 categories: Coffee, bread, shampoo and cereals. Of these, as already seen, cereals with Kellogg's included have their own peculiar picture with larger spending for Kellogg's and still decreasing NERS.

For the remaining brands we shall try and see to what extent NERS scores are influenced by marketing activities as reflected in the data available here.

1. Changing Spending and Changing NERS

For the three remaining categories, coffee, bread and shampoo, the overall level of advertising spending between brand categories varies dramatically. Therefore, to relate total advertising spending to total change in NERS scores makes little sense. However, if one relates change in spending within each of the particular markets and to the change in NERS within the same market, the data in Figure XI.1 result. At the overall level total spending decreases, but with the exception of Schulstad and Dove, the smaller the decrease in spending, the smaller the decrease in NERS.

Figure XI.1: Spending changes (without retailers' free sheets) in the last 6 months before measurement, and NERS score changes

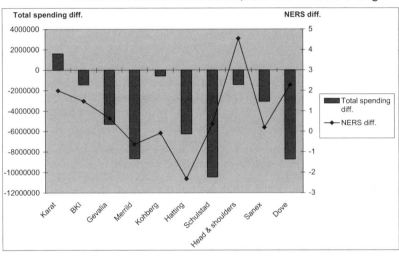

Of course, advertising spending in the last six month preceding the NERS measure can only be expected to account for a small proportion of the total NERS score obtained at the time. The efficiency of the campaigns in terms of their ability to generate awareness and persuasion may differ widely between brands. A host of other factors (some of which have been pointed at in the preceding section) such as merchandising for fast moving consumer goods, and special price activities may have played an important role. Still with few exceptions spending changes relate to changing NERS scores. This is a fairly direct relationship, illustrating the function of advertising in building and maintaining the emotional response towards the brand..

It is remarkable also how the two (Schulstad and Dove) of the three largest decreases in advertising spending do not result in similar NERS score changes. These traditionally heavily advertised brands probably profit from long term effects of past advertising.

A recent German study (Gierl and Praxmarer, 2006) provides data on how consumers react when brands are advertised through price messages rather than through more brand building messages. These authors studied the use of low price messages in advertising for 6 different brands and found systematically lower emotional responses for brands when advertised as "value for money" as compared to similar brands advertised without the stressing of price.

A similar analysis can be carried out covering the merchandising activities. These are available for the same fast moving consumer goods in both years. In Table XI.7 the change of the brands' NERS scores within each market and their spending on merchandising activities are illustrated. Here, it appears that a negative relationship with merchandising is suggested. Taken together with the observation based on Figure XI.1, the two analyses suggest that increasing brand building by advertising activity increases brand equity as reflected in NERS in the short run, whereas strong merchandising activity has the opposite effect.

Table XI.7: The relationship between average changes in TV spending and merchandise (measured as spending in retailers' free sheets) in the first half of 2004 (preceding the measurement of the last NERS scores) for FMCG with available data

Decreasing NERS

No. of brands	Average TV spending 2004 (mill. DKK)	Average free sheets spending 2004 (mill. DKK)
5	1.595	3.697

Increasing NERS

No. of brands	Average TV spending 2004 (mill. DKK)	Average free sheets spending 2004 (mill. DKK)
7	2.273	2.010

Again, as mentioned before a host of other factors influenced the data but still underlying it all, the basic effects of merchandising and advertising on brand equity can be seen: Heavy merchandising has a tendency to decrease the NERS score corresponding to the emotional component of the brand equity; and (mainly) TV advertising influences it positively.

2. Changing NERS Scores and Campaign Effectiveness

As discussed in Chapter X campaign effectiveness can be seen as composed of two elements: the ability to generate awareness and the ability to generate persuasion, the latter quantified by the ASTAS score. For 12 of the brands in the 2004 sample data were collected enabling a computation of awareness and ASTAS scores. The 12 are divided into those with positive changes in NERS scores between 2003 and 2004 and those with negative changes between the two years.

ASTAS and awareness scores for the two categories are shown in Table XI.8. Here, it can be seen that brands with improving NERS scores are characterised by having higher ASTAS. This suggests that more effective campaigns (higher ASTAS scores) tend to give higher NERS scores ($p \leq 0.05$). With the awareness score it is different. Here the score is practically the same for the two categories higher than those with decreasing NERS scores. However, particularly with regard to advertising awareness as discussed in Chapter VIII, a disturbing factor is the amount of advertising that the brand carries with it from preceding periods.

Table XI.8: Awareness and ASTAS for brands with increasing and decreasing NERS

Increasing NERS:

	2003	2004			NERS
	transf NERS	NERS	ASTAS	Awareness	Difference
Head & shoulders	-4,72	-0,17	94	20,9	4,55
Dove	-0,34	1,94	182	24,4	2,28
Karat	0,26	2,25	187	16,2	1,99
BKI	0,42	1,9	318	15,9	1,48
Gevalia	1,65	2,3	135	27,4	0,65
Schulstad	2,45	2,82	119	40,8	0,37
Sanex	2,04	2,23	160	21,9	0,19
Average	0,25	1,90	171	23,9	1,64

Decreasing NERS

	2003	2004			NERS
Kohberg	2,70	2,62	130	47,3	-0,08
Ota	2,50	2,41	140	13,7	-0,09
Merrild	2,93	2,3	137	17,1	-0,63
Kellog's	3,66	1,63	154	26,7	-2,03
Hatting	3,90	1,59	197	19,0	-2,31
Average	3,14	2,1	152	24,8	-1,0

C. Users and Non-Users

In Chapter VI it was documented that for all brands users score higher than non-users. As a consequence of this changes in market share for brands probably will reflect in the total NERS score of the brands, so that brands with increasing market share should have increasing NERS score.

At the general level we cannot really know what changes first – the market share or the NERS score. One can argue that the consumer decreases buying of a particular brand as a result of diminishing emotional response to the brand – but one can also argue that other factors induce the consumer to decrease buying and that the diminishing contact with the brand leads to a decline in emotional response.

In the preceding sections however, we have seen that activities of one kind or the other in the market seem to lead to changes in the NERS score – and therefore, eventually to changing market share.

In studying the differences between 2003 and 2004 we expect brands with an increase in total NERS to show an increasing market share also. We know about such changes from 2003 to 2004 in the case of Kellogg's where the decreasing distribution must have caused a decrease in market share. As a substitute for changes in market share we can look at changes in the proportion of users from 2003 to 2004. There are, however, only 12 FMCG for which such a computation can be made. Moreover, the difference between the two years in data collection methods (self administered printed questionnaire versus internet based questionnaire) gives some systematic changes in the proportion of users registered in the two years. On average, scores for usage and users in 2004 are 12% lower than scores for 2003. Adjusted for these systematic differences it is, however, possible to correlate the changes in NERS scores with the changes in users between the two years. This is done in Figure XI.2 where the relationship is estimated by:

$$\Delta \text{ Users (2004-2003)} = \quad 1.599 \ (\Delta \text{ NERS}) \quad R = .54, R^2 = 0.30$$
$$p \leq 0.10$$

Figure XI.2: Changes in users and change in NERS

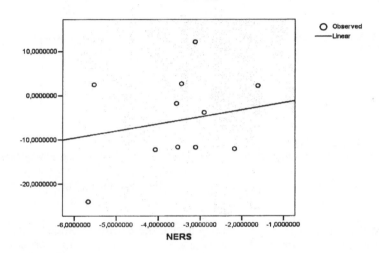

The regression indicates that changing numbers of users occur together with changes in NERS. The relationship is not very strong but as stated elsewhere, NERS can neither be expected to be the only driver of changes in usage the only driver of NERS. Considering the limited number of observations and the less than perfect quality of the data in the two years, the observation should not be overlooked.

We can also look at NERS scores from 2003 to 2004 among users and non-users in order to ascertain whether there is the tendency that frequent contact (= user) with the product does correlate with high NERS. This is done in Table XI.9.

There are systematic differences in these scores. In all cases users score higher than non-users, a phenomenon we shall analyse further in the following. Studying the scores by distributing the brands according to their position in the Rossiter-Percy grid, we find larger differences among the products in the different categories versus high involvement transformational products.

Marked differences are found also for some subgroups such as media where there are very large differences in NERS between users and non-users. Real estate dealers, glasses and gasoline on the contrary exhibit smaller differences in NERS, reflecting the lower degree of differentiation experienced between suppliers in these businesses. Also the typical FMCGs in the low involvement transformational category exhibit relatively smaller differences between users and non-users in NERS.

Two interpretations offer themselves, one is that media are having users much more strongly attached to them than fast moving consumer brands; the other is that most media generate much more animosity amongst non-users than do FMCGs.

Table XI.9: NERS score differences between users and non-users (2004 data) in the four Rossiter and Percy quadrants

Low involvement informational	Users NERS	Non-users NERS	NERS diff.	% users
Shampoo	2,26	0,12	2,14	100
Sanex	2,99	1,69	1,30	41
Garnier Fructis	2,88	0,15	2,73	27
Dove	2,65	1,74	0,91	22
Matas	2,59	1,65	0,93	34
Head & Shoulders	2,37	-0,71	3,08	17
Category average	2,63	0,77	1,85	40,30
Mobile phone handsets	-	-		-
SonyEricsson	3,43	1,20	2,23	24
Nokia	2,91	0,69	2,22	63
Siemens	2,57	0,00	2,57	25
Samsung	-	-		-
Category average	2,97	0,63	2,34	37,13
Butter	0,46	-1,35	1,81	89
Engholm	2,27	0,56	1,71	35
Lurpak	2,25	0,95	1,30	57
Bakkedal	1,63	-0,21	1,84	49
Kærgården	1,58	-1,00	2,58	87
Category average	1,64	-0,21	1,85	63,53
Gasoline	-	-		-
OK	1,80	0,14	1,66	65
Q8	1,44	0,09	1,35	55
Hydro	1,24	0,00	1,24	50
Statoil	1,10	0,12	0,98	57
Shell	0,48	-0,90	1,38	51
Category average	1,21	-0,11	1,32	55,52
Insurance	-	-		-
Fair forsikring	0,78	-1,77	2,56	5
Codan	0,53	-1,56	2,09	20
Topdanmark	0,51	-1,71	2,22	31
Tryg	0,36	-1,30	1,67	36
Alm. Brand	-1,18	-2,07	0,90	19
Category average	0,20	-1,68	1,89	22,25
Brand average	1,83	-0,01	1,84	41

Average difference
(users-non-users)=   1.84 (p ≤ 0.01)

Low involvement transformational	Users NERS	Non-users NERS	NERS diff.	% users
Coffee	4,51	0,88	3,63	93
Karat	3,43	1,71	1,72	36
Gevalia	3,23	1,61	1,62	46
Merrild	3,04	1,51	1,54	55
BKI	2,97	1,35	1,62	38
Category average	3,44	1,41	2,02	53,72
Bread	3,64	1,58	2,06	100
Kohberg	3,32	0,38	2,95	76
Schulstad	3,19	1,33	1,86	81
Hatting	2,14	0,23	1,91	71
Category average	3,07	0,88	2,19	82,00
Soft drinks	2,89	-1,49	4,39	89
Coca Cola	3,44	-1,36	4,80	79
Faxe Kondi	3,36	1,43	1,93	59
Fun Saftevand	3,23	-1,85	5,08	40
Rynkeby	2,70	2,01	0,69	80
Category average	3,13	-0,25	3,38	69,38
Cereals	2,51	0,45	2,07	83
Ota	3,06	1,92	1,15	48
Kellogg's	2,50	0,24	2,26	68
Category average	2,69	0,87	1,82	66,46
Candy	2,31	0,06	2,25	93
After Eight	3,50	1,83	1,67	62
Toms	3,12	1,33	1,80	85
Stimorol	3,04	1,60	1,44	61
SorBits	3,01	1,45	1,56	49
BonBon	2,89	0,64	2,25	53
Haribo	2,62	0,22	2,41	89
Malaco	2,35	0,42	1,93	74
Category average	2,86	0,94	1,91	70,89
Spirits	1,85	-1,71	3,56	85
Rød Ålborg	3,16	0,57	2,59	54
Gammel Dansk	3,13	0,37	2,75	52
Bacardi	2,62	0,62	2,00	55
Martini	2,54	0,65	1,89	44
Category average	2,66	0,10	2,56	57,94
Chips	0,75	-2,38	3,12	85
Kims	1,45	-1,29	2,74	85
Estrella	1,39	-0,22	1,61	60
Category average	1,20	-1,30	2,49	76,83
Brand average	2,86	0,72	2,14	62

Average difference= 2.14 (p≤0.01)

High involvement informational	Users NERS	Non-users NERS	NERS diff.	% users
Newspapers	-	-	-	-
Politiken	3,55	-0,15	3,70	30
Berlingske Tidende	2,79	-0,06	2,84	24
Urban	2,66	1,08	1,58	38
Jyllands-Posten	2,57	-0,84	3,41	39
MetroXpress	2,55	0,95	1,60	43
BT	1,70	-2,48	4,18	23
Ekstra-Bladet	0,37	-2,93	3,30	19
Category average	2,31	-0,63	2,94	30,75
Glasses	-	-	-	-
Thiele	2,79	0,84	1,95	22
Synoptik	2,05	0,12	1,93	38
Category average	2,42	0,48	1,94	30,28
Weekly magazines	-	-	-	-
Alt for Damerne	3,66	-0,51	4,17	25
Femina	3,60	-0,15	3,75	27
Billed Bladet	2,32	-2,46	4,79	19
Her og nu	1,37	-2,65	4,02	15
Kig ind	1,14	-2,84	3,98	11
Se & Hør	0,89	-3,20	4,09	15
Category average	2,16	-1,97	4,13	18,61
Mortgage credit	-	-	-	-
Nykredit	1,75	-0,41	2,16	22
BRF Kredit	0,97	-0,74	1,71	14
Realkredit Danmark	0,94	-0,56	1,50	29
Category average	1,22	-0,57	1,79	21,80
Banks	-	-	-	-
Jyske	3,61	-0,04	3,66	14
BG	2,05	-1,71	3,77	20
Nordea	0,96	-1,94	2,90	28
Danske	0,93	-2,13	3,05	28
Category average	1,89	-1,46	3,34	22,28
Real estate dealers	-	-	-	-
EDC	0,51	-0,92	1,43	24
Danbolig	0,20	-0,71	0,90	12
Home	-0,02	-0,80	0,78	23
Nybolig	-0,14	-0,85	0,71	22
Category average	0,14	-0,82	0,95	20,60
Mobile phone companies	-	-	-	-
Telmore	4,80	-0,88	5,68	35
CBB Mobil	3,76	-0,41	4,16	13
Orange	0,78	-2,18	2,96	11
Telia	0,21	-2,07	2,28	10
TDC Mobil	0,13	-2,22	2,35	43
Sonofon	-0,01	-2,11	2,11	19
Mobil 3	-0,10	-1,06	0,96	5
Debitel	-0,35	-2,22	1,87	8

High involvement transformational	Users NERS	Non-users NERS	NERS diff.	% users
Amusement parks	-	-	-	-
Legoland	6,84	4,98	1,86	23
BonBon-land	6,61	4,00	2,61	14
Tivoli	6,36	5,16	1,20	46
Bakken	5,23	4,30	0,92	28
Category average	6,26	4,61	1,65	27,59
Toys	-	-	-	-
Lego	5,65	4,10	1,55	49
Brio	4,82	3,31	1,51	34
Fisher Price	4,25	2,50	1,75	39
Category average	4,91	3,30	1,60	40,80
Charter companies	-	-	-	-
Spies Rejser	5,52	3,38	2,14	8
Tjæreborg Rejser	5,23	3,26	1,97	6
MyTravel	4,20	2,70	1,50	18
Star Tour	3,98	3,17	0,81	9
Category average	4,74	3,13	1,60	10,09
TV stations	-	-	-	-
DR 2	3,60	-0,42	4,02	82
Zulu	3,43	0,61	2,81	72
TV2	1,95	-0,31	2,27	97
TV3	1,60	-2,24	3,84	77
DR 1	1,54	-2,58	4,12	96
3+	1,49	-1,72	3,21	76
Category average	2,27	-1,11	3,38	83,29
Brand average	4,25	2,01	2,24	45

Differences in NERS scores between users and non-users for brands within the same categories may reveal differences in attachment to the brands. Some of the brands known from previous examples show up here again. Among the shampoo brands, Head & Shoulders has a larger difference between users and non-users than any other brand.

The same is the case with BG Bank in 2004 in the bank group. Among the newspapers it is remarkable that the two freely distributed newspapers (MetroXpress and Urban) have smaller differences in NERS scores when users are compared to non-users than the major national newspapers. However, in absolute terms they fare better than their major competitors, the tabloid papers BT and Ekstrabladet. The low 2004 NERS score for the Kellogg's brand discussed earlier is much more strongly expressed among the non-users – probably mirroring the association of the products with the obesity debate as discussed earlier.

Table XI.10: Difference in NERS scores for brands with most users in each category compared with remaining brands

	No. of brands	NERS			% users
		Users	Non-users	Diff.	
Most used brands	11	2.60	0.22	2.38	71%
Remaining brands	27	2.77	0.96	1.81	40%

By comparing most used brands in each category with the remaining brands (table XI.10), it appears that the larger brands have larger discrepancies between users and non-users than the smaller brands.

The double jeopardy phenomenon (Ehrenberg et al., 1997) appears here also. The larger brands are not only large in themselves; they have stronger emotional reactions attached to them with clear differences between the NERS amongst users and the NERS amongst non-users. This makes them much more difficult to attack for challenging competitors, since the pattern of emotional reaction can be seen as a barrier that the challenger has to overcome in order to "convert" the consumer.

D. NERS Scores for Leading Political Candidates

The sudden announcement of a general election in Denmark in early 2005 made it possible to look at NERS scores for leading political candidates immediately after the election had been declared and following the election. This provides a unique possibility to study the extent to which NERS scores change in a situation with a lot of marketing communication going on about the political spokespersons involved.

In Denmark (after the election) six political parties are represented in the parliament. It was decided to measure NERS score for the leading political spokespersons for each of the leading parties. A total of six candidates were identified for inclusion in the study (see Table XI.11). To measure the NERS scores, ten items out of the total list of 16 used for brands and products in the 2004 study were selected with a view to their relevance in connection with political spokespersons. To this was added an attitudinal question about the trustworthiness of the candidates. The items are seen in Table XI.11.

Data collection comprised approximately 1000 respondents and took place as part of data collection for Gallup/TNS' political index so that data could be weighted in a manner similar to that used in weighting political index. Fundamental in this weighting procedure is a weighting that secures that all respondents appear in the final data analysis with a distribution over political parties that corresponds to that of the last general election.

Table XI.11: Factor analysis of 10 emotional and one trustworthiness
items for 6 political candidates

	All spokes-persons		Fogh Liberal		Bendtsen Conserv.		Nielsen Soc. Pop.		Jelved Radical		Lykketoft Soc. Dem.		Kjærsgaard Danish Pop.	
	+	-	+	-	+	-	+	-	+	-	+	-	+	-
Joy	.80	.05	.80	.05	.82	.08	.80	.11	.78	.03	.81	.10	.79	.03
Fresh	.77	-.08	.80	-.12	.79	.04	.77	-.08	.75	.02	.74	-.20	.73	-.05
Success	.77	-.13	.72	-.30	.81	.04	.78	-.17	.78	-.02	.74	-.12	.80	.15
Healthy	.76	.03	.75	-.03	.72	.04	.74	.05	.74	.09	.77	.16	.75	.13
Pretty	.74	.23	.73	.24	.78	.23	.72	.24	.70	.35	.76	.23	.77	.27
Expectation	.68	.27	.70	-.27	.65	-.37	.69	-.21	.68	-.28	.70	.15	.67	.28
Trustworthy	.57	.53	.64	-.53	.52	-.55	.58	-.56	.52	-.55	.73	-.31	.48	-.55
Doubt	.12	.70	-.01	.75	.10	.66	.07	.72	.24	.71	.08	.64	.22	.60
Worry	.05	.73	-.12	.78	.18	.65	.09	.75	.21	.68	-.17	.69	.24	.63
Boring	-.07	.52	.06	.61	-.02	.64	-.11	.58	-.20	.63	.16	.61	-.07	.67
Annoyed	-.13	.75	-.20	.78	-.02	.74	-.03	.74	-.05	.77	-.35	.69	-.06	.71

For the computation of the NERS scores an overall factor analytical
solution identifying a positive and a negative emotional response dimension was conducted for each of the candidates. The result of this
is seen in Table XI.11. A clear positive and a clear negative emotional dimension emerge. Only trustworthiness fall out of the general
pattern being positively associated with the positively judged feeling
words, but equally strongly negatively associated with the negative
feeling words, obviously "trustworthiness" measuring something else
than sheer emotions. Other findings reported elsewhere suggest that
trustworthiness rather should be seen as a separate variable much in
line with what also is being discussed on attitudes towards the ad.
Factor analytical solutions for the individual spokespersons did not
deviate from this overall pattern, which consequently was applied for
the computation of NERS scores for all the six candidates.

Judged in comparison with the NERS scores so far reported the
magnitude of the differences between the voters preferring a party at
last election and that of the NERS scores for other candidates is remarkable. Obviously emotional attachment to the different candidates
plays a major role for the outcome of and election.

Table XI.12: NERS scores for 6 leading political candidates of the 2005 Danish national election early in the election period

Voting for at last election	Fogh Liberal	Lykketoft Soc. Dem.	Bendtsen Conserv.	Jelved Radical	Kjærsgård Danish Pop.	Nielsen Soc. Pop.	All voters
The Social Democrats	- 2.56	5.70	-1.04	3.24	-5.18	2.46	0.72
The Radical Party	-2.48	1.17	-1.44	7.67	-6.50	1.72	0.34
The Conservatives	11.54	-4.02	8.44	-3.13	-0.44	-1.75	1.75
Socialistic Populistic Party	-3.32	1.79	-1.13	3.55	-5.12	7.29	0.94
Danish Populistic Party	10.92	-3.49	3.36	-4.26	11.53	-2.24	2.37
The Liberal Party	13.50	-3.70	5.94	-2.81	1.22	-1.44	1.99
All voters	**4.73**	**-0.47**	**2.56**	**0.66**	**-1.91**	**0.75**	**1.10**
Own party	13.50	5.70	8.44	7.67	11.53	7.29	
All but own party	1.44	-2.08	1.72	-0.13	-2.77	0.28	

In Table XI.12 NERS scores for the candidates are shown. In the table the scores for each candidate are also broken down according to what the respondent voted at the last general election.

To interpret these scores it is necessary to say a few words about the political situation prior to the announcement of the election. The government was a coalition comprising the Conservatives and the Liberal Parties (Fogh and Bendtsen). It was supported by the extreme right wing party, Danish Populistic Party (Pia Kjærsgaard). The opposition was the two left-wing parties, Social Democrats and Socialistic Populistic Party together with the Radical Party.

Publicly it was assumed that the reason for having the election in early 2005 (it could have been delayed until late 2005) was the relatively strong standing of the government and its supporting right-wing party in the political indexes in the fall of 2004. This is reflected in the overall NERS scores where the candidates heading the government, Fogh and Bendtsen score overall much higher than any other political spokes person. Other relevant observations are the following:

The candidates with the lowest NERS score are on an overall basis Kjærsgaard for Danish Populistic Party and Lykketoft for the Social Democratic Party. There is however a marked difference in the situation of the two political leaders. Whereas Lykketoft is the spokesperson with the lowest NERS score among own voters of all spokespersons, Kjærsgaard is the one with the second highest score among own voters only outperformed by the leader of Liberal Party, Fogh.

The profile of Kjærsgaard thus is one of a highly loyal and attached following amongst party loyals, while voters for other parties, particularly the left wing parties, have strong negative emotions.

Remarkable is also the Radical Party's very strong standing with the Social Democrats and the Socialist Party. Political analysts have pointed to the contemporary political spectrum as being two dimensional rather than the "old-fashioned" one dimensional left-right wing. The two important dimensions are the political values dimension – from progressive to traditional – and a distributory dimension – from marked redistribution of income and a public sector providing lots of services to individuality where the individual provides his/her own social and medical security along with all other typical public services.

In this light it becomes easy to understand why the Radical Party – which in essence is a liberal party with a strong pacifist leaning, catering to the academic voter – appeals so strongly to the left wing parties. On the distributory dimension the Radical Party is very close to Social Democratic and Socialist viewpoints, however on values the party is much more progressive than the traditional Social Democratic working class values. The latter value proposition seems to appeal strongly to the contemporary Social Democrat and Socialist.

Based upon these observations, it is interesting to see the NERS scores after the election and the general outcome of the election. This is shown in Figure XI.13. Here it appears that the government parties largely maintain their strength whereas the Social Democrats and the Social Populists both loose voters (primarily to the Radical Central Party). These changes seem meaningful in relation to the NERS scores collected at the time at which the election was declared. Interesting is however also to see what changes occur in the course of the election as measured at the time of the first political poll following the election. Changes and the significance of these are indicated in the table.

Table XI.13: Election outcome and changes in NERS scores from before to after the election

Voting for/did vote for	Fogh Liberal	Lyk-ketoft Soc. Dem.	Bendt-sen Con-serv.	Jel-ved Radi-cal	Kjærs-gård Danish Pop.	Niel-sen Soc. Pop.	All vo-ters	Mandate before/af-ter election	
The Social Democrats	0.06	**-2.14**	0.24	1.14	**2.05**	-0.63	0.12	52	47
The Radical Party	**1.97**	-0.25	**1.78**	0.78	**1.33**	-0.31	**0.81**	9	16
The Conservatives	**-3.38**	**1.34**	-1.67	1.12	-0.60	0.53	-0.27	16	19
Socialistic Populis-tic Party	-0.27	-0.42	-1.16	2.08	-0.90	**-2.47**	-0.52	12	11
Danish Populistic Party	**-3.92**	1.45	-0.96	1.17	-1.85	1.35	0.04	22	24
The liberal Party	-1.32	0.92	0.49	**-0.53**	0.38	-0.04	0.09	56	52
All voters	-0.63	0.29	0.18	**0.69**	**0.62**	-0.31	0.24	175	175
Own party voters	-1.32	-2.14	1.78	0.78	-1.85	1.35			
All but own party	-0.09	1.00	0.32	0.42	0.66	-0.24			

Bold: indicates significant change (p≤ 0.05)

The largest total positive change occurs for Jelved (Radical Party). This change is the only total score, which is (almost) significant at the level of 0,066. It is also remarkable that Jelved for the Radical Party is the only one who maintains her standing with all competing parties but the Liberal Party. There are however several significant changes occurring in the matrix showing how the NERS scores change for different candidates among the voters of competing parties.

For Fogh and the Liberal Party negative changes occur relative to the Conservative Party and Danish Populist Party whereas a significant change in a positive direction is observed relative to the Radical Party. This corresponds to Jelved's (The Radical Party) only negative change and may be ascribable to a particular debate occurring in the election between Jelved and a senior person of the government, Harder, who was probably unrightfully criticized for his views on the integration issue by Jelved in an important television transmission.

Lykketoft (Social Democrats), the major looser is the only one who has a significant negative change in NERS scores among own voters. Kjærsgaard, in contrast, has a significant gain in NERS scores among social democratic voters and radicals. The gain amongst social democrats is probably ascribable to Kjærsgaard's position on the values dimension, where her party line is extremely traditional and conservative – appealing to the traditional working class voter of the social democrats. Her gain amongst radical voters may have to do with her strong views on distribution policy where particularly care for the elderly is very important, and that might well appeal to some of the Radical Party's older and more traditional voters.

All in all, the changes that occur are meaningful seen in the light of the outcome of the general election. By doing this, the results indicate that also in political decisions such as voting behaviour, the consumer does rely on stored emotional information for making decisions. The voter has a tendency to decide, probably more on holistic and emotional impulses than on detailed, rational weighing of the pros and cons of individual political spokespersons and the views of their respective parties. In this sense, spokespersons and their parties can be seen as close approximations to brands in a FMCG sense. The authors leave it to political decision makers to draw their own conclusions for future election campaigns from this.

E. Advertising Pre-Testing Experiences

In the preceding sections we have seen major changes in NERS scores being ascribable and explainable in terms of factual changes and developments in the markets studied. Most of these observations are either cross sectional in nature or they come from tracking changes over rather short periods of time.

So far, the available data do not provide any direct campaign tracking experiences covering extended periods of timebut another way of looking upon the sensitivity question is to look upon the use of feeling words for measuring feelings or underlying emotions as it has been done in advertising pre-testing.

1. 28 ELAM Pre-Tests

When looking at advertising pre-testing, emotions are seen from a somewhat different angle as compared to the NERS scores associated with brands, corporations etc. discussed so far. Here, the concern is with the emotional content of the advertising execution, the perceptions of this and to a lesser extent its effect upon NERS scores for the brands etc. Just as much conventional advertising testing is more concerned with advertising awareness than with brand awareness, we here find a concern with emotional effects generated by advertising rather than emotional effects as they may result in the form of changes in the NERS scores for the brand, product, party leader etc. An underlying assumption is that if advertising differs in the extent to which it generates emotional response tendencies, this eventually will influence the overall perception of the brand and eventually the extent to which the brand is chosen in a subsequent, appropriate buying situation.

The elaboration likelihood advertising model was introduced by Hansen (1997) based on the Petty and Cacioppo elaboration likelihood model (see Chapter II and IV). In an advertising test developed to measure degrees of central versus peripheral processing of advertising, a number of standard pre test measures such as advertising recall, brand recall, image linking, and attitudes towards the ads were included. Of particular interest for the purpose here, responses to feeling words were included.

The suggested test is carried out as a monadic hall test with 130 or more respondents being exposed to print or television advertising executions. As feeling words in the test were used 12 words taken from Gallup Robinson's standard procedure (METHA 1996) to reflect positive and negative emotions. In the years 1997-1999 a total of 28 tests were conducted with basically the same questionnaire used in all tests. The feelings words overlap with those used in the different NERS tests.

The majority of the tests were for FMCG. Data from these analyses were pooled for reporting effects of peripheral versus central information processing which was – as previously mentioned – the primary objective and purpose of the test (Hansen and Hansen 2001a). See also Chapter II.

Conducting a factor analysis on the pooled feeling word data across the 28 tests gave the results in Table XI.14. Here positive and negative emotional dimensions appear. The first factor predominantly combines positive feeling words, whereas the 2nd factor includes most of the negative feeling words.

Table XI.14: Forced two dimensional factor analysis of 12 feeling words used in 28 pre-tests. Explained variance 58%.

	Ad test	
	I	II
Happiness	**.70**	.01
Joy	**.67**	-.04
Pleasure	**.58**	-.21
Accept	**.56**	.08
Inspiring	**.54**	-.05
Hope	**.51**	.12
Surprise	.40	.19
Anger	-.01	**.67**
Fear	.17	**.65**
Sorrow	-.07	**.50**
Dominant	.23	**.44**

In the analysis respondents were classified as using predominantly central versus predominantly peripheral information processing based upon open-ended questions about their view on the advertisement. When this is done, the results in Table XI.15 appear.

Table XI.15: Frequency of positive and negative emotional scores for central vs. peripheral processing (Hansen et al., 2002). Figures in bold are significantly different with $p \leq 0.05$

(N = 4,456)	Central	Peripheral
Enjoyment	46.2%	**58.0%**
Happiness	27.4%	**41.2%**
Acceptance	22.2%	**33.5%**
Pleasure	26.4%	**40.0%**
Hope	28.5%	**33.4%**
Inspiring	28.8%	28.0%
Dominate	8.7%	**13.1%**
Surprising	18.7%	**23.3%**
Distrust	7.5%	9.0%
Anger	**11.6%**	6.9%
Fear	3.3%	5.3%
Sorrow	**6.9%**	4.6%
+ NERS	206.9%	270.5%
- NERS	29.3%	25.2%
NERS	**177.6%**	**245.3%**

Emotional responses occur both with central and informational processing. Most thought with informational processing. Of the eight positive feeling words seven show significantly larger scores (marked in bold in the table) when peripheral information processing occurs than when central information processing is used. When it comes to the negative feeling words however, a somewhat different pattern emerges. Here we find two feeling words (distrust and fear) scoring (not significantly) higher with peripheral processing and two (anger and sorrow) scoring significantly higher with central information processing.

The occurrence of central versus peripheral information process-ing is of course dependent on the dispositions of the individual in the testing situation and the actual ads being tested. Some ads were dominated by peripheral others by central information processing but the data suggests that the feeling words are sensitive to what kind of advertisement and what kind of information processing is at stake.

If one makes the assumption (which is not entirely unrealistic for many fast moving consumer goods) that the respondent has the same weight, say 1, on all evaluative dimensions, i.e. either they do have or they do not have the particular feeling associated with the test item, we can compute an overall NERS score for central and pe-ripheral information processing simply by adding the frequencies as shown in Table XI.15 in the bottom. It can be seen that on the whole when central information processing occurs the net emotional re-sponse strength is significantly lower than when peripheral informa-tion processing occurs.

The reporting of these findings here is complicated by the fact that the raw data from the tests do not exist any longer. However, it is still possible to have a picture of the overall sensitivity of the 12 feeling words in measuring emotional response by looking at the range of the scores reported in Hansen (1997). Here the number of times feel-ings words are rated in percentage of all ratings is computed. It can be seen that there are considerable variations in the occurrence of the feeling words (Table XI.16).

Table XI.16: Highest and lowest proportion found in different pretests. Highest and lowest percentage using different feeling words in evaluating 28 pretested adverts.

Emotional reactions (%)	Highest score	Lowest score
Pleasure	20%	45%
Hope	12%	45%
Acceptance	2%	36%
Happiness	10%	44%
Dominating	1%	18%
Enjoyment	67%	18%
Inspiring	50%	39%
Surprising	8%	48%
Distrust	0%	14%
Sorrow	0%	15%
Anger	0%	15%
Fear	0%	8%

Another example of feeling words (Hansen, 1998) used for testing two different mineral water advertisements, illustrates the different emotional responses generated by the ads, where one is based on a person in a thirst-aroused situation (central information), the other is based on associations with a mild and friendly landscape (peripheral information).The scores are shown in Table XI.17 where it can be seen that the landscape version scores positively higher on the emotional positive dimensions There are no real differences in the choice of negative words but the two ads provide very different NERS scores.

Table XI.17: Feeling words associated with two alternative mineral water commercials and derived NERS scores. Percentage of all respondents using the different feeling words in evaluating the two alternative adverts

Emotional reactions (%)	Version with person (N=132)	Version with landscape (N=135)
% positive words chosen	206.9%	290.5%
% negative words chosen	29.3%	25.2%
"NERS"	177.6%	245.3%

2. Experiences from International Pre-Testing

It is a common practice in contemporary pre-testing to include feeling words. Often the authors do not distinguish between feelings and emotions and the results of using these measures are interchangeably reported as feeling or emotional results.

Two internationally well-established pre-testing companies have lately reported findings demonstrating results from their use of feeling words in pre-testing. Du Plessis (2005a) and Hollis (2005) reports findings from a large number of Link-tests conducted by the Millward Brown Corporation using a battery of 16 feeling words divided into eight positive and eight negative ones.

The feeling words are shown in Table XI.18. In his reporting Hollis introduces what he calls a "feel good factor" which is the difference between the average positive and average negative emotional scores much like the NERS scores discussed here. From 150 tested ads he reports a maximum score of 50% and a minimum score of 4%.

Table XI.18: Feeling words used in later years in Millward Brown Link pre-testing

Positive/ 'Toward'	Negative/ 'Away from'
• Surprised	• Hatred
• Exited	• Repelled
• Attracted	• Annoyed
• Inspired	• Inadequate
• Confident	• Disappointed
• Proud	• Guilty
• Contented	• Unimpressed
• Affectionate	• Sad

The reporting for a particular ad is illustrated in Figure XI.3 where the scores of the ad are compared with average scores for the 150 test ads' database.

With these feeling words Hollis compute a total "feel good" score as the sum of the positive answers versus the sum of the negative answers. This score is in nature much like our NERS score. An example of such a score is shown in Figure XI.3.

Figure XI.3: Example of feeling words for a particular ad compared with averages for 150 ads (Hollis, 2005).

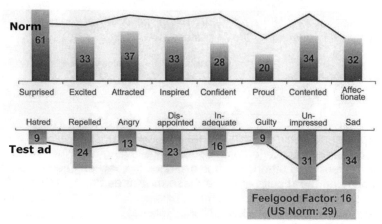

A noteworthy case of negative emotional response tendency is also reported by Nigel Hollis from a test in the US of a UK commercial. The working title of the commercial is Prisoner, and it shows a very unhappily looking woman imprisoned by cleaning duties in the household while her daughter is missing her. Here, different feeling words have been used in an earlier version of the Link test and from a database including 1544 US finished films, average scores and scores for the particular Prisoner spot are shown as the sum of the responses to the three negative feeling word; irritating, unpleasant, and disturbing. The emotional response by US consumers to this English commercial is remarkable and shown in Figure XI.4.

On a similar line the German institute GfK reports on the use of feeling words in advertising pre- and post-test. Public reporting does not include data.

Figure XI.4: Response distribution on sum of the three negative feel-
ing words for UK house cleaners. Commercials tested in
the US (Hollis, 2005)

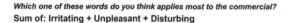

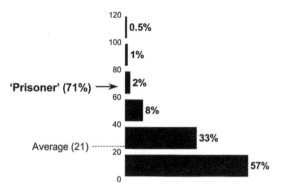

Base: 1544 USA - Finished Film ads

Also the examples of emotional responses to brand names in test situations using FMRI scanning may be recalled in this context, McClure et al. (2004) on Coca-Cola and Plassmann et al. (2005) on beer and coffee (Chapter IV.

Facial expressions play an important role in the study of emotional responses. Ever since the classical studies reported by Darwin, researchers have been concerned with facial expressions as they relate to underlying emotions. Ekman (1980) based his theory of feelings on facial expressions. And studies have been reported relating communication effects to facial expressions. For instance, Derbaix and Bree (2002) reports children's' facial responses to advertising, and standardised measures of facial expressions have been introduced into marketing research. Hazlett and Hazlett (1999) use electronic registration of the responses in facial changes as indications of emotional responses to advertising.

Facial expressions may be looked upon in different ways. It is possible – and so far that has been the major concern among researchers – to look at facial expressions and derive a hypothesis about underlying emotional states. In more recent times the almost opposite approach has been taken. Different research institutes and academic researchers have concerned themselves with the possibility of measuring effects to advertising material with the use of pictorial scales. Early work with such scales is reported by Morris (1995), and. furthermore Morris and McMullen (2000) demonstrated the use of their PAD based Sam pictorial test on TV commercials.

Another commercial approach is introduced by Ipsos-ASI (Charlton-Jones, 2005). Based upon what they report as extensive preliminary literature search, they arrive at a total list of more than 200 potential feeling words.

Figure XI.5: EMO faces describing 40 different feeling words (Ipsos-ASI 2005)

By using expert judges and multidimensional scaling of rated associations between the feeling words they arrive at a basic listing of 40 feelings each represented with three to six words. With these 40 feelings two different graphic artists were asked to illustrate each of them. The 40 different faces of EMO (as the depicted guy is called) are shown in Figure XI.5 where also the corresponding feeling words are indicated. It is obvious from this presentation that like the feeling words used in NERS testing they fall in two clearly separated segments on either side of the horizontal axis with negative feeling expressions on the left and positive feeling expressions on the right. The vertical axis seems to reflect arousal or a general activity or intensity level in connection with the feelings expressed. In the available reporting, Charlton Jones' (2005) - examples are presented showing high sensitivity of the measures in terms of their ability to discriminate among different ads. The scores are arrived at on an interactive basis on a computer with the respondent making choices among different faces On an unreported number of cases the relationship between a traditional purchase intention scale and average feeling words chosen are reported. Also a "persuasion score" is computed not unlike the NERS score discussed in previous chapters here. Persuasion is seen to decrease with the number of scores selected in the negative part of the diagram and increase with the number of scores selected in the upper as well as the lower quadrant of the right side of the diagram. This relationship is illustrated in Figure XI.6.

Figure XI.6: Average feeling word scores for EMO in different quadrants (Charlton-Jones, 2005)

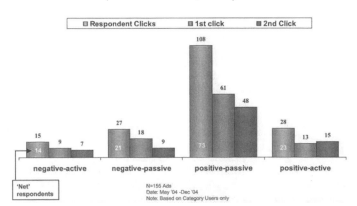

Another application of pictorially based measures of feelings used by TNS is reported by Desmet (2003b). Here the character Sam known from the traditional smiling scale applications is used. Of the 14 pictures (see Figure XI.7), the seven correspond to positive feeling words (desire, pleasant surprise, inspiration, amusement, admiration, satisfaction, fascination) and seven correspond to negative feeling words (indignation, contempt, disgusted, unpleasant surprise, dissatisfaction, disappointment and boredom). Here research departed in a listing of 347 possible feeling words but eventually these were boiled down to the 14 feelings expressed by the faces shown in Figure XI.7).

Figure XI.7: 18 PREMO picture scale faces (Desmet, 2003b)

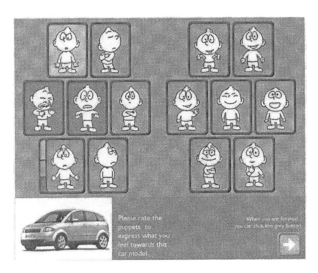

Measurement of the degree to which respondents feels the particular expression applies to what is being tested, can be scaled by the use of animation sequences like those shown in Figure XI.8.

Figure XI.8: Facial PREMO scale to measure degree of feelings (Desmet, 2003b)

Studies reported so far with these PREMO scales are based on relatively small samples and in the Desmet studies stimuli is not full advertising but rather pictures of products.

Among these studies one involves comparison of scores on pictures of cars from Japan and USA in the same countries and in the Netherlands. It was found that except for two feelings (desire and disappointment not working in Japan) the PREMO scale worked well in all three countries. Another interesting finding is reported in terms of very high correlations between the PREMO scores and scaling on corresponding verbal scales.

On the whole, experiences with this pictorial test seem to provide results in line with studies with more traditional verbal feeling words scales. The advantage is claimed to be that the respondent is not forced to apply cognitive processing in formulating his feelings. However, on the other hand one might suspect that the somewhat uncommon test situation and the many facial expressions may give rise to other speculations on behalf of the respondent which may influence responses in unknown ways.

A commercial application of the PREMO procedure is reported by Taylor Nielsen/nipo (Kuijten and Foekema, 2005) reducing the battery to five positive and five negative dimensions and computing a Net score, deducting negative from positive scores. They show positive, negative and Net scores (much like NERS) derived from Dutch data on political candidates. A sample of the results is given in Table XI.19.

Table XI.19: "Balanced results" (like NERS scores). Dutch study using promotions (Kuijten and Foekema, 2005)

	Score
Nelson Mandela	4.8
Kofi Anan	3.0
Queen Beatrix	3.0
Pope John Paul II	0.9
Tony Blair	0.5
Hu Jintao	0.1
Gerhard Schröder	-0.7
Jacques Chirac	-1.2
Jan Peter Balkenende	-1.3
Silvio Berlusconi	-1.4
Ariël Sharon	-1.8
Wladimir Poetin	-2.6
Robert Mugabe	-3.2
George W. Bush	-3.3
Kim Jung II	-3.3
Fidel Castro	-3.6

All in all it seems well documented that pictorial representation of faces can be used for measuring feeling response to stimuli such as advertising and products. It also seems that the findings resulting correspond very well to the findings derived with the use of verbal scaling of feeling words.

3. Emotional Responses to different Design Lines

Kristensen et al. (2000b) and Gabrielsen et al. (2000) reports on a series of tests conducted to evaluate different design lines. For the test a modified ELAM procedure (Hansen 1997) was used with a sequence of questions revealing central and peripheral information processing. Of particular concern for the reporting here is the inclusion of 12 feeling words, used in the advertising pre-testing context described previously.

In the test covering 220 graduate students taking introductory classes in the marketing programme, five experimental conditions were created. The test was monadic and had approximately 45 respondents included in each condition. The manipulation in each experimental condition consisted of presentation of a collection of design materials representing the particular company that was illustrated. The materials covered the façade of the company, its logo, an example of a letterhead copy from a company brochure front page, and an example of an invoice. The five conditions were; (1) Kilroy (a travel agency catering to young people), (2) the National Railway Agency, (3) a nonexisting, artificially created logo titled Subgate as a travel agency, (4) the students' book store at CBS and an artificially created book store with the name Subgate.

Emotional responses were obtained by asking the respondents to pick the four emotionally describing words, which they found associated the best with the design version which they were presented for.

In spite of the crudeness, a forced two-factor analytical solution was estimated across the different experimental conditions. This is represented in Table XI.20.

Table XI.20: Two emotional dimensions for different design lines (Hansen et al., 2001). Factor analytical solution (38% variance explained)

	Design	
	I	II
Happiness	**.72**	-.16
Joy	**.78**	-.03
Pleasure	**.75**	.03
Accept	.06	**-.55**
Inspiring	**.62**	.43
Hope	.43	-.30
Surprise	.16	**.81**
Anger	**-.84**	-.11
Fear	**-.73**	-.13
Mistrust	**-.71**	.07
Sorrow	**-.76**	-.31
Dominant	-.47	.30

It appears that here to a large extent positive and negative emotional responses seem to appear as opposites posed along the same first factor whereas the second factor, if anything, represents arousal (loading on surprise and lack of accept). A possible explanation for this special phenomenon may be the fact that the data collection procedure, forcing each respondent to choose four feeling words, all of the choices centred around the positively loaded feeling words and only few negative words were chosen for any of the five alternatives.

In terms of discrimination, the different design lines give rise to different combinations of feeling words being selected as illustrated below (Table XI.21) in the example comparing all Subgate responses with all Kilroy responses. The numbers are the frequencies with which the words were chosen as being suitable for the design line, and as in the advertising pre-tests a net emotional response strength score is computed as the aggregate sum of the frequencies - much like a NERS score. The existing Kilroy agency outperforms the artificial Subgate dramatically.

Still the finding reminds us that the preceding (Chapter V) debate concerning PAD (preference, arousal, dominance) versus PANAS (Positive versus negative affect) is not irrelevant.

F. Emotional Responses Explaining Evaluation of Sponsorships

In discussing effects of sponsorships, we do not purport to put forward documentation that covers all and any form that sponsorships may take. The terminology itself in sponsorship is not very clear; it seems that reported studies and practice uses the expression sponsorship to cover more or less anything from hospitality events via sponsored shows to adding logotypes to player jerseys and printed matters and even on to perimeter advertising in connection with sports events.

There is no doubt that sponsorship as an area has caught the interest of business and organisations for its assumed ability to play on the emotional reactions of participants or audience – an ability that sponsor professionals may even claim is much bigger than that of traditional forms of marketing communication.

In the studies that we report in this book the area under study is primarily an assumed low involvement, maybe even low attention exposure situation, since emotional responses are more important in low involvement situations and since that type of sponsorships seem to be by far the most common form, at least in Scandinavia.

Common to the published literature on sponsorship evaluation is an effect hierarchical thinking. One looks for effects in terms of awareness, liking of the sponsorship and persuasion in terms of convincing consumers of the superiority of the sponsored company or product. (Waliser, 2003, and Hansen and Halling, 2002).

1. First Sponsorship Study, 1999

To study how such traditional effect measures relate to measures of emotional responses to sponsorships, a project was carried out in 1999 where 27 well-known and established Danish sports sponsorships were evaluated by 52 first year undergraduate students at the Copenhagen Business School. Data were collected with a mail questionnaire.

Awareness was measured by asking respondents how well they knew the particular sponsorship. Liking was measured by asking respondents on a five point scale how well they liked the sponsorship and finally, persuasion was measured by a "self-rated change in purchase intention" question.

With these data a total sponsorship effect score was arrived at by computing the geometrical average of the three scores as indicated in formula XI.1 below.

Formula XI.1

Overall Effect Score = $\dfrac{\text{Awareness}}{\text{Avg. Awareness}} * \dfrac{\text{Liking}}{\text{Avg. liking}} * \dfrac{\text{Self-rated change in buying intention}}{\text{Avg. Self-rated change in buying intention}}$

The resulting scores are shown in Table XI.22.

Table XI.21: Total attractiveness score for 12 sponsorships and the components computed from Formula XI.1

Sponsor-sponsee combinations (N = 167)	Number of observations	Average awareness	Average liking	Average buying intention after knowledge	Combined Score
Faxe Kondi-Superligaen	143	1.20	1.16	1.05	1.45
MD Foods-Herrelandsholdet	123	1.21	1.13	1.06	1.44
SAS-Thomas Bjørn	39	1.10	1.15	1.06	1.36
Jolly Cola-Damelandsholdet i håndbold	98	1.10	1.01	0.97	1.08
Carlsberg-FCK	112	1.11	0.94	1.01	1.05
V6-Camilla Martin	144	1.05	0.96	0.95	0.96
Codan-Brønby	118	0.89	1.01	0.98	0.88
TV2-Camilla Andersen	32	0.91	0.94	1.02	0.86
Børsens Nyhedsmagasin-Kristian Pless	32	0.82	1.00	1.05	0.85
Spar-VM håndbold for kvinder	67	0.87	0.93	1.02	0.83
Scanbox-Brian Nielsen	65	0.90	0.89	0.89	0.72
Byggekram-Herrehåndboldligaen	65	0.84	0.89	0.94	0.71

Emotions were measured with the use of a slightly modified version of feeling words from the ELAM advertising pre-test described earlier. When forcing a two-factor solution upon the data the resulting factors looked as in Table XI.22. A clear negative and a clear positive evaluative dimension emerge, however with some slightly surprising loadings on accept and with no significant loadings on dominating and surprising at all. Suggesting that a third factor might reveal an arousal activation involvement kind of dimension.

Table XI.22: Two factor solution for feeling words associated with sponsorships

	Sponsoring	
	I	II
Happiness	.39	.03
Joy	.61	-.11
Pleasure	.48	.01
Accept	-.45	.01
Inspiring	.38	-.16
Hope	.33	-.02
Surprise	-.02	.16
Anger	-.07	.61
Fear	-.03	.45
Trust	-.32	.36
Sorrow	-.07	.40
Dominant	-.10	.08

In the study the combinations of sponsors and sponsees were selected in pairs so as to provide data on two soccer teams, two handball teams etc. It was possible to divide the sponsored objects into winners and losers. When this is done, the corresponding emotional scores are shown in Table XI.23. Also here it can be seen how the emotional scores make sense in this study in spite of the crude emotional measure where the respondent does not grade the emotions, but only choose what emotional words fit or do not fit. The NERS scores are computed at the aggregate level based on the difference between sums of positive and negative feeling words. In spite of this the scores relate clearly to the way in which the total evaluation varies among winners versus losers, soccer versus handball and different kinds of sponsorships.

Table XI.23: Emotional scores for winners and losers among sponsored parties. Average % of times positive respectively negative feeling words are chosen

	Joy/Enjoyment/Happiness	Fear/Anger/Grief	Difference in scores
Winners	21.21%	2.91%	18.30
Losers	9.31%	5.65%	3.75

2. Second Sponsorship Study, 2001

Based upon the experiences of this initial study it was decided to replicate it with a wider selection of sponsorships, with more feeling words used for the emotional measure and with a scaling of these. The sample was similar to that from the first year and consisted of 167 first year students. A total of 27 sponsorships were included divided equally on sports sponsoring, cultural sponsoring, social aid sponsoring and television programmes sponsoring.

In this test 27 different feeling words were used. These 27 feeling words were the same that eventually - with small modifications - developed into the battery earlier described for use in the 2003 data collection of NERS scores. In the reporting of these findings a four factor solution was chosen. This is illustrated in Table XI.24. Again here, it was possible to compute overall evaluations of the sponsorships based upon awareness, liking and persuasion in a manner similar to that described in the first sponsor test

Table XI.24: Four factor solution for feeling words associated with sponsorships showing factor loadings on the factors.

	"uncertainty"	"avoidance"	"approach"	"arousal"
	1	2	3	4
HOPE	0,59	-0,19	-0,19	-0,19
SORROW	0,57	0,16	0,01	0,00
WORRY	0,46	0,06	-0,03	-0,08
FEAR	0,45	0,14	0,04	-0,02
INSPIRING	-0,31	-0,15	0,00	-0,13
OPTIMISM	0,28	-0,27	-0,17	0,12
DOMINATING	-0,23	0,17	-0,06	-0,06
SATISFACTION	-0,16	0,09	0,12	-0,09
SHAME	0,00	0,54	-0,01	-0,04
LONELINESS	0,04	0,40	-0,04	0,11
ANGER	0,03	0,40	0,04	-0,11
SAD	0,15	0,40	-0,02	0,00
ENVY	-0,02	0,37	0,07	0,00
DESIRE	-0,07	0,34	-0,05	0,30
GUILT	0,03	0,34	-0,02	0,07
DISSATISFACTION	0,24	0,28	-0,02	-0,03
JOY	-0,06	-0,17	0,62	0,20
ROMANTIC LOVE	0,00	0,05	0,52	0,10
ENJOYMENT	-0,14	-0,05	0,51	0,00
HAPPINESS	0,14	0,00	0,49	-0,03
PEACEFULLNESS	-0,05	0,08	0,31	-0,18
EXCITEMENT	-0,12	-0,08	-0,17	0,64
SURPRISING	0,07	-0,03	0,02	0,44
TRUST	0,08	-0,11	-0,15	-0,40
ACCEPT	-0,08	0,10	-0,21	-0,35
RELIEF	0,04	0,10	0,01	0,22
PRIDE	-0,18	-0,07	-0,09	0,21

Extraction Method: Principal Component Analysis.
Rotation converged in 7 iterations.
Rotation Method: Varimax with Kaiser Normalization.

It will be seen that the second and the third factor represent the negative and positive evaluative dimensions whereas the fourth and the first factor most likely reveal arousal and uncertainty. We are reminded of the PANAS/PAD discussion again. It has not been possible to reanalyse these data in terms of a forced two-dimensional factorial solution but still, with the four dimensional solution when factor scores are used as independent variables in a linear regression analysis with the total sponsor evaluation as the dependent variable, the following relationships emerge:

(overall evaluation)= 1.0115+0.1124 (uncertainty) – 0.0030 (negative emotions) + 0.0016 (positive emotions) + 0.0011 (arousal)

Of the beta values in this equation only the one associated with arousal is not strongly significant (P=0.14). The multiple R for this equation is 0.81 and the adjusted R^2 is 0.60 suggesting that 60% of the variation in the overall evaluation of the sponsorship effect scores can be explained by the emotional responses to the sponsorship alone.

Thus, in these studies of sponsorship we find emotions playing an important role in determining how well different sponsorships perform. Basically, the data confirm the importance of the positive/negative dimensionality of emotion scores but we also find a separate effect ascribable to the arousal involvement type of variable.

3. Third Sponsorship Study, 2003

After the two initial sponsor effect studies with student samples were carried out, the opportunity arose to carry out a much larger study, both in terms of companies and sponsee institutions surveyed, and in terms of number and character of respondents.

The study was sponsored by the Danish Cancer Foundation (Kræftens Bekæmpelse) as part of this organisation's commitment to improve the knowledge of the effects of sponsorships in general and sponsorships of charitable institutions in particular. The sponsorship covered the data collection for the study which was carried out by TNS/Gallup.

A total of 472 respondents, aged 15+, were contacted as part of tns/Gallup's ordinary omnibus survey and requested to participate in a scientific project. Those that accepted – more than 64% of those selected – returned the self-completion questionnaire.

The basic issue of the study – apart from working with data from "real respondents" instead of student samples – was to provide NERS scores for both sponsees and sponsoring companies. Such scores, it was argued, can be used both by companies wanting to track the effect of their sponsoring activities – along the lines argued elsewhere in this book – as consumers realize and internalize the sponsor partnership, but also by companies that want their sponsorship strategy to produce certain results in emotional terms – to affect changes in consumers' emotional response to the companies as a result of "rub-off" from sponsee to sponsoring company.

Also the study would provide institutions seeking sponsorships valuable knowledge about what types of emotional reactions they generate.

The questionnaire consisted of a section with more traditional and cognitively based measurements of sponsorship liking and inclinations to buy products from sponsors.

Further it contained measurements on emotional responses towards 12 sponsored objects and 16 sponsoring companies. The 12 sponsored objects were divided between sports institutions, cultural institutions and charitable institutions since the two prior sponsorship studies clearly suggested that respondents reacted differently to organisations from different groups – and fairly similarly to organisations from the same group.

The actual objects include:

- 4 cultural institutions
- 3 sports institutions
- 6 charitable institutions

The 16 potential sponsors were selected to cover a broad spectrum of Danish companies that are both reasonably well known and currently involved in some form or other of sponsoring activities.

The list covers both FMCG companies and Business-to-business companies, physical products companies and service companies and physical as well as virtual companies.

The original batteries of feeling words were generated from the previously cited work. The 12 feeling statements covered the important feeling dimensions that were judged to be meaningful in relation to sponsorships and sponsored objects.

Although one might argue that cultural institutions, sports institutions and charitable institutions give rise to different feelings, it is our opinion that the type of fundamental emotional responses that we measure will be much more similar across these categories than dissimilar. A fundamental emotional response of the type "joy" is probably common to most of the institutions, just as sadness is the same type of emotional response, whether it concerns a lost game or the passing thought of suffering alleviated by charitable institutions. The variation probably is more in intensity than in nature.

In the further analysis of the data three separate forced 2-factor analyses were made on the data for sponsored objects as follows:

- 1 forced 2-factor analysis of emotional data for charitable institutions as one group with varimax rotation to obtain the final solution
- 1 forced 2-factor analysis of emotional data for cultural institutions as one group with varimax rotation to obtain the final solution
- 1 forced 2-factor analysis of emotional data sports institutions as one group with varimax rotation to obtain the final solution

In the factor analyses of emotional responses a number of variables were excluded in the final solutions since their loading on factors were very low.

These analyses make it possible to compute NERS for different sponsoring objects. Similar analyses were carried out for the sponsoring companies.

The variance explained by the 2-factor solution for emotional reactions varies across objects and sponsors, the lowest is 50% and the highest is 60%. Attempts at 3-factor solutions did yield higher explained variance – up to 67% - but the third factor generally resulted in dividing the positive factor from the 2-factor solution into two positive factors. These two positive factors could be seen as one factor being a general positive factor with the other a positive arousal factor. The interpretation, however, was not straightforward, so for this reason it was determined to continue with the forced 2-factor solution, just as in other work reported in this book.

When calculating the average scores on emotional responses to the potential sponsees, an interesting picture emerges, which again confirms the existence of both a positive and a negative dimension simultaneously. The results are given in Table XI.25:

Table XI.25: Aggregated NERS by category of sponsored objects

	Positive score	Negative score	NERS
Charitable institutions	11.27	14.11	-2.84
Cultural institutions	14.68	8.39	6.29
Sports institutions	17.14	10.06	7.08

First of all, it is worth noting that the NERS scores span – being averages of the categories – from sizable negative NERS to sizable positive NERS. Two factors account for this: The measurements were taken in the form of a self administered questionnaire left behind with the respondent's acceptance of participating in a scientific study, which accounts for a very thorough completion of the questionnaire, and the measurements were scaled somewhat differently than other examples in this book, therefore the numerical values, generally, are larger than for instance in the 2003/2004 studies.

The charitable institutions elicit an average negative NERS, consisting of a reasonably strong positive reaction illustrating probably feelings concerning the institutions' good deeds, but an even stronger negative reaction – probably concerning the ill phenomenon that the institution tries to alleviate.

The cultural and sports institutions exhibit the same type of positive NERS that we expect from most high involvement and transformational products/brands, interestingly enough, the sports institutions not only have a higher NERS score than the cultural institutions, reactions on both the positive and negative dimensions are stronger per se. It is worth noting the charitable institutions exhibit negative NERS scores.

The detailed emotional responses towards the companies in the study are shown in Table XI.26.

Table XI.26: Overall emotional responses towards potential spon-
sors, sorted by value of NERS score

		Positive score	Negative score	NERS
House of Prince	Tobacco	10.41	11.88	-1.47
Q8	Petrol	14.14	12.96	1.18
Sonofon	Telecom	13.67	11.53	2.14
Amagerbanken	Bank	13.76	11.40	2.36
Dansk Metal	Union	13.49	10.88	2.61
Gosh	Cosmetics	13.62	10.90	2.72
Tryg	Insur.	13.51	10.63	2.88
DSB	Rail	13.66	10.77	2.89
Novo Nordisk	Pharmac.	13.77	10.67	3.10
Microsoft		14.41	11.27	3.14
Netto	Discount retailing	14.72	11.24	3.48
Danske Bank	Bank	13.32	9.79	3.53
In Wear	Fashion	13.47	9.90	3.57
Matas	Chemist's retailing	14.10	10.18	3.92
Arla Foods	Dairy	13.75	9.38	4.37
Aarstiderne	e-fruit & vegetables	14.04	7.71	6.33

The measurements attempt to measure emotional reaction to the individual companies when they appear as sponsors. However, it is fair
to assume, that some respondents may not attach specific emotional
responses to these companies as sponsors apart from their general
emotional responses, so there might not be a large difference between the "sponsor-emotions" and the "corporation-emotions" that
they generate. However, when comparing the structure of the NERS
scores with the brand NERS scores, it does appear that the respondents to a large extent have tried to express emotions towards the
companies as sponsors. For instance, a company like Arla Foods has
a NERS score much larger than that of a cosmetic company like
Gosh, which runs counter to what one would assume, given the difference in involvement that the two product areas must exhibit. However, Arla Foods has sponsored the men's' national soccer team for a
number of years, and the NERS score seems to reflect this fact very
precisely.

One observation in particular spring to mind from examining the
table: There is only one company with a negative NERS as compared
to the institutions, where 5 charitable institutions generated large,
negative NERS scores. The other observation is the much smaller
range of NERS scores for the companies than for the sponsees. The
latter observation can be taken as an indication that companies still
are a lot less engaging and emotionally involving than charities, cultural landmarks and great sports teams.

A way to look for ideal sponsorship partners is to model the relationship between the individuals' responses and the degree to which
they would favour the sponsor and his products in future purchases.
The Sherif et al. (1965) Assimilation Contrast Model (Chapter II)
comes to mind here

Other factors than emotional responses influence the sponsorship value. It was attempted to account for some of these. This is done by introducing an attitude component into the model along with the emotional component.

The attitude component was measured basically the same way that the emotional component was measured, the battery of 12 attitude words relevant for sponsorships have been selected from more general 'attitude towards the ad' (A-ad) batteries (Mitchell and Olsen, 1981). The attitude data were factor analysed in the same manner as the emotional data and were forced into 2 factor solutions with an explained variance of between 55 and 65%, depending on the category or company.

It is remarkable that when the attitude toward sponsorship and emotional response variable are analyzed together they come out as separate factors in such a joint factor analysis, confirming that we are talking about two different classes of responses to which the consumers respond differently. This suggests that it is possible to use attitude (A-ad) and emotional variables (NERS) simultaneously when analysing communication effects.

The concept of sponsorship value takes as its basis that a good sponsorship can create awareness of the sponsoring company, generate liking of the company and eventually lead to increased probability that the individual will favour the sponsor's products in future purchases (Formula XI.1).

Based on the data collected, a model can be estimated by using a partial least squares (PLS) method (Fornell and Cha, 1994). This method has proven to be well suited for customer analysis based on structural modeling (Johnson and Gustafsson, 2000, p. 104). PLS estimates the performance level for each of the five latent variables and impact scores between the variables.

To exemplify the modeling approach, take the example of the sponsorship value model for Danske Bank, Denmark's leading bank. The parameters are illustrated in Figure XI.9.

Figure XI.9: The estimated Sponsorship Value for the "Danske Bank"

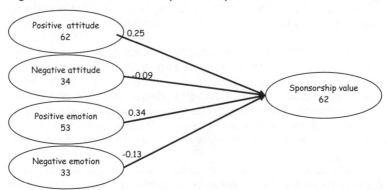

The model contains two types of parameters, the performance indices – written inside the ovals – and the impact scores, written along the arrows. The performance indices are the original emotional and attitudinal scores, rescaled to index form, spanning from 0 (lowest) to 100 (highest). In the illustration, Danske Bank is at 62% of maximum sponsorship value (awareness, liking and change in buying intention). This is created by a reasonably positive (62%) attitude score in combination with a reasonable emotional score (53%). The two negative scores, attitudes and emotions, are at a much lower level, indicating that respondents basically react neutrally to positive to the bank with some, but not overly many, negative reactions.

The impact scores show what effect on the performance score for sponsorship value can be achieved by one unit change in the emotional and attitude scores. For Danske Bank, a sponsorship that affects the positive emotional reaction would be the prime priority, since the impact score for that variable is 0.34. The second most important would be to improve on the positive attitude score, since its impact is 0.25.

Interestingly, the model also shows that the impact from improving on the negative dimensions is very small. So the Bank can concentrate on improving on the positive dimensions, since changing the negatives will not achieve much in the way of change.

The model has been estimated for all companies in the study (Christensen, 2005)

The signs of the impact scores are as would be expected: changes in positive emotional response affects the sponsorship value index positively, and the same holds for the attitude change. Increase in negative emotional response triggers a negative change in the performance index of sponsorship value, and the same goes for negative attitude change.

The model has also been estimated "the other way around", to model what contributions to a sponsor the various sponsee institutions can give. In this case the model shows how a sponsee can contribute to the sponsorship value of a company by the emotional and attitude reactions that it generates.

As was the case for the companies, positive change in positive emotional and attitude responses drive the index for the sponsor's sponsorship value up, and vice versa for the negative responses (Christensen, 2005).

More importantly, particularly for the charities in the study, negative emotional response has a non-significant impact on the sponsorship value, the impact is more or less nil. The negative attitude response only has a very limited impact, whereas the positive responses from emotions and attitudes are reasonably effective on the sponsorship value index. This is important for the charities, since we saw earlier that the typical charity has negative NERS score because of its area of effort. When charities seek sponsor partners, one of the arguments that companies want not to be associated with certain charities is, that the area of effort will – for instance cancer and cancer cure – will reflect negatively on the sponsor. This study shows that this is not the case, only the positive responses will affect the value of the sponsorship.

G. Conversion Model

The conversion model is described by Hofmeyr and Rice (2000). It departs in the observation that loyalty often does not predict behaviour and neither does satisfaction when taken alone. It is a common observation for marketing researchers that dissatisfied customers not always change brand and that satisfied customers sometimes do so.

The commitment scale is developed as an instrument to predict the extent to which different categories of consumers are more or less likely to move between brands. Commitment in this sense builds upon four dimensions influencing the consumers' attachment to brands in the market. The four dimensions are:

1. Satisfaction (how satisfied are the customers with the brand they are using right now?)
2. Attraction (how attractive are the brands of the competitors?)
3. Involvement (how important is the choice of brand or does the brand choice not mean anything to the customer?)
4. Ambivalence (to what extent are customers divided between choosing different brands and how much do they "shop around"?)

Based upon six relatively simple questions in relation to a particular brand, respondents are divided into first two categories depending upon whether they are customers or not for the brand. Among customers a subdivision is carried out according to the degree of commitment to the brand, and the non-committed are subdivided according to how uncommitted they are, in the sense that they may more or less easily be converted to competing brands. This produces 4 categories of actual customers.

Similarly, the non-customers are divided into 4 categories, available, ambivalent, differently available and unavailable. A 9th category is made up of those respondents who do not know the brand – basically these consumers are part of the available market, however they may be very difficult to reach (in the case of a large, well established brand with many years in the market those not aware of the brand probably are those consumers that are unexposed to any medium and therefore impossible to reach with traditional marketing methods) and they are probably more difficult to persuade to change brand compared to customers of competitors who are not very loyal and who are aware of the brand in question.

The model's identification of the categories and the most likely area of competition between brands are illustrated in Figure XI.10.

Figure XI.10: The conversion model's identification of area of competition between brands

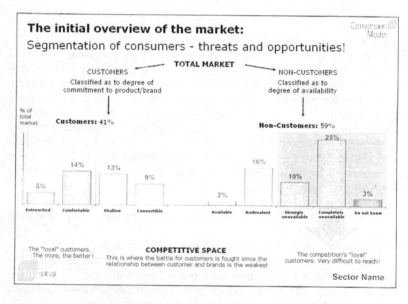

In the 2004 data collection the questions needed for categorising the customers in the eight categories in Figure XI.10 were asked with regard to bank customers. This makes it possible to compare NERS scores for each of the categories of conversion, thereby validating the NERS score as an indicator of the consumer's brand affinity.

The hypothesis is, that the more closely a consumer is attached to a brand, the higher the positive NERS score we would expect to find. And vice versa, the strongly unavailable consumers in relation to one particular brand should exhibit a very low NERS score, since those consumers are made up of those that are dissatisfied (to some extent) with that brand, are definitely not attracted to it (and rejection is the opposite of attraction) and finally are attached to another brand to a fairly high degree.

In Figure XI.11 we illustrate the general correspondence between consumers' availability for conversion for the major banks and the average NERS scores by conversion category for all banks.

When studying the distribution of NERS scores over conversion categories, the correspondence is very clear, and indeed confirms the hypothesis cited above. This serves as an excellent validation of the NERS score as a measurement of a given consumer's attraction to and relationship with a particular bank.

The logic in our findings seems to be: The entrenched and comfortable consumers show strong, positive NERS, the more association, the stronger the NERS. The shallowly attached consumers exhibit a much weaker, yet still positive NERS, whereas those consumers that are our customers but readily available for competitors to attract, show a negative NERS towards the brand that they are currently customers of. This should speak for itself when it comes to understanding, why these consumers may very well migrate to some other bank, given the right circumstances.

Amongst non-customers we find exactly the same pattern, although at a numerically lower level, which was to be expected. Those non-customers that are easily converted to our brand show a strong and positive NERS towards the brand. And the three other categories of non-customers that are increasingly difficult to convert, exhibit weak and even negative NERS. The higher level of NERS in the strongly unavailable category has a specific explanation – that we will illustrate below – since two of the banks, the niche banks, exhibit a positive NERS in this category, thus increasing the value of the average NERS for the four major banks.

To repeat, the above findings illustrate the correlation across all banks, so that in any category of conversion availability, we contain respondents who are in that category with respect to either of the 4 major Danish banks.

Figure XI.11: Correspondence between conversion availability and NERS scores for each of 4 major Danish banks.

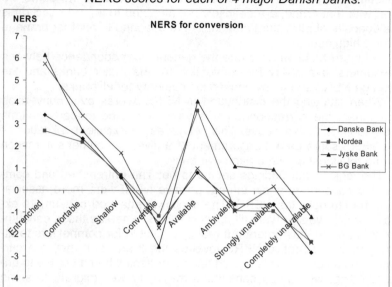

The graph shows the same correspondence between levels of NERS and the different categories of conversion availability for all four banks.

However, some interesting variations between the profiles of the banks occur. The two highest NERS scores in the Entrenched category are found for BG Bank and Jyske Bank. Both banks have been discussed in earlier chapters, where their characteristics as niche banks have been established. In the graph this is confirmed since their entrenched consumers show a much stronger emotional response than that exhibited by the two broader based banks' entrenched consumers.

Apart from the entrenched category, all 4 banks show almost identical emotional responses amongst their own customers in the other three conversion categories – apart from Jyske Bank's customers in the Convertible category to be the most negative of all bank customers. This probably illustrates a tendency towards Jyske Bank that goes with its niche – and some might even say maverick – image, customers either love it or hate it!

In the non-customer categories, we find a strong potential – in the shape of high positive NERS – for recruiting new customers for Jyske Bank and Nordea. For BG Bank the Strongly unavailable show a certain level of positive emotional reaction: these customers may be unavailable due to structural reasons (lack of availability for one, being bound to the present bank) and therefore BG Bank may have a potential if such structural reasons are diminished in importance.

Again Jyske Bank exhibits strong emotional reactions also in the Ambivalent and Strongly unavailable categories; actually the only non-customer group reacting with negative NERS to Jyske Bank is the Completely unavailable category.

H. Summary

In the present chapter we have looked at emotions as measured with NERS or similar scores as they respond to changes in the consumer environment. We have seen major and significant changes in the standing of brands and categories explained by factual changes in the market conditions. We have seen how NERS is sensitive to the frequency of use of the brands, to advertising and promotion activities and to the quality of marketing communication measured in terms of changes in campaign effect measured with NERS-type measurements and with attitudinal short-term advertising (ASTAS) effects.

In a broader consumer behaviour sense we have shown how voting behaviour and changes in the same can be understood departing in NERS scores for leading political candidates.

Also when applied to sponsorships the use of selected feeling words and computation of aggregated emotional NERS scores based on these makes sense and so does the use of feeling words in design and logo testing. Also here, NERS-like aggregated scores demonstrate marked differences in the emotional response to colours of logos and design lines.

Finally by comparing NERS scores with a commonly used conversion scale reflecting consumer attachment to brands, we find NERS scores meaningfully relating to this.

It is worth noting that the different findings reported in the chapter result from studies conducted by different researchers at different periods in time and with the use of somewhat different selections of feeling words. This confirms the observation made already in Chapter V and VI that the precise selection of feeling words is not so important as long as those used are meaningful to most respondents and tap positive as well as negative emotional tendencies. Of course when used over time ideally the same feeling words measured in the same manner should be applied.

Thus, in this chapter we have demonstrated that NERS scores do relate to important aspects of the consumer environment and to changes in conditions in it. Through this demonstration we have presented the arguments for tracking a brand's standing using NERS scores as a standard tool in order to provide measurement of successful and consistent brand development and early warning when brand stature is decreasing. We have also illustrated the potential of the NERS score as a communication (advertising) testing device.

Chapter XII

From Emotions to Feelings - and Back

CHAPTER OUTLINE

The dealing with emotional responses in this book in all other chapters are concentrated on a "two-dimensional" approach, positive and negative responses, and in the NERS measure, these two dimensions are further reduced to one number. In other contexts in the book we have discussed the alternative to add the positive and negative score (the acronym NUMS score denotes this construct) so that a measure of the total intensity of emotional response is maintained. But also this measure consists of one single number.

In marketing and advertising planning the decision maker will usually want a more detailed picture of consumer responses to enable him either to target more precisely or to track whether a particular effort is reaching its target. It is an expected critique - and one that the authors have already met - that NERS is too crude a measurement, since it only reports whether a brand organisation is on track or not.

In the present chapter we illustrate through a number of case examples how the feeling word measurements used in estimating emotional responses may be used either directly or through combinations of the specific feeling words into feeling dimensions to achieve a more detailed understanding of the "drivers" of NERS or NUMS.

Some of the cases are "new" in the sense that they have not been commented on, some of the cases have been dealt with in Chapter II, but in other scenarios. These cases should give the reader a good feeling for the potential value to the planner of applying emotional response measurements as a tracking tool for brand health.

CHAPTER OBJECTIVE

Our objective with the chapter is to demonstrate that emotional measurements do indeed lend themselves to a "diagnostic" use, provided of course that a sufficient number of feeling words are used in measurements and that consistency is applied over time to the feeling words actually used. Our aim in applying the measurements as suggested in the chapter, is to provide the decision maker not only with a very sensitive tracking tool in the form of NERS and its two emotional response components, but also with a sensitive diagnostic tool in the form of individual feeling words or groupings of feeling words into core feeling dimensions.

A. The Feelings that Emotions may Activate

In the classical S-O-R framework of psychology we may see the findings reported in Chapter V – VI as being concerned primarily with the O-R part of the relationship. The NERS we estimate is expected to guide subsequent choices. How these NERS scores become formed was of limited concern in these chapters.

In Chapter XI we have been concerned with attempting to determine what factors may have caused the different NERS scores we have estimated. It is the S-O part of the relationship.

In the organism (O), or more precisely for our purpose: brain, psychological processes occur. Brain scientists have taught us that these processes and phenomena are real and that they exist and they have given us insights into the way in which they function. These processes may be considered our (not quite) hypothetical intervening variables between S and R.

Answers to questions about feelings are seen as correlates of these intervening variables. By studying the answers systematically we can make better estimates of the real intervening variables in the organism. In Chapter XII we shall throw further light on what determines the NERS and how research findings about different aspects of affect such as cognitive feelings and moods can be seen in the light of emotional theories of the brain as they are discussed in this context.

In all of the preceding pages, when looking upon feelings and emotions, our focus has been on the two general emotional response tendencies, the positive and the negative. It is not that we have held that other emotions, based biologically or brain physiologically, than joy and sorrow do not exist. But for the study of the majority of consumer alternatives it provides a shortcut to concentrate on these, basic positive and negative behavioural response tendencies, particularly when the study is concerned with such relatively uninvolving matters as consumer choices.

We have made this position our fundamental assumption by relying upon questions about feelings from which we have deducted the underlying emotional response tendencies. In our discussions we have again and again stressed, that emotions occur before feelings and other relevant cognitive activities in response to actual stimuli or problems at hand. This of course does not mean that the cognitive conscious or unconscious feelings and other cognitive elements are of no importance. Our basic positive and negative emotional response tendencies may guide choices completely in very simple impulse and routinized choice situations. In other cases they may influence what feelings are activated and they may have impact on what enters into the total cognitive structure eventually guiding the choice. Over time emotions become modified by consumption and other experiences, and when relevant information appears, it is processed in a manner that builds traces in implicit memory. In this process feelings may play an important role by activating emotional responses acting as buffers between stimuli and emotions.

We can learn more about this by going back to our data from 2003 and 2004 in Chapter V and VI and ask what kinds of feelings are important for particular brands and categories. That is, we will look at what dimensions can be found in the answers to all of the 24 or 16 feeling words associated with different brands and categories. Basically we will study how feeling words are linked to emotions through more specific feelings associated with brands, categories etc. This is illustrated in the modified version of Figure VI.1 in Figure XII.1.

Figure XII.1 Groups of feeling words in the 2004 data collection

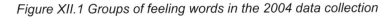
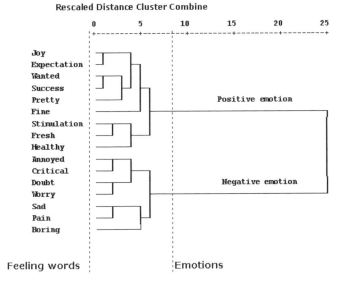

We shall look a little more at this analysis here. In Figure XII.1 we see that the two positive and negative emotional response tendencies are clearly separated in form of nine positive and seven negative feeling words. However, it is worth studying in a little more detail how the different feeling words cluster together. Starting from the top, one cluster comprises joy, expectations and fine. The grouping can be seen as centred on the pleasure experiences of the alternatives rated. We have labelled this overall feeling JOY which is in nature transformational. The joy feeling reflects the very general satisfaction derived from the products analysed.

The next feeling words grouped together are wanted, success, and pretty. They can be seen as reflecting the extent to which the use of the brand or product gives rewards in terms of social acceptability. It reflects the extent to which one expects to be in demand. We have labelled this grouping of feeling words SOCIAL REWARD. Also, this is transformational in nature. This component is closely related to the first but where JOY reflects feeling components closely related to one's own experience, then SOCIAL REWARD reflects feeling components of importance in the social world of the respondent. The two feelings resemble the distinction between inner-driven and outer-driven in a value context. The classical example of outer-driven social reward as a feeling is conspicuous consumption, which takes place to send signals to the social environment, it also plays in where the consumption in other ways may have influence upon the perception of the consumer by his environment. As seen in the figure the Joy and social reward feelings combine at a slightly higher level into an overall transformational feeling.

The third group of positive feeling words combines stimulating, fresh, and healthy. They have all to do with the functioning of the brand or product, refreshing deodorant, healthy food, stimulating coffee etc. We have labelled this grouping of feeling INSTRUMENTAL reward.

Among the negative feeling words two distinct groups can be identified. Starting with the last, sad, pain, and boring, like the first positive group of feeling words resembles JOY, this resembles the basic SORROW concept and we have labelled it so, in accordance with the thinking of Damasio (2003).

Other negative feeling words grouped together are annoyed, critical, doubt, and worry. They all reflect concern of one kind or another with the functioning of the product or the consequences of it and we have labelled this CONCERN.

Before using this clustering as a clue to the interpretation of the responses to the individual feeling words in the subsequent analysis, it makes sense to compare the results with a factor analysis conducted on the same data (all brands, all respondents, and all statements). This results in a four factor solution shown in Table XII.1.

Table XII.1: Factor analysis of feeling words for brands (all brands, all feeling words) explained variance 59%

	Component			
	Joy/social reward	Concern	Sadness/ sorrow	Instrumental reward
Expectation	.705	-.037	-.075	-.126
Joy	.695	-.122	-.048	-.046
Wanted	.650	.009	-.015	.155
Success	.553	.004	.110	.096
Stimulating	.537	.049	-.136	.275
Pretty	.462	-.035	.237	.209
Fine	.348	-.335	.176	.063
Critical	-.029	.730	.038	-.050
Annoyed	-.157	.626	.061	-.081
Doubt	.030	.589	.180	.019
Worry	.081	.540	.339	.003
Sad	. 062	.288	.639	.032
Boring	-.177	-.012	.627	-.169
Pain	.126	.180	.610	.138
Healthy	-.008	-.102	.091	.800
Fresh	.265	-.025	-.084	.684

The first factor combines the grouping of feeling words around JOY corresponding to that of the cluster analysis but including also some other transformational feelings, reflecting SOCIAL REWARD. A phenomenon as we shall see being common for some products.

The last factor combines the feeling words relating to functional performance of the product that we labelled INSTRUMENTAL reward. The second factor combines the feeling words associated with concern, mistrust etc. and is identical with the CONCERN feelings from the cluster analysis. The third factor combines the SADNESS-sorrow feeling words.

The correspondence of the results in Figure XII.1 and Table XII.1 is remarkable. Particularly the 16 feeling words were selected with a bias towards words reflecting positive and negative aspects. With a larger battery more detail in the description of feelings would probably result. Still the grouping here have face validity, seen in the light of the transformational informational grouping used here and in the light of positive versus negative émotions.

It makes sense in its own right to study what feeling words are used and enter into the specific NERS computation for various brands. To give an impression of the diversity with which these words are used, the average frequency with which they occur is computed in Table XII.2. Here, it can be seen that for the high involvement informational products, the critical CONCERN related words dominate. In contrast to the low involvement transformational products the IN-STRUMENTAL (fine, fresh, healthy etc.) feeling words dominate. Even more variance is found when single categories are looked at. Something we will use when we in the following look at the components entering into the computation of NERS scores for individual brands.

Still, it is remarkable that some rather general overall feelings seem to emerge when data are analysed across brands and feeling words. The feelings joy, social reward, instrumental reward, concern and sorrow appear in different combinations for different brands and product categories. In addition we will see product or brand unique feelings showing up in different cases.

Table XII.2: Frequency of occurrence of feeling words in the four Rossiter/Percy categories

Brand	Category averages, %			
	Low/Inf.	Low/Trans.	High/Inf.	High/Trans.
Annoyed	19	9	30	9
Boring	19	9	25	9
Critical	21	10	28	10
Doubt	11	5	12	4
Expectation	13	19	15	45
Fine	37	27	26	34
Fresh	15	22	6	12
Healthy	14	20	3	5
Joy	9	23	7	49
Pain	2	2	2	1
Pretty	7	2	4	7
Sad	4	3	5	3
Stimulating	6	29	8	30
Success	12	9	13	19
Wanted	16	18	10	25
Worry	9	8	9	7

In the following we shall explore the extent to which we can reconstruct these four groups of feeling words in the answering patterns for individual categories and brands and particularly the extent to which we find meaningful deviations from this general pattern, where by meaningful deviations we understand deviations that describe unique features of the brand or category in question.

We shall look primarily for the 3 positive and 2 negative elements as they stand out in Figure XII.1. In doing so we of course realize that the relative high degree of uniformness with which they reappear is a function also of the way in which we in Chapter V and VI have looked for feeling words focusing on the positive/negative evaluative elements in the emotional responses. Still it is remarkable that these five components of negative/positive emotions show up again and again. We believe that this reflects an underlying general pattern in the positive and negative emotion: Joy, social reward, instrumental reward, concern and sorrow.

That these and not other emotions known from more general emotional research such as fear, disgust, hate etc. dominate the picture, is of course a function of the fact that we focus on ordinary individual relations to trivial products and brands in the daily environment of the consumer. Here the negative emotions are much less important than in the struggle for life in a primitive world or in tragic cases the psychiatrist finds among his clients. The consumer may perceive risk in his alternatives and he may dislike them, and that is about all.

Similarly strong bases are human positive emotional phenomena such as love or all absorbing struggle for freedom are rarely occurring in the daily lives of consumers. He may feel the product provides instrumental satisfaction, social accept or sheer joy. It is in this context interesting to quote a recent study by Oh (2005), where he looks for feeling (emotion) dimensions in print apparel advertisements. Like us, departing in classical scaling work by Izard (1977), Plutchick (1980), Mehrabian and Russell's (1974) PAD instrument and others he arrive at 3 positive and 2 negative dimensions, that we in our terminology can name joy (items: joy, expectation, fine), Social (items: warm-hearted, sentimental, warm), instrumental (items: erotic, sexy, beautiful and sensual), critical (items: offended, humiliated, and distasteful), and sad (items: bored, dull, uninvolved)

To some extent differences in the kind of feelings associated with different product categories are evident from looking upon what feeling words actually enter in to the computation of NERS for the different product categories. This reflects individual particularities in the positive/negative emotional responses in individual cases.

That the concentration on 10 feeling words for each category leaves out in some cases nuances follow from the percentage of feeling word responses left out in the different categories. By redoing the factor analysis for brands of special interest involving all feeling words adds more detail to the picture drawn for such brands. An example illustrating this will be shown in the following (Table XII.3)

To understand the different importance of different feelings in different product categories and for different brands, it is however not enough to look at the loadings that the feeling words have on the positive and negative factors in the forced two-dimensional solutions for the different categories. It is also necessary to take into consideration how strongly the different feeling words are associated with the products or brands rated. Thus to look for the feelings activated by the choice of different brands one may look at factor analytical solutions including all significant factors (eigenvalue › 1). When this is done it gives the marketer of each particular brand the opportunity to go into much more detail in his performance analysis.

Other evidence of what determines the choice of the brands can be found if one looks at what feeling words are most important for the NERS scores for different brands. We shall in the following illustrate the nature of these two analyses and give some suggestions as to the relevance of the emerging findings.

B. Eleven Cases

1. The Nordea Case
In Table XII.3 this is done in terms of a five factor solution, which explains 51% of the variance in the data, for a bank: Nordea. With interview data of the kind used here it is not uncommon to be able to ac-

count for 60-70% of the variance in the data when all factors with an eigenvalue larger than 1 are extracted. Here and in the following we shall repeatedly see a somewhat smaller percentage variance explained. The reason for this is partly the difficulty of the rating task placing the respondents in some uncertainty as to what feeling words apply. Partly the uncertainties arising when all people are asked to rate the same feeling words on the same 5-point scale, even though many undoubtedly operate with less than 5 categories in the way they look at the feeling words. Finally, particularly to some minor brands, the limited number of responses generated plays a role.

Here, the first factor closely resembles the instrumental function dimension from the above general analysis. Combined with social instrumentality the second factor combines those items reflecting concern whereas the joy factor is illustrated in the fourth and the sadness/pain factor in the third factor. Finally, as a factor in its own right comes out the single term boring, which is negatively related to annoyed and joy.

Table XII.3: The feelings activated by brand emotion for Nordea by principal component analysis extracting factors with eigenvalues larger than one and subsequent varimax rotation (56% explained variance)

Factor name	Feeling words	Component				
		1	2	3	4	5
Instrumental + social	Fresh	**0.73**	-0.07	0.13	-0.04	-0.06
	Stimulating	**0.71**	-0.04	0.06	0.06	-0.05
	Pretty	**0.66**	0.00	0.04	0.38	0.00
	Healthy	**0.52**	0.16	0.00	0.16	0.06
	Success	**0.44**	0.11	0.27	-0.33	0.14
Worry (concern)	Critical	-0.14	**0.66**	0.07	0.17	-0.16
	Worry	0.06	**0.65**	0.08	0.35	0.08
	Doubt	0.10	**0.65**	-0.07	0.01	0.19
	Annoyed	0.10	**0.48**	-0.43	0.02	-0.45
Joy	Expectable	0.13	0.22	**0.77**	-0.12	-0.06
	Fine	0.01	-0.27	**0.68**	0.20	-0.12
	Wanted	0.38	0.17	**0.49**	-0.29	0.12
	Joy	0.35	-0.09	**0.40**	0.19	-0.25
Sorrow	Pain	0.22	0.22	0.02	**0.62**	0.01
	Sad	0.07	0.18	0.00	**0.60**	0.14
Boring	Boring	0.01	0.08	-0.15	0.16	**0.83**

All in all we find the general pattern of feelings but with boring being a rather unique feature for Nordea bank (as it turns out to be with the other two leading banks BG Bank and Danske Bank also).

A more detailed picture of the competitive situation among banks in terms of the emotions appears when one looks at the NERS computations as they were illustrated in Figure VI.1. This computation for banks is summarised in Table XII.4. Here we also take into account the importance assigned to the individual feeling words and thereby arrive at an estimate of the relative weight with which they are associated with the brands. Here it can be seen that the feelings joy and social reward are the only positive feelings that to any extent account for the difference in scores for the four brands analysed. Whereas the joy feeling does not vary greatly between the banks the perceived success (social reward) is much stronger for Jyske Bank and the smallest for Nordea and BG Bank (in 2003 this was even less contributing to the total NERS for BG Bank). The most important element however, are feelings reflecting concern. Again, here Jyske Bank fares better than the larger banks but they all come out quite negatively. Obviously most bank customers do not feel confidence in the banks with which they do business. To this should be added the special feeling of boredom, which does not enter into the NERS score directly but which pops up in the analysis of all the 16 feeling words. (Table XII.5)

Table XII.4: NERS score components for banks

	NERS				
Feeling words	Category	Danske Bank	Nordea	Jyske Bank	BG Bank
Wanted	0.16	0.18	0.13	0.27	0.15
Annoyed	-0.76	-1.17	-0.89	-0.61	-1.08
Fine	0.70	0.37	0.44	0.57	0.53
Doubt	-0.36	-0.31	-0.24	-0.26	-0.23
Fresh	0.03	0.03	0.05	0.18	0.04
Worry	-0.37	-0.23	-0.25	-0.15	-0.22
Success	0.34	0.36	0.19	0.75	0.27
Critical	-0.85	-0.84	-0.86	-0.54	-0.71
Joy	0.13	0.08	0.06	0.11	0.12
Expectation	0.34	0.23	0.26	0.15	0.16
Sum	**-0.65**	**-1.28**	**-1.11**	**0.46**	**-0.98**
Feeling groups					
Joy	1.17	0.68	0.76	0.83	0.81
Social reward + instrumental	0.50	0.57	0.37	1.20	0.46
Concern	-2.34	-2.55	-2.24	-1.56	-2.24
Sorrow	-	-	-	-	-

BG Bank showed a significant improvement in NERS scores from 2003 to 2004. The present analysis will enable us to find out exactly what feelings this builds on. Of the 10 items entering into the NERS score in 2004 eight can be found in the 2003 NERS computations. Scores on these show that the major improvement in the NERS score on behalf of BG Bank comes from its very large improvement on the feelings reflecting concern with the bank.

In summary, one may describe the feelings expressed concerning banks as first and foremost reflecting concern, doubt, or even mistrust. These apply not the least to the major banks and to a lesser extent to the bank concept as such. Among the positive feelings aroused by banks, the success/social reward element is the only one showing up with somewhat higher scores on behalf of the (obviously successful) largest bank, Danske Bank and the also commonly believed successful challenger, Jyske Bank.

As a special feeling unique to the bank sector, it is remarkable that a feeling of "boring" comes out. In emotional terms the negative emotions are first and foremost driven by concern (doubt and mistrust). The positive emotional responses are driven by social reward and to a very limited extent by joy or pleasure. There is no such thing as joy in the feelings associated with bank services provided to consumers.

White brings out very clearly, that this picture is in no way unique to the Danish bank sector. In a column on bank marketing in 'Admap' he presents very similar conclusions under the heading "No room for excitement" (White, 2005).

2. Gasoline

From Table XII.6 it can be seen, not surprisingly, that the feeling words accounting for the estimation of NERS for gasoline brands are different from those connected with banks. For illustration of the emotional and feeling structure inherent in this category, we have picked a major player whose values are around the average for the category.

Table XII.5: Feelings activated by Q8 gasoline (explained variance 56%)

Factor name	Feeling words	Component			
		1	2	3	4
Joy, social and Instrumental reward	Stimulating	**0.63**	0.13	-0.03	0.31
	Healthy	**0.61**	0,33	0.04	0.09
	Wanted	**0.61**	-0.10	-0.13	0.33
	Expectations	**0.59**	-0.01	0.09	-0.14
	Joy	**0.54**	0.03	-0.05	0.00
	Fresh	**0.49**	0.02	0.05	-0.26
	Success	**0.45**	0.09	0.03	0.11
Sorrow	Pain	0.46	**0.68**	0.28	0.13
	Sad	0.06	**0.68**	0.08	-0.01
	Pretty	0.47	**0.67**	0.25	0.11
	Boring	-0.27	**0.63**	-0.30	-0.03
Concern	Critical	-0.02	-0.06	**0.79**	0.08
	Doubt	-0.02	0.17	**0.64**	0.03
Worry	Annoyed	-0.04	0.06	-0.07	**0.64**
	Worry	0.10	-0.04	0.22	**0.60**
	Fine	0.40	-0.11	-0.10	**-0,46**

In Table XII.5 the four-factor solution for Q8 accounting for 56% of the variance in the data is shown. All positive feeling words combine into one factor reflecting overall positive feelings generated by the brand. Since the product is informational by nature, it does not give rise to more detailed specific or diversified positive feelings and the entire positive emotional response aroused is ascribable to one overall general positive joy, social and instrumental reward feeling, which, as shall be seen subsequently, is not very strong.

The negative feeling words partly represent the sorrow/sadness element (second factor) and worry/concern here represented by two separate factors (3 and 4), with the third factor reflects mistrust and the fourth concern. This picture is largely the same for all brands analysed, though the scoring of the brands on the 16 feeling words as seen in Table XII.6 vary.

Table XII.6: *Elements of which NERS score for gasoline brands are composed with a comparison of Category, Shell and Q8 (taken from basic NERS score computation like in Table V.6)*

Feeling words	NERS					
	Category	Shell	Hydro Texaco	OK Benzin	Statoil	Q8
Wanted	0.27	0.12	0.16	0.31	0.19	0.33
Annoyed	-1.13	-0.39	-0.27	-0.15	-0.26	-0.13
Stimulating	0.07	0.06	0.03	0.07	0.04	0.06
Fine	0.37	0.68	1.05	1.24	0.88	0.89
Doubt	-0.04	-0.11	-0.03	0.01	0.00	-0.07
Fresh	0.05	0.06	0.06	0.07	0.16	0.12
Pretty	0.03	0.01	-0.03	0.03	0.02	0.01
Critical	-0.42	-0.67	0.02	-0.04	-0.22	-0.19
Boring	-0.17	0.05	-0.13	-0.34	-0.16	-0.21
Healthy	0.02	0.01	-0.27	0.02	0.01	0.03
Sum	**-0.94**	**-0.19**	**0.62**	**1.21**	**0.68**	**0.83**
Feeling groups						
Joy	0.37	0.68	1.05	1.24	0.88	0.89
Social	0.30	0.13	0.13	0.34	0.21	0.34
Instrumental	0.14	0.13	-0.18	0.16	0.21	0.21
Concern	-1.59	-1.17	-0.28	-0.18	-0.48	-0.39
Sorrow	-0.17	0.05	-0.13	-0.34	0.16	-0.21

A more detailed picture of the brands emerges when we look at the elements of which the NERS score is build. Here we can see that for the category, the concern related items (annoyed, doubt, boring, critical) by far dominate the feelings towards the category and the transformational positive feeling words (joy, fine, success) and instrumentally related feelings (stimulating, fresh, health) cannot override the overall negative emotional contribution provided by the feelings of concern and mistrust. This undoubtedly also – besides the pollution issues – relates to the heavy price competition in the industry. As we shall see in connection with other FMCG brands, heavy promotional activity deteriorates the immaterial equity value of the brand.

It must be remembered here and in the following that the varimax rotated factor analytical solution including all significant dimensions like in Table XII.3, XII.7 and similar later tables in the following does not correspond completely with tables like XII.4, XII.9 and following where the elements entering into the NERS score are provided. The latter only include the 10 feeling words entering into the NERS computations for the particular category and they represent the actual scores weighted with the importance of the different feeling words.

Still, from Table XII.6 it can be seen that all the individual brands fare better than the category as such. The heavy advertising made for the major brands does have some effect for these.

A special comparison can be made between Q8 and Shell for critical and sorrow feeling elements. The results are shown in the bottom of Table XII.6. Here, it appears that Q8 do better on the negative concern-mistrust dimension but also slightly better on the positive feelings: joy, success and health. Seemingly, Shell is taking a beating on behalf of the industry as such, but even so, less than the overall industry It is of course impossible to determine from these data the extent to which the Brent Spar catastrophe still plays a role in the formation of feeling responses for Shell, however, it does offer itself as one possible part explanation for Shell's low scores compared to others in the industry. In the case of Q8, this company advertised itself with small sketches over some years focusing on two very folksy and rustic types who ran a very local gas station in competition with the shining Q8 station up on the highway. The better feeling scores for Q8 may similarly be reminiscences of this very different type of gasoline advertising still residing in implicit memory. In this category the major brands are fighting an uphill fight, but, in spite of price competition and pollution issues, still manage to draw a picture of themselves slightly better than that of the industry as such.

3. Coffee

Inspection of Table XII.7 shows that also coffee activates its own set of feeling words. We have singled out the brand Merrild for separate analysis. Here, a five factor solution explains 52% of the variance in the data.

Table XII.7: Feeling words aroused by emotions generated by the brand name, Merrild

Factor name	Feeling words	Component				
		1	2	3	4	5
Healthy	Pain	**0.83**	0.05	0.12	0.07	0.05
	Worry	**0.79**	0.09	0.28	-0.02	-0.01
	Healthy	**0.64**	0.32	0.04	0.13	0.06
	Pretty	**0.59**	-0.01	0.17	0.30	0.08
Joy	Stimulating	-0.03	**0.69**	-0.04	0.12	-0.07
	Fresh	0.26	**0.62**	-0.01	-0.12	0.14
	Expectation	0.02	**0.61**	0.17	0.21	-0.09
	Joy	0.19	**0.47**	0.02	0.30	-0.19
Concern	Doubt	0.11	0.01	**0.79**	-0.05	-0.02
	Critical	0.24	0.12	**0.66**	0.04	0.01
	Sad	0.15	-0.03	**0.52**	0.20	0.46
Social reward	Success	0.19	0.12	0.01	**0.77**	0.06
	Wanted	0.03	0.40	0.01	**0.62**	0.07
	Fine	0.19	-0.16	0.15	0.42	**-0.60**
Sad	Boring	0.00	-0.24	0.29	0.14	**0.58**
	Annoyed	0.33	-0.04	-0.08	0.09	**0.50**

The five factors relate closely to the five feelings identified at the overall level in Figure XII.I1, and the instrumental (health) element is contained in the first factor, the joy feeling comes out in the second factor, the concern in the third, the social reward in the fourth and the sadness in the fifth.

In terms of NERS scores the category elicits much better responses than any one of the analysed brands. This is most likely ascribable to the four brands included in the analysis, which are all national brands, are heavily promoted and widely distributed brands in the major retail chains.

Coffee being a transformational product generates positive feelings. As can be seen, the instrumental element (first factor in Table XII.7) combines positive (health, pretty) and negative (pain, worry). Possibly, the caffeine fear dominates this factor. For the category joy and the instrumental feeling stand out as the dominating elements. Looking at the components of the NERS score (not shown) the concern plays only a minor role and success/social reward generates most positive feelings for the analysed brand, Merrild. Also this brand scores lower on the two other groups of feelings in the analysis.

On the whole, coffee can be described as a category carried by positive emotions related to feelings of joy, performance (refreshing) and with small insignificant negative feelings being expressed. Social accepts plays a minor role and a very little role for the four brands analysed.

The four brands analysed are those most frequently on special offers in the supermarkets and they fare less well than the category as such and they do so on all feelings expressed. For the brands analysed here, undoubtedly the heavy merchandising activity deteriorates the potential positive brand value inherent in the category as such. It stands to reason that these products, being industrial products with heavy discounting as a major marketing tool, do not elicit the same type of emotional response that the concept of a quiet cup of coffee does.

4. Sweets

Another transformational product category is sweets, here illustrated with a four factor solution accounting for 49% of the total variance in the data in Table XII.8. The first factor primarily combines feeling words reflecting concern (sorrow, doubt, pain and worry), the second the joy feelings, the third the instrumental (health) and social reward elements combined and finally the sorrow element in the last. Feeling words reflecting worry and concern are very important, probably relating to various health issues with these products.

Table XII.8: Feeling words activated by emotions aroused by Stimorol chewing gum (four factor solution accounting for 49% of variance)

Factor name	Feeling words	Component			
		1	2	3	4
Sad	Doubt	**0.88**	0.16	0.17	0.06
	Pain	**0.87**	0.07	0.22	0.17
	Worry	**0.82**	0.12	0.05	0.05
	Sad	**0.61**	0.10	0.04	0.39
	Boring	0.41	-0.12	-0.08	0.07
Joy	Fine	0.07	**0.72**	-0.21	0.04
	Joy	0.03	**0.65**	0.17	-0.02
	Wanted	0.00	**0.64**	0.31	-0.01
	Expectation	0.08	**0.56**	0.33	0.06
Instrumental +	Healthy	0.10	0.09	**0.62**	0.06
Social reward	Success	0.02	0.14	**0.59**	0.16
	Stimulating	-0.01	0.27	**0.52**	-0.16
	Pretty	0.21	-0.07	**0.50**	0.41
	Fresh	0.02	0.03	**0.46**	-0.33
Critical	Critical	0.18	0.03	0.13	**0.79**
	Annoyed	0.18	0.02	-0.08	**0.77**

Turning to the NERS scores for the brand Stimorol and Sorbits and comparing them with the other brands in the analysis gives the scores shown in Table XII.9. Again these scores are derived from the kind of computations shown in Table V.6, where the computation of NERS for brands is illustrated. It is the instrumental (fresh, healthy, stimulating) feeling that comes out here, but also the joy aspect (pleasure and joy) has some importance. The social reward element plays a minor role and negative feelings are not important. Thus, Stimorol and Sorbits may be seen as sweets which functions through the feelings of stimulation and pleasure it arises. In contrast with this, a sweet like After Eight (a mint chocolate) gives rise to very different feeling. Here, the joy element is the dominating one, the instrumental (fresh and stimulating) is of some importance and also the social reward plays a role. Again, there are no negative feeling words activated. Looking at the category as such we find After Eight standing out with its NERS scores being the highest in the category. In promotion and brand communication After Eight has successfully explored the luxury transformational element of the product relative to the category.

Table XII.9: Elements of which NERS score are computed for candy brands (taken from basic NERS score computation like Table V.6.)

Feeling words	NERS							
	Category	Toms	Haribo	After Eight	BonBon	Malaco	Stimorol	Sorbits
Wanted	0.40	0.49	0.38	0.54	0.29	0.29	0.31	0.18
Annoyed	-0.24	-0.06	-0.10	-0.03	-0.28	-0.09	-0.09	-0.08
Stimulating	0.71	0.62	0.53	-0.45	0.29	0.29	0.62	0.69
Fine	-0.27	0.14	0.20	0.20	0.25	0.35	0.22	0.14
Doubt	-0.10	-0.05	-0.04	-0.02	-0.04	-0.07	-0.01	-0.02
Fresh	0.10	0.07	0.15	0.31	0.19	0.12	1.12	1.14
Critical	-0.45	-0.06	-0.17	-0.02	-0.15	-0.11	-0.05	-0.03
Joy	-1.00	1.09	0.75	1.01	0.81	0.66	0.25	0.15
Boring	-0.06	-0.04	-0.06	-0.06	-0.07	-0.08	-0.06	-0.11
Expectation	-0.51	0.60	0.65	0.49	0.48	0.47	0.14	0.13
Sum	**2.15**	**2.81**	**2.29**	**2.86**	**1.78**	**1.83**	**2.45**	**2.20**
Feeling groups								
Joy	-1.78	1.83	1.60	1.70	1.54	1.48	0.61	0.42
Social re-ward	-0.40	0.49	0.38	0.54	0.25	0.29	0.31	0.18
Instrumental	0.81	0.69	0.68	0.76	0.48	0.41	1.74	1.83
Concern	-0.79	-0.17	-0.31	-0.07	-0.47	-0.27	-0.15	-0.13
Sorrow	-0.06	-0.04	-0.06	-0.06	-0.07	-0.08	.-0.06	-0.11

5. The Cereals Category

In the comparison between 2003 and 2004 Kellogg's is seen to experience a strongly negative development in the NERS scores. It is interesting to look a little more into what underlies these changes. The feeling dimensions resulting from the analysis of the answers for this brand appear in Table XII.10.

Here, the negative doubt, concern, mistrust feelings come out first, followed by the sadness/sorrow element. Instrumentality health aspects come out third and finally the social reward/success and joy components appear in the last two factors. In terms of the elements in the NERS scores (Table XII.11) the feelings reflecting on the one hand joy, performance, healthiness and on the other hand concern and doubts are the only ones of any importance. The social accept feelings only appear in very low scores on the item "wanted".

Table XII.10: Feeling words activated by emotions towards Kellogg's brands (58% variance explained)

Factor name	Feeling words	Components				
		1	2	3	4	5
Sad	Pain	**0.73**	0.20	0.19	-0.05	0.12
	Sad	**0.72**	0.37	0.10	0.04	0.11
	Boring	**0.63**	0.01	-0.21	0.02	-0.15
	Pretty	**0.60**	-0.01	0.21	0.22	0.03
Critical	Critical	0.04	**0.72**	-0.01	-0.04	-0.10
	Worry	0.07	**0.71**	0.01	0.00	0.08
	Doubt	0.17	**0.59**	-0.09	0.09	0.10
	Annoyed	0.14	**0.52**	-0.14	0.13	-0.33
Functional	Fresh	0.03	0.00	**0.68**	0.08	-0.01
instrumentality	Healthy	-0.02	-0.19	**0.65**	-0.01	-0.05
	Stimulating	0.09	0.01	**0.56**	0.15	-0.02
	Joy	0.12	-0.01	**0.53**	0.07	0.36
Success	Success	0.18	0.00	0.01	**0.85**	-0.11
	Wanted	-0.03	0.07	0.32	**0.63**	0.26
	Expectation	0.02	0.19	0.26	0.41	0.41
Joy	Fine	0.05	-0.07	-0.10	0.05	**0.85**

The elements of which the NERS scores are composed are shown in Table XII.11 for both Kellogg's and Quaker Oats. For the latter it can be seen that the instrumental (health) and refreshing perception is by far dominant among the feelings activated by the products but joy (fine, wanted, joy) also plays a role as does concern in the negative direction. Here, Kellogg's stands out as being less instrumental (healthy) and giving rise to more concern feelings than its competitor. On the contrast though, it gives rise to higher joy feelings.

Table XII.11: Elements of which NERS scores are composed, for Cereals with a comparison of OTA and Kellogg's

Feeling words	NERS		
	Category	Kellogg's	OTA
Wanted	0.20	0.25	0.14
Annoyed	-0.29	-0.24	-0.06
Fine	0.38	0.30	0.23
Doubt	-0.16	-0.12	-0.03
Fresh	0.58	0.37	0.24
Worry	-0.14	-0.10	-0.06
Critical	-0.38	-0.29	-0.08
Joy	0.34	0.23	0.20
Expectation	0.22	0.16	0.09
Healthy	1.40	1.06	1.74
Sum	**2.17**	**1.63**	**2.41**
Feeling groups			
Joy	0.94	0.69	0.52
Social reward	0.20	0.25	0.14
Instrumental	1.98	1.43	1.98
Concern	-0.97	-0.75	-0.23
Sorrow	-	-	-

With this picture in mind it is interesting to turn to the 2003 data. Here, 26 feeling words were used. As discussed in Chapter V, many of these gave rise to very few actual responses. Still, however a factor analysis of the complete battery of the 26 items for Kellogg's gives a five factor solution explaining 61% of the variance in the data (Table XII.12). The factors in this analysis are quite similar to what we have seen in the analysis from the 2004 data.

Thus, basically we may envision the five feeling components as seen in the 2004 data underlying the choice of feeling words also in the 2003 data. In a straight comparison between the Kellogg's scores for 2003 and 2004 it makes sense to concentrate on those items that appear in both years. Among the 16 items in the 2003 battery, 13 can be found in the 2004 battery. Of the 10 items based upon which NERS scores for cereals are computed in 2004, seven appear in the 2003 data also. A straight forward comparison of the scores on these items shows that Kellogg's negative development stands out clearly in terms of increasing concern and mistrust.

6. Charter Travel Companies

In this category we have chosen the Spies company for further study. This is done since it has been a much "seen" contester in the Danish market. Its founder, mr. Simon Spies, created an image for the company as being daring, sexy, controversial and outrageous. Although he died more than 20 years ago and therefore has had no influence on the profiling of the company over the last many years, the company maintains its profile as maverick, keeping a lot of the nature of its original brand equity, and is the one with the highest NERS score among those analysed.

In Table XII.14 the three factor solution for Spies accounting for (only) 34% of the variance shows an overall grouping of positive feeling words and another of negative feeling words with joy and expectation standing out as a separate third, unique factor for this company, something that makes sense knowing the history and the general perception of the company among Danish consumers.

Table XII.12: Three factor solution feeling words for Spies Travel

Feeling words	Component		
	1	2	3
Stimulating	**0.66**	0.04	0.25
Success	**0.65**	-0.05	-0.01
Healthy	**0.65**	0.18	0.05
Fresh	**0.61**	0.12	0.18
Wanted	**0.55**	0.00	0.33
Pretty	**0.53**	0.17	-0.05
Fine	**0.46**	-0.02	0.04
Pain	0.28	**0.71**	0.12
Worry	0.15	**0.70**	0.04
Sad	-0.13	**0.59**	0.40
Critical	0.02	**0.54**	-0.01
Boring	-0.11	**0.53**	-0.17
Doubt	0.13	**0.52**	-0.25
Annoyed	0.09	**0.50**	-0.30
Expectation	0.19	-0.08	**0.75**
Joy	0.37	-0.14	**0.56**

Returning to the composition of the NERS scores (Table XII.13) we find that for the category, the dominant element is the basic joy feelings with social reward and functional elements being of minor importance. Among the negative feeling words those grouping around uncertainty and mistrust play a role. This is likely to be ascribable to a number of minor operators in the industry frequently closing down and leaving their clients without the promised travel arrangements.

Table XII.13: Elements of which NERS is composed for charter travel companies

Feeling words	NERS				
	Category	My Travel	Star Tour	Spies Rejser	Tjæreborg Rejser
Wanted	0.37	0.37	0.27	0.39	0.34
Annoyed	-0.27	-0.11	-0.08	-0.06	-0.03
Stimulating	0.28	0.17	0.26	0.23	0.22
Fine	0.38	0.26	0.09	0.26	0.29
Doubt	-0.14	-0.09	-0.02	-0.06	-0.04
Success	0.17	0.21	0.19	0.35	0.15
Critical	-0.33	-0.20	-0.14	-0.11	-0.08
Joy	1.45	1.06	1.16	1.23	1.23
Boring	-0.24	-0.04	-0.05	-0.14	-0.14
Expectation	1.74	1.32	1.45	1.27	1.40
Sum	3.41	2.95	3.12	3.36	3.35
Feeling groups					
Joy	3.57	2.64	2.70	2.76	2.92
Social reward	0.54	0.58	0.46	0.74	0.49
Instrumental	0.28	**0.17**	0.26	0.23	0.22
Concern	-0.74	-0.4	-0.24	-0.23	-0.15
Sorrow	-0.24	-0.04	-0.05	-0.14	-0.14

The feeling words entering in to the computation of NERS scores for charter companies are shown in Table XII.13.

For Spies the joy element is smaller than for the category as such, but this is made up by a stronger impression of feelings relating to social reward and with much lesser feelings of doubt expressed. The latter is most likely ascribable to the company being financially very solid and to the image of a company with joyful, social activities on their tours. Spies is the brand with the highest NERS score in the category. Only Tjæreborg, now a subsidiary of Spies has a similar high score.

7. Mobile Phone Companies

As the next example we shall have a look at the mobile phone companies (Table XII.14). A three factor solution accounting for 48% of the variance identifies one overall positive factor with feeling words corresponding to the overall underlying basic positive emotional response tendency including joy, social and instrumental effects. The two next factors represent partly the sorrow (pain/sadness) feelings and partly the concern feelings (doubt, critical, worry).

Table XII.14: Feeling words activated by emotions towards the category mobile companies (48%variance explained)

Feeling words	Component 1	2	3
Joy	**0.69**	0.16	0.00
Stimulating	**0.66**	0.19	-0.05
Pretty	**0.63**	0.43	-0.01
Fresh	**0.63**	0.19	-0.03
Wanted	**0.59**	-0.11	0.15
Success	**0.57**	-0.05	0.10
Healthy	**0.55**	0.48	0.03
Fine	**0.54**	-0.06	-0.17
Expectation	**0.54**	-0.14	0.20
Sad	0.11	**-0.61**	0.21
Pain	0.19	**0.57**	0.09
Boring	-0.05	**0.54**	-0.02
Annoyed	-0.21	0.40	0.22
Doubt	0.04	0.06	**0.72**
Critical	-0.03	0.06	**0.70**
Worry	0.11	0.31	**0.54**

NERS score in this category falls in two dominant groups. Feeling words associated with doubt and mistrust and feeling words associated with joy and pleasure. The negative feeling words by far outrate the positive ones. The very complex pricing policies of the mobile phone companies have taken their toll in terms of a considerable mistrust among the subscribers.

Only one company manages to come out with a positive NERS score: Telmore, a smaller company with rather special services and a limited clientele. This company, it seems, has managed to generate more joy (pleasure) feelings and to a smaller extent mistrust among its subscribers. Its concept of no subscription fee, cheap, straight pricing of traffic with no special discounts or varying rates across the day combined with a low SMS price – on of the lowest in the market - probably is the foundation on which the emotional response is built.

8. Hair Shampoo

In the hair shampoo category we earlier found the particular standing of the anti-dandruff brand Head & Shoulders. It should be interesting to look a little more in depth at the structure of the perception of this brand relative to that of its competitors. In terms of factor analytical structure, Head & Shoulders looks much like its competitors though it allows for the computation of five separate factors rather than three or four as for the remaining brands. The scree plot is shown in Figure XII.2. It can be added that the picture in Figure XII.2 looks almost identical for all other product categories analyzed.

Figure XII.2: Eigen values for different number of extract factors for five hair shampoo brands

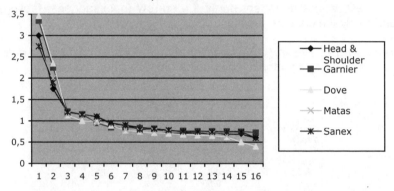

In terms of the factors the overall positive/negative ones emerge as always. For Dove they are the two first factors respectively. The third factor for Dove combines the social reward elements (fine, want, success).

The same picture holds true for Garnier, and also Matas is very much like Dove. Among the remaining brands Sanex gives rise to four factors.

Also here the feeling words accounting for the positive NERS score separate into two groups, one combining mostly joy elements (pretty, health, fresh and joy) and one combining social reward (success, expectation and want). That is, the social element stands out alone and the remaining joy elements combine in one factor.

The negative feeling words break into two groups. One carrying the bulk of the load combining concern (doubt, sad, pain and worried) and another with a negative loading on fine combined with boring and annoyed possibly reflecting the lack of excitement (joy) communicated by the brand.

Finally, Head & Shoulders comes out with five factors as shown in Table XII.15.

Table XII.15: *Five factor solution for feeling words activated by emotion aroused by the brand Head & Shoulders (56%
variance explained)*

Factor name	Feeling words	Component				
		1	2	3	4	5
Joy/social	Joy	**.693**	.251	-.026	.001	.102
Reward	Success	**.634**	.112	.083	-.067	.159
	Wanted	**.628**	.124	-.014	.910	.230
	Healthy	**.567**	.139	.039	.078	-.125
	Fine	**.527**	-.106	-.485	.083	-.199
Instrumental	Pretty	-.200	**.807**	-.123	.061	-.020
	Stimulating	.333	**.631**	.059	-.016	.034
	Expectation	.309	**.586**	-.063	.035	-.024
	Fresh	.367	.391	-.143	-.042	-.141
Critical I	Critical	-.180	-.062	**.659**	.286	.241
	Doubt	.102	-.126	**.626**	.175	-.022
	Annoyed	-.064	-.074	**.513**	-.252	.454
Critical II	Pain	.089	.063	.038	**.738**	.227
	Worry	-.017	-.003	.203	**.709**	-.009
Sad	Boring	-.073	-.054	-.094	.050	**.682**
	Sad	.188	.019	.018	.305	**.575**

Here again we see the positive feeling words dividing into two factors;
one transformational combining joy (success, wanted, healthy and
fine) and the other being instrumental, heavy loadings on pretty,
stimulating and expectation. The negative feeling words give rise to a
more specific perception of the brand. Concern feelings (critical,
doubt and annoyed) stand out as one factor and a second critical factor show high loadings on pain and worry. A third negative factor, boring and sad possibly reflects something special related to the dandruff element of the brand.

The composition of the NERS scores for the different brands is
shown in Table XII.16.

Table XII.16:Elements of which the NERS scores are composed, for the five deodorant brands in 2004

	Category	Dove	Head & Shoulders	Sanex	Matas	Garnier Fructis
Annoyed	-0,18	-0,18	-0,42	-0,12	-0,15	-0,61
Stimulating	0,22	0,14	0,11	0,20	0,12	0,19
Fine	0,40	0,34	0,44	0,26	0,46	0,29
Doubt	-0,14	-0,08	-0,32	-0,04	-0,07	-0,15
Fresh	0,91	0,81	0,30	0,70	0,51	0,89
Worry	-0,06	-0,04	-0,11	-0,04	-0,02	-0,03
Pretty	0,65	0,34	0,18	0,21	0,19	0,35
Critical	-0,32	-0,16	-0,59	-0,10	-0,11	-0,44
Joy	0,29	0,20	0,10	0,16	0,17	0,14
Healthy	0,49	0,57	0,14	1,00	0,87	0,25
Sum	**2,26**	**1,94**	**-0,17**	**2,23**	**1,97**	**0,89**
Feeling groups						
Joy	0,69	0,54	0,54	0,43	0,63	0,43
Social	0,65	0,34	0,18	0,21	0,19	0,35
Instrumental	1,62	1,52	0,54	1,90	1,51	1,33
Concern	-0,70	-0,46	-1,43	-0,31	-0,35	-1,23
Sad	-	-	-	-	-	-

The hair shampoo category is characterised by a large number of differentiated brands among which are some expensive and exclusive ones. Neither of these is included in the present analysis. Thus, it is not surprising that the category per se scores slightly higher than even the best scoring of the brands analysed. In the data it can be seen that the low score on Head & Shoulders comes particularly from the negative value of the concern (annoyed, doubt, worry and critical) feeling words. They together account for a negative component of the NERS score amounting to 1.44, which the positive feeling words cannot compensate for. The Garnier brand, too, generally scores lower on all feeling words than the other brands. Similar response profiles have been found in other situations, where the brands – just as is the case for Garnier - have a much smaller market share as compared with the leading brands. It probably is a general phenomenon that small brands will have lower emotional responses than major brands, when users and non-users are combined.

9. Amusement Parks

Turning to the amusement parks, a factor analysis of all statements used in 2004 give the same five factors as in Figure XII.1. The overall picture for the amusement parks can be read from Table XII.17 where it can be seen that Tivoli and Legoland score higher than the category per se and Bakken and BonBon Land slightly lower.

For Tivoli the differences in NERS scores between 2003 and 2004 is remarkable. The nature of the change in NERS for Tivoli between 2003 and 2004 can be analysed in more detail, since out of the ten feeling words upon which the NERS score for Tivoli in 2004 was computed, seven are available in the 2003 data also. Among these, the change first and foremost comes in the joy-related feeling words joy and expectation. In terms of contribution to the overall drop in NERS score, the drop in those two feeling words is 3.53, or slightly more than the total drop in the NERS score between the two years – leading to a score for Tivoli on the category average in 2004.

Table XII.17: Elements of which the NERS score for amusement parks are composed (2004)

Feeling words	NERS				
	Category	Tivoli	Legoland	Bakken	BonBon Land
Wanted	0.42	0.67	0.80	0.48	0.49
Annoyed	-0.24	-0.05	-0.08	-0.09	-0.30
Stimulating	0.66	0.52	0.55	0.42	0.45
Doubt	-0.04	-0.02	-0.01	-0.03	-0.02
Fresh	0.27	0.21	0.15	0.19	0.18
Worry	-0.05	-0.02	-0.02	-0.04	-0.03
Success	0.13	0.40	0.61	0.16	0.28
Joy	2.38	2.30	2.07	2.18	2.05
Boring	-0.17	-0.06	-0.06	-0.08	-0.10
Expectation	1.69	1.76	1.39	1.36	1.38
Sum	5.04	5.71	5.40	4.56	4.37
Feeling groups					
Joy	4.07	4.06	3.46	3.54	3.43
Social	0.55	1.07	1.41	0.64	0.77
Instrumental	0.93	0.73	0.70	0.61	0.63
Concern	-0.33	-0.09	-0.11	-0.16	-0.35
Sad	-0.17	-0.06	-0.06	-0.08	-0.10

Thus, the much higher joy and expectation expressed by a large number of respondents who have visited Tivoli – or at least have been exposed to Tivoli during the summer season in the fall of 2004- when the interviews were made as compared to those answering the questionnaire in the spring 2004 account for the difference in the NERS scores for Tivoli between the two years. (The gross number of visits to Tivoli with 4.3 million visitors in 2004 comes close to the size of the Danish population!).

That Legoland shows particularly high scores on positive social feelings may be ascribable to the fact that practically all visits to Legoland involve children in company with parents, grand parents and other adults.

10. Toys
The toy category is represented by three large manufacturers including the globally well known and dominant Danish LEGO brand. The factor analysis of the 16 statements used in 2004 again extracts the same five factors as in Figure XII.1.

LEGO's stature comes through in the emotional response measurement as an excellent brand in the sense that it is the only one that scores higher than the category (Table XII.18).

Table XII.18: Elements of which the NERS scores for toys are composed

Feeling words	NERS			
	Category	LEGO	Fisher Price	Brio
Wanted	0.26	0.73	0.36	0.49
Annoyed	-0.21	-0.08	-0.11	-0.04
Stimulating	1.13	1.21	0.98	1.10
Fine	0.38	0.57	0.24	0.39
Worry	-0.12	-0.02	-0.03	-0.01
Success	0.06	0.55	0.15	0.28
Critical	-0.31	-0.03	-0.08	-0.03
Joy	1.96	1.24	1.06	1.21
Boring	-0.09	-0.04	-0.06	-0.07
Expectation	0.88	0.69	0.68	0.50
Sum	**3.95**	**4.86**	**3.19**	**3.82**
Sums of elements				
Joy	3.22	2.50	1.98	2.10
Social	0.32	1.28	0.51	0.77
Instrumental	1.13	1.21	0.98	1.10
Critical	-0.64	-0.13	-0.22	-0.08
Sad	-0.09	-0.04	-0.06	-0.07

Considering the fact that LEGO as a company has been far less successful in financial terms over recent years, the high scores are remarkable and testify to a much-discussed phenomenon in corporate reputation contexts, namely whether the consumer can separate brand reputation and corporate reputation in cases where the same names are used – the argument is, that there will be a rub-off of one unto the other. In LEGO's case, consumers clearly separate the product essence and brand values of the company from the financial performance, at least in the short run. However, LEGO's excellent standing in the market in brand terms may be vulnerable, and there is a risk that the general Danish public's undoubted awareness of the problems of the LEGO Company will eventually reduce the favourable emotional responses that this flagship of Danish industry enjoys.

11. Mobile Telephones
As a last category to be illustrated here, we have chosen mobile telephones. The mobile telephone market, particularly in Denmark, is dominated by the two Nordic brands Nokia (Finnish) and Sony/Ericsson (Japanese/Swedish).

Table XII.19: *Elements of which the NERS scores for mobile phone companies are composed*

Feeling words	NERS				
	Category	Nokia	Sony/Eriksson	Samsung	Siemens
Wanted	0.61	0.87	0.70	0.41	0.37
Annoyed	-1.18	-0.34	-0.38	-0.08	-0.59
Fine	0.71	0.56	0.68	0.63	0.68
Fresh	0.09	0.09	0.06	0.05	0.03
Worry	-0.24	-0.08	-0.08	-0.06	-0.08
Success	0.33	0.72	0.54	0.31	0.25
Critical	-0.37	-0.25	-0.26	-0.17	-0.30
Joy	0.32	0.24	0.20	0.11	0.13
Doubt	-0.12	-0.06	-0.12	-0.21	-0.13
Expectation	0.32	0.34	0.39	0.42	0.26
Sum	**0.46**	**2.08**	**1.72**	**1.42**	**0.65**
Sums of elements					
Joy	1.35	1.14	1.27	1.16	1.07
Social	0.94	1.59	1.24	0.72	0.62
Instrumental	0.09	0.09	0.06	0.05	0.03
Concern	-1.91	-0.73	-0.84	-0.52	-1.10
Sad	-	-	-	-	-

Once again the analysis is focused on the NERS score components. These are shown in Table XII.19. In addition to the two Nordic brands, two other strong brands in the market, Samsung and Siemens are included in the analysis.

The dominant position of Nokia and Sony/Ericsson not only manifests itself in both brands scoring higher than the two other brands in the analysis in terms of NERS, but also in their higher score on the joy feeling word.

It can be seen that these four market leaders all score better than the category as such. The category is on the one hand dominated by the joy element, following from the use of the product, as expressed in answers to fine, joy, expectation (+1.35) against the negative element expressed in annoyed, worry, critical (-1.91), probably reflecting perceptions of confusing price offers made jointly with mobile phone operators.

The Nokia and Sony brands stand out by giving rise to less feeling of mistrust than the market as such. The relative advantage of Nokia over Sony Ericsson is to some extent ascribable to this brand's somewhat larger market share.

12. Summarising from Feelings to Emotions and Back

In the preceding examples we have illustrated how further analysis of the feeling words underlying NERS scores for brands and categories reveal some of the causes for the different standing of brands and for the way in which they have developed. Particularly we have observed some basic feelings activated identically by most products and brands. These are the feelings of:

- Joy as reflected in the feeling words joy, expectation, and fine.
- Instrumentality as reflected in feeling words like stimulating, fresh, and healthy.
- Social reward expressed by wanted, success, pretty,
- Sadness with the feeling words sad, pain, and boring
- Mistrust and uncertainty expressed by annoyed, critical, doubt, and worry.

For the marketer of a specific brand more information of this kind may throw further light on the emotional processes at work for his brand. Basic emotional processes, - the outcome of which may be predicted by the NERS score – may govern the choice of his brand when routine or impulse purchases are made. It is important for the marketer to know when and where and how frequently such purchases or consumption choices are made, and to know his brand equity in terms of NERS scores relative to those of his competitors. Also the feelings activated in choices when more elaborated choice processes occur are important - and to learn what basic feelings govern these and how his and competitors' alternatives are seen in terms of these feelings. Some such basic feelings have been illustrated in the preceding examples.

When the brand's important feeling dimensions are identified it is perfectly possible to analyse further - using qualitative and quantitative approaches as discussed in Chapter X – the specific nature of the feelings and cognitions that may relate to these. An example of such an analysis is given in the next section.

Emotions are important also in another context than that of generator of choice specific feelings. Emotions may also influence how the choice process takes form. As we have seen in an earlier section conflicting emotions may under different circumstances make choice processes more or less complex, and emotions of different intensity may determine the involvement in the choice, such as what kind of choice principle (compensatory versus conjunctive) is preferred.

C. NERS Scores as they Relate to Corporate Brand Character

Corporate branding is one of those things everyone believes is important, yet there is little consensus as to what it means. Words such as values, image and communication goals swirl around. For our purpose, we choose to regard the corporate brand as the name of the company as such. In some cases – such as LEGO – the corporate and the product brand are synonymous: The brand architecture strategy referred to as Branded House. In other cases, they are different – in the case of Proctor & Gamble's brands there is no overlap at all: The brand architecture strategy referred to as House of Brands. In the former case, we will usually expect a clear rub-off between the two uses of the brand, in the latter case, the rub-off must be expected to be zero.

In previous sections we have suggested that the NERS scores may reveal the immaterial elements of brand equity. In this section we shall analyse the extent to which NERS scores for companies may relate to what is normally being considered their corporate brand character or corporate brand value.

In 2001, replicated in 2005, a study among first year business school students was conducted evaluating ten major Danish corporations along 38 dimensions each believed to describe elements of their corporate image or corporate character. Items were selected based upon earlier work by Whitehead (1968), Berlo et al. (1969), Newell & Goldsmith (2001), Hansen and Kock (2003) and Keller (2003). This selection was done based upon the notation of Keller that a corporate brand encompasses a wider range of associations in the mind of the consumers. The selection procedure and the data analysis are described in further detail in Schnoor (2003).

In 2001 data collection included 185 students. Factor analysis conducted on the total battery of 38 items resulted in the identification of five factors (explaining 67% of the variance in the data). The five factors as they were identified in the 2001 and replicated in the 2005 study by applying identical analytic criteria, appear in Table XII.20.

Considering the similarity of the factors in the two years, - and the limited sample size in each year it was decided to carry out a joint analysis for the two years. The result of this is shown in the last column of Table XII.20.

Table XII.20:Statements used and how they factor out (2001 study, 2005 study, and total). 1 to 5 represents factor 1 to 5.

Statements	2001	2005	Total
Successful	1	1	1
Purposeful	1	1	1
Strong	1	1	1
Ambitious	1	1	1
Intelligent	1	1	1
Professional	1	1	1
Powerful	1	1	1
Self-confident	1	1	1
Visionary	1	1	1
Competent	3	1	1
Efficient	1	1	1
Decisive	1	1	1
Serious	3	1	1
Admirable	1	1	1
Knowledgeable	1	1	1
Organized	3	1	1
Colourful	2	2	2
Energetic	2	2	2
Cheerful	2	2	2
Extrovert	2	2	2
Active	2	2	2
Correct	3	3	3
Trustworthy	3	3	3
Just	3	3	3
Honest	5	3	3
Original	5	3	3
Open-minded	5	3	3
Sympathetic	5	5	3
Arrogant	4	4	4
Boastful	4	4	4
Superficial	4	4	4
Authoritative	4	4	4
Aggressive	4	2	4
Thoughtful	5	5	5
Capable of admitting Mistakes	5	5	5
Warm	5	5	5
Sensible	3	5	5
Responsible	3	1	5

The factors derived in the final joint analysis only deviate slightly from the factors of the two separate analyses, thus it is warranted to suggest that dimensions along which corporations are evaluated did not change between the two years in samples of young first year business school students.

The first factor combines strong, purposeful and successful, and could be labelled professionalism. The second factor reflects a kind of charisma ascribed to the company: powerful, energetic, cheerful, extrovert, and active. The third factor has to do with trustworthiness judgements such as trustworthy, just, correct, serious, earnest, original, open minded and dominate. The fourth factor combines elements relating to arrogance, authoritativeness, aggressiveness whereas the fifth combines elements much like Aaker's warmth dimension (Aaker et al., 1986).

Table XII.21 Development in the evaluation of 10 corporate brands (Significant (p<0.01) changes in bold; weak significant (p ≤ 0.05) changes in bold italics)

		Factor 1	Change	Factor 2	Change	Factor 3	Change	Factor 4	Change	Factor 5	Change
Byggekram	2001	-0.273	**-0.501**	-0.181	-0.101	-0.155	-0.016	-0.217	**-0.301**	0.097	-0.169
	2005	-0.774		-0.282		-0.171		-0.518		-0.072	
DSB	2001	-0.268	0.014	0.008	-0.106	0.026	0.001	0.288	**0.323**	0.453	-0.060
	2005	-0.254		-0.098		0.028		0.611		0.393	
EasyJet	2001	-0.148	**0.233**	0.365	**0.741**	-0.189	**-0.211**	-0.128	**-0.361**	-0.208	**-0.307**
	2005	0.085		1.106		-0.400		-0.489		-0.515	
Jubii	2001	-0.062	**-0.337**	0.984	**0.277**	-0.048	**0.408**	-0.014	-0.085	-0.285	-0.214
	2005	-0.399		1.262		0.360		-0.1000		-0.500	
Microsoft	2001	1.022	**0.688**	-0.188	-0.139	-0.427	**0.243**	0.665	0.045	-0.559	***0.2410***
	2005	1.709		-0.327		-0.184		0.709		-0.318	
PostDanmark	2001	-0.15	0.108	-0.242	-0.138	0.457	**0.399**	-0.165	0.173	-0.002	0.035
	2005	-0.05		-0.379		0.856		0.009		0.033	
SAS	2001	0.41	-0.088	-0.283	***-0.221***	0.216	**-0.515**	-0.135	**0.254**	0.214	**0.310**
	2005	0.33		-0.504		-0.300		0.119		0.525	
Silvan	2001	-0.25	**-0.270**	0.076	0.074	0.002	0.177	-0.182	-0.076	0.112	-0.201
	2005	-0.52		0.1500		0.179		-0.259		-0.089	
TopDanmark	2001	-0.08	0.094	-0.319	***-0.215***	0.020	**-0.319**	-0.116	0.095	-0.090	0.201
	2005	0.01		-0.534		-0.299		-0.021		0.111	
Tryg	2001	-0.20	0.060	-0.220	-0.174	0.099	-0.166	0.004	-0.066	0.267	0.164
	2005	-0.14		-0.394		-0.068		-0.062		0.431	

In spite of the stability in the dimension along which corporations were evaluated, several significant changes in their image were identified between 2001 and 2005. These are beyond the topic of this presentation but a discussion of these may be found in Christensen et al. (2005).

In the 2005 data collection emotional response scores for the corporations were measured. A selection of feeling words was made based on the words used in the 2004 data collection (Chapter VI). Four of these made less sense in a corporate context and were deleted. With the remaining feeling words two emotional response dimensions emerge. They are illustrated in Table XII.22. The dimensions are the negative and positive emotional response tendencies seen earlier.

Table XII.22:Two emotional response dimensions (one negative and one positive) for corporations

	Component	
	1	2
Joy	**.730**	-.053
Happiness	**.634**	-.087
Inspiring	**.605**	-.063
Enjoyment	**.527**	-.118
Hope	**.479**	.141
Trust	**.385**	-.278
Surprising	**.363**	.141
Anger	-.051	**.722**
Fear	.041	**.662**
Grief	-.032	**.562**
Dominating	.092	**.380**
Accept	.179	**-.359**

The loadings on the two factors allow for the computation of NERS scores on behalf of each respondent for each of the ten corporations included in the study. With these NERS scores as the dependent variable and with the factor scores for each respondent on each of the five factors as independent variables, correlation analysis was conducted for each of the ten companies included in the study. The result of this analysis is summarised in Table XI.23. Here for each corporation the NERS scores are correlated with the factor scores on the five dimensions. The Beta scores in the table reflect how much each of the 5 corporate identity dimensions adds to the explanation of NERS scores.

Table XII.23: Beta values for ten correlation analyses between NERS scores and individuals' perception of corporations in terms of their factor scores on five factors entering into the description of corporate identity. (Significant coefficients (p<0.01) in bold. Weak significance (p ≤ 0.05) in bold italics)

Corporate brand	DSB	SAS	Tryg	Silvan	Easy-Jet	TopDK	Jubii	Microsft	Post DK	Bygge-kram
NERS score	*0.107*	*1.009*	*0.403*	*1.016*	*1.010*	*0.592*	*1.300*	*0.824*	*0.607*	*0.932*
Factor 1 "Success"	**0.237**	**0.523**	0.160	**0.500**	**0.254**	**0.246**	**0.356**	**0.305**	0.209	**0.581**
Factor 2 "Credibility"	**0.281**	0.113	**0.248**	0.170	**0.458**	0.090	**0.232**	**0.420**	0.313	**0.208**
Factor 3 "Extrovert"	0.095	**0.345**	0.120	-0.021	*0.183*	-0.039	**0.324**	**0.227**	0.045	**0.223**
Factor 4 "Forceful"	**-.365**	*-.161*	**-.228**	-.154	**-.261**	-.181	0.055	**-.263**	**-0.427**	-0.032
Factor 5 "Warmth/caring"	**0.334**	0.047	**0.414**	0.152	0.082	**0.429**	*0.213*	**0.203**	**0.307**	**0.346**
R (R²)	.672 (.451)	.704 (.495)	.558 (.312)	.614 (.377)	.639 (.408)	.557 (.310)	.618 (.382)	.738 (.545)	.706 (.498)	.711 (.505)

From the relatively high correlations (R), from a low of .557 to a high of .738, it can be seen that the NERS scores to a large extent can be explained by the way in which people evaluate the different corporations. From Table XII.23, it also appears that for the different corporations different corporate value factors account for the explained variance in the NERS scores.

Thus, we can conclude that the NERS score as a measure of immaterial aspects of corporate brand equity to a large extent is explainable in terms of the dimensions along which the corporations are evaluated. And more importantly, we can understand the emotional response to a corporation as being driven by traditional evaluation criteria in the sense that, an obvious interaction between the way in which people think and feel about corporations and their more immediate emotional response to the same is established.

We would expect changes in the NERS scores related to the changing corporate values found between 2001 and 2005 of the corporations but since NERS measures are not available from the 2001 data collection, we cannot document this. We may, however, conclude that NERS scores for corporations rely heavily upon the way in which the same corporations are evaluated on credibility, successfulness, extraversion, forcefulness and warmth. Moreover, it is evident that different corporate value dimensions account for the NERS scores for different corporations.

Thus it is warranted to conclude that the basic underlying differences in net emotional response potentials for corporations may be seen in the light of cognitive evaluations, consciously or unconsciously of the corporations along the five dimensions included.

The emotional responses to the cooperation give rise to cognitive elements as described by the five factors. Similarly the perception along these dimensions most likely result in changes in implicitly stored information of importance for later emotional responses.

D. Summary

In the preceding chapters we have almost only used feeling words to predict underlying fundamental positive/negative emotional response tendencies. In this last chapter we have reconsidered the more detailed information that may be gained from studying exactly what feeling words and combinations of feeling words account for the overall positive/negative or NERS scores of brands. We find that in the selection of feeling words, with which we have worked, the positive as well as the negative ones tend to cluster in meaningful ways. Among the positive feelings we almost always find a feeling of "joy" and secondly we find feelings of social rewards associated with the use of the brands and the product. A third category of positive feeling words, identified in many product areas, are feelings relating to the actual use and in some instances concern with the consequences of the use of the product.

Among the negative feeling words for many products, we find a group reflecting the sheer negative experience associated with the use. This we have labelled sorrow. But, for many product categories we find a second dimension concerned with the possible malfunctioning of the product. With these more detailed analyses of feelings underlying the basic emotional response tendencies we can add to the explanatory power of the total analysis already provided in earlier chapters.

How NERS scores may relate to even more removed values and beliefs, than what is represented by the feeling words in their own right, is demonstrated in a study of the perception of the corporate identity of major Danish companies. Here it is found that the values associated with different companies have important influence on the NERS scores for the companies, suggesting that modified NERS scores may result from activities aimed at influencing the way in which the company is perceived.

Chapter XIII

Concluding Remarks

The present book, Emotions, Advertising and Consumer Choice, presents a body of knowledge that is widely accepted amongst both academics and practitioners of advertising and marketing, namely the thinking that goes into classical consumer behaviour modeling: Much processing is cognitive in nature, processing takes place at a certain level of consciousness, the consumer "solves problems" – although problem solving can span from complex to limited and routine – in short, the consumer behaves fairly rationally in the quest for a maximization of his or her utility.

This rationality is not seen as the classic economic idea of economic rationality, rather the consumer has differing objectives of different types: some economic, some self-centered, some depending on the thoughts and ideas of others. At some times the consumer strives to maximize his own physical well-being, at another time he wants to project a certain image and style in his clothing towards a group of friends or co-workers, at yet another time he works on re-mortgaging his home at the cheapest interest expense obtainable and balancing this objective against the wish to have a fixed interest rate for as long into the future as possible.

The models describing this type of thinking are well known, they are very well researched and all of them are very well documented through experiments and large and small scale studies. They form the basis of market research driven marketing work: We may not know what objectives are actualized by the consumer, but with clever market research we can find out, and then optimizing the marketing effort for maximum market share gain is plain sailing.

The corresponding theory of advertising and advertising's effects clearly has its origins in the concept of a rationally utility-maximizing individual. The concept of information processing that follows a – more or less – strict sequence of steps from initial awareness over the awakening of interest via formation of an irresistible desire to the action of purchasing the wanted product or service gives the advertising planner a well defined tool with which to reach well defined objectives. And there is nothing wrong with that.

The whole idea of formulating advertising objectives in terms of measurable and actionable quantities has lifted the level of the advertising profession from being one of the lower art forms to a level of true professionalism, where intended results are created by planned efforts, based on thorough research and prior knowledge about how consumers act.

Research work in the 70's and 80's began to make small cracks in this picture of the consumer as a cognitive, conscious individual who is driven towards goal fulfilment in a reasonably rational fashion – and who processes commercial communication in a way that can be modelled by the traditional hierarchy of effects.

Many different ideas have been put forward, partly to try something new and different – a key effort in any process of marketing – partly to overcome some of the shortcomings that practitioners increasingly were stumbling across in the pursuit of marketing and advertising. The hierarchy of effects, formulated in its simplest form: Learn, feel, do gave rise to the idea, that there was not one hierarchy of effects, but rather 4 different hierarchies, depending on the sequence in which the three building blocks appeared.

In research terms, what had happened was the realization that consumers may do many things – and over the years the number of tasks performed and stimuli processed have increased exponentially – but they do not do all of them at the top of their mental capacity with all brain cells churning away, neither do they necessarily pay close attention to all stimuli that arrive in front of them, and basically – as it has once been expressed – "the Vietnam war is more important to most people than the choice between one- and two-ply toilet tissue."

In spite of these realizations and attempts at modeling them for practical use, little actually happened. Textbook writers and business schools keep teaching sequential consumer behaviour models and hierarchies of effects models, not because they don't know the other models, but probably because of some variation on the theme: To break the rules, you have to know them. So in order to do away with the idea of cognitive and conscious consumers processing information in a strict hierarchy of effects, the students have to know about them first.

Many writers and researchers have tried to break through the clutter with different ideas as to how consumers make up their minds and how they manage to deal with the flood of advertising that barges in on them every awakening moment of the day. It is our impression that a number of concepts have been more instrumental in achieving the reorientation that we perceive as happening today, and that this book is a manifestation of.

First of all, the realisation of different levels of consumer involvement, simplified down to high and low involvement gave researchers and practitioners alike a completely new insight into how consumers function when shopping or watching advertising in various media. Add to this the idea (Petty & Cacioppo, 1986c) of a central (cognitive, probably also conscious) route to persuasion versus a peripheral (affective, probably not very conscious) route to persuasion, and marketing managers had gotten a whole new tool box for planning communications and marketing programmes. And in recent years the advent of brain scanning technology of a type, which makes it feasible to study brain activity when the individual is exposed to commercial stimuli in settings, that are not weird, laboratory type settings with tubes and mysterious machinery.

The combination must have struck many traditionally bred marketing managers as a bomb shell: Think of fashion advertising that consists of a picture of a beautiful female or male, and the name of the company and verbal information of the type: Paris, Rome, Munich under the logo. And then imagine a traditionalist marketing manager trying to make sense of this, using sequential models of consumer choice: where is the necessary information with which the consumer must compare products, availability, prices etc.? And how do the consumers manage to come from awareness along the way to at least purchase intention, when there is no price in the ad? The fashion moguls stated that their ads were supposed to project an image as their rationale for this type of advertising. The Benetton advertising of the 80's completely lacked any reference to the collections, only the logo remained as a clue as to what the consumer was supposed to think and do.

But once you realize, that consumers basically do NOT pay attention to advertising to any large degree, that consumers do NOT necessarily compare products or prices etc., that consumers do NOT make conscious deliberations to arrive at the decision to enter a shop and buy a blouse, then the fashion advertising, which really lead the way, begins to make sense. Even Benetton's shock advertising begins to make sense.

Once you accept that the traditional theories and models are all very well for understanding basic principles underlying some consumer choices and information processing activities, but that mechanisms of the brain are at work that do NOT quite resemble the way a computer programme would work at problem solving, then you may even begin to notice how much research effort has been put into developing other theories and models of consumer choice.

In Chapter III of this book, we have made a review of the literature that has dealt with the broad concept of affect. It is noteworthy that not only has such work been published starting all the way back in the mid-80's without having had a profound impact on the way marketing is taught and practised, but also has such an amount of original research been going on, that might show a better way to understand consumer behaviour, without this work having a real effect on the mainstream thinking and practising of marketing.

The idea of affect as a mediating function in consumer data processing, as stated, is not new. Researchers and practitioners alike began to realize, that the mood a given consumer was in, seemingly had a quite noticeable effect on his or her choices. Upscale restaurants have known this for ages: the better the client mood, the bigger the tips.

As we showed, affect as a concept covers a lot different ideas and concepts which have at least one thing in common, they have nothing to do with cognition. They are not necessarily the opposite of cognition, they actually collaborate with cognition, but are seen as many different forms. Eric du Plessis recently expressed the role of affect in the following elegant way: "To appreciate the implications for advertising practices one must understand the old paradigm (emotions interfere with rationality) versus the new (emotions guide rationality, and cause attention)" (Du Plessis, 2005b).

Market researchers and others in latter years have made many experiments in order to document that consumers actually perceive things that they don't perceive, so to speak. Experiments with exposing advertising material at the fringe of peripheral vision while the respondent is busy keeping watch over two lines right in front of his/her nose show that they do recognize the ad at a later time. Actually experiments have shown that attitude change is stronger amongst the respondent group that recognizes the ad than among the respondent group that recalls the ad.

In a small experiment, French researchers have shown a similar mechanism with web banners on a computer screen – the banners being exposed out of focus led to positive attitudes towards the fictitious brand that was shown, the more exposures, the better the attitude.

It is observations such as these that have led to a rethinking of Zajonc's (1968) mere exposure theory: You may not believe it, but research results indicate that it works. Although the results may not give the full explanation of how it works, they indicate that more exposure leads to more positive responses.

Back to affect as such. Probably the single most important development in consumer behaviour and information processing thinking are the increases in our understanding of, how the brain works. This development comes from the medical sector of research, particularly neuro-physiology and neuro-psychology. Most of what we were taught back in the 60's and 70's about how the brain works turns out to be wrong. And some of what we thought in the 80's turns out to be wrong, too. Remember hemispherical lateralization?? Whole consulting companies grew up on that idea.

The new developments have been fuelled by neurologists, such as LeDoux (1998 and 2002) and Damasio (1994, 2000, and 2003). Their observations of very unfortunate patients with grave physical and psychological disorders have led to a much deeper understanding of the workings of the brain in general and the role of emotions and the limbic system in particular. At least the present authors were very inspired by their thoughts and theories when formulating a similar conceptual framework for the understanding of consumer behaviour and information processing.

It turns out that the thinking capacity of the brain is – evolution-wise – of fairly recent age, whereas the "original" elements in the brain are much more for classification purposes and subsequent action control so as to increase the probability that the individual can survive: Is it dangerous? Can it be eaten? Is it something new that I must be careful about? etc. This almost reptile-like working of the brain controls the escape and attack mechanisms, as well as other more or less automatic reactions.

And these patterns seem – on the surface at least – to have a lot in common with consumer choice on autopilot without attention and cognition: Do I like it? Have I seen something similar before? Does it taste awful? The basic approach and avoidance tendencies that we argue are fundamental to the human system and fundamental in choice situations. Of course the matters that we choose between are most definitely not of life threatening nature, but the lightning quick and un-bothering way to control action seems well suited to the enormous number of choices that we have to make every day on more or less trivial matters.

With this sketchy picture of how consumer behaviour might take place, let us reflect a little more on the theories about how advertising works. We have argued that the mainstream thinking of advertising and how to persuade consumers rests on a fundamental assumption that the consumer processes information fairly consciously and using cognitive faculties to perceive and decode messages. Most practitioners tend to work as if the consumer is going to decode more or less as was encoded, since consumers are "thinking beings" and will react favourably to messages that present the case at hand convincingly in relation to the consumer's choice mechanisms.

Whether this type of theory then has driven practices in advertising testing or whether advertising testing has driven the formulation of theories of how advertising works will never be clarified – and neither does it seem to be worthwhile to discover what was the hen and what the egg in the development.

It does seem that there is a close connection between what has been measured – or is easily measurable – in traditional questionnaire based research and what is thought to represent good advertising. The measurement of awareness provides a wonderful metric, which all practitioners know clearly differentiates between ads with a lot of GRPs as backing and ads with very few GRPs behind them. It also – in the form of unaided recall – differentiates between clearly executed ads and cluttered and "fact-stuffed" ads. And the reason we all argue that ads should be simple and clear in their message structure may be precisely because we know that will mean that they will score well in awareness testing – not necessarily that we have any knowledge about those ads' performance in the process of persuasion.

The same argument can be raised about other measurements linked to the classic hierarchy of effect: It is wonderfully logical to assume that awareness must precede interest, and that interest must precede desire and that desire is the necessary prerequisite for action. And therefore it is logical also to argue that that is the way in which advertising works. But again and again in academic research and in practical work with advertising, it turns out that this model may not be completely appropriate – and that other sequences of the effects of the hierarchy may actually not be much more appropriate.

Most importantly, it has become increasingly clear that affect played an important role in the consumer's processing of information from advertising. One of the stumbling blocks from this understanding to a fundamental change in the view on how advertising works has probably been the lack of precise knowledge about how the brain works. But that has changed. Another stumbling block has been – given that affect is important – what more precisely is affect in relation to how advertising works, and how can we measure the relevant constructs in affect. It is amazing that early thorough advertising testing such as the ARF's copy-testing project turned out with the conclusion that the measurement that most discriminated between good or bad ads in relation to persuasion was ad liking. That, if anything, can only be seen as a very simple, basic and affective response to advertising stimulus. Actually, it closely resembles the kind of positive / negative type of reaction to brands that we argue is fundamental to consumer choice.

And with what we know of advertising testing along lines of the ELM routes to persuasion of Petty, Cacioppo et al. (1986), we can so to speak regenerate that knowledge of information processing as an unconscious process with very little cognition involved, a process that again seems to resemble consumer choice on autopilot a lot.

In broader circles, the term: Emotion in advertising has been used to denote the idea that the consumer is looking for an idea rather than a load of facts. Supermarket retailers for years have interpreted this in such a way that supermarket advertising across the western world consists of pictures of packs and a gigantic price, supposedly an exceptionally low price. Only the simplest facts are served, no explanation, no brand building effort, nothing except a picture and a price.

Most of the work on affect that we have reviewed point in the same direction, namely that there are two basic emotional response mechanisms – positive and negative - that in all probability guide much more of the consumers' choice than we have so far been aware of. In the literature as well as in our own research, we can identify more emotions than just the two. However, they all can be boiled down again to the two dimensions: Approach and avoidance, positive and negative.

In our own research, we have based the analysis on modeling consumer responses as happening on the two dimensions, the positive emotional response tendency and the negative emotional response tendency. We have demonstrated that these responses can be seen as part of the consumers' reaction to brands, as part of their reactions to politicians at an election, as part of their reactions to sponsoring companies and to corporations in general, as a reaction to organisations that look for sponsorship support. We also demonstrate in a number of examples that it is possible to look at more detailed feeling responses that form the two basic responses. This we do, because for the practitioner it will provide a richer analysis and thereby opening up more alternatives to actions that may develop the desired response patterns. We also do it to illustrate, that the two basic responses are there at all times and guide the choices that the consumer makes and the way he or she reacts to advertising.

Brain scanning – as EEG or QEEG, fMRI or other abbreviations – is coming of age as a tool that can be used in connection with research into consumer behaviour phenomena. It is still cumbersome, still fraught with the risk of creating artificial situations, but nevertheless studies are beginning to appear in published sources that illustrate not only what parts of the brain are at work in various tasks, but that a lot of the theoretical underpinning of the emotional theory of consumer choice is in fact there. The Pepsi Challenge study, McClure et al. (2004), shows in graphic detail that blind tasting the two colas is a process for that part of the brain that takes care of reward experiences such as having a beverage. But the branded tasting activates the old parts of the brain where the emotional processes reside, the hippocampus amongst others.

Our work also measures the fundamental emotional processes that reside in the oldest parts of the brain such as the hippocampus. We do not do it with a brain scanner, but rather have developed a questionnaire based instrument that – in contrast to the brain scanning – allows for large samples of respondents. Of course such an instrument does not have the precision that the medical apparatus has. Since it works with samples of respondents, it has random errors of a different kind that EEG measurement have.

But it is not cumbersome, it is easy and cheap to administer. It tells the decisions maker what the respondent actually likes or is attracted to, where the brain scanner's primary function is to tell us where activity occurs in the brain, and consequently, what type of process is taking place – but not, whether the respondent likes the experience.

We demonstrate in the book that this instrument is reasonably robust with respect to changes in actual number of words used. It is reasonably robust to changes in respondent contact methodology. And we demonstrate that it captures changes in emotional responses in a number of cases, where such changes can be ascribed to actual changes in the market situation, in the marketing mix or in the competitive situation. And we demonstrate that it can be used across a number of study fields: Brands, election behaviour, sponsorship effects and corporate branding.

Much more research is needed in order to develop actual recommendations to marketers on what types of stimuli in-store, on-line, in print or broadcast media will produce desired results. We also need to do more research in order to determine the sensitivity of the measurements with respect to changes in the types of communication or media involved. And also to do more research to determine the sensitivity with respect to changes in the amount of advertising money spent. And then more research in order to establish models that tie emotional responses and other elements of the brand equity to actual purchasing, so that measurements of how advertising works can be further refined from the short term, medium term and long term effects that are discussed in the book.

But most of all, we need marketers and advertising people to adopt the ideas and the theory. Because when that happens, experience will develop, and the researchers will get the data with which to develop the emotional theory further.

We need tracking studies to tell us how emotional responses in target groups develop as markets and marketing programmes change over time. We need advertising testing to determine how better to advertise to build brand equity. We need sponsors to work with planned sponsorships in order to improve on emotional responses amongst consumers and we need the sponsors to do tracking studies to tell them how their sponsorship programmes work.

We need the advertising community to accept that advertising works at low attention and with low involvement, but that it is possible to influence the way consumers react to brands, products and services. The emotional responses can be changed and increased so that marketers with attractive marketing programmes can capitalize on changed customer mindsets. And we need the advertising community to develop creative approaches that will work at low attention levels, with low involvement and consequently with little cognitive effort.

And then we need research to build knowledge about how various types of messages and information structures can effect emotional responses and changes in the responses. We need to do the research with in-store media that are increasingly of importance in FMCG retailing. We need research on print media, on broadcast media and on on-line media. Particularly on-line media that for most companies are increasingly used as branding medium are an important medium to do research on: It is multimedia, it is interactive and most of all, it's demanded by the consumer, not pushed to him or her.

Reference List

"Advertising Works", Advertising Effectiveness Awards, Regularly 1981-, IPA

AAKER, D. A., CARMAN, J. M. (1982): Are you Over Advertising?, Journal of Advertising Research, 22, 4 (August/September)

AAKER, D. A., STAYMAN, D. M. & HAGERTY, M. R. (1986): Warmth in Advertising: Measurement, Impact and Sequence Effects, Journal of Consumer Research, 12, pp. 365-381, March 1986

AAKER, J. L. & LEE, A. Y. (2001): "I" Seek Pleasures and "We" Avoid Pains: The Role of Self-Regulatory Goals in Information Processing and Persuasion, Journal of Consumer Research, Vol. 28, June

AAKER, J. L. (2000): Accessibility or Diagnosticity? Disentangling the Influence of Culture on Persuasion Processes and Attitudes, 26 (March)

ABEELE, P. V. & MACLACHLAN, D. L. (1994): Process Tracing of Emotional Responses to TV Ads: Revisiting the Warmth Monitor, The Journal of Consumer Research, Vol. 20, No. 4, Mar.

ABRAHAM, M. & LODISH, L. (1999): A Study of Advertising Effectiveness and the Resulting Strategic and Tactical Implications, In: Advertising Works, Information Resources, Inc.

ACKOFF, R. L. & EMSHOFF, J. R. (1975): Advertising at Anheuser-Busch, Inc. (1963-68), Sloan Management Review, 16, 2 (Winter), 1-16

ADAVAL, R. (2003): How Good Gets Better and Bad Gets Worse: Understanding the Impact of Affect on Evaluations of Known Brands, Journal of Consumer Research, Vol. 30, No. 3, Dec.

ADDISON, T. (2005): More science: more sense, or nonsense?, Admap, May

AGRES, S. J., EDELL, J. A. & DUBITSKY, T. M. (1990): Emotion in Advertising – Theoretical and Practical Explorations, Quorum Books, New York

AJZEN, I. & FISHBEIN, M. (1977): Attitude-Behaviour Relations: A Theoretical Analysis and Review of Empirical Research, Psychological Bulletin, Vol. 84, No. 5, pp. 889-918, September 1977

AJZEN, I. (1991): The theory of planned behavior, Organizational Behavior and Human Decision Processes, 50, pp. 179-211

ALBA, J. W. & HUTCHINSON (1987): Dimensions of Consumer Expertise, 13, (March) 411-454

ALLEN, C. T., MACHLEIT, K. A. & KLEINE, S. S. (1992): A Comparison of Attitudes and Emotions as Predictors of Behavior at Diverse Levels of Behavioral Experience, Journal of Consumer Research, 18, pp. 493-504, March 1992

AMBACH, G. (2005): Inside the black box: Understanding what should go in and come out of econometric models, In: Proceedings from The 2005 European Advertising Effectiveness Symposium, Budapest, June

AMBLER, T. (2000): Persuasion, Pride and Prejudice: How Ads Work, International Journal of Advertising 19

ANDERSEN, L. P. (2004): The Rhetorical Strategies of Danish TV Advertising, Copenhagen Business School

ANDERSEN, O. E. (2006): Product Placement, Research Paper No. 1, Center for Marketing Communication, Copenhagen Business School, Copenhagen

ANDERSON, L., & SHIMAMURA, A. P. (2005): Influences of emotion on context memory while viewing film clips, American Journal of Psychology, Fall, 188(3), 323-37

ANDERSON, S. J., GLANTZ, S. A., LING, P. M. (2005): Emotions for sale: cigarette advertising and women's psychosocial needs, Tobacco Control, Apr., 14(2), pp. 127-35

ANDREASEN, A. R. (1965): Attitudes and Customer Behavior - A Decision Model, in: PRESTON, L. (Ed) New Research in Marketing, University of California at Berkeley, Institute of Business and Economic Research.

APPEL, V., S. WEINSTEIN & C. WEINSTEIN (1979): Brain Activity and Recall of TV-Advertising, Journal of Advertising Research, Vol. 19, pp. 7-15.

ARS (2005): Superior Performance of Ads in the HeartZone and MindZone Regions, Unpublished manuscript, RSC the quality measurement company.

ASHTON, R. H. (1980): Sensitivity of Multi-Attribute Decision Models to Alternative Specifications of Weighting Parameters, Journal of Business Research, Vol. 8, No. 3, pp. 341-60, September 1980

ASSMUS, G., FARLEY, J. U. & LEHMANN, D. R. (1984): How Advertising Affects Sales: Meta-Analysis of Econometric Results, Journal of Marketing Research, 21 (February), 65-74

AXELROD, J. N. (1966): Attitude Measures That Predict Purchase, Journal of Advertising Research, pp. 3-12.

AYELSWORTH, A. B. & MACKENZIE, S. B. (1998): Context is Key: The Effect of Program-Induced Mood on Thoughts about the Ad, Journal of Advertising, 27 (2), 17-27.

BACHE, E. & F. HANSEN (1975): A Pretest Procedure which Works - Pre-testing and Post-testing and Informational Campaign. In Proceedings from ESOMAR annual Conference, Amsterdam.

BAGOZZI, R. P. (1986): Attitude Formation under the Theory of Reasoned Action and a Purposeful Behavior Reformulation, British Journal of Social Psychology, 25, pp. 95-107

BAGOZZI, R. P., BAUMGARTNER, H. & YI, Y. (1992): State versus Action Orientation and the Theory of Reasoned Action: An Application to Coupon Usage, Journal of Consumer Research, Vol. 18, No. 4, Mar.

BAGOZZI, R. P., GOPINATH, M. & NYER, P. U. (1999): The Role of Emotions in Marketing, Journal of the Academy of Marketing Science, Vol. 27, No. 2, pp. 184-206, 1999

BARFOD, B. (1964): On Optimal Advertising, National Økonomisk Tidsskrift

BARONE, M. J, MINIARD, P. W & ROMEO, J. B (2000): The Influence of Positive Mood on Brand Extension Evaluations, Journal of Consumer Research, Vol. 26, No. 4, Mar.

BARRY, T. E. & Howard, D. J (1990): A review and critique of the hierarchy of effects in advertising, International Journal of Advertising, Vol. 9, No. 2

BATRA, R. & AHTOLA, O. T. (1990): Measuring the Hedonic and Utilitarian Sources of Consumer Attitudes, Marketing Letter 2 (2), pp. 159-170, 1990

BATRA, R. & RAY, M. L. (1986a): Affective Responses Mediating Acceptance of Advertising, Journal of Consumer Research, Vol. 13, Sep., pp. 234-249.

BATRA, R. & RAY, M. L. (1986b): Situational Effects of Advertising Repetition: The Moderating Influence of Motivation, Ability, and Opportunity to Respond, Journal of Consumer Research, 12 (March)

BATRA, R. & STAYMAN, D. M. (1990): The Role of Mood in Advertising Effectiveness, Journal of Consumer Research 17, pp203-214, September 1990

BAUMEISTER, R. F. (2002): Yielding to Temptation: Self-Control Failure, Impulsive Purchasing, and Consumer Behavior, Journal of Consumer Research, Vol. 28, No. 4, March

BAUMGARTNER, T., ESSLEN, M, & JANCKE, L (2005): From emotion perception to emotion experience: Emotions evoked by pictures and classical music, International Journal of Psychophysiology, Jul 1

BEARDEN, W. O. & WOODSIDE, A. G. (1977): Situational Influence on Consumer Purchase Intentions, in: WOODSIDE, A. G., SHETH, J. N. & BENNETT, P. D. (eds.) (1977): Consumer and Industrial Buying Behaviour, pp. 167-78, New York: North-Holland, 1977

BEAUMONT, L. (2003): Effective Frequency – Does One Size Fit All?, ASI. Communication Effectiveness Symposium, Frankfurt

BEAVER, J. D., MOGG, K., & BRADLEY, B. P. (2005): Emotional conditioning to masked stimuli and modulation of visuospatial attention, Emotion, Mar, 5(1), pp. 67-79

BECHARA, A. & DAMASIO, A. R. (2005): The Somatic Marker Hypothesis: A neural theory of economic decision making, Games and Economic Behavior, Vol. 52, Issue 2, August, pp. 336-372

BECHARA, A. (2003): Decisions, Uncertainty, and the Brain: The Science of Neuroeconomics, Journal of Clinical and Experimental Neuropsychology, Vol. 25/7), pp. 1035-

BECKMANN, S. C. & KILBOURNE, W. E. (1998): Review and critical assessment of research on marketing and the environment, Journal of Marketing Management, vol. 14, no. 6, pp 513-532

BELCH, G. E. & BELCH, M. A. (2004): Advertising and Promotion – An Integrated Marketing Communications Perspective, McGraw Hill

BELK, R. W, WALLENDORF, M. & SHERRY, J. F. JR. (1989): The Sacred and the Profane in Consumer Behavior: Theodicy on the Odyssey, Journal of Consumer Research, 16, pp. 1-38, June 1989

BELK, R. W. & POLLAY, R. W. (1985): Images of Ourselves: The Good Life in Twentieth Century Advertising, Journal of Consumer Research, Vol. 11, No. 4, pp. 887-97, March 1985

BELK, R. W. (1988): Possessions and the Extended Self, Journal of Consumer Research, Vol. 15, Sep., pp. 139-168.

BELK, R. W., SHERRY, J. F. JR. & WALLENDORF, M. (1988): A Naturalistic Inquiry into Buyer and Seller Behavior at a Swap Meet, Journal of Consumer Research, 14, pp. 449-470, March 1988

BENTLER, P. M. (1969): Semantic Space is (approximately) Bipolar, Journal of Psychology, 71, 33—40

BERLO, D., LEMERT, J. B. & MERTZ, R. J. (1969): Dimensions of Evaluating the Acceptability of Message Sources, Public Opinion Quarterly 33, pp. 563-76

BERLYNE, D. E. (1960): Conflict, Arousal and Curiosity, McGraw-Hill, New York

BERMPHOL, F., PASCUAL-LEONE, A., AMEDI, A, MERABET, L. B., FREGNI, F., GAAB, N., ALSOP, D., SCHLAUG, G. & NORTHOFF, G. (2005): Attentional modulation of emotional stimulus processing: An fMRI study using emotional expectancy, Human Brain Mapping, Nov. 29

BETTMAN, J. R & PARK, C. W. (1980): Implications of a Constructive View of Choice for Analysis of Protocol Data: A Coding Scheme for Elements of Choice Processes, Advances in Consumer Research, Vol. 7, pp. 148-53, 1980

BETTMAN, J. R. (1979): An Information Processing Theory of Consumer Choice, Addison-Wesley Publishing Company, Boston

BETTMAN, J. R., LUCE, M. F. & PAYNE, J. W. (1998): Constructive Consumer Choice Processes, Journal of Consumer Research, 25, pp. 187-217, December 1998

BIRCH, K. (2003): Analysing Effects of Advertising Using Conditional Logistic Regression, In: Branding and Advertising, CBS Press

BIRCH, K., OLSEN, J. K. & TJUR, TUE (2005): Regression Models for Market-Shares, Preprint No 1/2005, Center for Statistics, Copenhagen Business School

BITHER, S. W. & WRIGHT, P. (1977): Preferences Between Product Consultants: Choices vs. Preference Functions, Journal of Consumer Research, Vol. 4, No. 1, pp. 39-47, June 1977

BLACKBURN, J. D., CARTER, L. E. & CLANCY, K. J (1984): LITMUS II: A New Model to Help Optimize Marketing Plan for New Products and Service. In Proceedings of ESOMAR Seminar on Are Interviewers Obsolete? Drastic Changes in Data Collection and Data Presentation, November, Amsterdam: ESOMAR (European Society for Opinion and Marketing Research).

BLAIR, M. H. (2000): An Empirical Investigation of Advertising Wearin and Wearout, Journal of Advertising Research, (November/December), pp.95-100

BOURTCHOULADZE, R (2000): Memories are made of this, The biological building blocks of memory, Columbia University Press.

BRAEUTIGAM, S. (2005): Neuroeconomics-From neural systems to economic behaviour, Brain Research Bulletin, Nov, Vol. 67, Issue 5

BRAUN, K. A. (1999): Postexperience Advertising Effects on Consumer Memory, Journal of Consumer Research, 25 (March)

BREMS, H. (1951): Product Equilibrium under Monopolistic Competition, Cambridge Mass.: Harvard University Press, p. 116

BRISOUX, J. E. & LAROCHE, M. (1980): Evoked Set Formation and Composition: An Empirical Investigation under a Routinized Response Behaviour Situation, Advances in Consumer Research, Vol. 8, pp. 357-61, 1980

BROADBENT, S. (1979): One Way TV Advertisements Work. Journal of the Market Research Society, Vol. 21, No. 3, pp. 139-166.

BROADBENT, S. (1984): Modeling with adstock, Journal of the Market Research Society, Vol. 26, pp. 295-312.

BROADBENT, S. (1989): The Advertising Budget – The Advertiser's Guide to Budget Determination, NTC Publications Ltd., London

BROADBENT, S. (1999): When to Advertise, Admap Publications, Henley-on-Thames

BROADBENT, S., SPITTLER, J. Z. & LYNCH, K. (1997): Building Better TV Schedules: New Light from the Single Source, Journal of Advertising Research, Vol. 37, 4, July-August.

BROADBENT, T. (1998): Review of Advertising Research Directions, Campaign, 24 July, p.18

BROWN, G. H. A. (1989): Findings from Ad Tracking, Esomar Conference Proceedings.

BROWN, S. P. & STAYMAN, D. M. (1992): Antecedents and Consequences of Attitude Toward the Ad: A Meta-Analysis, Journal of Consumer Research, Vol. 19, 1, pp. 34-51.

BRUNER, G. II & HENSEL, P. J. (1992): Handbook of Marketing Scales: A Compilation of Multi-Item Measures, Vol. 1, Mason, OH: Southwestern Publishing

BUCK, S. (2001): Advertising and the Long-term Success of the Premium Brand, World Advertising Research Center

BURKE, M. C. & EDELL, J. A. I (1989): The Impact of Feelings on Ad-Based Affect and Cognition, Journal of Marketing Research, 1 (February), 69-83.

CACIOPPO, J. T., BUSH, L. K, & TASSINARY, L. G. (1992): Micro-expressive facial actions as a function of affective stimuli: Replication and extension, Personality and Social Psychology Bulletin, 18, pp. 515-526

CAMERER, C. F., LOEWENSTEIN, G., & PRELEC, D. (2004): Neuroeconomics: Why Economics Needs Brains, Scandinavian Journal of Economics, Vol. 106, Issue 3, pp. 555-579

CAMERER, C. F., LOEWENSTEIN, G., & PRELEC, D. (2005): Neuroeconomics: How Neuroscience Can Inform Economics, Journal of Economic Literature, March, Vol. 43, Issue 1, pp. 9-64

CAMPBELL, M. C. & KIRMANI, A. (2000): Consumers' Use of Persuasion Knowledge: The Effects of Accessibility and Cognitive Capacity on Perceptions of an Influence Agent, Journal of Consumer Research, 27 (June)

CAMPHORN, M. F. (1996): Where does Your Ad Work, Journal of the Market Research Society, vol. 38, no. 1.

CARMONE, F. J. & GREEN, P. E. (1981): Model Misspecification in Multi-Attribute Parameter Estimation, Journal of Marketing Research, Vol. XVIII, pp. 87-93, February 1981

CAROLL, J. (2005): 10 principles for marketing in the age of engagement, Admap, February

CELUCH, K. G. & SLAMA, M. (1993): Program Content and Advertising Effectiveness: A Test of the Congruity Hypothesis for Cognitive and Affective Sources of Involvement, Psychology & Marketing, 10, pp 28-299, 1993

CHANDY, R., TELLIS, G. J., MACINNIS, D. & THAIVANICH, P. (2001): What to Say When: Advertising Appeals in Evolving Markets, Journal of Marketing Research, 38, 4 (November), 399-414

CHANG, M. K. (1998): Predicting unethical behavior: a comparison of the theory of reasoned action and the theory of planned behavior, Journal of Business Ethics, 17, pp. 1825-1834

CHARLTON-JONES, J. (2005): Capturing emotions in advertising and benefiting from the knowledge, Proceeding from The 2005 European Advertising Effectiveness Symposium, Budapest, June

CHEN, K. M, LAKSHMINARAYANAN, V & SANTOS, L. (2005): The Evolution of Our Preferences: Evidence from Capuchin-Monkey Trading Behavior, Cowles Foundation, Yale University

CHESNEY, M. A., DARBES, L. A., HOERSTER, K, TAYLOR, J. M., CHAMBERS, D. B, & ANDERSON, D. E. (2005): Positive emotions: exploring the other hemisphere in behavioral medicine, International Journal of Behavioral Medicine, 12(2), pp. 50-8

CHRISTENSEN, L. B., SCHNOOR, P. & HANSEN, F. (2005): NERS Determined by Corporate Identity Perceptions, Research Paper, Center for Marketing, Copenhagen Business School

CHRISTENSEN, S. R. (2006): Measuring Consumer Reactions to Sponsoring Partnerships Based upon Emotional and Attitudinal Responses, International Journal of Market Research, Vol. 48, Issue 1, pp. 1 -20

CHURCH, N. J., LAROCHE, M. & ROSENBLATT, J. A. (1985): Consumer Brand Categorization for Durables with Limited Problem Solving: An Empirical Test and Proposed Extension of the Brisoux-Larouche Model, Journal of Economic Psychology, Vol. 6, pp. 231-53, 1985

CLARK, L. H. (ed.) (1955): Consumer Behaviour, Vol. II, New York City, University Press

CLARKE, D. G. (1976): Econometric Measurement of the Duration of Advertising Effects on Sales, Journal of Marketing Research, 13 (November), pp. 345-57

COHEN, J. B. & ARENI, C. S. (1991): Affect and Consumer Behavior, In: Handbook of Consumer Behavior (eds.) ROBERTSON, T. S. & KASSARJIAN, H. H, Englewood Cliffs, NJ, Prentice Hall, pp. 188-240

COLLEY, R. H. (1961): Defining Advertising Goals for Measured Advertising Results, New York: Association of National Advertisers.

COPAGE, A. (1998): Pre-testing for Other Media, Admap, The Advertising Association, January, Church House Conference Centre, London.

COTE, J. A., MCCULLOUGH, J., REILLY, M. (1985): Effects of Unexpected Situations on Behavior-Intention Differences: A Garbology Analysis, Journal of Consumer Research, 12, pp. 188-194, September 1985

COY, P. (2005): Why Logic Often Takes a Backseat, Business Week, Issue 3926, pp. 94-95

CROONE, P. & HORSFALL, J. (1983): Advertising: Key to the Success of Kellogg's Super Noodles, In Advertising Works 2. Papers from the IPA Advertising Effectiveness Awards. Edited by S. Broadbent. London: Holt Rinehaart and Winston, pp. 83-102.

CURRY, D. J & MENASCO, M. B. (1983): On the Separability of Weights and Brand Issues and Empirical Results, Journal of Consumer Research, Vol. 10, No. 1, pp. 83-95, June 1983

CYERT, R. M & MARCH, J. G. (1963): A Behavioral Theory of the Firm, Englewood-Cliffs, New Jersey, Prentience Hall, Inc.

DAEYEOL, L. (2005): Neuroeconomics: making risky choices in the brain, Nature Neuroscience, Sep., Vol. 8, Issue 9, pp. 1129-1130

DAMASIO, A. (1994): Descarte's Error: Emotion, reason, and the human brain, Grosset/Putnam, New York

DAMASIO, A. (2000): The feeling of what happens, Vintage

DAMASIO, A. (2003): Looking for Spinoza: Joy, Sorrow, and the Feeling Brain, Harcourt

DARWIN, C. (1872): The expression of the emotions in man and animals, London, John Murray

DARWIN, C. (1872, 1865): The expression of emotions in man and animals, University of Chicago Press, Chicago

DEIGHTON, J. HENDERSON, C. M & NESLIN, S. A. (1994): The Effects of Advertising on Brand Switching and Repeat Purchasing, Journal of Marketing Research, Vol. XXXI, February

DEIGHTON, J., ROMER, D. & MCQUEEN, J. (1989): Using Drama to Persuade. Journal of Consumer Research, Vol. 16, December.

DEKIMPE, M. G. & HANSSENS, D. M. (1995): The Persistence of Marketing Effects on Sales, Marketing Science, 14, 1-21

DEPPE, M., SCHWINDT, W., KUGEL, H., PLASSMANN, H. & KENNING, P (2005): Nonlinear Responses Within the Medial Prefrontal Cortex Reveal When Specific Implicit Information Influences Economic Decision Making, Journal of Neuroimaging, Vol. 15, pp. 171-182

DERBAIX, C. & BREE, J. (1997): The Impact of Children's Affective Reactions Elicited by Commercials on Attitudes Toward the Advertisement and the Brand, International Journal of Research in Marketing, Vol. 14, pp. 207-229.

DERBAIX, C. & BREE, J. (2002): The Impact of Children's Affective Reactions, in: HANSEN et al. (2002): Children – Consumption, Advertising and Media, Copenhagen Business School Press

DESMET, P. M. A. (2002): Designing Emotions, Technical University Delft

DESMET, P. M. A. (2003a): a Multilayered Model of Product Emotions, The Design Journal, 6(2)

DESMET, P. M. A. (2003b): Measuring Emotions, In: BLYTHE, M. A., MONK, A. F., OVERBEEKE, K. & WRIGHT, P. C. (EDS.): Funology: from usability to enjoyment, (pp. 111-123). Dordrecht: Kluwer Academic Publishers.

DETENBER, B. H., SIMONS, R. F. & BENNETT, G. G. Jr. (LINK): Roll'em!: The Effects of Picture Motion on Emotional Responses, www.udel.edu/psych/rsimons/rollem.htm

DHAR, R. & SHERMAN, S. J. (1996): The Effect of Common and Unique Features in Consumer Choice, 23 (December)

DICHTER, E. (1964): Handbook of Consumer Motivations, McGraw-Hill Book Company, New York.

DONOVAN, R. J., & ROSSITER, J. R. (1982): Store atmosphere: An environmental psychology approach, Journal of Retailing 58, pp. 34-57

DORFMAN, R. & STEINER, P.O. (1954): Optimal Advertising and Optimal Quality, American Economic Review, December, pp 826-836

DU PLESSIS, E. (1994a): Understanding and using likeability, Journal of Advertising Research, September/October

DU PLESSIS, E. (1994b): Recognition Versus Recall, Journal of Advertising Research, May/June.

DU PLESSIS, E. (2002): Low involvement Processing: Is it HIP Enough?, Admap, July

DU PLESSIS, E. (2005a): The Advertised Mind, Kogan Page

DU PLESSIS, E. (2005b): Advertisers' new insight into the brain, Admap, May

DUBÉ, L, CHATTOPADHYAY, A. & LETARTE, A. (1996): "Should Advertising Appeals Match the Basis of Consumers' Attitudes?" Journal of Advertising Research, 36(6), pp. 82-89

DUBÉ, L. & MORGAN, M. S. (1998): Trend effects and gender differences in retrospective judgements of consumption emotions, Journal of Consumer Research 23, pp. 156-162

DUBE, L., LEBEL, J. L. & LU, J. (2005): Affect asymmetry and comfort food consumption, Physiology and Behavior, Nov. 15, 86(4) pp. 559-67

DUBOW, J. S. (1994): Recall Revisited: Recall Redux, Journal of Advertising Research, May/June.

DUHACHEK, A. (2005): Coping: A Multidimensional, Hierarchical Framework of Responses to Stressful Consumption Episodes, Journal of Consumer Research, Vol 32, No. 1, June

DUNN, B. D., DALGLEISH, T., & LAWRENCE, A. D. (2005): The somatic marker hypothesis: A critical evaluation, Neuroscience and Biobehavioural Reviews, Sep 26

DYSON, P., FARR, A. & HOLLIS, N. S. (1996): Understanding, Measuring, and Using Brand Equity, Journal of Advertising Research, Vol. 36, No.6, pp.9-21.

EASTLACK, J. O. JR. & RAO, A. G. (1989): Advertising Experiments at the Campbell Soup Company, Marketing Science, 8 (Winter), 57-71

EDELL, J. A. & BURKE, M. C. (1987): The power of Feelings in Understanding Advertising Effects, Journal of Consumer Research, Vol. 14, Dec., pp. 421-433

EDWARDS, W. (1955): Personality Preference Schedule, Annual Review of Psychology, Vol. 2, Alto, California

EHRENBERG, A. & SCRIVEN, J. (1997): Added Values or Propensities to Buy, Admap, Jan., pp. 11-13, NTC Publications Ltd.

EHRENBERG, A. S. C. & BARNARD, N. R. (1994): Justifying our Advertising Budgets, AdMap, Jan., pp.11-13.

EHRENBERG, A., BARNARD, N. & SCRIVEN, J. (1997): Justifying our Advertising Budgets, the Weak and Strong Theories. JOAB Report No. 8, South Bank University, London.

EHRLICHMAN, H. & WEINBURGER, A. (1978): Lateral Eye-Movements and Hemispheric Asymmetry: A Critical Review, in Psychological Bulletin, Vol. 85, 5, pp. 1080-1101.

EKMAN, P. & DAVIDSON, R. J. (1994): The Nature of Emotion: Fundamental Questions, New York: Oxford University Press

EKMAN, P. (1980): Biological and cultural contributions to body and facial movement in the expression of emotions, in: RORTY, A. O.(Ed) Explaining Emotions, University of California Press, Berkeley

EKMAN, P. (1994): Moods, emotions, and traits. In: EKMAN, P & DAVIDSON (Eds.): The Nature of Emotion, fundamental questions (pp. 56-58). Oxford: Oxford University Press

ENGEL, J. F., KOLLAT, J. & BLACKWELL, R. D. (1971): Consumer Behavior, The Dryden Press Series in Marketing

EPHRON, E. (1998): The fog of battle – there are different methods of targeting TV campaigns, Admap, Vol. 33, No. 8, Issue 387, pp. 28-30

EREVELLES, S. (1998): The Role of Affect in Marketing, Journal of Business Research, 42, pp. 199-215, 1998

ERK, S., SPITZER, M. WUNDERLICH, A. P., GALLEY, L. & WALTER, H. (2002): Cultural objects modulate reward circuitry, NeuroReport, Vol. 13, No. 18, 20 December

ESCALAS, J. E. & STERN, B. B. (2003): Sympathy and Empathy: Emotional Responses to Advertising Dramas, Journal of Consumer Research, 29, pp. 566-578, March 2003

ESCH, F. –R., LANGNER, T., REDLER, J. (2005): In-Store Advertising: An Examination of the Impact of Emotion, Brand Strength, and Product Category in Display Promotion on Buying Behavior, EMAC Conference Proceedings (forthcoming)

ESSLEN, M. (2002): Human brain imaging of emotion and language using low resolution brain electromagnetic tomography, Zentralstelle der Studentenschaft, Zürich 2002

EVANS, F. B. (1959): Psychological and Objective Factors in the Prediction of Brand Choice: Ford versus Chevrolet, Journal of Business, Vol. 32, pp. 340-69, 1959

FASEUR, T. & GEUENS, M (2004): Different Positive Feelings Leading to Different Ad Evaluations: The Case of Cosiness, Excitement and Romance, Working paper 280, Ghent University, Belgium

FAZIO, R. H., POWELL, M. C. & WILLIAMS, C. J. (1989): The Role of Attitude Accessibility in the Attitude-to-Behavior Process, Journal of Consumer Research, 16, pp. 280-288, December 1989

FELDWICH, P. (1998): A Brief guided Tour through the Copy-Testing Jungle, Admap, The Advertising Association, January, Church House Conference Center, London.

FERBER, R. (1954): The Role of Planning in Consumer Purchases of Durable Goods, American Economic Review, Vol. 44, 1954, pp. 854-76

FERBER, R. (1967): Research on Household Behavior, In: Surveys in Economic Theory, Vol. III, The Royal Economic Society, New York: Macmillian

FESTINGER, L. (1957): A Theory of Cognitive Dissonance, Stanford, Calif., Stanford University Press

FIELDING, N. G. & LEE, R. M. (1991): Using Computers in Qualitative Research, London: Sage.

FISHBEIN, M. & AJZEN, I. (1975): Belief, Attitude, Intention and Behaviour, Reading, MA: Addison-Wesley, The Journal of Consumer Research.

FISHBEIN, M. & MIDDLESTADT, S. E. (1995): Noncognitive Effects on Attitude Formation and Change: Fact or Artefact? Journal of Consumer Psychology, Vol. 4, pp. 181-202.

FISHBEIN, M. & MIDDLESTADT, S. E. (1997): A Striking Lack of Evidence for Nonbelief-Based Attitude Formation and Change: A Response to Five Commentaries, Journal of Consumer Psychology, Vol. 6, 1, pp.107-116.

FISHBEIN, M. (1965): A Consideration of Beliefs, Attitudes and Their Relationships, in: STEINER, J. & FISHBEIN, M.(Eds) Current Studies in Social Psychology, Holt, Reinhart and Winston, New York

FOLKES, V. S. (1984): Consumer Reaction to Product Failure: An Attributional Approach, Journal of Consumer Research, 10 (4), 398-409.

FOOTE, N. N. (1961): Household Decision-Making – Consumer Behavior , Vol. IV, New York University Press

FOTHERGILL, J. E. & EHRENBERG, A. S. C. (1965): On the Schwerin Analysis of Advertising Effectiveness, Journal of Marketing Research, Vol. 2, August.

FRANZEN, G. & BOUWMAN, M. (2001): The Mental World of Brands, NTC Publications

FRANZEN, G. (1994): Advertising Effectiveness. Findings from Empirical Research. Henley-on-Thames, Oxfordshire, UK: NTC Publications Ltd.

FREEMAN, F. S. (1962): Theory and Practice of Psychological Testing, Holt, Rinehart and Winston, New York

FREUD, S. (1925): The unconscious. In Collected papers, London, Hogarth

FRIJDA, N. H (1988): The Laws of emotion, American Psychologist, 43 (5), pp. 349-358

FRIJDA, N. H. (1986): The Emotions, Cambridge, England: Cambridge University Press

FRIJDA, N. H. (1993): The Place of Appraisal in Emotion, Cognition and Emotion, Appraisal and Beyond: The Issue of Cognitive Determinants of Emotions, 7 (3/4), pp. 357-387. Hove: Lawrence Erlbaum Associates

FRIJDA, N. H. (1994): Varieties of affect: emotions and episodes, moods, and sentiments. In: EKMAN, P & DAVIDSON (Eds.): The Nature of Emotion, fundamental questions (pp. 59-67). Oxford: Oxford University Press

GABRIELSEN, G., KRISTENSEN, T. & HANSEN, F. (2000): Corporate design: a tool of testing, Corporate Communication, Vol. 5, No. 2, 2000, pp.113-118

GARDNER, M. P. (1985): Mood States and Consumer Behavior: A Critical Review, Journal of Consumer Research, 12 (December), 281-300.

GARG, N., INMAN, J. J. & MITTAL, V. (2005): Incidental and Task-Related Affect: A Re-Inquiry and Extension of the Influence of Affect on Choice, Journal of Consumer Research, Vol. 32, No. 1, June

GAZZANIGA, M. S. (1998): The Mind's Past, Berkeley, CA, University of California Press

GEE, P., COVENTRY, K. R., & BIRKENHEAD, D. (2005): Mood state and gambling: using mobile telephones to track emotions, British Journal of Psychology, Feb, 96(Pt 1), pp. 53-66

GIBSON, L. (1996): What Can One Exposure Do?, Journal of Advertising Research, March/April, 9-18

GIERL, H. R. & PRAXMARER, S. (2006): The Effects of Value Propositions in Advertising. Paper presented at the 5th International Conference on Research in Advertising, Bath, June

GLIMCHER, P. W. (2003): Decisions, uncertainty and the brain: The science of neuroeconomics, MIT Press, Cambridge, Mass.

GLIMCHER, P. W., DORRIS, M. C., & BAYER, H. M. (2005): Physiological utility theory and the neuroeconomics of choice, Games & Economic Behaviour, Aug., Vol. 52, Issue 2,

GOLDBERG, M. E. & GORN, G. J. (1987): Happy and Sad TV Programs: How they Affect Reactions to Commercials, Journal of Consumer Research, Vol. 14, Dec., pp. 387-403

GOLDIN, P. R., HUTCHERSON, C.A.C., OCHSNER, K. N., GLOVER, G. H., GABRIELI, J. D.E. & GROSS, J. J. (2005): The neural bases of amusement and sadness: A comparison of block contrast and subject-specific emotion intensity regression approaches, NeuroImage, 27, pp. 26-36

GOLDMAN, A. I. (1993): The Psychology of folk psychology, Behavioral and Brain Sciences 16, pp. 15-28

GOODE, A. (2001): The Value of Implicit Memory, Admap, Dec., 2001, Iss. 423

GOODSTEIN, R. C. (1993): Category-based Applications and Extensions in Advertising: Motivating More Extensive Ad Processing, Journal of Consumer Research, 20, pp. 87-99, June 1993

GOODYEAR, M. (1998): Qualitative research. In: MCDONALD, C. & VANGELDER, P (EDI.): ESOMAR Handbook of Market and Opinion Research, 4th Edition, 1998)

GRAYSON, K. & SHULMAN, D. (2000): Indexicality and the Verification Function of Irreplaceable Possessions: A Semiotic Analysis, Journal of Consumer Research, 27, pp. 17-30, June 2000

GRAYSON, K. & VEHILL, K. (1997): How Does Advertising Mean What it Does? The Impact of "Real Consumers" in Commercials, London Business School, Centre for Marketing Working Paper No. 97-501, February.

GREENBERG, A. & SUTTON, C. (1973): Television Commercial Wearout, Journal of Advertising Research, 13 (October), 47-54

GREENE, J. D., SOMMERVILLE, R. B., NYSTROM, L. E., DARLEY, J. M. & COHEN, J. D. (2001): An fMRI Investigation of Emotional Engagement in Moral Judgment. Science, Vol. 293, 14 September

GREENE, W. F. (1991): Hearts and/or Minds: What Drives Commercial Liking?, Eight Annual ARF Copy Research Workshop, The New York Hilton, Sep. 11.

GREENWALD, *M. K.,* COOK, E. W. & *LANG, P. J. (1989): Affective Judgment and Psychophysiological Response: Dimensional Covariation in the Evaluation of Pictorial Stimuli, Journal of Psychophysiology, 3(1), 51-64.*

GRØNHOLDT, L. & MARTENSEN, A. (2004): Validating and applying a customer-based brand equity model, Proceedings from the 33rd EMAC Conference, Mucia, Spain, May

GRØNHOLDT, L. (1996): Advertising Effect Modeling, A tool for Optimizing the Media Plan, from ESOMAR Seminar, Rome (Italy), November.

GULLEN, P. & JOHNSON, H. (1986): Relating Product Purchasing and TV Viewing, Journal of Advertising Research, Vol. 26, 6, pp. 9-19.

GULLEN, P. (1998): Art, Science or Dangerous Black Magic?, Admap, The Advertising Association, January, Church House Conference Centre, London

HAIR, J. F., ANDERSON, R. E., TATHAM, R. L. & BLACK, W. C. (1998): Multivariate data analysis, 5. ed., Prentice-Hall

HALEY, R. I. & BALDINGER, A. (1991): The ARF Copy Research Validity Project, Journal of Advertising Research, Vol. 31, No 2.

HALL, B. F. (2002): A New Model for Measuring Advertising Effectiveness, Journal of Advertising Research, March – April, 2002, pp.23-31

HANSEN, F. & CHRISTENSEN, L. B (2005): Share of Voice/Share of Market and Long Term Advertising Effects, Journal of International Advertising, Vol. 24, No. 3, pp. 297-320

HANSEN, F. & CHRISTENSEN, L. B. (2003): Long-term Advertising Effects and Optimal Budgeting, paper presented at "The 2003 ASI Conference", Frankfurt, Germany

HANSEN, F. & HALLING, J. (2002): Estimation of emotional and evaluating effects of sports sponsorships, published in proceedings from EMAC, Annual conference, Bergen, May 2001

HANSEN, F. & HANSEN, L. Y. (2001a): The Nature of Central and Peripheral Advertising Information Processing, Research Paper, Copenhagen Business School, Department of Marketing

HANSEN, F. & HANSEN, L. Y. (2001b): Advertising and promotion effectiveness – learnings from a five-year study. Department of Marketing, Research Paper No. 10, June 2001, presented at the ASI International Advertising Symposium, Copenhagen

HANSEN, F. & KOCK, C. (2003): Evaluation of Public Spokes Persons, Nordicom Review, 1

HANSEN, F. & OLSEN, J. K. (2001): "Separating Recall Effects and Short Term Sales Effects in Personal Interview Data on Self-reported Ad Recall and Purchases". The Marketing Institute, Copenhagen Business School.

HANSEN, F. (1972): Consumer Choice Behavior: A Cognitive Theory, The Free Press, New York

HANSEN, F. (1976): Psychological Theories of Consumer Choice, Journal of Consumer Research, Vol. 3. no. 1, 1976, pp.117-42

HANSEN, F. (1979): Measurement Problems in the Social Sciences – on Single and Multidimensional Scaling, Arnold Busck

HANSEN, F. (1981): Hemispheral Lateralization: Implications for Understanding Consumer Behaviour, Journal of Consumer Research, Vol. 8, no. 1, 1981, pp.23-27

HANSEN, F. (1984): Towards an Alternative Theory of the Advertising Communication Process?, International Journal of Research in Marketing, Vol. 1, no. 1, 1984, pp.69-80

HANSEN, F. (1987): Forbrugeradfærd og –beslutning, Nyt Nordisk Forlag Arnold Busck, Copenhagen

HANSEN, F. (1997): Quantifying Creative Contributions: Advertising Pre-testing's New Generation, In: ESOMAR Conference Proceedings, Edinburgh, September

HANSEN, F. (1998): "Advertising research: testing communication effects" in ESOMAR Handbook of Market and Opinion Research

HANSEN, F. (2000): Attitudinal measures of advertising effects, Proceedings from ACR, Asia-Pacific Conference, Queensland

HANSEN, F. (2005): Distinguishing between feelings and emotions in understanding communication effects, Journal of Business Research, 58, pp. 1426-1436

HANSEN, F., ARNAA, K., RANDRUP, R. & BECKMANN, S. C. (1998): Profiling media users: An operational instrument for the measurement of cultural values in a wide variety of cultures, In: Proceedings of the Worldwide Media Research Seminar and Exhibitor, Towards Total Communication Strategies: Is Media Research Keeping Pace with Change? Amsterdam and Mexico City

HANSEN, F., HALLING, J. & CHRISTENSEN, L. B. (2006c): Choosing Among Alternative Parties to be Sponsored for Supporting Brand Strategies, Based Upon Emotional Responses, Journal of Consumer Behaviour, Vol. 5, Issue 6

HANSEN, F., HANSEN, L. Y. & GRØNHOLDT, L. (2002a): Modeling Purchases as a Function of Advertising and Promotion, International Journal of Advertising, Vol 21, No. 1

HANSEN, F., HANSEN, L.Y. & GRØNHOLT, L. (2002b): STAS and Logit Modeling of Advertising and Promotion Effects. Research Paper, Center for Marketing Communication, Copenhagen Business School

HANSEN, F., OLSEN, J. K. & LUNDSTEEN, S. (2006a): The effects of print vs TV advertising, documented using short-term advertising strength (STAS) measures, International Journal of Advertising, Vol 25, No. 4

HANSEN, F., RASMUSSEN, A. & HALLING, J. (2001): Emotional responses to advertising sponsoring and design, Preceedings from ACR Berlin, June

HANSEN, L. & ANDERSEN, L. (1993): The Creativity Factor as an Important Variable in the Understanding of Campaign Effect, In: Proceedings 46th ESOMAR Marketing Research Congress, September, Copenhagen.

HANSEN, T. (2002): The Effect of Physical Surroundings in Usage Situations on Consumer Perception of Food Quality and on Consumer Emotions, Journal of International Consumer Marketing, Vol. 15(1), 2002, pp. 31-51

HANSEN, T., BRUUN-CHRISTENSEN, A. & SCHAUMAN, J. (2006b): Consumers' emotions, cognition and approach/avoidance behaviour in relation to scented food products, Procedings from the ESCP-EAP Conference, 2006

HANSEN, T., JENSEN, J. M. & SOLGAARD, H. S. (2004): Predicting online grocery buying intention: a comparison of the theory of reasoned action and the theory of planned behaviour, International Journal of Information Management, 24, 2004, pp. 539-550

HANSSENS, D. M. & PARSONS, L. J. (1993): Econometric and Time-Series Market Response Models. Chapter 9 in ELIASHBERG, J. & LILIEN, G. L. (eds.): Handbooks in Operations Research and Management Science, Vol. 5: Marketing. Amsterdam: North-Holland/Elsevier Science Publishers.

HARE, T. A., TOTTENHAM, N, DAVIDSON, M. C., GLOVER, G. H., & CASEY, B. J. (2005): Contributions of Amygdala and striatal activity in emotion regulation, Biological Psychiatry, Mar 15, 57(6), pp. 624-32

HAVERMANS, J. (2005): Online research gains ground, Research World, ESOMAR, April 2005

HAVLENA, W. J. & HOLBROOK, M. B. (1986): The Varieties of Consumption Experience: Comparing Two Typologies of Emotion in Consumer Behavior, Journal of Consumer Research, Vol 13, No 3

HAZLETT, R. L. & HAZLETT, S. Y. (1999): Emotional Response to Television Commercials: Facial EMG vs. Self-Report, Journal of Advertising Research, 35, March/April 1999, pp. 7-23

HEATH, R. (2001): The Hidden Power of Advertising, Admap Publications

HEATH, R. (2004): Measuring the hidden power of emotive advertising, Market research society conferences

HEATH, R. (2006): Emotional persuasion, Admap, July/August

HEIDER, F. (1958): The Psychology of Interpersonal Relations, New York, John Wiley and Sons, Inc.

HERR, P. M & PAGE, C. M. (2004): Asymmetric Association of Liking and Disliking Judgments: So What's Not to Like? Journal of Consumer Research, 30, pp. 588-601, March 2004

HESS, ECKARD. H. (1972): Pupillometrics: A Method of Studying Mental, Emotional and Sensory Processes, in GREENFIELD, N. S. & STERNBACH, R. A. (eds.): Handbook of Psychophysiology, New York: Holt, Rinehart and Winston.

HIRSCHMAN, E. C. (1990): Secular Immortality and the American Ideology of Affluence, Journal of Consumer Research, 17, pp. 31-42, June 1990

HIRSCHMAN, E. C. (1992): The Consciousness of Addiction: Toward a General Theory of Compulsive Consumption, Journal of Consumer Research, 19, pp. 155-179, September 1992

HOFMEYR, J. & RICE, B. (2000): Commitment-Led Marketing – The Key to Brand Profits is in the Customer's Mind, John Wiley & Sons, Ltd

HOLBROOK, M. B. & BATRA, R. (1987): Assessing the Role of Emotions as Mediators of Consumer Responses to Advertising, The Journal of Consumer Research, Vol. 14(3), Dec., pp. 404-420.

HOLBROOK, M. B. & HIRSCHMAN, E. C. (1982): The Experimental Aspects of Consumption: Consumer Fantasies, Feelings, and Fun, Journal of Consumer Research, Vol. 9, Sep., pp. 132-140

HOLLIS, N. (1992): The Link between TV Ad Awareness and Sales. New Evidence from Sales Response Modeling, Journal of the Marketing Research Society.

HOLLIS, N. (2005): Measuring the Power of Emotions, Proceeding from The 2005 European Advertising Effectiveness Symposium, Budapest, June

HOVLAND, C. I & JANIS, I. L. (eds.) (1959): Personality and persuasibility, by: JANIS, I. L., HOVLAND, C. I., FIELD, P. B., LINTON, H., GRAHAM, E., COHEN, A. R., RIFE, D., ABELSON, R. P., LESSER, G. S., KING, B. T., New Haven and London, Yale University Press

HOVLAND, C. I., JANIS, I. L., & KELLEY, H. H. (1953): Communication and Persuasion. New Haven: Yale University Press

HOWARD, D. J. & GENGLER, C. (2001): Emotional Contagion Effects on Product Attitudes, Journal of Consumer Research, 28, pp. 189-201, September 2001

HOWARD, J. A. & SHETH, J. N. (1969): A Theory of Buyer Behavior, John Wiley and Sons, New York

HUANG, G. T. (2005): The Economics of Brains, Technology Review, May, Vol. 108, Issue 5, pp. 74-76

HUANG, M.-H. (2001): The Theory of Emotions in Marketing, Journal of Business and Psychology, Vol. 16, Winter 2001

HÜBER, J. & PUTO, C. (1983): Market Boundaries and Product Choice: Illustrating Attraction and Substitution Effects, Journal of Consumer Research, Vol. 10, No. 1, pp. 31-44, June 1983

HULL, C. L. (1943): Principles of behaviour, New York, Appleton-Century-Crofts

INSKO, L. (1967): Theories of Attitude Change, Appleton-Century-Crofts, New York

IZARD, C. E. (1977): Human emotions, New York, Plenum Press

IZARD, C. E. (1992): Basic Emotions, Relations Among Emotions, and Emotion-Cognition Relations, Psychological Review, 99 (3), pp.561-65

JACOBY, J. (1977): Information Load and Decision Quality: Some Contested Issues, Journal of Marketing Research, Vol. XIV, pp.569-73, November 1977

JAGGER, S. (1998): The Pursuit of the Holy Grail, Admap, The Advertising Association, January, Church House Conference Centre, London.

JAMES, W. (1890): Principles of psychology, New York, Holt

JAMES, W. (1894): The physical basis of emotions, Psychology Review, 1, 516-529

JANISZEWSKI, C. & MEYVIS (2001): Effects of Brand Logo Complexity, Repetition, and Spacing on Processing Fluency and Judgment, 28 (June)

JANISZEWSKI, C. (1988): Preconscious Processing Effects: The Independence of Attitude Formation and Conscious Thought, Journal of Consumer Research, 15, pp. 199-209, 1988

JANISZEWSKI, C. (1990): The Influence of Print Advertisement Organization on Affect toward a Brand Name, Journal of Consumer Research, 17, pp. 53-65, 1990

JANISZEWSKI, C. (1993): Preattentive Mere Exposure Effects, Journal of Consumer Research, Vol. 20, No. 3, Dec.

JAYNES, J. (1976): The Origin of Consciousness in the Breakdown of the Bicameral Mind, Princeton University

JEDIDI, K., MELA, C. F. & GUPTA, S. (1999) : Managing Advertising and Promotion for Long-Run Profitability, Marketing Science, 18, 1, 1-22

JOHN, D. R. (1999): Consumer socialization of children: A retrospective look at twenty-five years of research, Journal of Consumer Research, 26, pp. 183-216.

JOHNSON, A. R. & STEWART, D. W. (2004): A Re-Appraisal of the Role of Emotion in Consumer Behavior: Traditional and Contemporary Approaches, Review of Marketing Research, 1, Armonk, N.Y.: M.E. Sharpe, Inc., pp. 1-33

JOHNSON, E. J. & MEYER, J. A. (1984): Compensatory Choice Models of Non-Compensatory Processes: The Effect of Varying Context, Journal of Consumer Research, Vol. 11, No. 1, pp. 528-41, June 1984

JONES, J. P. & BLAIR, M. H. (1996): Examining "Conventional Wisdoms" about Advertising Effects with Evidence from Independent Sources. Journal of Advertising Research, Vol. 36, No. 6, November-December.

JONES, J. P. (1990): Ad Spending: Maintaining Market Share. Harvard Business Review, Jan-Feb 1990, pp 38-42

JONES, J. P. (1995): When Ads Work: New Proof that Advertising Triggers Sales. New York: Lexington Books/The Free Press.

JONES, J. P. (1997): What Does Effective Frequency Mean in 1997? Journal of Advertising Research, Vol. 37, No. 4, July-August.

JONES, J. P. (1998): Pre-testing - the Agony of Misconceptions, Admap, NTC Publications Ltd. January.

JONES, J. P. (2003): Advertising Works - the Last Secret, Prentice-Hall

JUSTER, F. T. (1964): Anticipations and Purchases: An Analysis of Consumer Behavior, Princeton, N.J.: Princeton University Press

KAHN, B. E. & ISEN, A. M. (1983): The Influence of Positive Affect on Variety-Seeking Behavior Among Safe, Enjoyable Products, Journal of Consumer Research 19, pp. 257-270

KAHNEMAN, D & TVERSKY, A. (1984): Choices, values and frames, American Psychologist 39 (4), pp. 341-350

KAHNEMAN, D. (1994): New Challenges to the Rationality Assumption, in: KAHNEMAN, D & TVERSKY, A. (eds.) Choices, values and frames, Cambridge University Press, New York, pp. 758-774

KAHNEMAN, D. (2002): Maps of Bounded Rationality: A Perspective on Inuitive Judgment and Choice, Nobel Prize Lecture, Stockholm

KAMP, E. & MACINNIS. D. J. (1995): Characteristics of portrayed emotions in commercials: When does what is shown in ads affect viewers?, Journal of Advertising Research, 35(6), pp. 19-28.

KASSARJIAN, H. H. & KASSARJIAN, W. M. (1979): Attitudes under Low Commitment Conditions, in: MALONEY, J.C. & SILVERMAN, B. (eds.) (1979): Attitude Research Plays for High Stakes, Chicago.

KATONA, G. & MUELLER, E. (1964): Consumer Expectations, 1953-63, Ann Arbor, Michigan: Institute for Social Research

KATONA, G. (1955): The Predictive Value of Consumer Attitudes, In: L. H. Clark (ed.): Consumer Behavior, Vol. 2. New York: New York University Press, 1955

KATZ, E. & LAZARSFELD, P. F. (1955): Personal Influence. The Part Played by People in the Flow of Mass Communications, New York, Free Press

KEITZ, B. VON (1988): Eye Movement Research: Do Consumers Use the Information They are Offered? European Research, Vol. 16, No. 4.

KELLER, K. L (1993): Conceptualizing, measuring, and managing customer-based brand equity, In: Journal of Marketing, Vol. 57, pp. 1-22

KELLER, K. L. (2003): Strategic Brand Management. Building, Measuring and Managing Brand Equity, International Edition, Prentice Hall

KELLER, P. A., LIPKUS, I. M. & RIMER, B. K. (2002): Depressive Realism and Health Risk Accuracy: The Negative Consequences of Positive Mood, Journal of Consumer Research, Vol. 29, No. 1, June

KELLER, P. A., LIPPUS, I. M, & K. RIMER, B. K. (2003): Affect, Framing, and Persuasion, Journal of Marketing Research, 40 (February), 54-65.

KENNING, P., PLASSMANN, H. (2005): Neuroeconomics: An Overview From An Economic Perspective, Brain Research Bulletin, 67, pp. 343-354

KIRMANI, A. (1997): Advertising Repetition as a Signal of Quality: If It's Advertised So Much, Something Must Be Wrong, Journal of Advertising, 26, 3 (Fall), 77-86

KITCHEN, P. J. & SPICKETT-JONES, G. (2003): Information Processing: A critical literature review and future research directions, International Journal of Market Research, Vol. 45, Quarter 1, 2003, pp. 73-96

KJÆR-HANSEN, M. (1960): Salgets driftsøkonomi, Einar Harcks Forlag, København

KOPONEN, A. (1960): Personality Characteristics of Purchasers, Journal of American Research, Vol. I, No. 3, 1960, pp. 6-12

KOTLER, P. (1980): Principles of Marketing, Prentice- Hall, Inc., Englewood Cliffs

KOYCK, L. M. (1954): Distributed Lags and Investment Analysis. Amsterdam: North-Holland Publishing Company.

KRISTENSEN, T., GABRIELSEN, G., HANSEN, F. & HALLING, J. (2000c): Developing a Tool for Testing, Diagnosing and Providing Creative Input for Corporate Communication, Advertising research group. Research paper, nr.7, Copenhagen Business School

KRISTENSEN, T., HANSEN, F. & GABRIELSEN, G. (2000b): Design Testing: A Competitive Tool for Designers and Management, New Product Development & Innovation Management, Dec./Jan. 2000

KRISTENSEN, T., HANSEN, F., GABRIELSEN, G. & HALLING, J. (2000c): The Meaning of Colours in Design, Advertising research group. Proceedings from International Association for Research in Economic Psychology, Vienna, July

KROEBER-RIEL W. (1975): Konsumentverhalten, Verlag Franz Vahlen, München

KROEBER-RIEL, W. (1979): Activation Research: Psychobiological Approaches in Consumer Research, Journal of Consumer Research, 5, March, pp. 240-250

KROEBER-RIEL, W. (1987): Analysis of 'Non-Cognitive' Behavior Especially by Non-Verbal Measurement, Institut für Kon..... und Verhaltensforschung, Universität des Saarlandes.

KROEBER-RIEL, W. (1993): Bildkommunikation (Pictorial Communication), Vahlen, Munich, English summary provided by LANGNER, T., Justus-Liebig-University, Giessen, Aug, 2001

KRUGMAN, H. (1977): Memory without Recall, Exposure without Perception, Journal of Advertising Research, Vol. 17, No. 4 pp.7-12

KRUGMAN, H. E. (1971): Brain wave measures of media involvement, Journal of Advertising Reseach, Volume 11, Number 1, February

KUBOVY, M. (1999): On the Pleasures of the Mind. In KAHNEMAN, D., DIENER, E & SCHWARZ, N. (Eds.): Well-being: The Foundations of Hedonic Psychology, New York, Russell Sage Foundation, 1999

KUIJTEN, A. & FOEKEMA, H. (2005): Emotions in Politics – International politicians from another point of view, presentation material from TNS-NIPO, The Netherlands

KUMAR, A. & KRISHMAN, S. (2004): Memory Interference in Advertising: A Replication and Extension, Journal of Consumer Research, 30, pp. 602-611, March 2004

LA BARBERA, J. & TUCCIARONE, J. (1995): GRR Reconsidered, Journal of Advertising Research, Vol. 35, No. 5, pp. 33-53.

LAIRD, J. D. (1974): Self-Attribution of Emotion: The Effects of Expressive Behavior on the Quality of Emotional Experience, Journal of Personality and Social Psychology, 29, 475-486.

LANCASTER, K. (1971): Consumer Demand – A New Approach, New York, Columbia University Press

LANG, P. J. (1985): The Cognitive Psychophysiology of Emotion: Anxiety and the Anxiety Disorders, Hillsdale, NJ: Lawrence Erlbaum

LANG, P. J. (1995): The Emotion Probe – Studies of Motivation and Attention, American Psychologist, May

LANG, P. J., GREENWALD, M. K., BRADLEY, M. M., & HAMM, A. O. (1993): Looking at Pictures: Affective, facial, visceral and behavioural reactions, Psychophysiology, 30, pp. 261-273

LAROCHE, M., BLIEMEL, F. & RANSOM, R. K. (1985): The Economic Impact of Price-Quality Evaluations on Brand Categorization: An Examination of the Microcomputer Market, Journal of Economic Psychology, Vol. 5, 1985

LAROS, F. J. M., STEENKAMP, J-B E. M. (2005): Emotions in consumer behavior: a hierarchical approach, Journal of Business Research, 58, pp. 1437-1445

LARSEN, J. T., MCGRAW A. P. & CACIOPPO, J. T. (2001): Can People Feel Happy and Sad at the Same Time?, Journal of Personality and Social Psychology, October 2001, Vol. 81, No. 4, pp 684-696

LARSEN, R. J. & DIENER, E. (1987): Emotional Response Intensity as an Individual Difference Measure, Journal of Research in Personality, 21, pp. 1-39

LASSEN, N. A., INGVAR, D. H. & SKINHØJ, E. (1978): Brain Function and Blood Flow, Scientific American, October.

LAURENT, G. & KAPFERER, J. -N. (1989): Thresholds in Brand Awareness, Developments in Advertising and Communication Research, ESOMAR.

LAYBOURNE, P. & LEWIS, D. (2005): Neuromarketing: the future of consumer research?, Admap, May

LAZARUS, R. S. (1982): Thoughts on the Relations beyond Emotion and Cognition, American Psychologist, 37 (9), pp. 1019-1024, 1982

LAZARUS, R. S. (1991): Emotion and Adaptation, Oxford: Oxford University Press

LAZARUS, R. S. (1999): Stress and Emotion: A New Synthesis, New York, NY: Springer Publisher Co.

LAZARUS, R. S., KANNER, A. D. & FOLKMAN, S. (1980): Emotions: A Cognitive-Phenomenological Analysis, In: Emotion: Theory, Research and Experience, eds. PLUTCHIK, R & KELLERMAN, H., New York, Academic Press, pp 189-217

LEDOUX, J. (1998): The Emotional Brain, Phoenix

LEDOUX, J. (2002): Synaptic Self: How Our Brains Become Who We Are, Viking, New York

LEDOUX, J. E. (2000): Emotion Circuits in the Brain, Annual Review of Neuroscience, 23, pp. 155-184

LEE, A. Y. & STERNTHAL, B. (1999): The Effects of Positive Mood on Memory, Journal of Consumer Research, Vol. 26, No. 2, Sep.

LEE, D. (2005): Neuroeconomics: making risky choices in the brain, Nature Neuroscience, Sep, Vol. 8, Issue 9, pp. 1129-1130

LILIEN, G. L., KOTLER, P. & MOORTHY, K. S. (1992): Marketing Models. Englewood Cliffs, New Jersey: Prentice-Hall.

LIPSTEIN, B. (1985): An Historical Retrospective of Copy Research, Journal of Advertising Research, Vol. 24, No. 6.

LODISH, L., ABRAHAM, M., KALMENSON, S, LIVELSBERGER, J., LUBETKIN, B., RICHARDSON, B. & STEVENS, M. E. (1995): How T.V. Advertising Works: A Meta-Analysis of 389 Real World Split Cable T.V. Advertising Experiments, Journal of Marketing Research, Vol. XXXII (May 1995) pp. 135-139

LOEF, J, ANTONIDES, G. & RAAIJ, W. F. VAN. (2001): The effectiveness of advertising matching purchase motivation: An experimental test, Research paper, Erasmus University, The Netherlands

LOEWENSTEIN, G. (2000): Emotions in economic theory and economic behavior, Am. Econ. Rev. 90

LOEWENSTEIN, G., & SCHKADE, D. (1999): Wouldn't It Be Nice? Predicting Future Feelings, in: KAHNEMAN, D., DIENER, E., & SCHWARZ, N. (eds.): Well-being: The foundations of hedonic psychology, New York, Russell Sage Foundation Press, pp. 85-105

LUCE, M. F. (1998): Choosing to Avoid: Coping with Negatively Emotion-Laden Consumer Decisions, Journal of Consumer Research, Vol. 24, No. 4, March

LUNDSTEEN, S. & HANSEN, F. (2006): Tracking shifts in emotional responses to brands – a comparison of two studies, Proceedings from ICORIA 2006, Bath

LUTZ, R. J. (1977): An Experimental Investigation of Causal Relations Among Cognitions, Affect, and Behavioral Intention, Journal of Consumer Research, Vol. 3, No. 4, pp. 197-208, March 1977

LUTZ, R. J. (1985): Affective and Cognitive Antecedents of Attitude Toward the Ad: A Conceptual Framework, in: Psychological Processes and Advertising Effects, eds. ALWITT, L. F. & MITCHELL, A. A., Hillsdale, NJ: ERLBAUM, LAWRENCE, pp. 45-64

MACINNIS, D. & RAO, A. G. & WEISS, A. M. (2002): Assessing When Increased Media Weight Helps Sales of Real World Brands, Journal of Marketing Research, 39 (November), pp. 391-407

MACINNIS, D. J & PARK, C. W (1991): The Differential Role of Characteristics of Music on High- and Low-Involvement Consumers' Processing of Ads, Journal of Consumer Research, Vol. 18, No. 2, Sep

MADDEN, T. J., CALLEN, C. T. & TWIBLE, J. L. (1988): Attitude Toward the Ad: An Assessment of Diverse Measurement Indices Under Different Processing 'Sets'. Journal of Marketing Research, Vol. 25, No. 3, pp. 242-252.

MADSEN, B. O. (1964): Familiens Ökonomiske Livslöb, Copenhagen, Denmark: E. Harch's Forlag

MALJKOVIC, V. & MARTINI, P. (2005): Short-term memory for scenes with affective content, Journal of Vision, Mar. 18, 5(3), pp. 215-29

MAMMUCARI, A., CALTAGIRONE, C., EKMAN, P., FRIESEN, W., GAINOTTI, G., PIZZAMIGLIO, L., & ZOCCOLOTTI, P. (1988): Spontaneous facial expression of emotions in brain-damaged patients, Cortex, 24(4), Dec., pp. 521-533

MANDLER, G. (1982): "The Structure of Value: Accounting for Taste", in Affect and Cognition: The Seventeenth Annual Carnegie Symposium on Cognition, ed., Hillsdale, New Jersey: Lawrence Erlbaum, pp. 3-36

MANO, H. & OLIVER, R. L. (1993): Assessing the Dimensionality and Structure of the Consumption Experience: Evaluation, Feeling and Satisfaction, Journal of Consumer Research, Vol. 20, No. 3, Dec.

MANSTEAD, A. S. R., FRIJDA, N. & FISCHER, A. (2004): Feelings and Emotions – The Amsterdam Symposium, Cambridge University Press

MARECK, M. (2005): The battle for media measurement, Research World, ESOMAR, July/August

MARTENSEN, A. & GRØNHOLDT, L. (2002): From People to Profit: How Loyal Employees and Customers Improve the Bottom Line, In Proceedings from the 5th International Conference on Quality Management and Organisational Development, Busan

MARTENSEN, A., GRØNHOLDT, L. & HANSEN, F. (2001): A new approach to modeling the effect of advertising, Proceedings from EMAC 2001, Bergen

MAXWELL, J. S., SHACKMAN, A. J., DAVIDSON, R. J. (2005): Unattended facial expressions asymmetrically bias the concurrent proceeding of nonemotional information, Journal of Cognitive Neuroscience, Sep, 17(9), pp. 1386-95

MAZIS, M. B., AHTOLA, O. T. & KLIPPEL, R. E. (1975): A Comparison of Four Multi-Attribute Models in the Prediction of Consumer Attitude. Journal of Consumer Research, Vol. 2, June, 38-52.

MCCARTHY, E. (1968): Basic marketing: A managerial approach (3rd ed.), Homewood, IL, Irwin

MCCLURE, S. M., LI, J., TOMILIN, D., CYPERT, K. S., MONTAGUE, L. M. & MONTAGUE, P. R. (2004): Neural Correlates of Behavioral Preference for Culturally Familiar Drinks, Neuron, Vol. 44, October 14, pp. 379-387

MCDONALD, C. (1969): Relationships between Advertising Exposure and Purchasing Behaviour, Market Research Society Conference, pp. 67-98.

MCDONALD, C. (1971): What Is the Short-Term Effect of Advertising?, Marketing Science Institute Report, No. 71-142, Cambridge, MA: Marketing Science Institute

MCDONALD, C. (1995): Where to Look for the Most Trustworthy Evidence, Short-term Advertising Effects are the Key. Admap, The Advertising Association. January.

MCDONALD, C. (1996): How Frequently Should you Advertise, Admap, The Advertising Association, July/August.

MCDONALD, C. (1997a): From "Frequency" to "Continuity" - Is It a New Dawn?, Journal of Advertising Research, Vol. 37, No. 4, July-August.

MCDONALD, C. (1997b): How Advertising Works, A Review of Current Thinking. The Advertising Association in Association with NTC Publications Ltd., London.

MCGAUGH, J. L. (2003): Memory and emotion - The making of lasting memories, Columbia University Press, June

MCGUIRE, W. J. (1976): Psychological Factors Influencing Consumer Choice, in: FERBER, B. (Ed) Selected Aspects of Consumer Behavior

MCQUARRIE, E. F. & MICK, D. G. (1996): Figures of Rhetoric in Advertising Language, Journal of Consumer Research, Vol. 22, No. 4, March

MEDIA SCAN (2005): What are we waiting for?, ESOMAR Research World, Vol. 13, 7-8

MEHRABIAN, A & RUSSEL, J. A. (1974): An Approach to Environmental Psychology, Cambridge, Mass.: The MIT Press

MEHRABIAN, A. (1995): Framework for a comprehensive description and measurement of emotional states, Genetic, Social, and General Psychology Monographs, 121

MEHRABIAN, A. (1997): Comparisons of the PAD and PANAS as Models for Describing Emotions and for Differentiating Anxiety from Depression, Journal of Psychopathology and Behavioral Assessment, 19, 331-357.

MELA, C.F., GUPTA, S. & LEHMANN, D.R. (1997): The Long-Term Impact of Promotion and Advertising on Consumer Brand Choice, Journal of Marketing Research, vol. XXXIV, May, pp 248-261

MELOY, M. G. (2000): Mood-Driven Distortion of Product Information, Journal of Consumer Research, Vol. 27, No. 3, Dec.

METHA, A. (1994): How Advertising Response Modeling (ARM) can increase Ad Effectiveness, Journal of Advertising Research, May/June, pp. 62-74.

MEYERS-LEVY, J. & TYBOUT, A. M. (1997): Context Effects at Encoding and Judgment in Consumption Settings: The Role of Cognitive Resources, Journal of Consumer Research, 24, pp. 1-14, June 1997

MICK, D. G. & BUHL, C. (1992): A Meaning-based Model of Advertising Experiences, Journal of Consumer Research, Vol. 19, No. 3., Dec., pp. 317-338

MICK, D. G. (1986): Consumer Research and Semiotics: Exploring the Morphology of Signs, Symbols, and Significance. Journal of Consumer Research, Vol. 13, Sep., pp.119-213.

MICKWITZ, G. (1959): Marketing and Competition, Helsingfors, Finland: Societas Scientarium Fennica

MILLER, D. W & STARR, M. K. (1960): Executive Decisions and Operations Research, Prentice-Hall, Englewood Cliffs, N. J.

MILLER, G. (2005): Economic Game Shows How the Brain Builds Trust, Science, Vol. 308, Issue 5718, p. 36-36

MILLER, G. A. (1956): The Magic Number Seven, Plus and Minus Two: Some Limits on Our Capacity for Processing Information, Psychological Review, Vol. 63, pp. 81-97, 1956

MILOTIC, D. (2003): The Impact of Fragrance on Consumer Choice, Journal of Consumer Behavior, Vol. 3, 2, 2003, pp.179-191

MINIARD P. W. & BARONE, M. J. (1997): The Case for Noncognitive Determinants of Attitude: A Critique of Fishbein and Middlestadt. Journal of Consumer Psychology, Vol. 6, No.1, pp.77-93.

MINIARD, P. W. & COHEN, J. B. (1981): An Examination of the Fishbein-Ajzen Behavioral-Intentions Model's Concepts and Measures, Journal of Experimental Social Psychology, Vol. 17, pp. 309-99, May 1981

MINIARD, P. W. & COHEN, J. B. (1983): Modeling Personal and Normative Influences on Behavior, Journal of Consumer Research, Vol. 10, No. 2, pp. 169-80, September 1983

MITCHELL, A. A. & OLSON, J. C. (1981): Are Product Attribute Beliefs the Only Mediator of Advertising Effects on Brand Attitude?, Journal of Marketing Research, Vol. XVIII, pp. 318-32, August 1981

MOORADIAN, T. A., & OLIVER, J. M. (1997): "I can't get no satisfaction": The impact of personality and emotion on postpurchase processes, Psychology & Marketing 14, pp. 379-393

MOORMAN, C. (2002): Consumer Health under the Scope, Journal of Consumer Research, 29, pp.152-158, June 2002

MORRIN, M., & RATNESHWAR, S. (2000): The Impact of Ambient Scent on Evaluation, Attention, and Memory for Familiar and Unfamiliar Brands, Journal of Business Research, 49, 2000, pp. 157-165

MORRIS, J D., ROBERTS, M. S., & BAKER, G. F. (1999): Emotional Responses of African American Voters to Ad Messages, in: KAID, L. L. & BYSTROM, D. G. (eds.): The Electronic Election: Perspectives on the 1996 Campaign Communication, Mahwah, NJ: Lawrence Erlbaum Associates

MORRIS, J. D. & MCMULLEN, J. S. (1999): Measuring Multiple Emotional Responses to a Single Television Commercial, Proceedings from the 1999 Conference of the American Academy of Advertising

MORRIS, J. D. (1995): Observations: SAM – The Self-Assessment Manikin: An efficient Cross-cultural Measurement of Emotional Response, Journal of Advertising Research, 35 (6), pp. 63-68

MORRIS, J. D., BRADLEY, M. M., WAINE, C. A., & Lang, J. B. (1992): Assessing Affective Reactions to Advertisements with the Self-assessment Manikin (SAM), paper was presented at Southern Marketing Association Conference.

MORRIS, J. D., STRAUSBAUGH, K. L., NTHANGENI, M. (1996): Emotional Respone to Advertisements (or commercials) across cultures, proceedings Of The 1996 Conference Of The American Academy of Advertising

MOSELEY, S. & PARFITT, J. (1987): Measuring advertising effect from the AdLab panel, Admap, June

MUCHA, T. (2005): Why the Caveman Love the Pitchman, Business 2.0, April, Vol. 6, Issue 3, pp. 37-39

MUELLER, E. (1958): The Desire for Innovation in Household Goods, In: L. H. CLARK (ed.): Consumer Behavior, Vol. 3, New York, New York University Press

MURRAY, H. A. (1938): Explorations in Personality, New York, Oxford University Press

MURRY, J. P. JR. & DACIN, P. A. (1996): Cognitive Moderators of Negative-Emotion Effects: Implications for Understanding Media Context, Journal of Consumer Research, Vol. 22, March 1996

MURRY, J. P., LASTOVICKA, J. L. & SINGH, S. N. (1992): Feeling and Liking Responses to Television Programs: An Examination of Two Explanations for Media-Context Effects, Journal of Consumer Research, Vol. 18, No. 4, Mar.

NACCACHE, L., GAILLARD, R., ADAM, C, HASBOUN, D., CLEMENCEAU, S., BAULAC, M., DEHAENE, S., & COHEN, L. (2005): A direct intracranial record of emotions evoked by subliminal words, May 24, 102(21), pp. 7713-7717

NAKAMURA, K., KAWASHIMA, R., ITO, K., SUGIURA, M., KATO, T., NAKAMURA, A., HATANO, K., NAGUMO, S., KUBOTA, K., FUKUDA, H, & KOJIMA, S. (1999): Activation of the Right Inferior Frontal Cortex During Assessment of Facial Emotion, Journal of neurophysiology, Sep, 83(3), pp. 1610-1614

NAPLES, M. J. (1997): Effective Frequency - Then and Now. Journal of Advertising Research, Vol. 37, No. 4, July-August.

NEIDELL, L. A. (1969): The Use of Non-Metric Multidimensional Scaling in Marketing Analysis, Journal of Marketing, Vol 33, pp. 37-43

NETER, J., WASSERMAN, W. & KUTNER, M. H. (1989): Applied Linear Regression Models, pp. 578-626, Irwin USA

NEWELL, S. J. & GOLDSMITH, R. E. (2001): The development of a scale to measure perceived corporate credibility, Journal If Business Research, pp. 235-247

NICKERSON, R. S. (1968): A note on Long-term Recognition Memory for Pictorial

NICOSIA, F. M. (1966): Consumer Decision Process, Englewood Cliffs, N.J.: Prentice-Hall Inc.

NILSSON, O. S. & OLSEN, J. K. (1993): 'Sales Plan' - A Forecasting and Decision Support System for Fast Moving Consumer Goods. In Proceedings of ESOMAR/EMAC/AFM Symposium on Information Based Decision Making in Marketing, Paris, 17-19 November.

OH, H. (2005): Measuring affective reactions to print apparel advertisements: a scale development, Journal of Fashion Marketing and Management, Vol. 9, No. 3, pp. 283-305

ÖLANDER, F. (1986): Comment on the paper by H. Keith Hunt: Consumer Satisfaction/Dissatisfaction and the Consumer Interest, The International Conference on Research in the Consumer Interest, Racine, WI, USA, August 13-16, 1986

OLIVER, R. L. (1980): A Cognitive Model of the Antecedents and Consequences of Satisfaction Decisions, Journal of Marketing Research, Vol. XVII, pp. 460-69, November 1980

OLSEN, J. K. & HANSEN, F. (2002): An Interview-based measure of Short-term Advertising Effects, International Journal of Advertising, Vol. 21(4)

ORTONY, A. & TURNER, T. J. (1990): What's basic about basic emotions? Psychological Review, 97, pp. 313.

OSGOOD, C. E., SUCI, G. J. & TANNENBAUM, P. H. (1957): The Measurement of Meaning, Urban, Ill., University of Illinois Press

OSWALD, L. R (1999): Culture Swapping: Consumption and the Ethnogenesis of Middle-Class Haitian Immigrants, Journal of Consumer Research, 25, pp. 303-318, March 1999

OTTESEN, O. (1969): Problem, Midler og Beslutninger i Foretakets Markedskommunikasjon, bind I, Oslo, Norway: Instituttet for Markedsforskning

OTTESEN, O. (1973): Studier i Virksomheders Mediabeslutninger, Nyt Nordisk Forlag, København

PACKARD, V. (1957): The Hidden Persuaders, New York, David Mackay Company

PAGE, G. (2005): The challenges for neuroscience in ad research, Admap, September

PALDA, K. S. (1964): The Measurement of Cumulative Advertising Effects. Doctoral Dissertation. Englewood Cliffs, New Jersey: Prentice-hall.

PALDA, K. S. (1969): Economic Analysis for Marketing Decisions, Englewood Cliffs, N.J. Prentice-Hall Inc.

PARKINSON, B. (2005): Do facial movements express emotions or communicate motives?, Personality and Social Psychology Review, 9(4), pp. 278-311

PAULUS, M. P. & FRANK, L. R. (2003): Ventromedial prefrontal cortex activation is critical for preference judgments, Neuroreport 14

PAULUS, M. P. (2005): Neurobiology of decision-making: Quo vadis?, Cognitive Brain Research, 23, pp. 2-10

PECHMANN, C., STEWART, D. W. (1992): Advertising Repetition: A Critical Review of Wearin and Wearout, Current Issues and Research in Advertising, 11, 2, 285-330

PEDRICK, J. H. & ZUFRYDEN, F. S. (1991): Evaluating the Impact of Advertising Media Plans: A Model of Consumer Purchase Dynamics Using Single Source Data, Marketing Science, 10, 2 (Spring), 111-130

PENN, D: (2005): Could brain science be peace broker in the "Recall Wars"?, Admap, September

PERCY, L. (1997): The Importance of Flexibility in Pre-Testing Advertising, Working Paper, University of Oxford.

PERCY, L. (2004): Advertising and the seven sins of memory, International Journal of Advertising, Vol. 23, No. 4, pp. 413-427

PERCY, L. (2007): Advertising Strategy, Greenwooed Press, Westport CT, United States

PERCY, L., HANSEN, F. & RANDRUP, R. (2004): Emotional responses to brands and product categories, Proceedings from ESOMAR, Lissabon

PETER, J. P. & OLSON, J. C. (1987): Consumer Behavior – Marketing Strategy Perspectives, Irwin, Illinois

PETERSON, R. L. (2005): The neuroscience of investing: fMRI of the reward system, Brain Research Bulletin, Nov 15, 67(5), pp. 391-397

PETTY, R. E. & CACIOPPO, J. T. (1986a): The Elaboration Likelihood Model of Persuasion Advances in Experimental Social Psychology, Vol. 19, pp. 123-205.

PETTY, R. E. & CACIOPPO, J. T. (1986b): Communication and Persuasion, New York, Springer-Verlag

PETTY, R. E., CACIOPPO, J. T. & SCHUMANN, D. (1983): Central and Peripheral Routes to Advertising Effectiveness: The Moderating Role of Involvement, Journal of Consumer Research, Vol. 10, No. 2, pp. 135-146, September 1983

PHAM, M. T, COHEN, J. B., PRACEJUS, J. W. & HUGHES, G. D. (2001): Affect Monitoring and the Primacy of Feelings in Judgment, Journal of Consumer Research, 28, pp. 167-188, September 2001

PHAM, M. T. & AVNET, T. (2004): Ideals and Oughts and the Reliance on Affect versus Substance in Persuasion, Journal of Consumer Research, Vol. 30, No. 4, Mar.

PHELPS, E. A. (2006): EMOTION AND COGNITION: Insights from Studies of the Human Amygdala, Annual Review of Psychology, 57, pp. 27-53

PHELPS, E. A., & LEDOUX, J. E. (2005): Contributions of the amygdala to emotion processing: from animal models to human behavior, Neuron, Oct 20, 48(2), pp. 175-187

PIETERS, R. & WARLOP, L. (1999): Visual attention during brand choice: The impact of time pressure and task motivation. International Journal of Research in Marketing, 16(1), 1-16

PINE II, B. J. & GILMORE, J. (1998): Welcome to the Experience Economy. Harvard Business Review, Jul./Aug. 1998, pp. 97-105.

PLASSMANN, H., KENNING, P., DEPPE, M., KUGEL, H., SCHWINDT, W. & AHLERT, D. (2005): The fire of desire: Neural correlates of brand choice, Proceedings from EACR 2005, Göteborg, June

PLUTCHIK, R. & KELLERMAN, H. (1974): Emotions Profile Index – Manual, Western Psychological Services, Los Angeles

PLUTCHIK, R. (1980): Emotion: A Psychoevolutionary Synthesis, New York: Harper & Row

POELS, K. & DEWITTE, S. (2006): How to Capture the Heart? Reviewting 20 Years of Emotion Measurement in Advertising, Journal of Advertising Research, Vol 45, No. 1, Mar, pp. 18-37

POLLATOS, O, KIRSCH, W. & SCHANDRY, R. (2005): On the relationship between interoceptive awareness, emotional experience, and brain processes, Brain research. Cognitive Brain Research, Dec, 25(3), pp. 948-62

POPAI (POINT OF PURCHASE ADVERTISING INTERNATIONAL) (1999): European consumer buying habits study, Weinheim

PROHOVNIK, I, SKUDLARSKI, P, FULBRIGHT, R. K, GORE, J. C, & WEXLER, B. E. (2004): Functional MRI changes before and after onset of reported emotions, Psychiatry Research, Dec 30, 132(3), pp. 239-50

RAGHUNATHAN, R. & IRWIN, J. R. (2001): Walking the Hedonic Product Treadmill: Default Contrast and Mood-Based Assimilation in Judgments of Predicted Happiness with a Target Product, Journal of Consumer Research, Vol. 28, No. 3, December

RANDRUP, R. (2004): Why newspaper ads are effective, Admap, June, Issue 451, pp 47-49

RASMUSSEN, A. (1977): Pristeori eller parameterteori, Nyt Nordisk Forlag – Arnold Busck, København

RAY, M. L. (1976): Marketing Communications and the Hierarchy-of-Effects, in New Models for Communication Research, New York.

RAY, W. J. & OLSON, J. C. (1982): Perspectives on Psycho physiological Assessment of Psychological Responses to Advertising, ESOMAR Congress, Vienna.

REYNOLDS, T. J., OLSON, J. C. & ROCHON, J. P. (1997): A Strategic Approach to Measuring Advertising Effectiveness. In Measuring Advertising Effectiveness, ed. William D. Wells, Mahwah, N.J., Lawrence Erlbaum Associates.

RICE, M. & DAVIS, B. (1993): The Canadian Media Directors' Council Television Commercial Awareness Model. In Proceedings of ESOMAR/EMAC/AFM Symposium on Information Based Decision Making in Marketing, Paris, 17-19 November.

RICHINS, M. L. (1997): Measuring Emotions in the Consumption Experience, Journal of Consumer Research, Vol. 24, Sep., pp. 127-142.

ROBERTS, A. (1997): Optimising Advertising and Promotions. Paper presented at The 1997 European Advertising Effectiveness Symposium

ROBERTS, A. (1998): Linking Sales to Advertising Activity, Admap, The Advertising Association, January, QEII Conference Centre, London.

ROBERTS, A. (1999): Recency, Frequency and the Duration of the sales effects of TV advertising, Proceedings from ASI, 1999

ROBERTS, A. (2000): tvSpan: The Medium Term Sales Effects of TV Advertising for FMCG products, Proceedings from ASI Conference, 2000

ROBERTS, M. L. & BERGER, P. D. (1989): Direct Marketing Management, Prentice-Hall, Inc.

ROGERS, E. M. (1962): Diffusion of Innovations, New York: The Free Press

ROMANIUK, J. & SHARP, B. (2004): Brand Salience – What it is and why it matters, R&D Initiative Research Report, Number 16, March,

ROSBERGEN, E., PIETERS, R. & WEDEL, M. (1997): Visual Attention to Advertising: A Segment-Level Analysis, Journal of Consumer Research, Vol. 24, No. 3.

ROSENBERG, M. J. (1959): A Structural Theory of Attitude Dynamics, Public Opinion Quarterly, Vol 24, No. 2, pp. 319-340

ROSSITER, J. & BELLMAN, S. (2005): Marketing Communications, Prentice Hall

ROSSITER, J. (2004): A theory of two level emotions in advertising, ICORIA 2004, p. 11

ROSSITER, J. R. & EAGLESON, G. (1994): Conclusions from the ARF's Copy Research Validity Project, Journal of Advertising Research, Vol. 34, No. 3, May/June.

ROSSITER, J. R. & PERCY, L. (1997): Advertising Communications and Promotion Management. McGraw-Hill, New York.

ROSSITER, J. R. & PERCY, L. (1998): Integrated Marketing Communication, Prentice-Hall, New Jersey

ROTHSCHILD, M. L., REEVES, B., THORSON, E., MCDONALD, D., HIRSCH, J. & GOLDSTEIN, R. (1984): Attention to Television: Intrastimulus Effects of Movement and Scene Changes on Alpha Variation over time. Working Paper, Graduate School of Business, University of Wisconsin- Madison.

ROUSSET, S., DEISS, V. JUILLARD, E., SCHLICH, P. DROIT-VOLET, S. (2005): Emotions generated by meat and other food products in women, The British journal of nutrition, Oct, 94(4), pp. 609-619

RUECKERT, L. (2005): A Web-based study of cerebral asymmetry for perception of emotion, Behavior research methods, May, 37(2), pp. 271-276

RUMELHART, D. E. (1984): "Schemata and the cognitive system", In: WYER, R. S, and Srull, T. K (HG.) (1984): Handbook of social cognition, Hillsdale/NJ: Lawrence Erlbaum Associates, p. 161-188

RUSO, J. E. & LECLERC, F. (1994): An eye-fixation analysis of choice processes for consumer nondurables, In: Journal of Consumer Research, Vol. 21, pp. 274-290

RUSSELL, J. A. & CARROLL, J. M (1999a): The Phoenix of Bipolarity: Reply to Watson and Tellegen (1999), Psychological Bulletin, Vol. 125, No. 5

RUSSELL, J. A. & CARROLL, J. M. (1999b): On the Bipolarity of Positive and Negative Affect, Psychological Bulletin, Vol. 125, No 1

RUSSELL, J. A. & MEHRABIAN, A. (1977): Evidence for a three-factor theory of emotions, Journal of Research in Personality 11, pp. 273-294

RUSSELL, J. A., LEWICKA, M. & NIIT, T. (1989): A Cross-cultural Study of a Circumplex Model of Affect, Journal of Personality and Social Psychology, 57, pp. 848-856

RYAN, M. J. & BONFIELD, E. H. (1980): Fishbein's Intentions Model: A Test of External and Pragmatic Validity, Journal of Marketing, Vol. 44, No. 2, pp. 82-95, Spring 1980

RYAN, M. J. (1982): Behavioral Intention Formation: The Interdependency of Attitudinal and Social Influence Variables, Journal of Consumer Research, Vol. 9, No. 3, pp.263-78, December 1982

SAWYER, A. (1981): Repetition, Cognitive Responses and Persuasion, In: Petty, R. E., Ostrom, T. M. & Brock, T. C. (eds): Cognitive Responses in Persuasion, Hillsdale, NJ, Lawrence Erlbaum

SCHACTER, D. (2001): How the mind forgets and remembers - The seven sins of memory, Souvenir.

SCHIFFMAN, L. G. & KANUK, L. L. (1978): Consumer Behavior, Prentice-Hall, Inc.

SCHLINGER, M. J. (1979): A Profile of Responses to Commercials, Journal of Advertising Research, 19 (2), pp. 37-46, 1979

SCHNOOR, P. (2003): An Evaluation of Corporate Brand Character, In: HANSEN, F. & CHRISTENSEN, L. B. (2003): Branding and Advertising, Copenhagen Business School Press

SCHROEDER, G., RICHARDSON, B. C. & SANKARALINGAM, A. (1997): Validating STAS Using BehaviorScan. Journal of Advertising Research, Vol. 37, No. 4, July-August.

SCHWARZ, N. (1997): Moods and Attitude judgments: A Comment on Fishbein and Middlestadt. Journal of Consumer Psychology, Vol. 6, No. 1.

SCOTT, C, KLEIN, D. M & BRYANT, J. (1990): Consumer Response to Humour in Advertising: A Series of Field Studies Using Behavioral Observation, 16 (March), pp. 498-501

SETHURAMAN, R. & TELLIS, G. J. (1991): An Analysis of the Tradeoff Between Advertising and Pricing, Journal of Marketing Research, 31, 2 (May), 160-174

SHAROT, T.D., MAURICIO, R., PHELPS, A. E. (2004): How emotion enhances the feeling of remembering, National Neuroscience, 7

SHAVER, P., SCHWARTZ, J, KIRSON, D. & O'CONNOR, C (1987): Emotion Knowledge: Further Exploration of a Prototype Approach, Journal of Personality and Social Psychology, Vol. 52, No. 6, 1987, pp. 1061-1086

SHEIKHIAN, M. (1982): Pictorial Information Processing: A Selective Review. Institut für Konsum- und Verhaltensforschung, Universität des Saarlandes.

SHEPPARD, B. H., HARTWICK, J., & WARSHAW, P. R. (1988): The theory of reasoned action: a meta-analysis of past research with recommendations for modifications and future research, Journal of Consumer Research, 15, pp. 325-343

SHERIF, C. W., SHERIF, M. & NEBERGALL, R. E. (1965): Attitude and Attitude Change: The Social Judgement-Involvement Approach, Philadelphia, Saunders

SHIIMP, T. A., EASTLICK, M. A., LOTZ, S. L., & WARRINGTON, P. (2001): An online prepurchase intentions model: the role of intention to search, Journal of Retailing, 77, pp. 397-416

SHIMP, T. A. & KAVAS, A (1984): The Theory of Reasoned Action Applied to Coupon Usage, The Journal of Consumer Research, Vol. 11, No. 3, Dec. 1984

SHIV, B. & FEDORIKHIN, A. (1999): Heart and Mind in Conflict: The Interplay of Affect and Cognition in Consumer Decision Making, Journal of Consumer Research, Vol. 26, No. 3, Dec.

SHUGAN, S. M. (1980): The Cost of Thinking, Journal of Consumer Research, Vol. 7, No. 2, pp. 99-111, September 1980

SHWEDER, R. A. (2004): Deconstructing the Emotions for the Sake of Comparative Research, In: MANSTEAD, A. S. R., FRIJDA, N. & FISCHER, A. (2004): Feelings and Emotions – The Amsterdam Symposium, Cambridge University Press

SIEMER, M. (2001): Mood specific effects on appraisal and emotion judgements, Cognition and Emotion, 2001, 15 (4), 453-485

SIM, T. C. & MARTINEZ, C. (2005): Emotion words are remembered better in the left ear, Laterality, Mar, 10(2), pp. 149-159

SIMON, J. L. & ARNDT, J. (1980): The Shape of the Advertising Response Function, Journal of Advertising Research 20, pp. 11-28

SINGH, A. (2003): From the periphery to the center: An emotional perspective of the elaboration model, Thesis, University of Florida

SOLOMON, M., BAMOSSY, G. & ASKEGAARD, S. (1999): Consumer Behaviour – a European Perspective, Prentice Hall Inc

SPERRY, R. (1982): Some Effects of Disconnecting the Cerebral Hemispheres, Science, Vol. 217, pp. 1223-26, 1982

SPIELMAN, H. M. (1988): Meeting the Multi-National Companies' Demand for Global Advertising Research Tool. ESOMAR Annual Conference.

SPINELLA, M. & LESTER, D. (2005): Predicting credit card behavior: a study in neuroeconomic, Perceptual & Motor Skills, Jun., Part 1, Vol. 100, Issue 3, pp. 777-778

SQUIRE, L. R. & KANDEL, E. R. (1999): Memory: From mind to molecules, New York: Scientific American Library

STAPEL, J. (2000): Advertising Effects and their Attitudinal Background, Admap, Jun

STEWART, D. W. & FURSE, D. H. (1982): Applying Psychophysical Measures to Marketing and Advertising Problems, in J.H. LEIGH & C.R. MARTIN, JUNIOR (eds.): Current Issues and Research in Advertising, University of Michigan, Ann Arbor, Michigan.

STEWART; D. W. (1984): Physiological measurements of Advertising Effects: An Unfulfilled Promise, Psychology and Marketing, 1 (1), 43-48.

SWINYARD, W. R. (1993): The Effects of Mood, Involvement, and Quality of Store Experience on Shopping Intentions, Journal of Consumer Research, 20, pp. 271-280, 1993

TELLIS, G. J. (1988a): Advertising Exposure, Loyalty and Brand Purchase: A Two Stage Model of Choice, Journal of Marketing Research, 15, 2 (May), 134-144

TELLIS, G. J. (1988b): The Price Elasticity of Selective Demand, Journal of Marketing Research, 25, (November), pp. 331-341

TELLIS, G. J. (2003): Effective Advertising – Understanding When, How, and Why Advertising Works, Sage Publications

THORSON, E. (1991): Likeability: 10 years of Academic Research, in proceeding from the Eight Annual Copy Research Workshop, N.Y.

THURSTONE, L. L. (1953): Examiner Manual for the Thurstone Temperament Schedule, Chicago, Science Research Associates

TIWSAKUL, R., HACKLEY, C. & SZMIGIN, I. (2005): Explicit, non-integrated product-placement in British television programmes, International Journal of Advertising, 24(1), pp. 95-111

TOMKINS, S. S. (1962): Affect, imagery, consciousness, New York, Springer

TVERSKY, A. & KAHNEMAN, D. (1974): Judgment under uncertainty: Heuristics and biases, Science, 185, pp. 1124-1131

TVERSKY, A. (1969): Intransitivity of Preferences, Psychological Review, Vol. 76, pp. 31-48, 1969

URBAN, G & HAUSER, J. (1983): Product Development, McGraw Hill, New York

URBAN, G. L. & HAUSER, J. R. (1980): Design and Marketing of New Products, Englewood Cliffs, New Jersey, Prentice-Hall, Inc

US TODAY (1996): Business Section, May 11th.

VAN RAAIJ, W. F. (1983): Affective and Cognitive Reactions to Advertising, Papers on Economic Psychology, Number 26, Erasmus Universiteit Rotterdam

VAUGHN, R. (1979): How Advertising Works: A Planning Model, Journal of Advertising Research, Vol. 20, No. 5, October 1980, pp. 27-33

VERMA, R., DAVATZIKOS, C., LOUGHEAD, J. INDERSMITTEN, T., HU, R., KOHLER, C. GUR, RE, & GUR, RC (2005): Quantification of facial expressions using high-dimensional shape tranformations, Journal of Neuroscience Methods, 141(1), Jan 30, pp. 61-73

WALKER, D. & DUBITSKY, T. M. (1994): Why Liking Matters, Journal of Advertising Research, May/June

WALLISER, B. (2003): An International Review Of Sponsorship Research, International Journal of Marketing, vol. 22, no. 1, 2003

WALTER, H., ABLER, B. CIARAMIDARO, A. & ERK, S. (2005): Motivating forces of human actions, Brain Research Bulletin, Vol. 67 (5)

WALTERS, C. G. (1978): Consumer Behavior – Theory and Practice, Irwin, Illinois

WARD, S. & SAWYER, A. (1976): Carry-Over Effects in Advertising Communication: Evidence and Hypotheses From Behavioral Science, Cambridge, MA: Marketing Science Institute

WARING, T. (2005): Can the power of magazines be measured? Proceedings from ASI Conference; Budapest, June

WÄRNERYD, K. E. (1959): Ekonomisk Psykology, Institute for Economic Research, Stockholm School of Economics.

WATKINS, D. (2004): Economics 101, Scientific American, Jan. Spec. Edt, Vol. 14, Issue 1, pp. 99-99

WATSON, D., CLARK, L. A. & TELLEGEN, A. (1988): Development and validation of brief measures of positive and negative affect: The PANAS scales, Journal of Personality and Social Psychology 54, pp. 1063-1070

WATSON, D., WIESE, D., VAIDYA, J. & TELLEGEN, A. (1999): The two general activation systems of affect: Structural findings, evolutionary considerations, and psychobiological evidence, Journal of Personality and Social Psychology, 76, pp. 820-838

WEBSTER, J. & WIND, Y (1972): Organizational Buying Behavior, Prentice-Hall, Inc., Englewood Cliffs, New Jersey

WEI, L.- P. (1993): Assessing cross-cultural Transferability of standardized global advertising: an emotional response approach, Thesis, University of Florida

WEILBACHER, W. M. (2001): Point of view: Does advertising cause a "hierarchy of effects"?, Journal of advertising research, Vol. 41, No. 6, November/December

WEINER, B. (1985): An Attributional Theory of Achievement Motivation and Emotion, Psychological Review, 92 (4), pp. 548-573

WEINER, B. (2000): Attributional Thoughts about Consumer Behavior, Journal of Consumer Research, 27 (December)

WEINSTEIN, S., WEINSTEIN, C. & DROZDENKO, R. (1984): Brain wave analysis: An electroencephalographic technique used for evaluating the communications-effect of advertising, Psychology and Marketing, 1(1), pp. 17-42

WELLS, W. D., LEAVITT, C. & MCCONVILLE; M. (1971): A Reaction Profile for TV Commercials, Journal of Research, 11 (December), 11-17.

WESTBROOK, R. A. & OLIVER, R. L. (1991): The Dimensionality of Consumption Emotion Patterns and Consumer Satisfaction, 18 (June), pp. 84-91

WEXLER, B. E. & HENINGER, G. (1981): Perceptual Asymmetry, Field Dependence and Performance Subtests of the WAIS, Working Paper, Yale University, School of Medicine.

WHITE, R. (2005): No room for excitement? Admap, July/August

WHITEHEAD, J. L. JR. (1968): Factors of Source Credibility, Quarterly Journal of Speech 54, 59-63

WILDGRUBER, D., RIECKER, A., HERTRICH, I., ERB, M., GRODD, W., ETHOFER, T., & ACKERMANN, H. (2005): Identification of emotional intonation evaluated by fMRI, Neuroimage, Feb 15, 24(4), pp. 1233-1241

WILDNER, R. & KINDELMANN, K. (1997): TV Advertising Effectiveness. How to measure and judge TV ads effectiveness with single source data, ESOMAR

WILLIAM, J. (1884): What is an Emotion?, Mind, 9, pp. 188-205.

WILLIAMS, M. A., MCGLONE, F., ABBOTT, D. F., & MATTINGLEY, J. B. (2005): Differential amygdala responses to happy and fearful facial expressions depend on selective attention, Neuroimage, Jan., 15, 24(2), pp. 417-25

WILLIAMS, P. & AAKER, J. L. (2002): Can Mixed Emotions Peacefully Coexist? Journal of Consumer Research, Vol. 28, No. 4, March

WOODSIDE, A. G. & CLOKEY, J. D. (1974): Multi-Attribute/Multi-Brand Models, Journal of Advertising Research, Vol. 14, No. 5, Oct., pp 33-44

WORCESTER, R. & MCINTYRE, I. (1979): Strategic Decision Research: Its Communications and Use at ICI, paper presented at the ESOMAR Congress, Brussels, September 1979

WRIGHT, P. (1980): Message-Evoked Thoughts: Persuasion Research Using Thought Verbalizations, Journal of Consumer Research, Vol. 7, No. 2, pp. 151-75, September 1980

YOO, BOONGHEE & MANDHACHITARA, R. (2003): Estimating Advertising Effects on Sales in a Competitive Setting, Journal of Advertising Research, Sep.

YOUNG, C. B. (2004): Capturing the Flow of Emotion in Television Commercials: A New Approach, Emotion in Advertising - Journal of Advertising Research, June 2004

ZAICHKOWSKY, J. L. (1985): Measuring the Involvement Construct, Journal of Consumer Research, Vol. 12, No. 3, pp. 341-52, December 1985

ZAJONC, R. B. & MARKUS, H. (1982): Affective and Cognitive Factors in Preferences, Journal of Consumer Research, Vol. 9, No. 2, Sep., pp. 123-31

ZAJONC, R. B. & MARKUS, H. (1985): Must All Affect Be Mediated by Cognition?, Journal of Consumer Research, Vol. 12, No. 3, pp. 363-64, December 1985

ZAJONC, R. B. (1968): Attitudinal Effects of Mere Exposure, Journal of Personality and Social Psychology, Vol. 9, No. 2, June

ZAJONC, R. B. (1980): Feeling and Thinking: Preferences Need No Inferences, American Psychologist, 35, pp. 151-175, 1980

DATE DUE